WHAT EVER HAPPENED TO BABY PEGGY ?

ALSO BY

DIANA SERRA CARY

The Hollywood Posse

Hollywood's Children

To Brenda —

from

Diana Serra Cary

Baby Peggy

4/17/2000

St.
Martin's
Press
New York

*The Autobiography of Hollywood's
Pioneer Child Star*

WHAT EVER HAPPENED TO BABY PEGGY

Diana Serra Cary

PUBLISHED BY THOMAS DUNNE BOOKS
An imprint of St. Martin's Press

What Ever Happened to Baby Peggy?

Design by Songhee Kim
Photo insert by Barbara Bachman

Library of Congress Cataloging-in-Publication Data

Cary, Diana Serra, date
    What ever happened to Baby Peggy?: the autobiography of Hollywood's
pioneer child star / Diana Serra Cary. —1st ed.
        p.   cm.
    "A Thomas Dunne book."
    ISBN 0–312–14760–0
    1. Cary, Diana Serra, 1918–   . 2. Motion picture actors and actresses—
United States—Biography. I. Title.
PN2287.C32A3   1996
791.43'028'092—dc20
    [B]   96–23290

First edition: October 1996

10 9 8 7 6 5 4 3 2 1

To that unsung host of heroes—film historians, archivists, and movie buffs—who, with infinite patience, continue to gather the widely scattered pieces of motion-picture history which Hollywood so heedlessly threw away

CONTENTS

HOLLYWOOD REVISITED

Honey, do you realize you're the youngest self-made millionaire in the entire history of the world till now?" asked an awestruck girl reporter interviewing me for a movie magazine. It was a question quite beyond the ken of any three-year-old, and I recalled it as I returned to Hollywood some sixty years later to attend an awards dinner taking place only three blocks from my childhood home. At age three I had earned enough to purchase a tony address on what was still inhabited by Beverly Hills's haut monde—Crescent Drive.

Like Mary Pickford, I was one of that new breed of multimillionaires, owing their phenomenal wealth to the fact that movies existed as much as to our own special gifts. It would take most of my life for me to come to terms with the anguish which that bonanza cost me and my family, as well as the host of other children and their families who followed the trail I blazed, convinced it led to the same gold mine where Baby Peggy was the first to strike it rich.

Sometime between two and two and a half years of age, already a movie veteran, I came to consciousness inside a huge structure with a dark sky sown with a multitude of tiny distant stars. This I accepted as my world. Narrow, black walkways formed a maze of iron latticework between myself and that starry host twinkling above—walkways inhabited by shadowy figures tending what appeared to be bright flowers on spindly black stalks. I gradually learned the beings above were crewmen, answering to the same name as those working the lights below—gaffers—but they handled the overhead spots instead.

Then, without warning, I discovered that this world was not what I thought it was at all. One day the myriad pinpoints of light I believed were stars suddenly began to melt before my eyes. While torrential rain hammered down outside, propmen and grips rushed about setting out buckets to catch the silvery trickles threatening to ruin the set. It was then I realized my distant stars were actually an entire galaxy of leaks in the sievelike roof of Century Studio's very large, very old, and fast-disintegrating fifth-hand Barn.

Not long after that I found myself in yet another world, where I now spent most of my waking hours. It was much more extensive than the Barn, and far less constrictive than the area I now knew as "home." Once introduced to it, the only space I cared to inhabit was this zany realm peopled by frenzied men, women, and animals, all of them engaged in a kind of nonstop, knockabout flying circus where film was rationed, money short, and time forever running out. It was also a world where everyone except me seemed not only willing but eager to work without a net.

This bewitching, Oz-like kingdom had many names—"the lot," "the back lot," "the studio," "Century," "the set," "location," or most often simply "work." But by whatever name, there the very air crackled with excitement, and every task demanded of me was innovative, chancy, frightening, or downright death-defyingly dangerous. Happily for all concerned I possessed a naturally adventurous nature which seemed to thrive on risk and dares.

Perhaps because its owners, brothers Julius and Abe Stern, had flipped a coin to choose between running a five-and-dime store and a nickelodeon, Century Studio exuded an off-the-cuff, luck-of-the-draw atmosphere. In fact, all the dozen or so fly-by-night independent studios lining Sunset Boulevard immediately east of Century, known collectively as Poverty Row, breathed a similar dicey air. For some reason, turning out slapstick comedies engendered this go-for-broke attitude, making otherwise sane actors and directors eager to risk life and limb. It was no secret that these here-today, gone-tomorrow film companies ran more on luck and nerve than brains and money.

To many newcomers this seedy stretch of Sunset seemed reminiscent of the Last Chance saloons that once lined the streets of California gold camps and tent cities. Because the First World War and its aftermath had shut down movie production abroad, from 1914 to 1919 the United States had virtually cornered the world market on films. By 1920 Hollywood was no longer a clutch of inexperienced film pioneers tinkering with an untried medium: the motion-picture bonanza had turned it into a twentieth-century boomtown.

But tonight's awards dinner took precedence in my thoughts. As the guest of my good friend Roddy McDowall, I was here to celebrate a milestone in his career.

Joining the glittering crowd in the ballroom's lobby, I was impressed by how completely the Hollywood of my earliest memories had transformed her public image. She had risen from her grubby slapstick origins as a barely literate, pie-throwing hoyden to become a stately bejeweled doyenne. Presiding over tonight's affair, she was every inch a queen, long past the golden jubilee of her reign as movie capital of the world.

A host of former matinee idols gradually joined those of us already in the lobby chatting and sipping champagne. The men's perennially handsome features were only enhanced by the light frost of age. Beside them were elegantly coiffed and remarkably young-looking female counterparts—stars all. It seemed a reprise of one of those 1930s art deco premieres where fans begged autographs and stars obliged while arc lights swept the starry, utterly smog-free night sky above.

It was apparent these products of the legendary studio system—now a casualty of change—came from an era when great stars knew they were ensuring their own fame by going the extra mile for their public. They comported themselves in that same spirit of gracious noblesse oblige in which I too had been reared.

When Roddy stepped into the spotlight to accept the industry's Distinguished Achievement Award for a forty-year career that took him from child star to veteran actor, I marveled at the fortunate time frame destiny had bestowed on those of us who survived child stardom.

I grew up with Hollywood, having entered films in 1920, a mere eight years after it became the hub of moviemaking. Its infancy was my own. As late as 1941, the year eleven-year-old Roddy arrived as a war refugee from firebombed London, I was still in my early twenties.

In 1943 I left Hollywood, returning rarely, each visit coinciding with a time of tumultuous change in the industry.

When I finally settled in nearby San Diego in 1971, I had been away nearly thirty years, ten of them spent outside the country as a working journalist. I was disoriented by the freeways and bewildered by the vast demographic and geographic changes. But throughout the seventies and eighties, my greatest shock came from seeing Hollywood's rich film legacy being systematically demolished by those who headed major studios. When research, book tours, or other work brought me to town, I discovered that irreplaceable films were being heedlessly lost, pirated, or deliberately destroyed.

On one unforgettable night I checked into the Holiday Inn to appear in, and work with the producers of, a PBS television documentary based on my book *Hollywood's Children: An Inside Account of the Child Star Era*. After the bellman had deposited my bag and departed, I walked to the window of my suite and gazed down upon the after-dark world of today's Hollywood Boulevard. It was an eerie, neon-lit jungle of pimps, prostitutes, hustlers, pushers, "adult" bookstores, and runaway or homeless children.

I knew the Hollywood Chamber of Commerce had spent lavishly on several ambitious cleanups. They had studded the sidewalks with bronze stars to honor past and present celebrities. They revived Santa Claus Lane, where more than once I rode as honored guest in Santa's sleigh, waving back at beaming Rinso-white families lining the curbs on either side. But despite all the face-lifts, the boulevard I remembered had become a cruel, Norma Desmond–like mockery of itself.

What had become of the hamlet that called itself Hollywood after the Spanish toyon bush that flourished here? What became of the spirit of those teetotaling Midwesterners who had founded it forty years before I arrived in their midst?

I had first encountered them sipping lemonade and watching reproachfully from their verandas as the Baby Peggy company filmed slapstick comedies on their front lawns. I had grown up believing their passion for pastel-colored stucco houses had to be their sole vice. In retrospect, I realize that outsiders like myself, whom they scorned as "camera gypsies," had already taken over the quiet streets of their town.

Known to each other as "picture people," the newcomers were vagrants all, bound together solely by their common obsession with moviemaking. They were rough-cut originals, drawn from every race, culture, social stratum, and nation on the globe: drifters, shop girls, immigrant moguls, vaudeville dandies, con men, courtly cowboys, pale brooding thespians, grave-faced Indians, and stranded circus folk.

Lost in this gaudy crowd, but equally fixated on film and fame, were plenty of bound-for-glory parents (kids in tow)—and a few born-old movie children like me.

ACKNOWLEDGMENTS

I owe thanks to silent-film historian and reviewer John DeBartolo, who launched a one-man global campaign to find my "lost" comedies in film archives worldwide. Movie buff Richard Batt donated a print of my early comedy *Sweetie*, directed by Alf Goulding, while Kristan Caruso located rare early interviews with both myself and Jackie Coogan. Film buffs Richard A. Davis and Marge Meissinger sent me photos of everything from Baby Peggy handbags, stationery, and jewelry to lobby posters and a rare 1927 vaudeville flyer. Doll expert Billie Nelson Terrell introduced me to the world of celebrity dolls and the going price for dolls of Baby Peggy, circa 1923.

Marc Wanamaker of Bison Archive has been unfailingly helpful. Longtime studio friend Lee Hanna surprised me with a videotape of *Peg o' the Mounted* from a Netherlands archive. Former child actor and childhood coworker Frank "Junior" Coghlan filled me in on some early details which had eluded me. Steve Potts gave me two extremely rare lobby cards of *The Darling of New York*.

Ron Magliozzi of New York's Museum of Modern Art sent me clippings, song sheets, and videotapes of my long-missing 1921 *Circus Clowns* and *Miles of Smiles*. In addition he compiled the filmography that appears on page 325. In appreciation for his kindness and that of his equally generous colleague Mary Corliss, the museum's Baby Peggy archive has been augmented by stills from my collection, with more to come.

I owe a lifelong debt to countless strangers who have written me from every corner of the world—fans, movie buffs, and readers of my books and articles. Some sent what I had believed were irretrievable photos. To all of them, whose names I never knew or have forgotten but whose generosity I have not, I extend the heartfelt thanks of both Baby Peggy and myself.

I am particularly grateful to my agent, Pauline Fox, to Chuck Morrell of St. Martin's Press, and to my publisher, Thomas Dunne, and editor Jeremy Katz for the faith and enthusiasm all of them brought to this manuscript.

Lastly, I thank my husband and son for their encouragement, and Sister Francisca, OCD—godmother, friend, and Carmelite nun—for the cloud of fervent prayers she has offered on my behalf over many stormy years.

PART 1

1920 – 1923

"SHOOT IT IN GRIFFITH PARK"

1

In the green-lumber cubicle that passed for an office, feet resting on a much-abused desk which no further punishment could harm, and munching a box-lunch sandwich, he studied the frosted glass in the upper half of the closed door with a dreamy look in his mischievous blue eyes. There he saw his own name: Fred Fishbach, Director.

Not that the letters were really there—not yet. But after almost a dozen years in the nascent motion picture business, Fishbach's imagination had been sharpened to an uncanny degree. He could visualize virtually any scene, character, or situation.

It was precisely this knack for seeing what wasn't there that had landed him this job as a comedy director at Century Studio, earning $150 a week. Over here, on the west bank of Hollywood's Poverty Row, that princely wage was twice what Mack Sennett had been paying him over at Keystone. Now, in April of 1920, he considered himself a success at last.

When the war broke out in 1914, Hollywood's European competitors had been forced to cease production, so Fishbach had been kept busy churning out low-budget one- and two-reelers with such popular comics as "Fatty" Arbuckle, Mack Swain, Marie Dressler, and the cross-eyed clown Ben Turpin. The move up to Century had enabled him to marry his steady girl, Ethel Lynne, who played ingenues in the comedies produced by Al Christie at his studio across the street, on the northwest corner of Sunset and Gower.

Only after Fishbach's repeated demands for a private place to work on his comedy scripts did Century's notoriously stingy president, Julius Stern, finally grant him this shabby office. "Who needs an office to write in?" Julius chided him. "Century comedies are put together by our gagmen right on the set!"

Nearly every member of the first generation of movie moguls, the majority of them Jews from Germany, Eastern Europe, and Russia, had crossed the Atlantic in steerage and passed through Ellis Island. Not long after their arrival, they noticed how quickly their fellow immigrants took to the primitive "flickers" showing in America's nickelodeons.

These "galloping tintypes" were openly disdained by most American entrepreneurs as the lowest class of entertainment, suitable only for the ignorant masses. But the potential for profit was not lost on the more prescient foreigners. They not only understood the mentality of nickelodeon patrons, they could see that storefront "nicks" were doing a fire-sale business in the nation's largest cities.

Typical of this sharp-eyed breed was Julius Stern's brother-in-law, Carl Laemmle. He had arrived in America in 1884 at the age of seventeen, with only a few dollars to his name. After twenty years of clerking in a Wisconsin clothing store, he grew sick of being a "salary slave." On a visit to Chicago he spent one whole day standing in front of a nickelodeon, counting customers by moving a single dried bean from one pocket to another. Multiplying the beans by five, he found the day's take astronomical for the times.

Utterly astounding to Laemmle was that every nickelodeon patron prepaid for the item he had gone in to see, but *not one* carried his purchase out. The goods remained, to be sold and resold a thousand times over. What other product in history had ever been merchandised this way? Nickelodeons were a perfect business.

The following day Laemmle risked his entire life savings of three thousand dollars to purchase his first nickelodeon. His wife's two brothers, Julius and Abe Stern (immigrants like himself), were about to invest a nest egg of their own in a five-and-ten-cent store when Laemmle advised them to join him instead. A tossed coin launched their film career. Nine years later Laemmle's Universal in the nearby San Fernando Valley opened as Hollywood's preeminent studio, providing product to his growing network of theaters. Meanwhile, on Sunset Boulevard's Poverty Row, the Stern brothers' humble fiefdom was Century Studio.

A self-made man like Fred Fishbach (himself a Romanian Jew from Bucharest) understood this immigrant-film connection well. It not only explained but justified the cost-cutting methods of producers like Julius Stern, and made working for this fiscal tyrant far less stressful for Fishbach than it was for Century's American-born employees.

But while Fishbach shared the Sterns' Atlantic crossing, he was not cursed with their obsessive drive for money and power. From childhood he had helped support his family, but in his early teens he left New York to make his own way in the world. Landing in Los Angeles in 1909, he found his first job working as a movie extra. A few months later, all of fifteen years old, he moved up to propman for Thomas Ince. After quietly observing how it was done, he got a job directing for Sennett. Now, barely twenty-six, he was already a movie veteran. Best of all, he was being paid handsomely for doing what he enjoyed most (and what few mortals had ever done before him!) turning out three or four crackerjack slapstick comedies a month.

Today, besides his idle lunch-hour game of visualizing his name on the office door, Fishbach was also trying to solve a long-standing casting problem. He needed to find a comedienne to play opposite one of Century's most popular contract stars. He had written a two-reeler that Julius liked and was prodding him to make, but he had spent three frustrating months in a futile search for just the right costar.

A propman rapped on his door and called, "Mr. Fishbach! Your company's ready in the Barn!"

Lowering his feet from the desk, he shouted back, "Okay! Tell 'em I'll be right there!"

What was referred to at Century as "the Barn" was precisely that. The lot occupied the former site of a rambling farmhouse and outbuildings which once had stood in open country, a full day's wagon trip to Los Angeles. But forty years of development had landed the old homestead here in the middle of Hollywood. The Sterns knocked down the old house and built a couple of high, windowless stages on the grounds. Spared (to save money) was the farm's original cavernous, hip-roofed barn, which was large enough to allow several companies to shoot inside simultaneously. A small wooden bungalow on Sunset Boulevard, built during the brief term of Century's predecessor, L-KO (short for "Lehrman's Knockout Pictures"), served as the studio's front office.

As Fishbach entered the Barn and headed toward a far corner where his cluster of actors, cameraman, and crew waited inside a circle of lights, spots, and cables, an angular dark-haired woman rushed up to intercept him. "Oh, Mr. Fishbach!" she cried. "You may not remember me, but I'm Margaret Campbell. I worked as an extra on one of your Rainbow Comedies last week, but the cashier didn't have enough cash to pay us all off. She told me to come back this week and get my three dollars and twenty cents directly from you!"

"Of course I remember you, Margaret," he replied affably, flashing a broad smile of recognition as he peeled five singles from the roll of crisp bills he carried in his trouser pocket. "Sorry it cost you a second trip up here on the trolley. Please keep the change!"

Joining his company, the director was informed that one of his comics had gone home for the day with a severe case of "klieg eyes." Kliegs, as these primitive lights were called after their inventor, were cumbersome metal-backed monsters, four or five feet high, mounted on wheels for mobility. They were fitted with several vertical glass tubes through which flowed a gaseous substance that gave off a vibrant blue-white light. It also emitted actinic rays, the villains that so painfully inflamed the eyes of stage actors, new to both moviemaking and the treacherous kliegs.

Although "klieg eyes" was a common affliction at Century, causing copious tears for several days, any player's absence required working around him. After shooting a couple of scenes, Fishbach called a short recess to figure out how he could make the most time-saving camera setups with the principals he had left.

He strolled away from the set, past the usual number of wonder-struck tourists who, for various reasons, the front office routinely granted permission to watch pictures being shot in the Barn.

Head down, eyes half-closed in thought, he stumbled directly into an electrician's high stool which stood all by itself in the dusky center of the Barn. Brought up short, he was astonished to find himself looking into the dark eyes of a very small child who appeared to have staked out the spot as her own. Dressed in a simple cotton frock, she sat with her hands folded in her lap, ankles neatly crossed. Meeting his gaze forthrightly, she seemed far less flustered than he by their surprise encounter.

"Sorry if I scared you, honey," he said reassuringly, his hands steadying her to make sure she didn't tumble off the tall stool. "Whose little girl are you anyway?"

She smiled agreeably but made no other response. In fact, he had never seen a mere toddler remain utterly motionless and self-contained for such a long period of time. He saw she didn't have a doll or toy of any kind to occupy her, but no matter how he baby-talked or otherwise coaxed her, she refused to reply and stuck gamely to the stool. She was not intimidated, he saw, and he had dealt with his share of cowed as well as cheeky picture kids in his time.

Suddenly he pushed up the white felt sun visor he always wore and stared at her. "Of course!" he muttered under his breath. *"She's the one!"*

She had the perfect square face, turned-up nose, and quirky smile. Her whole demeanor was almost clownishly self-deprecating, and he detected more than a spark of humor in her expressive brown eyes. Even her black hair—cut in short bangs in front and barely touching her ears on either side—was comical enough to make him want to laugh out loud! It hardly seemed possible. Here on a stool in Century's own Barn was the very child he had ransacked every studio in town trying to find.

He turned at the approach of a pretty young woman in a gray silk suit with a straw boater pinned atop her pompadoured chestnut hair. "I hope my little girl isn't bothering anyone?" she asked nervously. "I put her over here so she'd be out of the way while I watched a picture being filmed. I've never been inside a movie studio before."

"Oh, your child's no bother. In fact, I couldn't coax her to say a word or move from this stool. How in the world do you get her to do that?"

Vastly relieved, the young mother blushed and laughed lightly. "Oh, that!" she exclaimed. "I just told her to sit here and keep quiet till I came back. And of course she did."

"Is she always this obedient?"

"Oh, yes. She's been taught to do exactly what she's told. My husband is a very strict disciplinarian."

"I'd like to use your little girl in a picture I plan to make," Fishbach ventured softly, half afraid of scaring off the child's timid mother. "Would you please give your name and phone number to the girl in the front-office bungalow when you leave?"

For a moment the woman was speechless; then she asked hesitantly, "And your name, sir?"

"Fred Fishbach, the director. And yours?"

"Marian—I mean, *Missus* Jack Montgomery."

Embarrassed at having to introduce herself to such an important personage while dressed in the same suit in which she had been married five years earlier, Marian hoped to summon greater dignity by stressing her married name. But as soon as the director walked away she realized she had invoked her husband's accusatory presence instead. She could hear Jack's repeated warning, "Don't you ever go near a Hollywood studio! Working as a stuntman these past three months has really opened my eyes. A movie set's no place for a lady."

Today, behind his back, she had defied his wishes. Worse yet, she knew she didn't possess the strength of will not to leave her name in the front office. Although he had never laid a hand on her in anger, she was terrified of what he would say, for weathering one of Jack Montgomery's Othellian rages was a truly fearsome experience.

2

Y ou see, Marian? What did I tell you?" Margaret Campbell exulted as the two women emerged from Century's front-office bungalow onto Sunset Boulevard. "It's like I keep saying, over here in Hollywood lightning strikes somebody every day! Tomorrow it may be me!"

Shading her eyes against the brilliant California sun as she shepherded her two small daughters before her, Marian was only half listening to her starstruck companion. She was still in a panic of fear at having set in motion God only knew what unholy chain of events by leaving her name at the front office. She had gone against the strict moral precepts by which her Victorian grandmother had raised her, and disobeyed her husband.

Of course, she lectured herself, I'm flattered the director found my little girl appealing. Any mother would be. But perhaps he only said that to make me feel good. And even if he was serious about using her in a picture, what

could that lead to? After all, she's only nineteen months old. What can a toddler *that* small possibly do before a camera that would interest anyone?

"Now aren't you glad I talked you into coming up here with me while I
collected my pay?" Margaret rattled on. "You've got the best-behaved two
kids I've ever seen. Today proves you don't have to stay home in your flat
all the time because there's no one to leave the children with."

Margaret and her widowed mother had been kind and generous neighbors ever since Marian and Jack moved to Los Angeles. They were always
glad to loan a cup of sugar or a bit of baking powder when Marian needed
to bake a cake. Looking back on the last three months, Marian had to admit
only the Campbells had made them bearable.

Although the two women had scarcely exchanged more than the time of
day, the past few minutes had changed Margaret into both a willing accom-
plice and star witness to the most fateful act of Marian's entire life.

"But Margaret, you don't understand. Jack is going to be absolutely furious when he finds out what I've done without asking his permission!"

"You just have to learn how to handle men," Margaret counseled. "Jack
will come around once he sees there's money in it. Just think! Peggy could
earn enough to pay for her own college education and even travel around
the world."

"But ever since he's been doing stunts at Mixville," Marian continued,
"he's kept railing against the awful mothers who drag their youngsters
through the studio trying to get them in pictures. He'll swear I did all this
deliberately."

"Well, then, figure it this way," Margaret advised, "Jack was off at work
and doesn't even know you came with me. And certainly the kids won't
breathe a word if you tell 'em not to. So don't tell him anything until the deal's
all signed and sealed." Then she added with a wicked wink, "Besides, honey,
you're a real looker yourself. A second Marion Davies if you ask me. Some
director might just take a long look and decide to put *you* in pictures."

Marian turned scarlet. For the spinster daughter of saintly Mother Campbell who took in sewing, Margaret seemed scandalously wise about men. Of
course, she does work as a wisecracking waitress at the Pig 'N Whistle
restaurant in downtown Los Angeles, Marian told herself, and she takes
movie jobs every chance she gets, so naturally she's a lot more worldly than
a sheltered wife and mother like me.

Although Margaret was plain-looking and her figure had fewer curves
than the road to Bakersfield, Marian had to admit she did have a certain
sparkle about her. And certainly for a woman so eager to be discovered her-

self, she was more than generous in celebrating someone else's lucky break.

But good-hearted as her companion was, Marian was secretly relieved when, boarding the red trolley on Hollywood Boulevard, Margaret spied a fellow female extra across the aisle and chose to sit with her and trade studio gossip. Marian was badly shaken by this visit to Century and needed time alone to sort things out. With four-year-old Louise minding the baby and the trolley rocking eastward at a fast clip, this was the perfect opportunity.

Marian had grown up cosseted by her grandmother and a host of relatives, the family males all thrifty merchants and bankers who virtually ran the little town of Lancaster, Wisconsin. The unfenced lawns and spreading maples of their adjoining estates formed what was more a rambling park than one little girl's backyard. When Marian was three, her father had placed her with his sixty-year-old mother in this bastion of nineteenth-century propriety because, as the matriarch informed her neighbors and kin, the poor child's own mother had died in the bloom of youth.

While Grandmother Baxter honored her version as gospel, a deathless rumor wafted from one Lancaster veranda to another, hinting that the restless young wife and mother had actually run off with another man and abandoned her child. If Marian overheard such gossip (and time would prove she had), she clung doggedly to the early-death version which better suited her own prudish and self-protective nature. Her motherless childhood also fostered in her what she regarded as a well-deserved self-pity, which she would have demanded be catered to by whatever man she married. Unhappily, the mate she chose was not of a nature to dance attendance.

At eighteen Marian moved to the Chicago suburb of Villa Park, staying with her father and stepmother while attending secretarial school. After a courtship of several months it was understood she and the young man who lived with his parents next door would soon announce their engagement. Ed Montgomery, handsome and prospering, held a seat on Chicago's Corn Exchange and was the kind of steady good provider for which her Midwestern, middle-class, nineteenth-century Congregationalist upbringing had prepared her. Then into this comfortable setup burst the Montgomery family's notorious black sheep. Marian knew only that Ed's brother had run away from home at thirteen and gone west to Calgary, Canada, to become a cowboy. Now, after an absence of a dozen years, during which his family had not known if he was alive or dead, he made a prodigal's return. Ed proudly introduced his girl to his dashing older brother. The instant Jack laid eyes on her the die was cast.

With her willowy figure, delft-blue eyes, patrician profile, and rich chestnut hair swept up into a pompadour, Marian epitomized the era's model of femininity as well as Jack's own romanticized vision of the ideal woman. Although he soon realized she espoused the very same conservative values against which he himself had always been in rebellion, he also understood from the way his own sisters had been reared that this was the mold in which "real ladies" *had* to be formed. As a consequence he immediately elevated Marian to the high moral pedestal where every "good woman" belonged. After all, out west he had seen enough of the other kind.

Despite, or perhaps because of, the fact that Jack had no real trade and few skills except horsemanship and personified all the risky, unstable character traits her relatives had warned her against, Marian was fascinated by the tall, dark, ruggedly handsome cowboy fresh from the open range of half a dozen western states. She hung on his tales of derring-do in the untamed West, applauded his rebellious spirit, and was mesmerized by the exotic aura of adventure that clung to him like the scent of wild sage. In the face of growing family disapproval, she also revealed an unsuspected rebellious streak of her own.

After a six-week whirl of well-chaperoned dances and tours of Chicago's White City amusement park, as they waltzed to "You Wore a Tulip," the jobless, stone-broke cowboy asked her to marry him.

They were married in June of 1915, in a home ceremony at her grandmother's residence. To the naive bride, steeped in total Victorian denial of sex, her grandmother gave a parting word of advice: "In about a year, in a pink or blue envelope, a baby girl or boy will be sent to you in the mail." The following June a much wiser Marian gave birth to a daughter in the time-honored fashion.

Quitting the Chicago job he hated, Jack moved his family to Rockford, Illinois, where he found work he enjoyed and at which he excelled, doing what he described as "topping off green broncs." He appealed to his anxious wife's patriotic nature by giving his singular occupation a mantle of respectability, telling her the vicious horses he was gentling would become remounts for the U.S. Cavalry.

In 1917 the cavalry went overseas to fight in Europe's Great War, and Jack hastened to enlist in what was called the Rainbow Division, composed of volunteers from various National Guard units. (This luckless force was soon rushed into battle and virtually annihilated in France.) Being the father of an infant child, Jack was turned down, but the recruiting officer urged him to help fight the war as a civilian. Troop training centers like Camp Kearny in San Diego, California, paid well, he said, and had a crying need for carpenters.

Marian pushed hard for San Diego. To her *any* job was preferable to the suicidal, bone-breaking business of "topping off" murderous horses every day, no matter how red-white-and-blue Jack painted it. They headed west, but not long after their arrival in San Diego Marian fell ill. The doctor she consulted diagnosed an abdominal tumor and scheduled her for surgery the following Monday. On Friday his young assistant called, explaining that her doctor had suffered a heart attack and she must be reexamined before her operation.

"Well, I'm sure you'll be relieved to know you positively do *not* have a tumor," the smiling young assistant assured her following his examination. "Actually, you're three months pregnant instead!"

Marian bore her second daughter in October 1918, but two weeks later the war ended and Jack's army job with it. He promptly hauled his family off to the great Chowchilla Ranch in the San Joaquin Valley, where years before he had been a top hand. But things had changed mightily: there were no riding jobs. Here it suddenly dawned on Marian that cowboys might be romantic, but they were as obsolete as covered wagons, a hard truth she decided not to share with her husband.

Jack soon landed a job with the National Park Service as a temporary forest ranger in Yosemite Park. Overnight Marian became a pioneer mother. The family was housed in twin tents—one for living quarters, the other a cookhouse, the only luxuries wooden platforms under the tents and Coleman lanterns for light. Jack was given "valley floor duty," which entailed checking public campgrounds and policing the flow of tourists. To her horror Marian learned he was also required to fight forest fires, one of which he survived only by half burying himself in the forest's floor while the firestorm roared overhead.

By day two-year-old Louise was tied to a tree outside the tent, which kept her in sight. The baby's "playpen" was a remodeled Campbell Soup carton Jack fashioned to contain her. Tourists poured through the ranger's tent all day, asking Marian a thousand questions. When she brought Louise in at night, she found her pockets filled with half-dollars, given her by visitors, grateful for her mother's kindness to them. In early autumn Jack was promoted and transferred to the Grand Canyon's south rim. Arriving by train, Marian soon learned that at this outpost tent life came with subzero temperatures and real snow. Come summer the tents were invaded by creatures Marian had not even dreamed existed—scorpions, rattlesnakes, centipedes, and Gila monsters. The Havasupai Indian Reservation was also close by. Although an eminently peaceful people, the Havasupais were in her mind secretly planning the wholesale massacre of every white woman and child on the canyon's lonely south rim.

The nearest town was Williams, thirty miles distant. A government nurse rode in on horseback every three months to visit the Indians. Others living on the rim were free to seek her help as well, *if* they timed their ailments to coincide with her reservation call. But despite the job's inconveniences, Jack was glad to be working on horseback again. Marian now realized this circumstance was indispensable to his happiness. She also discovered he dealt with the public well. He was witty, told riveting true stories of treacherous river crossings and longhorn stampedes, all spiced with the heroism of men he'd known while trailing the last great herds. His supervisor assured him that Park Service precursors like himself would soon begin to reap rewards in better pay, decent housing, and a generous pension upon retirement. Marian was willing to play pioneer mother a few more seasons in return for such lifelong security.

But Jack's temper had a short fuse. One day a pompous major, left over from the army regime which ran the Grand Canyon before it became a national park, ordered Ranger Montgomery to "cuff off my mount and polish my boots!" Jack's scathing, graphically worded response and stubborn refusal to apologize spelled the end of his Park Service career.

Once more the family boarded the train, this time bound for the City of Angels, which was enjoying a postwar building boom. Jack quickly found work as a carpenter, but while it gave him a paycheck and fed his family, he was miserable working on foot.

Still, his luck had not entirely run out. One day he was hailed on the street by "Handlebar" Hank Bell, a Texas cowhand with whom he had "ridden the river" for years. Hank had just delivered three carloads of white-faced steers to L.A. and now he too was afoot and out of work. But Hank had heard tell of a former whiskey mill, aptly called the Waterhole, in the nearby town of Hollywood. Despite Prohibition, here they still served the real McCoy, sub rosa, and not surprisingly this owl-hoot saloon was a magnet to former cowpunchers and vaqueros from all the western states, Canada, and northern Mexico.

At the Waterhole Jack and Hank caught up with several cowboy friends who had also found themselves displaced around 1913 when the country began running on wheels. But miraculously enough, right here in town they had found work which demanded their otherwise obsolete riding skills.

"We're riding in Western movies out at Universal Studios in the Valley and over at Tom Mix's studio in Edendale," one former Chowchilla cow-puncher assured them expansively. "These picture people need seasoned horsemen. Come out with me to Mixville tomorrow, and I'll see if I can get you on!"

As Jack described it to Marian later, Mixville had its own barns, corrals, tack, bunkhouse, and sizable horse herd. Two days later he announced, "I've turned in my hammer! From now on I'm doing stunts and falls with the boys at Mixville."

"But you might as well be back in Rockford, topping off spoiled broncs!" Marian cried. "Only now you'll be breaking your neck for a paltry three dol-lars and twenty cents a day!"

Jack turned a deaf ear to Marian's protests. Two weeks later he became Tom Mix's double, doing all the Western star's dangerous stunts, for which he was now paid a handsome $7.50 a day. Best of all he was in the saddle again, doing what he did best and riding with cowboys he knew and respected and who in turn respected him.

Over the past three months Marian had learned to steel herself, trying not to jump out of her skin every time the hall phone rang, afraid it was the stu-dio calling to say Tom Mix's double had just been dragged to death by some runaway horse and she was now a penniless widow with two small children.

The most enigmatic contradiction in a character riven with them was Jack Montgomery's lifelong obsession with obedience. He was single-minded in exacting it from every man, woman, child, and creature who fell under his domination. Ironically, he himself had routinely *dis*obeyed every-one who had ever held authority over him. Perhaps his compulsion to main-tain total control over his life was rooted in the fact that he had possessed *no* control over the most traumatic event of his childhood—his mother's di-vorce. In 1902 *any* divorce in America was socially taboo, but Jack's mother, who was an upright Episcopalian wife and mother of four, had the poor judg-ment to fall in love with her husband's brother—in, of all places, Lincoln, Nebraska! (Marrying an in-law in that era was still branded "incest" by church and state alike.) She would have caused less outrage if she had walked naked down the town's main street. But it was no less unsettling to him than his own wife's abandonment by her mother.

When his mother took the Montgomery name a second time—following the beclouded birth of an infant son—the family moved to the welcome anonymity of Chicago's Villa Park, where Jack's stepfather held a high post in a local bank and owned a handsome home.

Two years of open warfare with his erstwhile uncle ended when thirteen-year-old Jack took his piggy bank's twenty-five dollars and bought a one-way ticket to Calgary, on the Canadian frontier. Several character traits had now taken deep root in the rebellious youth. Thanks to his mother's "betrayal," he nursed a deep distrust of women, he convinced himself the eighth grade was as high as any self-made man need go, and by his own actions he had proved that if you're not happy in one place all you have to do is head for another.

His defiant nature flourished on the open range. If he was snubbed up too tight here or dealt an abrasive ramrod there, he took horse and bedroll to another spread. Commitment to a single brand was not demanded by the fractious cattlemen, who honored every man's right to move on. Like most of his peers, Jack was pridefully independent and disinclined to obey orders, and while he was willing to bestow friendship on some and fealty on a few, there was no man on earth to whom he need render obedience.

Every horse he owned was taught instant compliance, from coming when it was called to remaining "ground-tied" wherever Jack dropped his reins. He trained each pet dog to perfection. The creature had no choice but to render to Jack what he demanded, its whole-souled devotion to its master. As a consequence, Marian suspected, he concluded that obedience and love were two sides of the same coin.

Since these methods had produced so many top "cutting" horses and tractable dogs, when Jack became a father he naturally applied them to his daughters. It was really very simple, he told Marian. All that was needed, starting in infancy, was to lay out the rules, set limits, issue clear commands, deal out swift punishment for noncompliance, and be consistent. Lifelong love and total obedience from the child were the inevitable rewards.

Unskilled at earning a living for herself and totally dependent on that authoritan and not always reliable breadwinner, Marian was understandably tempted by Mr. Fishbach's offer. Now, as the trolley neared its downtown terminal, Marian hit upon a temporary way out of her quandary. She would fall back on a trick she had used at the Grand Canyon whenever Jack was in a foul temper—bake his favorite devil's food cake. Then, when he was relaxed and in a mellow mood, she would explain what had taken place—all by accident!—at Century today.

3

Marian had barely got back to her flat in the Beaudry Arms when the communal phone in the hall began to ring. It was the secretary at Century informing Marian her little girl had an interview with Mr. Fishbach's assistant tomorrow morning.

In a secret sugar bowl Marian had squirreled away five dollars against some dire emergency. Simple logic told her *this* was the extremity. Then, having sworn both children to silence about today's events, she took Peggy out and bought her a brand-new dress and bonnet for tomorrow's interview and neglected to tell Jack of her plans.

Fishbach's assistant had his office in the front bungalow. When Marian was ushered in, she beheld a stocky, coarse-featured man behind a desk wearing an expression of perpetual distrust and anger. He signaled mother and child to a chair, then sat scowling at them through a scrim of blue cigar smoke. Eyes narrowed, he appraised Peggy as if she were a two-headed calf that some blind contestant had mistakenly entered in a county fair.

"She ever been onstage?" he growled at last. "Any acting experience?"

"Of course not," Marian replied. "She's only nineteen months old."

"No picture work, either, I suppose?"

"No, but she learns fast and minds extremely well."

He rose slowly, walked to a side door, and opened it. In bounded a short-haired, brindle-brown mongrel terrier about the size of a small police dog. As though on cue, he rushed over to the baby and licked her face. Terrified by the dog's sudden appearance out of thin air, Peggy let out a scream of terror and tearfully backed away.

The man gave a wry smile. "Well, that settles it," he sneered. "She's sure as hell afraid of dogs. She'll never work with Brownie."

Marian jumped to her feet. "But you didn't give her any warning." The man moved his hand in a gesture of dismissal. Fuming and without another word, she flounced out of the office, the baby casting a reproachful glance back at the lolling tongue and wagging tail of one of Century's brightest stars, Brownie the Wonder Dog.

That evening, with yet another dilemma facing her, Marian finally resorted to her devil's food cake strategy. After serving Jack a big wedge of his favorite dessert, she took a deep breath and began pouring out the whole story, asking for his help in deciding what they should do. When she got as far as today's failed interview, Jack's reaction surprised her.

"Who does that son of a bitch assistant think he is?" he demanded, rising to his feet. His rage was directed at Fishbach's assistant for disbelieving the integral bravery of Jack Montgomery's daughter. "Hell, she's not afraid of anything that wears hair."

Marian interrupted, trying to calm him enough to hear her out. For not one hour ago Mr. Fishbach had himself called to apologize for scaring her with the dog, and scheduled another interview tomorrow with him. Jack, to Marian's relief, cooled down at once and insisted that he take Peggy to her second audition.

The next morning Jack found himself in director Fred Fishbach's office, demonstrating—through his nineteen-month-old daughter's instant responses—the merits of unquestioning obedience to his authority.

Fishbach marveled as Peggy fearlessly played with Brownie.

"I told her not to be afraid," Jack offered, spreading his hands in a gesture indicating it was simplicity itself.

"I'm sure we'll have no problems with her minding," Fishbach concluded. "This comedy is only two reels long, so it won't take more than four or five days to finish."

Before getting to his feet, and almost as an afterthought, Jack asked, "And what will the Stern brothers be paying her?"

"The standard five dollars a day is all they ever pay," Fishbach explained with a shrug.

"Well, now, that's a real problem, I'm afraid. I'm getting seven-fifty a day for doubling Mix. I don't mind taking these few days off to bring her to the studio, but I can't afford to lose two-fifty a day on top of that!"

Fishbach glanced at Peggy and then back at Jack. "Mr. Montgomery, Julius Stern wouldn't pay her seven-fifty if she were the original Little Eva."

A tense silence fell between them, and then Fishbach rose and walked around the desk to his visitor. "I really *do* want your little girl for this film, so on my word as a gentleman, I'm willing to pay you the extra two-fifty a day out of my own pocket to get her. But it's a private deal, strictly between the two of us. Okay?"

He offered his hand and Jack took it. He had liked Fred Fishbach from the moment they met, and this was the way he was used to closing deals out west. But he still felt ill at ease, for it was the first time he had ever done business with a Jew. Out west the only ones he had ever seen close up were rare Jewish peddlers, hardy souls who braved vast distances and capricious climes to sell such things as notions and pocket watches off the tailgate of a wagon on the streets of small cow towns.

The cavalier cowboys held these peddlers in the same veiled contempt as they did every other man who worked on foot—farmers, sheepherders, and the "carpet knights" who took rake-offs at gambling tables, and on sporting houses. Well, whatever the pecking order had been back on the long gone open range, Jack had been in Hollywood long enough to know that the picture business was a rare equalizer of men, however diverse their backgrounds might be. And for a Gentile like himself, with only an eighth-grade education, that circumstance had its advantages.

"It's a deal," Jack said. "That's damned decent of you and I appreciate it."

Playmates was the comedy Fishbach had written about a baby and a dog. Of course, Brownie was not just some mutt off the street. Smart as a whip, he could execute any trick imaginable from opening doors to riding a bicycle. His Wonder Dog series was one of Century's most popular.

On this set there were actually three directors—Brownie's trainer and Peggy's father, who each guided his own puppetlike creature with hand signals and spoken commands, and Fishbach, who had little more to direct than camera setups. Five days later, when the film was in the can, Fishbach called Jack into his office. "Jack, Julius and Abe Stern are both as enchanted with the baby as I am."

Although pleased that Peggy had proved herself suitably intrepid, Jack was more interested in collecting her one-time check, returning her to a normal baby's life at home with her mother, and getting on with his own career at Mixville.

"Few people know this," Fishbach continued, "but I discovered Jackie Coogan, and tested him, only Julius didn't take to him." He grinned. "But I've hit the jackpot this time. Julius plans to sign her to a seven-year contract at seventy-five dollars a week! He wants to see you first thing next week to sign the papers." With a warm smile, the director held out his hand. "My congratulations, Jack!"

As far as the movie business was concerned, Jack and Marian were still living back in the early daguerreotype age. The only movie Peggy's father had seen before coming to Hollywood was *The Great Train Robbery*, which he saw in 1905 and remembered vividly. Because of her strict Victorian upbringing, Marian had never attended either a vaudeville theater or a nickelodeon in her life. They were not considered places for nice girls or ladies to be seen. Also, given the remoteness of both Yosemite and the Grand Canyon from the nearest town, motion pictures might as well have not been invented as far as Marian and Jack Montgomery were concerned.

Not surprisingly, then, Fred Fishbach's announcement of their daughter's long-term movie contract and her awesome three-hundred-dollar-a-month salary struck them both like a thunderbolt from a cloudless sky. Their immediate reaction was not exploitive but an instinctive desire to retain their child's "real identity." When their first daughter was born, Jack had named her Jack-Louise (he had desperately wanted a son; Louise was in honor of his own mother). But when the second arrived, Marian made sure she did the naming herself. Peggy-Jean was her choice, one that was challenged by the mother superior of Saint Joseph's Hospital in San Diego where she went to give birth. (Not that stoutly anti-Catholic Marian had *wanted* to go there, but because of the flu epidemic, it was the only place that had a spare bed.)

"Peggy is a pagan name," the nun counseled her gently. "You should christen her Margaret, a saint's name."

Marian always bragged she had taught Sunday school back in Lancaster, but not a word of Scripture, hymn, or prayer had ever rubbed off on her. She was as untouched by Christian doctrine as a Borneo headhunter, probably because the subject was too mystical for her brass-tacks nature. As usually happened when her dander was up, she refused to give Saint Margaret the time of day, and the nun bowed out of the arena gracefully. Now both parents wanted the studio to call their discovery Peggy-Jean, but Fishbach insisted that Baby Peggy was pure magic on the marquee, so they lost that round.

Moving from their Los Angeles flat, they rented a small California bungalow on nearby Vista del Mar Avenue, and Jack bought a secondhand Franklin touring car. But upward bound though they now were, there were compromises. Jack flatly refused to allow Marian to take Peggy to the studio. (In his naïveté he equated the actresses he'd seen on the sets with cowtown sporting women and dance-hall tarts.)

However, Jack hated giving up what he considered his own nascent film career to ride herd on his daughter's. Marian did not consider it a sacrifice at all. His leaving Mixville relieved her of the constant worry that he would be crippled or killed and she would end up a penniless widow. (This fear proved so deep-seated it remained her favorite tragic scenario throughout the rest of her life.)

So now the scene was set for a whole new chapter, a life of wealth, comfort, and the all-American pursuit of happiness which up to now had eluded them. But first Jack had a dilemma to work out, a compromise far more complex than turning his back on Mixville. He began to sense, however vaguely, that he was putting his life and future as a man into the hands of his own nineteen-month-old daughter. His self-respect cringed at the prospect. How would people view him? The Jewish producers Peggy was working for? His longtime cowboy friends now working at other studios? His own wife?

He and Fred Fishbach had gotten along famously throughout the making of *Playmates*. Maybe it would go on like that. But he must find a way to preserve his identity in the process, to prove he was still in command of his own destiny as well as Peggy's rising star. If he could no longer further himself, he must prove that all her talent and courage depended *solely* on his guidance. For a variety of reasons—both valid and fancied—he set about making himself indispensable to her career. The higher he pushed her, the more she achieved, the greater the credit redounding to him.

Jack had never even heard of Svengali when he set out to transform himself into a benign, inexpendable version of Du Maurier's malevolent hypnotist, an iron-willed puppeteer wielding absolute physical, moral, and psychic control over another human being. But he didn't have time to choose Svengali as a role model or even read the book: over the next eighteen years he would be too engrossed in making the movie version.

4

My workday—six days a week—began shortly after seven-thirty every morning, with the punctual arrival of my father and myself at Gower and Sunset. The boulevard was broad and lined with young fan palms which had not yet grown much taller than I. As automobiles were few and traffic far lighter in those early days, Father's usual parking space at the curb was always empty and waiting. We alighted from the Franklin (my small tooled-leather makeup case in hand) directly in front of Christie Studio, whose high gray battlements made it seem more like a fortress than a film factory.

Farther west on Sunset one could find a number of imposing California stuccos and Spanish-style residences painted pink, salmon, or pale green, a growing vogue among longtime Hollywood residents and newly arrived picture people alike. But here at the busy, studio-dominated intersection of Sunset and Gower, budgets, not beauty, defined the style. Every office, bungalow, fence, or wall was painted battleship gray. If once gaily colored, they

had long since been sun-bleached and weather-beaten back to a dingy util-
itarian white. The four corner lots at Sunset were occupied respectively by
Christie Studio and the Napoli Cafe on the north side, Century and a drugstore on the south. Far from being interlopers, both restaurant and pharmacy
were an integral part of Poverty Row's movie industry, catering almost ex-
clusively to a studio clientele. (At that time only lordly Universal had its own
private restaurant.) The corner drugstore did a flourishing trade in movie
makeup and backed onto a clutter of stages and offices which mogul Harry
Cohn would later piece together to form Columbia, the first major studio
on Poverty Row.

Those working at Century entered not by the front-office bungalow at
6100 Sunset but past a gateman in a small security booth on the Gower Street
side. From here a wooden walkway led past several frame bungalows, converted into cutting rooms and storage vaults, their windows heavily barred
for security. Here round silver cans containing finished films were stored.
The passage between these bungalows was always ripe with the sharp,
smoky-sweet smell of raw film. But, as I would soon learn, scents changed
dramatically as one traveled across the lot.

We usually took a shortcut through the huge prop department, which was
a treasure house to a child. It was crammed with flats, furniture, suits of armor,
tapestries, bits and pieces of castles, drawbridges, and dungeons from every
period of history since the Pharaohs. There were African masks, Roman
shields, jury boxes, Western saddles, breakaway barroom furniture, pow-
dered wigs, Turkish interiors, cigar-store Indians, and bronze Chinese cer-
emonial gongs. This was the vast arsenal where Julius stored all the weaponry
of make-believe essential to his small army of directors: many items in it
would later turn up on my own sets. Despite Century's comparatively modest size, it produced an amazing variety of serials—Chinese, animal, Western, jungle, and mystery—all requiring a wide assortment of backgrounds.
The prop department gave off a distinctive musty smell of old paint and gathering dust which told me where I was, even with my eyes closed.

My dressing room, about eight by ten feet, was little more than an over-
size crate put together with green lumber. An iron rod in one corner served
as both closet and clothesrack. A prewar army cot, with its rock-hard
stretched canvas surface, was my bed, not a luxury but a necessity demanded
by the California child labor laws for a working child's daily nap. (Luckily
I was never given time to take a nap, so I never had to use it!) For wintry
mornings, or when I worked nights, a squat kerosene heater, resembling a
rusted institutional-size coffee can on legs, was brought out to be lit. Its fee-

ble blue-and-gold flames gave off precious little heat, but the rank stench of kerosene hung over the room for days afterward.

A rough-hewn makeup bench ran along one wall, a mirror above it edged with naked lightbulbs encased in wire cages. The air was pungent with the mixed odors of lead-based greasepaint and Stein's pre-nickelodeon, rancid-smelling brand of theatrical cold cream that came in a big blue can. Father was in charge of all facets of my career except choosing what dresses I wore when I wasn't at work, a prerogative Mother retained. He drove me to and from work, chose the food I ate, the costumes I wore, and the barber who cut my hair, and as my director it also fell to him to apply my makeup.

There were no studio makeup departments in those days, and only major stars, such as Mary Pickford, hired their own personal experts. Getting presentable for the camera was a case of every man for himself. It was then a far more complicated chore than it later became, mainly because greasepaint came only in six-inch-long, paper-wrapped cylinders and had to be applied by rubbing the solid stick over the face. On chilly mornings, when greasepaint was especially firm, it felt as if the cold stick would take my entire face with it before any color rubbed off.

Purple eye shadow went on more easily, lifted by a little finger from the stick and gently applied. A bright spot of lip rouge on the tip of a toothpick was placed at the inner corner of each eye. Then, despite the fact that I was barely two, lip rouge spread on with Father's little finger gave me much the same cupid's-bow lips as Pola Negri and Theda Bara. Once the heavily leaded powder was firmly patted on over the lead-based greasepaint, every pore was sealed and my face encased in a firm mask. As the day wore on the mask grew even heavier as more leaden powder was applied before each new camera setup to kill the shine from the heat of the spots. One of the earliest self-restraints I mastered was never to touch my hair or disturb my makeup in *any* way.

It was surprising Father learned to tackle this exacting ritual at all, for he had discovered the secrets of makeup the hard way. Only three months earlier, when first hired to double Tom Mix, he was told to apply greasepaint to increase his resemblance to the star. At day's end he turned to the same veteran stage actor who had helped him apply it and asked, "Now how in hell do I get this damned bear grease off my face?"

"Nothing to it," the older man assured him. "Just pick up some cold cream tonight on your way home."

At home, after half an hour's struggle before the bathroom mirror, Jack had finally called Marian for help. She hurried in to find his face a solid white mask.

"An old stage actor told me cold cream would take this stuff right off," he fumed, "but it's not even making a dent!" Only then did Marian notice, sitting on the sink, the small half-pint bottle of chilled dairy cream which Jack had innocently picked up at the corner grocery store!

Century was ruled from the top, but Julius Stern allowed himself no more creature comforts or perquisites as president than his lowliest employee. The raw, unpainted cubicle in which he worked was not one iota less spartan than any office or dressing room on the lot. His penuriousness was thoroughgoing and evenhanded, and while it scorned preferential treatment, it also made grousing about one's own stark accommodations an exercise in futility.

As recently transplanted Easterners, Julius and Abe Stern dressed strictly according to the dictates of the season. It was white shoes and straw boaters from May to October, dark shoes and hard-topped derbies the rest of the year. Both worked in brightly gartered shirtsleeves, but always formalized with starched collar and tie.

Not long after I went to work on the lot, author Edgar Rice Burroughs closed a deal with Julius to produce the first movie version of *Tarzan*, featuring Elmo Lincoln as the Ape Man and Louise Lorraine as the original movie Jane. On their first visit to the studio, Ed and Emma Burroughs were introduced to Father and me, and it was the start of a long association between our two families.

Too miserly to keep on renting animals by the day from Charles Gay's lion farm in nearby Del Monte, Julius followed the precedent set by his brother-in-law, Carl Laemmle, at Universal, and formed his own zoo right on the lot. He started out with a jackass, a billy goat, and a large brown bear. For the upcoming Tarzan films, he purchased two of Gay's African lions, a nearly toothless tiger, and an ancient elephant, all for a song. The disconsolate roars and rank odors emanating from the big cats' cages and the elephant's corral gave ample warning to anyone approaching this corner of the lot that danger and even stronger odors lay ahead.

These venerable four-legged thespians formed a handy source of animal extras for Julius, all under the seasoned guidance of longtime circus "bull handler" and lion trainer "Curly" Stecker. But there was one genuine star in this menagerie, the remarkably clever chimpanzee Joe Martin. Trained and directed by both Stecker and his wife, the chimp had achieved worldwide renown starring in Century's popular "Joe Martin" two-reelers. Although my father cautioned me to stay clear of the zoo and keep a watchful eye out for Joe Martin, over the next eighteen months I was required to work with nearly every frightening member of this animal farm, two of whom were to die during that time under tragic circumstances.

A raised walk of plain wooden planks snaked around the dusty lot. In summer it was possible to disregard this boardwalk, but in winter, when seasonal rains turned the entire lot into a sea of mud, it provided the *only* means of getting from one building to another. Like everything else at Century, from leaky roofs to the sun-rotted awnings which hung in faded shreds at each grimy window, this antiquated walkway was in such an advanced state of disrepair and decay that in countless places individual planks had disintegrated and entire sections had disappeared. While the unwary adult might sprain an ankle or possibly even break a leg in one of these gaping holes, a small child could virtually drop from sight. To avoid these hazards Father took to carrying me like a satchel, hands clasped above my head to form a handle, knees bent to clear the ground. Because I was barely two feet tall, it came to be the handiest way for us to get around the lot and to cross downtown streets and intersections as well.

As costars, Brownie and I turned out a veritable blizzard of fast-paced two-reelers. These were true slapstick comedies which some theater managers ran as "chasers"—screening them as one audience was exiting the house and the next coming in. Referred to on the lot as "five-day wonders," they were produced at what seemed the speed of light, at an average cost to the studio of less than three thousand dollars each, and sold to exhibitors at vastly inflated prices, earning Century enormous profits.

One morning, after working with the dog for more than a year, I was told that poor, tireless Brownie had died in his sleep. Saved from a dogcatcher by his trainer, Charlie Gee, Brownie had made his debut with Charlie Chaplin in a 1918 comedy-drama entitled *A Dog's Life;* it made him a star. He died in early 1922, in the canine equivalent of his eighties.

Father was concerned that Brownie's death could spell the end of my rapidly ascending career. But while Fred Fishbach was saddened by the animal's death, he was jubilant about the possibilities it opened up for his own career and mine.

"We've mined out the dog-and-baby format," Fishbach told Father over lunch at the Napoli, where we always ate.

"But they *did* put her on the map, Fred," Father countered. I was beginning to be interviewed by magazine reporters, my fan mail was snowballing, and Sid Grauman had already featured me in a solo skit on the stage of his Million Dollar Theater in downtown Los Angeles.

"That's exactly why it's time for a change," Fishbach enthused. "Julius knows he has to groom a successor to replace the income Brownie used to generate, so I've already suggested to him we star her in an all-new series of her own, Baby Peggy Comedies. She deserves better than playing second fiddle to a dog."

Jack was flattered but visibly shaken at the heady prospect of Peggy becoming a serious rival to Jackie Coogan.

My own lunch finished, I was quietly occupied with playing an imaginary game of tic-tac-toe with myself on the Napoli's Italian-style red-and-white-checked tablecloth. Fred Fishbach placed his hand fondly on my head as he spoke. "Alf Goulding and I have a whole string of absolutely fresh story ideas that will mean a real step up from what she's been doing. We'll advertise her as the youngest comedienne in entertainment history—which is certainly no lie!"

Julius Stern brought in a new terrier look-alike as a hedge against the possibility that Peggy might not make it on her own and also in the faint hope he could keep Brownie's lucrative series going with a stand-in. Nevertheless, he *did* agree to try out the two directors' innovative concept. My brief apprenticeship was over. Now I would be up there with all the other daredevil knockabout comedians on the lot, working without a net to catch me if I fell.

5
—

Alf Goulding's contribution to this series consisted of takeoffs on classic fairy tales, famous novels, and even grand opera. Interspersed with them were such favorites as *Hansel and Gretel, Little Red Riding Hood, Carmen, Jr.,* and scathing two-reel parodies on the social evils of the day—unwed mothers, yellow journalists, bribe-taking politicians. His fertile imagination also conjured up satires of leading screen stars in their most famous films— Pola Negri as the femme fatale in *Kiss Me, You Fool,* Rudolph Valentino as *The Sheik,* Mae Murray's vampish *Merry Widow.* Playing the major satirical adult roles—both male and female—was two-and-a-half-year-old Baby Peggy.

These original screenplays were full of gaping holes and intentionally so. Julius had not been far wrong when he claimed that Century comedies were put together by gagmen on the set. Following the proud tradition of slapstick comedy, an art form he himself had pioneered at Keystone, Fishbach purposely left these gaps in the script so that he, his gagman, and often the comedians themselves could flesh out the films with fresh silent business and sight gags on the spot. This procedure kept the action cracking and was guaranteed to keep alive the sparkle of spontaneous humor which alone made good slapstick work.

Far to the west of Century, at what was regarded as Charlie Chaplin's classy La Brea Studio, the Little Tramp had metamorphosed into a lordly, exacting genius who took months on end to turn out everything from a two-reeler to a feature-length masterpiece. Seventy to a hundred versions of a single scene were not uncommon during the year-long making of *The Kid*, his 1919 classic which shot his five-year-old costar, Jackie Coogan, to fame overnight. But at Century, as far as I could tell, the penalty for filming even *one* scene twice had to be tantamount to being boiled in oil, so strictly was the one-shot rule observed. The reason, of course, was rooted in the high cost of film per foot and Julius Stern's standing order not to waste an inch of the stuff. Father explained this fact to me when I first started working with Brownie. "In the picture business," he said, *"time is money."* My reputation for being "one-take Peggy" was soon noised about the lot, and my zeal for saving film won me high points with both Julius and Abe.

Most visitors to my set were amazed at my instantaneous response to any order given me. Although I invariably put my own personal twist on every emotion, expression, or bit of business I acted out, the truth was that all the rules and limits had been learned in infancy, and any breach of either, having been promptly punished, had driven the lesson home.

Fortunately, I did not have a willful nature, so having learned obedience, learning to act was made easier. These visitors also forgot I had the example of adults all around me who had to follow orders just as promptly as I. When the director called "Hold the hammers!" before a take, carpenters building sets in other parts of the same stage immediately stopped banging. At his command of "Ready! Action! Camera!" every actor responded right along with me. If role models mold childrens' values, I had them a-plenty. At Century even the animals practiced instant obedience!

Significantly, I had *no* other children pressuring me to conform with what might have been disruptive common peer-group interests. The only child I had ever played with was my older sister, Louise. Most movie children who worked with me were every bit as businesslike as I. But there were others who staged tearful scenes or threw outright tantrums on the set, refusing to perform until they were bribed with ice cream or candy. Even at two I was completely outraged by these irresponsible outbursts of temper which brought nothing but my own and everyone else's contempt down upon their heads. I saw no rewards and countless disadvantages in behaving in such a selfish and unprofessional manner.

Some visitors jumped to the false conclusion that my responsiveness to Father's direction was driven by fear of severe reprisal. When they overheard him say to me just before a take, "Okay, now, do it right, or I'll beat you with a two-by-four," their fears were confirmed. This was our own private joke. I don't remember his ever laying a hand on me at work, and I did not strive for excellence out of fear. It was simply my nature to take everything in life seriously and to be single-minded in whatever I did.

Father studiously avoided open praise for fear of spoiling me, and I never expected or asked for special favors. A grip brought me my vanilla milk shake from the corner drugstore every morning at the stroke of ten because it was good for me, regardless of whether our work went well or poorly. I never chewed gum, drank soft drinks, or snacked between meals (although candy was allowed at home), so I neither missed these nonessentials nor considered them treats. Having no experience with treats or expectations of reward, I was confused to see that children could lose all control of themselves and forfeit every shred of dignity by screaming for such bribes. My sole motivation was to earn Father's approval and that of my coworkers, from the director down to the crew. From my colleagues I only wanted acceptance on equal terms.

The only difficult situation I faced with adults lay outside the working relationship entirely, when I had to deal with tourists visiting the set, or be interviewed by a sob sister from one of the growing number of movie magazines. I hated having to watch grown men—often learned, highly respected professors, judges, bankers, and lawyers—cast aside all the dignity and reserve I expected from adults and reduce themselves to the level of doting grandfathers while they ohhed and ahhed over a celebrity named Baby Peggy. I saw her on the daily rushes, and I knew I was the one who, in the final analysis, made her tick. But I was self-aware enough to realize that in a certain sense she was not the *real* me. She was the larger-than-life projection of Baby Peggy these moviegoers *saw* but whom they did not *know*. I was made uncomfortable by their adulation because it was not being lavished on me for anything I had done, but as though merely being a child were somehow a noble achievement, deserving in itself. The gushing and patronizing fans and reporters made me feel deeply embarrassed for them.

We were set to begin shooting the new series early in 1922, as soon as Fred Fishbach finished putting together a special stock company composed of reliable performers he knew from Educational, Ince, and Keystone. His first priority in recruiting these character actors was size—he wanted men, women, and animals whose bulk or height would emphasize the diminutiveness of his lilliputian star. His first acquisition was a dignified Great Dane named Teddy, who had built quite a career for himself as a comic at Keystone. As he was a very large example of his breed, experienced and well trained, he fit Fishbach's criterion perfectly.

Blanche Payson was a strapping, statuesque amazonian actress who stood six feet two and weighed well over two hundred pounds. Handsome and sweet-tempered, on-screen she came across as hostile and formidable. A former Los Angeles policewoman, Blanche had turned in her badge to accept a curious position with Mack Sennett, working on the lot as a female turnkey. Her job was to watch over the luscious but elusive bevy of "bathing beauties" he had recently put under contract. Pursued by a small army of the movie equivalent of stage-door Johnnies, none of these aspiring Gloria Swansons seemed inclined to put up much of a fight anytime their own virtue was at stake. After waging a losing battle to keep this fickle flapper harem virginal, or at least under lock and key, Blanche gave up and was glad to accept Fishbach's offer to work as a foil for Baby Peggy.

Fishbach bagged another stock-company steady when he spotted him visiting the lot—a lantern-jawed Polish Jewish youth from El Paso, Texas, named Jake Earle. He confessed to Fishbach he had never acted a day in his life and was so sensitive and shy he would have made himself invisible if that were possible. But he had *one* striking quality that made him positively priceless to Fishbach—he stood within a few inches of being *eight feet tall*. As Fishbach gained Jake's confidence, he learned the nineteen-year-old was so deeply depressed about his incurable glandular condition that his watchmaker father had treated him to this trip to Hollywood, hoping a visit to the studios would take his mind off himself. When Jake mentioned his longing to be independent and earn his own living at some decent job, Fishbach offered him steady work playing giants in Baby Peggy comedies. To Jake it was manna from heaven, no matter how paltry the pay. Needless to say, any actor to whom money was no object was a man after Julius Stern's heart. Jake was hired on the spot and paid about forty dollars a week. Over the next few months he appeared in twenty-five of my films.

When working with Brownie we had stayed fairly close to the studio, but now going on location became the order of the day. It was on these location excursions that the always hectic and perilous pace of moviemaking reached new heights of excitement and danger.

Teddy worked with me in *Seashore Shapes,* an early solo-flight comedy that came close to being my last. We were working on the beach at Santa Monica where the waves were running more than ten feet high. The Great Dane was to pick me up by the back of my one-piece wool bathing suit, carry me out to the breaking waves, hold me under a few seconds, and then trot back to the camera, holding me securely in his massive jaws. I had never been in any form of water deeper than a bathtub, nor had I ever seen a wave up close. Father's test-walking me along the strand did nothing but convince me that an ocean was a whole lot bigger and more powerful than I. I wasn't too keen on trusting my life out there to a dog I had only just met. But "the story called for it," as the pat phrase went, and at Century that was cause enough for any actor to walk on or under water.

Teddy and I reached the waves together without incident, but once he dipped me in the surf, he seemed to lose track of time. At first I held my breath as I had been told to do, but as the seconds passed, half the ocean seemed to rush into my lungs. I choked, gasped for air, and lost my breath completely. Without even knowing the word "drowning," I realized that was precisely what I was doing. Terrified, I finally blacked out. I came to again in bright sunlight and heard Teddy's trainer calling out to him to drop her right in front of the camera. Teddy obliged and the director called, "Okay! It's a take!" No one asked how I had fared in the brine, so I didn't bother to explain to anyone. I was glad to be alive and to find out we wouldn't have to shoot the scene again.

On another location I worked with the studio goat. The animal, saddled and standing upright, was wired to the bed of a pickup truck. I was placed astride him and wired to the saddle. Another wire around one ankle secured me to the truck bed. The idea was to drive the truck over a bumpy road while the camera, mounted on a camera car moving alongside, filmed from the waist up a pint-size cowboy riding a bucking bronc. Typically, they hired a teenage kid off the street to drive the truck, and off we went to find a bumpy farm road leading through a plowed bean field.

Father gave strict orders not to exceed twenty miles an hour, but once the boy got his hands on the wheel, he turned into another Barney Oldfield (the champion race car driver), sending the truck bounding over the rutted road while Father and everyone else on the now-speeding camera car yelled at him to slow down. Heedless or deaf to their orders, he merely pressed down harder on the gas and barreled on, doing over fifty. One of the wires holding the goat in place snapped and the terrified animal went down, throwing me over the edge of the truckbed. I hung precariously upside down, held fast by the single wire around my ankle, my other leg free and kicking, arms waving wildly. All the while, barely six inches from my nose, the truck's left rear wheel spun dizzily before my eyes.

"Don't move your arms!" Father shouted to me from the racing camera car, frantic I would unwittingly plunge an arm between a spoke in the turning wheel and have it torn from my body. "Hold both arms tight against your chest!" he commanded. "No matter what happens, *don't move!*"

The camera car's wild pursuit of the truck through the bean fields, twin dust plumes whirling a mile behind both vehicles and me dangling overboard upside down, was like a scene out of one of Century's own cliff-hanging serials. The bizarre chase lasted nearly three minutes more, until they finally flagged down the driver and cut me free. But the entire time I had followed Father's orders not to move. My habit of instant, unquestioning obedience always served me well. This time it saved my life. I don't think the teenage hot-rodder fared as well.

On location in the beach town of Venice, filming *Miles of Smiles*, I was playing twins separated in infancy. As the poor lost twin, I was shown working as a railroad engineer, complete with striped bill cap and overalls, driving the engine of a miniature railroad train. The narrow-gauge track encircled an artificial lagoon which the city's founders had built to make Venice, California, resemble its Italian model. The company was set up in a park, which had been duly closed to all foot and bicycle traffic while we were shooting there. I was waiting in my small director's chair, and when Father called me to come over to the engine, I started across the gravel path which ran through the park. Without warning, a boy on a speeding bicycle, who had somehow slipped through the studio's barrier, came hurtling through the trees, striking me with tremendous force. The impact itself would have been bad enough, but my engineer's overalls got caught in the bicycle's rear spokes and I was dragged along the gravel path for almost thirty feet before the cloth finally tore loose and released me. The rider, apparently unaware he had hit anyone, sped on out of sight.

My overalls were made of tough fabric, but the gravel chewed it up thoroughly and worked similar havoc with me. I suffered severe abrasions over most of my body. When Father picked me up and saw the damage, he took me in his arms and ran to the nearest medical aid, unfortunately a quackish doctor working in a makeshift emergency station at the end of Venice pier. His magic potion for warding off what he seemed to think was an imminent case of lockjaw was to paint the entire skinned surface of my body with white iodine!

Father sat me down on the cot and peeled off what was left of my clothes. "This is going to hurt a lot," he warned, "but it's got to be done, and you're *not* going to cry."

I took him at his word and endured this barbarous cure in agonized silence, mostly because I didn't want to embarrass either Father or myself by making a scene.

On yet another memorable location shoot at the Pasadena train station, Fred Fishbach and Father were preparing to do a sequence featuring me, dressed as a hobo, riding the rods underneath a Pullman car. But Father and Fishbach were in sharp disagreement over how we were to do it.

"I insist they disconnect the engine from the cars first!" Father argued hotly. "I refuse to risk putting the baby under there until they do."

"Jack, how many times do I have to tell you?" Fishbach retorted angrily. "The stationmaster has absolutely guaranteed the engine won't move an inch until we've finished shooting and she's completely clear of the train."

While the two men argued, I noticed that the long passenger train, which had been standing there for the past fifteen minutes waiting for us to make up our minds, began slowly pulling out of the station. I tugged at the director's trouser leg to get his attention. "Look, Mr. Fishbach!" I cried, pointing to the cars. "The engineer didn't even wait for us to do the scene!"

Both men looked up, saw the moving train begin gathering speed, and turned positively ashen. "Oh, my God!" Fishbach cried. Sinking into his chair, he buried his face in his hands and burst into tears. Regaining his composure momentarily, he called out in a hoarse voice, "Company dismissed!"

In one comedy whose title I never knew, I worked all one day in a bathtub supposedly foaming to the brim with soapsuds. But instead of suds the director used whipped cream. Under the hot lights the cream soured, the taste and smell making me deathly ill. For years thereafter just the sight of whipped cream nauseated me. When I walked into the banquet room of New York's Biltmore Hotel filled with five hundred guests celebrating my fifth birthday, and glimpsed a table lined with pie wedges topped with whipped cream, only Father's firm admonition, "Don't you *dare* get sick!" saved the day.

We enjoyed many lighter moments making Baby Peggy comedies, and most of the time it was Julius Stern himself who provided them. Like his fellow immigrant movie producer, Samuel Goldwyn, Julius was renowned for his malaprops. It was said he had first wanted to name his company Miracle Pictures and honestly believed he had found the perfect motto to go under the logo: "If it's a good picture, it's a miracle!"

For all he knew about what made good comedy, he was utterly mirthless when it came to real life. When a rival producer jokingly disparaged his two-reelers, Julius declared with a perfectly straight face, "Century comedies are *not* to be laughed at!"

Alf Goulding asked to take the Baby Peggy company all the way to Yosemite Valley to film *Peg 'o the Mounted,* a spoof on the Royal Canadian Mounted Police, with the park's soaring granite walls and towering pines providing the spectacular background. In response to this request the penny-pinching Julius uttered his oft-quoted classic, "A rock's a rock! A tree's a tree! Shoot it in Griffith Park!"

When one of his directors, making a Western serial, asked Julius to rent a North American mountain lion for a scene in which a hungry puma is shown stalking the heroine, Julius countered stubbornly, "Lions we've got on the lot."

"But a puma is a sleek animal," the director explained patiently. "Our zoo cats are *African* lions, with those big ruffs around their necks. They simply will not do!"

At that point Julius came up with his solution. "Shave 'em! Disguise 'em! But, goddamn it, use 'em!"

In making *The Little Flower Girl,* on a set inside the Barn, with a pretty dark-haired Century ingenue, we filmed a scene in which we played French flower vendors. To lend atmosphere the assistant director brought in the studio jackass, bearing on his back two baskets stocked with paper flowers. He was a bad-tempered creature given to biting anyone who displeased him. In the middle of our scene, when the actress was to pluck a flower from one of the baskets, he laid back his ears, bared his teeth, and turned on her.

Badly frightened, the poor girl fled the set, but the angry beast lit out after her, chasing her the full length of the Barn. At last, caught between the jackass and the far wall, she scampered up the electricians' iron ladder leading straight up the Barn wall to the walkways above. But she was not *quite* fast enough. With a final lunge the jackass sank his teeth into the only fleshy part of her anatomy still within his reach, stripping off her full skirt and every other stitch of clothing she had on below the waist.

Furious and smarting, she raced from the Barn in tears, demanding to see Julius. Waiting in her dressing room, she lay facedown on a cot, covered by a sheet, suffering as much from mortification as physical pain. When Julius appeared she delivered her ultimatum: "Julius Stern, you get rid of that god-damned fire-breathing dragon or I swear I'll never set foot on this lot again!"

"But darling," Julius pleaded, "we need him. He's the only ass we've got!"

"And this," she stormed, touching her wounded posterior, "is the only ass *I've* got! Get rid of him!"

Making two-reel comedies was a dangerous occupation, but it was also creative, challenging, and understandable. It was in my other life at home that I began facing problems far too complex for any child to grasp but which, with my exaggerated sense of responsibility, I felt called upon to solve.

6
***

In our family, due to the convergence of several curious circumstances, my mother led the sheltered life of a child, not I. Father had picked up where Grandmother Baxter left off with the task of keeping her protected from the real world. He made it clear a lady never cut her hair but wore her crowning glory piled atop her head. Neither did a lady smoke, drink, wear short skirts, work outside the home, or drive a car. These restraints were simply his way of keeping his wife safely on her proper pedestal of moral virtue—and securely chained to it.

Because we were constantly together, and almost of one mind in everything, I quickly acquired Father's protective attitude toward Mother, concocting sugar-coated half-truths in response to her bright, "So, what happened at the studio today, honey?" When I came home from my mishap in Venice, wrapped in more bandages than King Tut's mummy, I downplayed the extent of the accident *and* the pain of its cure. Needless to say Father and I never even mentioned such close calls as the train-station incident and my upside-down bean-field chase. Since they left no visible scars, why frighten her?

But in spite of our efforts Mother could not entirely avoid being caught up in my spotlight. She watched my appearance at Grauman's Million Dollar Theater, sitting out front in an agony of worry, certain no child *that* small, and all alone on a stage, could muster the courage to face this vast audience, not to mention remember a monologue. Dressed as a washerwoman, bending over a small tin tub and scrubbing clothes on a miniature washboard, I delivered the opening line in this brief solo skit, "All ye ladies with babies, bring your washing to me!"

At that, the slippery bar of Fels Naphtha squirted from my fingers and skidded downstage. I spent the next few moments on hands and knees in a determined search for the soap. Finally fishing it out of the footlights, I held it up to the audience in silent triumph, then returned purposefully to the tub and picked up my lines exactly where I had left off. Mother sat in stunned disbelief. While the stuntman in Father believed Baby Peggy could execute *any* feat mortal man could conceive, Mother still saw her as a helpless toddler, so small she was not yet even steady on her feet.

But whenever Marian *was* in the public eye, she always remained the staunch Victorian. Asked by reporters to comment on her daughter's success, she invariably cast any inelegant facts in a more tasteful, genteel light. Describing my discovery and why she took me with her to the studio that day, she ad-libbed, "I couldn't leave Peggy at home because it was *our maid's day off*." Father became an expert at spot-cleaning family history as well, telling reporters he'd become a Yosemite Park ranger because doctors advised him to take the sickly infant Peggy to the mountains for her health. He left his ranger post at the Grand Canyon, I discovered, because doctors said his wife "was too frail to stand another winter there."

In one interview Mother invented a fairy story version of my eight-hour-day working life. "Peggy works, if you can call it work, only four hours a day, never at night, and never on Sundays. She considers her work play, and nothing is ever said or done to make her feel otherwise: she believes she's only *playing*!" Father informed the press, "Acting in pictures has never been a joyous game to Peggy. It has been work, good hard work, from the first day." Of course, this toilsome version place Jack Montgomery squarely in the driver's seat, as the hidden hand and secret force behind Peggy's much-vaunted genius, a talent which he insisted was nothing more than simple obedience to his commands.

Unfortunately for Father, my older sister, Louise, was living proof that obedience, like hypnosis, requires a reasonably convinced, or at least a *willing* subject. On several occasions at home, when guests pressed him to test his theory, he set out to prove its merit by calling Louise into the room. Her nature was the exact opposite from mine. Where I was outgoing and self-confident, she was painfully sensitive and shy. When Father tried to put her through my fast-paced, snap-of-his-fingers routine, barking out commands to express various emotions—"Laugh! Cry! Anger! Surprise!"—she became rattled and ran from the room in tears. After a few such fiascos, Father was careful not to try demonstrating his theory with anyone but me.

As one perceptive woman interviewer observed in *Picture Play* magazine, "Mr. Montgomery might make a fortune writing books on child training. But he is making one fortune now managing Peggy." Then she added with remarkable insight and prescience, "The future of Baby Peggy doesn't seem to me so much of a question as the future of Mr. Montgomery. . . . I have a feeling there will come a day when she will stop taking orders from her father. When that day comes, it will be Mr. Montgomery who will feel the blow most. . . . She has been not only the darling of his heart—she has been his gold mine. Managing her has been his career, and in a way she has been the clay which he molded and through which he expressed himself. Unfortunately for him, dominating parents are not being tolerated by girls over twelve or fifteen this generation."

Although low salaries, physical hardships, and violent quarrels had troubled the home life of Jack and Marian long before they were caught up in the limelight, they had not quarreled over money. But Marian knew that Jack had an extremely jealous nature and that his threshold for both anger and pain was exceedingly low. In Los Angeles after he started work at Mixville, he had gone to a back-street, low-priced credit dentist who bungled a simple extraction. When the wound became dangerously infected, Jack went temporarily out of his mind with the pain. Taking out his revolver, he vowed he must kill Marian and both children before putting himself out of his misery. In the fierce struggle that ensued, Marian wrested the gun from him and hid it, saving our entire family from being snuffed out only days before Margaret Campbell's "Hollywood lightning" had a chance to strike.

Now, however, there were powerful new forces at work to undermine the marriage of this mismatched couple whom outsiders regarded as fortune's darlings. In retrospect I realized they did not understand the rootless community in which they were living nor comprehend the immense social changes wracking the postwar world. As a consequence they tended to personalize and blame each other for outside pressures that made them feel unhappy and insecure. Jack, handsome, witty, and vital at thirty, found himself constantly in the company of such alluring ingenues as Louise Lorraine, Virginia Valli, and Florence Lee, each of whom had, oddly enough, played Baby Peggy's mother. To Jack's surprise, he discovered he was attracted by and attractive to the opposite sex. Ironically, these independent young moderns who intrigued him so were the very same free spirits Jack was afraid Marian would emulate if he let her visit the studio.

The naive young mother who had greeted Fred Fishbach wearing the same suit she had worn on her honeymoon suddenly woke up to fashion. Since she had all day in which to do practically nothing, Marian began visiting the dress shops lining quiet but swank Hollywood Boulevard. Salesladies told her she had the perfect pencil-thin, boyish figure that was the height of fashion in the early twenties. It slowly dawned on Marian that her rich chestnut hair, falling to her waist, and the pompadour in which she wore it were both passé and déclassé in up-to-the-minute Hollywood. One day, without telling anyone, she called on my barber and asked him to bob her hair and give her one of the popular new permanent waves.

Father was livid. That quarrel lasted an entire week. At last he drowned his anger, not in drink, but in the purchase of two brand-new cars—an elegant Lincoln limousine for Mother (he hired a chauffeur to go with it) and a Pierce Arrow touring car for himself and to take me to and from the studio—beginning a compulsive and increasingly expensive hobby.

Expanding our lifestyle, we moved from the rented Vista del Mar bungalow and bought a three-acre ranch out in the remote San Fernando Valley. At that time the Valley was a vast expanse of fields, tilled mostly by Japanese truck gardeners, its flat landscape broken by windbreak rows of eucalyptus trees and an occasional peach and apricot orchard. Our new acquaintance Edgar Rice Burroughs was behind this move, for he had just built his own dazzling pink Spanish stucco mansion on a knoll overlooking our property and had advised Father to invest in Valley real estate. The Burroughses called their hilltop estate Tarzana after Ed's jungle hero, and soon our two families were best friends, visiting each other every weekend.

Now we had not only two cars and a big home but our own saddle horses and whitewashed stables in which to keep them. White Man was Father's high-stepping gray; Redwing, a little brown mare he bought for Mother and Louise to share. Tim—a jet-black midget Mexican horse that stood barely thirty-six inches high—was the singular mount Father purchased for me. I rode him in several of my comedies, and Father and I often took Sunday-morning rides together along the bridle path that ran down the center of Sunset Boulevard as far west as Whittier Boulevard. The seventeen-hands-high White Man and the miniature Tim, with their strikingly dissimilar riders, proved a traffic-stopping sight for residents and tourists.

In addition to the usual work schedule at Century, I was suddenly in demand by movie-magazine writers and as an honored guest at evening banquets, theater openings, and society horse shows. I even entered a Baby Bathing Beauty contest at Santa Monica Beach. Naturally, Century saw to it I was photographed when I won.

About this time Hollywood was unexpectedly hit by a landslide of scandal. Movie idol Wallace Reid died from his tragic addiction to morphine. Thomas Ince's alleged murder, while cruising aboard William Randolph Hearst's private yacht, rocked the movie colony. At the apex of his fame, Fatty Arbuckle stood trial for the rape and death of an actress in his hotel suite. This was followed by the suicide in Paris of Olive Thomas, Jack Pickford's wife, who was also on drugs. The murder of Desmond Taylor exposed him as a Lothario linked to drug dealing and sexual liaisons with two famous movie actresses. This, combined with a spate of shocking movie star divorces, caused the morally bankrupt industry to be threatened with a nationwide boycott by irate church groups and outraged women's clubs.

Julius Stern made sure that he and "angelic" Baby Peggy were photographed with Will Hays the instant that worthy was named censorship czar of the endangered industry. In a similar example of using a child star's innocence to cleanse Hollywood's tarnished image, a photo of Jackie Coogan hugging Arbuckle, the Coogans' longtime vaudeville pal, was circulated when a third jury found the comic innocent. In 1923 the Hollywood Chamber of Commerce chose Baby Peggy to grace their flower-covered float in the annual Pasadena Rose Parade. I rode with the impeccably virtuous May McAvoy, who had just returned from a private audience with the pope. Driven snow could not have been purer! But years later I learned that the ribald joke making the rounds at the time had it that the Rose Parade was actually the chamber's *second* choice. First, the story went, they tried to stage an impressive parade of virgins down Hollywood Boulevard as a show of moral strength, but it was called off because May McAvoy caught the flu and Baby Peggy refused to march alone.

I came to regard the grueling business of "touring the realm" as an obligatory task to be carried out by me with the same sense of duty as that shown by the crowned heads of Europe whom I had seen in newsreels, waving, nodding, and smiling at their subjects as they rolled by in their gilt-trimmed, horse-drawn carriages. These after-hours visitations opened up an entirely new dimension of responsibility to me, the obligation owed one's fans. Astounded at the volume of fan mail I was now receiving, Mother sometimes read aloud to me portions of the more poignant passages.

Usually written in English (no doubt by some bilingual scribe), these letters came from all parts of Europe, from Australia, New Zealand, China, Japan, and Russia. I knew that silent films were shown all over the world and titles translated into each country's language, but I was profoundly impressed by this odd, one-sided human connection around the globe. These total strangers all wrote as if they knew me well, and although I had never laid eyes on any of them, I felt an invisible bond *had* been forged between us. Thousands of copies of Baby Peggy photos, reproduced from an original bearing my scrawled signature, were sent out in response to requests from these fans.

Because my parents did their quarreling at home, either in my presence or within earshot, it was clear to me that my earnings were the main bone of contention. Jack accused Marian of spending too much money on furs and clothes. She hit back by ticking off his own list of luxuries: sport togs, country club memberships, golf clubs, monogrammed silk shirts, horses, and automobiles. In self-defense he claimed he had to develop what he called "important industry contacts" on the golf links. She nagged him to be more aggressive in negotiating a higher salary for Peggy and in finding a business manager who saw to it she was paid what she was worth.

It was no secret, even to such financial innocents as my parents, that Baby Peggy's box-office ratings were now way up there with Coogan's and Chaplin's and that the Stern brothers were making out like bandits at her expense. Each two-reeler in which she starred cost the studio a mere $5,000 to $7,000 to make. In turn Universal Studio paid Century $50,000 for distribution rights before releasing each comedy worldwide.

Having circled the globe, each two-reeler racked up for Uncle Carl Laemmle between $300,000 and $500,000. Not a bad return on my $75-a-week salary. Furthermore, due to both the business and blood relationship between them, the Stern brothers were given a generous share of Laemmle's final take. At that point Century systematically *burned* the comedies overseas exhibitors returned, to extract the $2.50 worth of silver nitrate the film contained.

Many foreign companies chose *not* to return films to Hollywood: considering them a valuable new art form, they conserved them in their own vaults. For this reason alone, decades later, film archivists were able to retrieve the few Baby Peggy comedies to escape the flames.

The brilliant Alf Goulding not only directed me in more comedies than anyone else but was responsible for those that were the most successful. (He would later launch the great comedy team of Laurel and Hardy.)

In Goulding's script *Taking Orders,* the chimp Joe Martin was cast as my patient in a dentist-office sequence in which I played a comically small dental assistant. I was terrified of Joe. My skin crawled whenever the chimp put his hairy arm around my shoulders or flashed an entire keyboard of yellow ivories in a grimace known the world over as "Joe Martin's smile." But Curly Stecker, his trainer, assured Father he was absolutely safe. I *was* impressed by his remarkable patience, having to wear clothes and work under the blazing heat of the spots. Fortunately, I only had to endure his company for five days. The following Monday I was due to start a new film, and Joe would be working on a different stage.

But come Monday, shortly after we started shooting, the panic-stricken director from Joe Martin's set suddenly came running onto our stage, which also served as a shortcut to the Stern brothers' offices.

"I've got to find Julius!" he shouted frantically to Goulding as he ran. "Joe Martin just turned on Mrs. Stecker and bit her on the arm! Curly was there and went berserk. He picked up a crowbar and beat Joe over the head until the chimp went limp, then dragged him off to the prop department. We've got to stop him or he'll kill poor Joe!"

Seconds later Julius Stern came racing across our set, going the other way, his face white, right hand clamped onto his straw boater, red-striped tie streaming behind him. By now chaos had broken out all across the lot. We could hear bloodcurdling screams emanating from the prop department. These in turn set off every other animal in the zoo: Old Charley began trumpeting wildly from his corral over by the Barn. The jackass started braying incessantly, and the three big cats kept up a frantic, sympathetic roaring.

When Julius reached the prop department, he found Joe Martin strapped down in the very same dental chair he had occupied in last week's scenes with me. His enraged and powerfully built trainer was bending over him.

"No, Stecker, no!" Julius pleaded. *"Please, not his trademark!"*

But he was too late. Using a pair of ordinary pliers, the infuriated Stecker had already pulled out every tooth in poor Joe's head. Then, as though emerging from a trance, the trainer realized what he had done. Looking into the animal's pain-crazed eyes, he knew if he ever let him free now, the murderous chimp was capable of tearing any man to pieces. As Julius turned away in anguish, Stecker drew the pistol he always carried in his belt, and with a single shot put Joe out of his agony. That bullet also put an end to one of Century's most successful series. As a studio ad had long proclaimed, there was only *one* Joe Martin.

Several weeks later, Father and I were sitting in a far corner of what had once been the old Barn's hayloft. We were there because it was a quiet spot, and Father was trying to teach me to pronounce certain words correctly. He had no patience with baby talk, so while looking down on Charley, he drilled me in carefully pronouncing "elephant" instead of "efosom." Curly Stecker kept a small amount of hay up there for Charley, and on this day he was pitching a few forkfuls of it down to land just inside the gate of the elephant's corral, in the shadow of the Barn.

Stecker confided to Father that he disliked working with Charley. "We've got a long feud between us," he said. "He turned on me once back in our circus days, and I had to take a chain to beat him off. That's twenty years ago, but he's never forgotten. My wife can work with him, but he'll have no part of me." He chuckled as he looked down at the elephant, who always had one foot chained to a heavy post planted deep in the center of the corral. "I almost never go inside, but toss hay down to him like this. And I *always* carry that." He pointed to a high-powered elephant gun standing in a corner of the loft.

A week or so later, I was working on an outdoor set for *Hansel and Gretel* with several tame deer Julius had reluctantly hired for the sequence. The crew was about to wrap things up for the day when two of the deer leaped high into the air as though someone had put springs under them. Only then did the rest of us catch the sound of Charley's fearful trumpeting and the chilling scream of a man in mortal terror. "Stop him! For God's sake, *somebody stop him!*"

"That's Stecker!" Father cried.

"Good God! Run for your lives!" Alf Goulding shouted to everyone on the set. "Charley's loose!"

Panic ensued; Father picked me up and ran directly to the old Barn, knowing it would be the safest place on the lot with Charley escaped and running amok. When we reached the loft and looked down, we were astounded to find Charley still safely inside his corral but dragging the heavy uprooted post to which one leg was still chained.

Suddenly Father ordered me sharply, "Don't look!" as he caught sight of Stecker's crushed and broken body lying in Charley's shadow. While I obediently kept looking the other way, a propman found Stecker's big gun where the luckless trainer had left it, just inside the gate beside a small pile of hay. Three blasts from the powerful weapon and the angry, swaying hulk of Old Charley lay in the bloodied dust beside the fatally incautious bull handler on whom he had wreaked his long-delayed vengeance at last.

7

As I entered my third year with Century, my own and my family's lifestyle began to soar and, Father having won some hefty increases from Julius, so did my salary. Father made use of his natural animosity toward "cow-town" Jewish peddlers to take me from seventy-five to five hundred dollars a week. Now, added to my other spare-time chores of being seen and touring the realm, I was required to play hostess to an endless parade of dignitaries, reporters, or just plain sightseers who trooped onto my set every day.

On weekends I walked through "home layouts," movie magazines' newly created means of showing fans where and how stars lived inside their own posh palaces. Partly to mine a richer lode of real estate, and partly to better match the image my fans expected, Father sold the ranch in San Fernando Valley and purchased a more impressive home in Beverly Hills. The magazine photographers always got the fanciful glimpses of "normal" home life they had come for—photos of me reading a big book of fairy tales or playing with my large collection of dolls. Since the truth was I had not yet learned to read and my dolls were all gifts from fans (I only played with bears), in essence these home tours fell considerably short of reality.

One Sunday afternoon my parents took me to a premiere at Grauman's Egyptian Theater on Hollywood Boulevard. Also attending were the Jack Coogans and Jackie. Some reporter came up with the suggestion that Jackie and Peggy should appear in a movie together—perhaps Shakespeare's *Romeo and Juliet*. Both fathers dryly dismissed any such pairing as "absurd." Despite their widely disparate backgrounds, the two Jacks managed to be friends, but each jealously guarded the singular identity of his respective breadwinner. Neither the former cowboy nor the one-time vaudeville hoofer would permit even a publicity picture to be taken of three-year-old Peggy and eight-year-old Jackie together.

After the show we retired to the popular Montmarte Café across the street, which was so crowded that the two families had to settle for separate tables. Halfway through our meal I looked up and saw Jackie coming in from the balcony, striding directly to where we were sitting. Banging his small fist on our table, he looked me straight in the eye and said accusingly, "I am *too* younger than you!" Then, without a word of explanation, he strode back to his own table outside.

Perhaps the most demanding of all my mounting publicity chores was being quizzed, tested, and analyzed by child psychologists. Because the popularization of the Freudian movement coincided with the public's fascination with movie personalities, they had a field day sifting the minds of Hollywood's two famous child stars, Jackie Coogan and Baby Peggy. Many reporters, besotted with sentimentality, called Jackie "a masterpiece of life," "an inspired artist," and "the Boy King." They sang my praises as "the darling of the universe," but "child genius" was their most extravagant term for us both.

The road to high expectations thus paved, it was not surprising that half a dozen fledgling experts invited me into their classrooms or offices. There they proceeded to ask a long list of complicated, misleading questions about everything I saw, heard, or did at the studio. Shortly after each interview, my parents received in the mail a densely worded report and the psychologist's assessment of Peggy's intelligence quotient and possible "genius level." Of course my parents did not understand how each erudite Ph.D. arrived at his conclusions, but it sufficed to know their daughter possessed the rare IQ of 145 points! This they felt was cause for considerable personal pride. Over the years, when proudly quoting this statistic in speeches and letters, Father always interpreted and wrote it "Eye Cue," which, considering my film career, made much more sense to him.

On a less exalted level, when questioned by another savant to tell him what swearing meant to her, Peggy answered in pure studio jargon, "Oh, that's what they say when they want to move the lights!" The baffled professor had to have Father translate that one for him.

Meanwhile, the tutor whom Mother hired had my sister to herself all day, but she found Peggy a rapidly moving target with little time to apply her vaunted IQ to the labor of learning to read and write. Worse still, the tutor got virtually no cooperation from either parent. Both were quite content to let my education slide or, more accurately, let it rest on my impressive psychological laurels. Certainly Father had never held schooling in high regard. Now that the Freudians assured him a bona fide genius like me could pick up anything from calculus to Sanskrit without benefit of tutors, he considered the problem of my education solved. Of course he knew a child labor law required that two hours a day be set aside for schooling, but he also knew the studios honored it only in the breach. As a consequence my education was put on ice, and I never did have a teacher at Century.

Incredibly enough, to his dying day my father never even asked me how I—not yet able to read or write—had performed so flawlessly. In retrospect, I think I developed a simplistic technique of learning in the round, taking the objects around me as symbols, signals, or markers, as opposed to acquiring knowledge through devoted and structured sequential learning time. As an intelligent child, it was not enough for me to follow orders. I, not the orders, had to figure out how to execute commands in ways that seemed safe, reasonable, and believable to me. It was a skill I came by subconsciously, grounded as it was in pure instinct and self-protection.

By the time I was three, I had worked so consistently I could not imagine any other kind of childhood. With tourists or reporters I often made polite conversation by asking what pictures *they* had made when they were children. Excepting my own parents and Louise, all of whom I knew relied on me, I thought every other adult in the world had worked in pictures when they were little.

Although she did not work, not even Louise was allowed to play with other children, lest she catch some childhood disease and pass it on to me. Skates and bicycles were taboo for Baby Peggy (skinned knees and broken arms were not in my contract), so Louise had to forgo them too. I was rarely at home, and in fact, I didn't much like staying home. It bored me. Most of all I hated being put down for naps. I *never* took naps on the set or on location, and I grew very anxious trying to sleep in broad daylight when I felt I should be up and working.

One rare weekday when I could not go to the studio due to some delay in finishing a set, I was in our backyard with Louise when I heard a great commotion in the yard next door. Climbing up on a box so I could see over the ivy-covered wall, I beheld an appalling sight. Perhaps as many as twenty children were romping about on the lawn, riding teeter-totters, sliding down slides, eating ice-cream cones, and laughing and shouting at each other.

"What in the world are they doing?" I asked Louise.

Thinking I must have eyes in my head, she replied matter-of-factly, "What do you think they're doing? It's a party and they're *playing*!"

"But it's a *weekday*!" I cried, genuinely outraged at the children's shift-lessness. "Why aren't they working? Who will take care of their parents?"

At Century, at least, I now had a child companion on the set. He was not a playmate but a fellow actor, which of course explained why we got along so well. Blond, six-year-old Alfie Goulding, the director's handsome little son, was cast as my leading man in several riotously funny satires on adult situations which his father directed. Goulding, a widower, had no one to care for the boy at home.

When I was introduced to Alfie on the set of *Carmen, Jr.*, I was told it was his first time ever before a camera. In our first scene we were to do a Spanish dance together, and this being his first picture, I was concerned that he needed help and guidance. Conscientiously, I kept whispering helpful instructions and cues while we danced. Years later a grown-up Alfie described to me the Baby Peggy he had worked with that first day as "the youngest little old lady" he had ever met.

It was 1922, and the two-reeler entitled *Peg o' the Mounted* was now set to be directed by Alf Goulding. Julius had finally agreed to let him shoot it on location in Yosemite Park. Little Alfie came along, even though he wasn't in the film, as did Jake Earle, who was playing yet another giant. Mother and Louise accompanied us as well, a rare treat for them.

The reason Jack allowed Marian to be part of the Mountie location was that *this* trip to Yosemite was special. It marked the triumphal return of the former lowly ranger who had dry-nursed tourists and fought forest fires for a paltry eighteen dollars a week! Now, a mere two and a half years later, he and his wife were celebrities, the proud, and *very* well-to-do, parents of a famous child star whose name was, as the press said, "a household word in every civilized country in the world."

In this parody of the Royal Canadian Mounted Police, in addition to being the Mountie hero, I also played a hapless part-Indian woman. In the latter role I wore a ragged cotton dress and had to wear my hair in wisps tied by tightly twisted strips of rags. It was extremely painful to my scalp.

One evening when we finished work, Father told me the camp's owner, Dave Curry, had asked me to give a special personal appearance for his guests in a small amphitheater in the center of camp. I was still in my Indian costume at twilight when Father and I mounted the little stage.

I knew what was coming, as I'd done it countless times before: a quick run through the usual series of commands to register expressions and emotions—surprise, anger, fear, laughter, tears. But tonight I was tired and my head really ached from my hair being pulled all day.

Surprise, anger, fear all came off without a hitch, but when Father demanded, "Cry!" something inside of me snapped. I had an inner mechanism that always produced real tears on order, but I didn't feel like reaching down to prime that pump. Always willing, tonight I felt cranky and very much put upon.

"I won't!" came my answer, loud and clear, the first time in my three years of life I had ever dared utter those forbidden words to Father. I could not have picked a more inappropriate time and place to challenge his authority than here in front of Dave Curry and all his former ranger friends. He stared down at me in utter disbelief. As if to prove he had misunderstood, he asked slowly, "What did you say?"

"I won't!" I sang out again. I heard my stout refusal hit the valley's sheer granite walls all around us, liking the sound of it as two faint echoes came ricocheting back to me.

At this point Father picked me up, spanked me soundly, and set me back down on my feet. As I gulped down my tears, he issued his next command, "Now, *laugh!*"

I laughed.

$\mathscr{8}$

Even at this early date, in 1922, it seemed to me that Hollywood was already a throwaway society. If every building was a series of flats and false fronts hammered together by carpenters one day, only to be torn down the next, what was permanent? My own case seemed to prove my point. At three and a half I had already made a score of two-reel comedies. I had outlived Brownie, Joe Martin, Curly Stecker, and Old Charley. Fred Fishbach had moved on to another studio and our family had changed addresses four times, all since starting my career a little over twenty-four months ago. Small wonder, then, that I was so impressed when we worked on location at the one-hundred-year-old Spanish mission of San Fernando Rey in San Fernando Valley. Even half ruined it was an imposing structure, with its arched cloisters, stout roof beams, and thick adobe walls. For the first time in my life I felt I was inside of something the prop department couldn't *possibly* have put up overnight. It was one location that seemed protective in-

stead of threatening, in stunning contrast to my hit-and-run life at the studio and constant strife at home.

But another transient movielike set in my life was about to be struck. The
Baby Peggy stock company Fishbach had put together began falling apart.
First Blanche Payson returned to the LAPD. Next we lost our resident giant,
Jake Earle. While working on *Jack and the Beanstalk*, Jake fell in love with
a pretty waitress at the Napoli Café. She was a petite five feet tall, while Jake,
now twenty, stood eight feet six and was *still growing*. Shy though he was,
he decided to propose to her. Later, in tears, he confessed to Father that the
girl had reacted to his proposal by backing away, screaming, and then running from him as if he were some kind of monster.

Always quiet, after this incident Jake fell into a deep melancholy. We had
made forty-eight comedies together, and while making our forty-ninth, he
fell fourteen feet from a scaffold attached to one of Century's so-called comedy cars. As he crashed to the ground, he was struck a hard blow by a falling
two-by-four. Rushed to the hospital, he woke up the next morning with a
broken nose and blurred vision. That soon degraded into blindness. His parents arrived and took him home with them to El Paso. Another fast-moving
chapter in my life had closed.

I never had any problems with good behavior and manners at the studio
or in public. It was only at home that I unwittingly made serious social blun-
ders. Our butler and maid were a married couple. William was a very dark
Negro, while Juanita, being part Cherokee, was lighter. William was elegant to his fingertips, but their marriage was tempestuous, for Juanita had a
fiery temper. I loved them both and had never thought of them as being different from me in any way.

But I returned home from the studio one evening, after a day of working
in old-fashioned black cork, surrounded by a group of real Negro children
at a banquet table. As they were my own age, their color made a great impression on me.

After my bath and before donning my pajamas, an astounding realization
struck me. Still in the buff, I ran downstairs to the butler's pantry and confronted William.

"Look, William!" I said as though I had just discovered the secret of life
itself. "I'm all white, and you're a nigger!"

"Don't you ever call me that!" William cried angrily. Brushing past
Juanita, he headed for the living room. Seconds later Father appeared, picked
me up bodily, and carried me up to where the razor strop hung on a hook
inside the bathroom door. Suddenly realizing I must have said something

taboo, I decided to plead my case. "But Daddy, William *is* black like those children on the set today! You heard yourself that's what everybody was calling them!"

Stumped, Father gravely replaced the strop. "Well, it's not a polite word. It's—" He floundered. "It's bad manners and—if you use it—well, people won't like you!"

Whenever I was at home, Louise functioned as my unofficial bodyguard. One Saturday she left me in the backyard momentarily while she ran into the house for something. When she returned seconds later, I had disappeared. She searched the hedges and flower beds, but in vain. In tears she reported to Mother, who ran to the neighbors asking if any of them had seen me. One woman *had* observed a moronic-looking youth loitering near our house moments before. Another said she saw a long black limousine cruising slowly down the street. It could have picked Peggy up! Beside herself, Mother phoned Father at the studio. By the time he had blazed across town at ninety miles an hour, the front lawn was swarming with police, newspaper reporters, and photographers, while guilt-ridden Louise and an anguished Marian sat on the front steps weeping quietly.

In the midst of this confusion William ran down Crescent Drive, thinking I might have wandered off toward the trolley tracks. Just as he reached Beverly Hills Park, he caught sight of Juanita, strolling home proudly under the trailing pepper trees, head high, shopping basket on her arm. Skipping along beside her, blissfully unconcerned, was the object of the citywide dragnet!

Breaking into a run, he confronted us, his face contorted with anguish and rage. With no explanation, he snatched me up and into his arms. "You fool black nigger squaw!" the always impeccably mannered William screamed at his poor unsuspecting wife. "What do you mean, *stealin' this child?*"

Juanita's responding rage was so great it seemed to me she was giving off light. I was aghast, for all she had done was to grant my request to accompany her to market. It was a treat Louise enjoyed *every day*, but because I was always working, *I* never got to go.

If William hadn't turned and run for home with me in his arms, I think Juanita would have torn him apart on the spot, her fury was so intense. As we drew closer to the scene of utter chaos on our front lawn, now nearly two hours old, it dawned on me I must have done something terribly wrong. In the midst of a crowd of reporters, neighbors, and curiosity seekers, Father's newest car was parked in the driveway, all four doors wide open, and Father was surrounded by policemen. "Oh, William, please don't tell Daddy!" I begged. At which point a newsboy ran past us with a bundle of newspapers under his arms, shouting: *"Extry! Extry! Baby Peggy kidnapped in Beverly Hills! Child star missing! Read all about it!"*

When William delivered me to my hysterical parents, Father was so overjoyed to find me alive he did not even scold me. Louise was forgiven for her dereliction of duty, and Mother clasped me to her like I was made of solid gold. The incident passed, but my kidnapping scare cost us our two sterling servants, and William and Juanita, their marriage.

At the time I was completely unaware of the massive publicity campaign launched by Julius and Abe Stern once they saw how popular my two-reelers had become. Full-page ads for Baby Peggy comedies appeared regularly in the leading trade journnals.

Abe Stern announced he had commissioned the firm of Louis Auberg to issue *two* bisque-headed Baby Peggy dolls, one pensive, the other smiling, both the living image of the star dressed as Red Riding Hood, the film Century was promoting nationwide. Box-office boosters, such as Peggy look-alike contests, "with her doll as first prize!" were well advertised and staged by theater managers across the country. By 1922 Century began marketing my two-reelers to theaters in handy "six-packs" and admonishing distributors in full-page ads, "Dont *ever* miss a Baby Peggy!" Every Christmas week Julius celebrated a "Century Week," usually showing my films at his New York flagship theater.

But in November of 1922 *Motion Picture News* reported that "Baby Peggy, the three-year-old Century comedy star, and the youngest star in the world, is dangerously ill with pneumonia." Work on the film *Grandma's Girl* (a parody of Harold Lloyd's *Grandma's Boy*) was suspended. In December Alf Goulding, the film's director, collapsed and his doctor ordered him to take a long, much needed rest. The film was canceled. The exhausting pace of grinding out our seemingly effortless five-day wonders was beginning to take its toll. This, my first serious illness, must have shaken my parents and may have been the reason that Father decided to try to obtain a release from my contract with Century. Still outraged at the disparity between my now $750-a-week salary and the fortune Century was making from my thrifty five-day wonders, in the fall of 1922 Father decided to go directly to Uncle Carl Laemmle at Universal. It turned out Father had picked a most propitious time to approach Carl Laemmle. He alone seemed aware of a hitherto unguessed resource in comedienne Baby Peggy—her potential worth as a tragedienne.

He knew two-reelers had won her a huge following. As one of Universal's own ads in the *Saturday Evening Post* magazine stated, "She is a better actress than a lot of older people who draw aristocratic salaries. Exhibitors are booking her right and left, and there isn't a pretentious theater in the country that doesn't regard her as a great drawing card."

To his amazement Father learned Uncle Carl was not interested in adjudicating any feuds. Instead he wanted to take Peggy away from Century and out of comedy. His plan was to bring her over to Universal to star in feature-length dramatic films. Uncle Carl was playing a hunch and bidding for much higher stakes by grooming Peggy as the Tragic Muse to run against Jackie Coogan's Tearful Waif. Laemmle knew well that child stars, like racehorses, had short track lives, but Peggy was a mere colt while Jackie, going on nine, was already long in the tooth. My new "aristocratic salary" at Uncle Carl's Universal was an impressive ten thousand dollars a week.

Moving from Century to Universal was like going from a tattered tent show to the Metropolitan Opera House. The entry and front office were cream-colored stucco, done in Spanish mission style, although with a certain boxiness that kept the walls from achieving true loftiness and the arches from soaring. Still, it was imposing in its own way. There was a large fountain and pond before the entrance, in which goldfish darted. Indeed, it was there on my first day that I was greeted personally by the elfin fifty-five-year-old Laemmle, who took time to show me the pond's bright orange denizens and then proudly led Father and me on a guided tour of his fabulous domain.

Unlike Century, Universal was a city in its own right. It boasted its own large, incredibly busy restaurant, its own street-cleaning company, police and fire departments, a private reservoir, a chicken ranch, and a sizable zoo. There was an enormous tack room, with enough saddles to put a large company of cavalry in the field. Father, who had worked there during his brief career as a stuntman, was already familiar with the cowboys' lounge. It was equipped with two or three round, saloon-style gambling tables, and there, between scenes, cowboy actors and extras could play their brand of poker or the well-remembered frontier favorite, Jick, Jack, Jinny, and the Bean Gun.

To the far left of the studio's wrought-iron entrance gates was a large wire-enclosed pen, where cowboys willing to kill time in this informal labor pool were hired to fill any instant Western posse's ranks. The back lot was a triumph of trompe l'oeil; the Paris streets for Lon Chaney's *Hunchback of Notre Dame* and the solid-looking brick façades of the old New York street could have deceived even the natives.

Directly behind the back lot rose a round grassy hill, providing a perfect

Western location in the studio's own backyard. At almost any time of day I could see a cattle stampede, Indians pursuing covered wagons, or outlaws holding up a lone stagecoach on those slopes. As a Universal star, I was presented with my own large dressing room, handsomely furnished and carpeted, and with what, after my dark cell at Century, I regarded as pure luxury—a window!

But there were many other things at Universal not visible to the naked eye. Laemmle made an annual pilgrimage back to his German birthplace of Laupheim, where he was honored as its most generous benefactor. The lot swarmed with close to a hundred relatives from there, hence the name Uncle Carl. "Uncle Carl Laemmle / Has a very large faemmle," quipped Ogden Nash. Due to his lavish nepotism offset by occasional bouts of Century-like austerity and followed by orgies of prodigious spending, Hollywood wags dubbed Universal "the Bottomless Pit."

There were countless stories circulated about Uncle Carl's eccentricities. Although gladly giving up the garment business for films, he never lost his sharp eye for haberdashery. When an agent brought a good-looking leading man to him for an interview, Uncle Carl circled the actor, studied him carefully, but failed to hire him for the part. When the agent later asked why he had turned the man down, Laemmle replied, "Handsome he is, act he can, maybe—but, my God, who made his buttonholes?"

My debut as a pint-size Divine Sarah was a feature-length film entitled *The Darling of New York*. Directed by well-known actor-director King Baggott, then at the zenith of his career, it was the story of poor Italian immigrants coming through Ellis Island and settling in a grim New York tenement building, where all manner of tragedies overtake them.

While chases, pratfalls, and pie-in-the-face antics were the order of the day at Century, Universal was a bastion of melodrama. *The Darling of New York* was a classic Laemmle weeper that offered its tormented star limitless opportunities to spurn the cheap deceit of glycerine and prove to the world she could generate plenty of "real tears." "To be taken seriously," Uncle Carl said delightedly after watching a day's rushes, "a child star *should* make you cry." To help his actors emote, Uncle Carl provided each company with its own three-piece orchestra—usually a portable organ (or concertina), a violin, and a bass viol. The musicians rendered such tearful ballads as "My Buddy," "Roses of Picardy," "Danny Boy," and "I'll Take You Home Again, Kathleen," known generically as "cry music."

But life at Universal, even caught up in melodrama, still proved dangerous to the lachrymose child star. The sequence in which the tenement catches fire was the high point of the film. In it Gladys Brockwell's double, with a Baby Peggy dummy in her arms, jumped from a fourth-floor window into a fireman's net. Drenched with water from the fire hoses, we shivered through two or three cold nights' work on the New York street, doing close-ups for these fire scenes. Then we moved inside for interiors of the same blaze.

For my own inside fire scenes, the window frames and doorjambs were primed with kerosene-soaked sawdust. Just before the camera rolled, they were all set aflame, except for the door leading into the tenement hall. It was *not* to be fired, for it was through this one safe exit that the panic-stricken immigrant child I was playing manages to escape from the burning room.

When the scene began, I ran dutifully from window to window seeking a way out, and then made straight for the door. But when I opened it a crack, I saw it was also ablaze and realized the propman had misunderstood his orders and fired it as well. Having been warned it would be impossible to retake this scene without rebuilding the entire set, I slammed the door shut. Seeking some other way out, I chose the window nearest the camera, for its sill was not burning as fiercely as the rest.

From behind the camera neither Father nor King Baggott could see that my other exit was in flames, so they kept shouting at me, "Go back to the door! Get out *now, through the door!*" I ignored them, grimly following my own instinct for survival and putting all my energy into clambering over the windowsill, which put me right in the camera's eye. It was not until the scene was over and I showed them the charred doorjamb that they understood. But my ad-lib escape provided Baggott with a realistic close-up of a trapped child frantically finding her way out of a blazing room.

Uncle Carl's decision to bet a bundle on his "immigrant hunch" paid off in a big way. Baby Peggy's largely immigrant audience was ripe for a three-handkerchief melodrama recapping their own recent encounters with Atlantic crossings and big-city disasters. The film was a box-office hit. In Europe, where my following was already strong, moviegoers planning to risk that fateful voyage saw in me a symbol of hope and courage, and *The Darling of New York* was as popular abroad as it was at home.

Fast approaching four, and working harder than ever in films, I realized, in retrospect of course, that the real goal I was striving to achieve did not lie at the studio. There I accomplished every day what I set out to do: gratification was virtually built in. But all the while, in the back of my mind, I struggled to accomplish something of far greater importance to me—trying to make Jack and Marian Montgomery stop fighting and be happy.

Perhaps because I knew they depended on me financially, I convinced my-self that the burden of insuring their happiness devolved solely upon me. I regarded Mother as especially helpless and dependent, while Father on the other hand dominated my entire world to the farthest horizons. Knowing no other God, I gave him the same respect others give the Almighty, for it would not have surprised me to learn he had created the universe. Nevertheless, I knew from what I overheard that *I* was the root cause of their unhappiness, a discovery which only added guilt to the fact that I couldn't make them happy.

An idyllic marriage and blissfully happy home life was the polished image they presented to outsiders. The perfect 1920s attractive young couple, cast in the mold of Scott and Zelda Fitzgerald, they attended premieres and nightclubs and were the hit of their own parties and those given by the Bur-roughses, Fishbachs, and Coogans.

At the Burroughses' parties, Jack and Marian gaily threw themselves into the eerie game of Murder, all the rage in Hollywood at the time. The game was fueled by a potent mixture of bootleg liquor and a total blackout of the entire house, with players being forced to grope their way through the dark-ness of sprawling Tarzana in a search for both murderer and victim. At these curiously juvenile orgies, guests were known to fall downstairs or into foun-tains and lily ponds, easy to do given the amount of alcohol consumed amid the absence of light. As Mother told me many years later, at the game's end more than one tipsy couple was discovered lying naked together in a con-venient double bed or—as on one occasion—ensconced in a considerably less comfortable bathtub.

When entertaining at home, Father was impeccably turned out in black tie, wing collar, and tuxedo. He started the evening off by performing the host's lively ritual of agitating a mixture of gin, orange juice, and ice in a sil-ver cocktail shaker the prescribed number of times. Then he filled crystal highball glasses on a silver tray which the butler gravely served to the guests.

Father was a natural raconteur, drawing on his eventful days as cowboy and ranger. Mother, also in formal dinner dress, played counterpoint to him, amusingly filling in the distaff side of his adventures. Oh, the water buck-ets she had carried! The hardships she had endured while living in a tent with two babies in the wilderness, fighting off wild Indians, rattlesnakes, and Gila monsters! Invariably, her closing line, delivered with a heavenward glance of saintly patience, was, "And of course, wouldn't you know? Every time I needed him most, Jack was off somewhere, fighting a forest fire or going down the canyon with those damned mules of his!"

European-born Fred Fishbach found their well-polished tragicomic duet wonderful. Eccentric dancer Jack Coogan, who knew what audiences liked, told them more than once, "You two would make a helluva great two-spot team in vaudeville!"

Jack and Marian had "made the scene," but behind the hum of constant partying, the buzz of conflict sounded. Father was hopelessly ill-equipped to handle money and desperately needed to find someone trustworthy to name vice president of the Peggy-Jean Corporation, a difficult task in this sharper's paradise. After I moved to Universal, he had hired one highly recommended business manager who not only embezzled ninety thousand dollars of my earnings but wisely decamped to Brazil with his loot.

Finally, in sheer desperation, Father fell back on what many picture people had found a safe solution: hiring a relative to manage the money for him. It had worked for Charlie Chaplin, whose financially shrewd brother, Syd, handled his affairs, and for Mary Pickford, whose scrappy mother, Charlotte, made Mary's millions multiply like rabbits. Father's choice, however, was especially noteworthy because the relative he selected to handle Peggy's mind-boggling earnings was the Villa Park banker, his erstwhile nemesis, uncle, and stepfather, J. G. Montgomery.

Mother tried to persuade Father to change his mind. The two men had hated each other ever since they met. But deep down, Jack felt this was his opportunity to bury the hatchet between himself and J. G. He regretted having put his mother through a dozen years of grief after he ran away from home, and this would make up for that. J. G. accepted the job as vice president of my coporation. In late 1922 he and my grandmother came west by train to move in with us.

Of course, this meant investing in a much larger house. A newly hired local "investment advisor" cautioned him to "get out of Beverly Hills because it's becoming a common address." The fourteen-room mansion and estate complete with rock gardens, gazebo, and stables he saw for sale in Laurel Canyon was five times costlier than the house on Crescent Drive. The big real-estate futures were in Malibu, the Miracle Mile of West Wilshire, and in exclusive Laurel Canyon.

PART 2

1923 –1926

THE GOLDEN EGG

"What do you want to be when you grow up—an actress?"

Peggy shook her head. "No, I want to be a lady."

"And can't you be both?"

"I'm afraid," she said, twisting the corner of her small jacket, "I'm afraid I'm not big enough."

"Seen but Not Heard: An interview with three-year-old Baby Peggy."
Motion Picture Classic,
October 1922

9

On the afternoon of October 26, 1923, the grand ballroom of New York's Biltmore Hotel was crowded to capacity with newspapermen and -women, photographers, actors, writers, producers, and financiers of the motion-picture industry. Hosting this banquet for five hundred distinguished guests was the National Press Association. Among the glittering celebrities was Sol Lesser—a man much better known today than he had been yesterday. Newspapers had just run a nationally syndicated story about an extraordinary three-picture contract to which he had signed a major star.

> Film salary $1,500,000 a year! One and a half million dollars a year for baby to spend, in addition to a little romper money just for dolls, scoops and lollipops! Such is to be the good fortune of Baby Peggy. . . . Mr. Sol Lesser, who has contracted for the services of Baby Peggy for

three years, says the $500,000 "bonus" was just "to give the contract a good start!"

That morning's *New York Sun Globe* saw the controversial deal in a more interesting historical context:

> Baby Peggy has reached the mature age of five. But . . . holds a contract by which baby makes as much in the next five years as all the Presidents since Lincoln have drawn from the Treasury of the United States.*

Standing on her thronelike chair in order to be seen above an enormous four-tiered birthday cake with five tall candles was guest of honor Baby Peggy. She obligingly froze in the fake pose of cutting her cake to give each of a dozen photographers holding a T-shaped metal container filled with combustible "flash powder" above his head sufficient time to snap a picture. Each loud explosion and blinding burst of light sent clouds of acrid ochre-colored smoke soaring upward.

The speeches were brief. Well-known Eastern financier Joseph Schenk spoke a few words praising the star of *Captain January,* my first film under the new contract. It was to be a costly production which was soon to be released nationwide. Next, author George Bye stood up and wittily explained that he had just completed writing the young star's official biography—"all five turbulent years of it!"

Producer Sol Lesser rose to express immense satisfaction with his new star, and proudly introduced her father, Mr. Jack Montgomery. Although he was always gripped by stage fright whenever asked to speak in public, Father held forth about how talent, genius, and "Eye Cue" all boiled down to "plain old-fashioned obedience."

When asked to share equally cogent maternal tips on how to raise a self-made boy millionaire, pretty and plump Lillian Coogan rose to her feet and sang out brazenly, "Well, you all know me! I'm the goose that laid the *other* golden egg!"

At this shockingly indiscreet remark, an embarrassed hush fell over the room. The Press Association host sprang to his feet, cut off Mrs. Coogan with gallant applause for her speech, and announced it was time for Baby Peggy to cut her cake.

---

*In fact, the extravagant terms of this contract caused such a public outcry from outraged male adult breadwinners, Lesser was at last obliged to issue a statement that "false stories" about Peggy's million-dollar-plus salary "were entirely out of reason and unfounded." Nevertheless, the terms remained unchanged.

Following the banquet, a police escort raced me and my family to Macy's department store, where I posed with a brand-new Baby Peggy papier-mâché composition doll ($2.50) and greeted the hundreds of fans buying this fresh-from-the-factory item. From there I visited New York's famous F A O Schwarz toy store, where I was met by another horde of children. Told by the manager I could have any toy I fancied, I fell in love with a fire engine big enough to drive. But Father cautioned softly, "No. We're traveling and it's too heavy for the road!" Already worn out from the long day, I was deeply disappointed and close to tears, but I knew better than to question his judgment or appear to cross him in public.

The following morning, flanked by six motorcycle policemen with sirens, we screamed across town to visit the New York Foundling Home, bringing with us the enormous top tier of yesterday's birthday cake to be shared with a roomful of incredulous orphans and beaming nuns. Just before leaving, Father initiated a well-intentioned ritual he was to repeat in many other orphanages in coming years—tossing quarters and fifty-cent pieces into the center of a large room where the youngsters scrambled and fought each other for the coins. (It made me feel uneasy. I would have felt insulted had I been in their place, and I thought there must be a better way to make a donation.)

From there we whirled on to visit two children's hospitals. I had no trouble smiling at orphans, who were obviously overjoyed with my visit, but no one had prepared me for the emotional ordeal—especially for a young child—of going from ward to ward, bed to bed, trying to cheer up children that I could see were chronically ill, crippled, or even dying, although I gave it my best. Minutes later I was in Newark, confidently delivering a short speech on what most adults regarded as an unsettling new medium—radio. After lunch it was off to Bryant Park, where I marched down a long line of towering policemen, reviewing "New York City's finest."

That night, wearing a silver lamé dress edged with satin rosebuds, I stepped out of a gigantic Fabregé-like golden egg on the cavernous stage of New York's Hippodrome Theater to face an audience of six thousand people. That stage (which actually measured 110 feet deep by 200 feet long) was alive with scores of chorus girls and boys made up and costumed as dolls and toy soldiers. As I stepped forward to the footlights, they danced around the stage singing the lyrics to Victor Herbert's "Toyland." All one hundred of Leo Singer's world-famous midgets joined the huge company, adding their squeaky falsettos to the gigantic presentation. My solo "personal appearance speech" followed, delivered in front of the drawn black velvet curtains.

The Hippodrome, the largest theater of its day, was noted for its gargantuan spectacles. An almost circuslike atmosphere hovered over everything, for in addition to the production showcasing me upstairs, an enormous basement housed a semipermanent sideshow billed as Midget City. Here patrons strolled through a long arcade lined on either side with curious lilliputian-size stores, barbershops, beauty parlors, hotels, cafes, and, yes, even private homes. Each separate establishment had the wall that faced the arcade completely cut away, so the interiors could be viewed like large dollhouses, open on one side only. To the gaping public's perpetual wonderment, here is where Mr. Singer's one hundred midgets actually resided! I visited this bizarre underground city several times during my weeklong Hippodrome engagement and never ceased to be amazed at what I saw. A large sheet of plate glass on either side of the arcade gave the midgets their only touch of privacy, while a steady stream of visitors observed the diminutive denizens going about the business of their lives, seemingly oblivious of the crowds.

The busy week of my birthday was only the opening shot of a vast publicity and print campaign, as well as the kickoff for a nationwide personal-appearance tour. Lesser has been credited with originating the "In Person" tour, and it was he who inspired the blizzard of Baby Peggy dolls, dresses, sweaters, hats, handbags, jewelry—even canned spinach and peaches!—which appeared in stores just as my tour began. These franchised manufacturers paid for the privilege of using my name on their products, and royalties from their sale were to be split between Lesser and the Peggy-Jean Corporation. A leading jeweler circulated a publicity portrait of me wearing a million dollars' worth of diamond, pearl, emerald, and ruby bracelets, the caption capitalizing on the controversy over the Million Dollar Baby's contract.

I believe Sol Lesser was also the first to dream up the movie tie-in publication of a book. He persuaded the publisher of Laura E. Richards's nineteenth-century children's classic, *Captain January*, to bring out a new Baby Peggy edition, lavishly illustrated with production stills from the film. This too he timed to coincide with the movie's release in July of 1924.

For six months after that I was sent hurtling through the dozens of celebrity hoops Lesser had lined up for me all across the country, but it was only half as hectic as the bizarre family events which had preceded it.

I had just finished work on my third feature at Universal when we moved into the big Laurel Canyon house. Not only did Grandmother and J. G. settle in with us, but like a bit of human flotsam came their thoroughly spoiled twenty-year-old son, Graham. From the moment the elder Montgomerys arrived, there was nothing but dissension and trouble. J. G., fifty-five, pompous and portly, had a round face, divided by a brush mustache. Grandmother, a statuesque woman a year or two older than he, was blessed with a luxurious head of pure white pompadoured hair. Both were culturally out of their element. Hollywood was not only the mecca of star-struck shopgirls, stage mothers, and "flesh peddlers" but the home for mavericks of every stripe, Jew and Gentile alike. It was also a theological variety store. Jeremiahs, Pharisees, and mesmerizing messiahs jammed every square block. Rich and well-fed Indian swamis, gurus, and self-proclaimed avatars planted more Lotus Lands, onion-domed temples, and of-this-world nirvanas in Southern California than they had left behind in poor starving India. It was all a far cry from orderly Villa Park, where conformity and orthodoxy prevailed.

Still a devout Episcopalian, despite the fact that her divorce and remarriage had placed her beyond the pale, Grandmother was scandalized to find I had never been baptized and floored to learn Louise and I had never stepped inside a church in our lives.

Our Sundays were given over to such impieties as enjoying the "funnies" and then spending the rest of the day at a private rodeo, staged at his ranch every Sunday afternoon, weather permitting, by cowboy star and Father's good friend Hoot Gibson. In Gibson's arena, Father worked the gates of the bronc chutes, where he could hobnob with his old cowpuncher friends. From overhearing Mother's furious accusations, and Father's proud admissions, I learned that around the chutes he routinely handed out twenty-five-, fifty-, and hundred-dollar loans here and there to help out old cowboy friends who were "gimpy" or down on their luck—loans which his sense of cowboy chivalry prompted him to forget. Louise and I watched the show with Mother from the bleachers.

Graham was proving a problem. By later standards, 1920s Hollywood was hardly a truly wicked town, but it didn't take long for Graham to find what nacent wickedness there was to get himself into trouble. He had a weakness for pretty young women with round heels, a type as common out here as fan palms. He was forced to marry in haste, for the usual reason, and so was mercifully out of our lives for a time. When he did resurface, it was in the form of a surprising phone call from the Los Angeles city jail.

It seemed Graham had left his first wife (and infant child) to marry a look-alike second, but having neglected the small formality of divorce, he was now being sued for bigamy. Father went his hefty bail. Posting Graham's bail became a leitmotiv in our lives. While other men become habitual bank robbers or lifelong safecrackers, Graham was that rarity, a serial bigamist.

It also soon came to light that Grandmother and J. G. were anything but compatible. They were, in fact, on the brink of divorce. Now instead of one unhappy couple we had two, both under the same roof! One day Grandmother intervened when Father was punishing Louise, accusing him of being too severe. Her needling triggered his explosive temper, and in a virulent exchange of words, he told his mother to mind her own business. In high dudgeon she packed her bags and prepared to move out, whereupon Father put her up in style, at our expense, in the fashionable sugar-white Garden Court Apartments on Hollywood Boulevard. There she might have been accused of "going Hollywood," for once settled in, she sued J. G. for divorce, took up watercolor painting, and succumbed to the blandishments of one of Hollywood's most unorthodox but popular religions, Unity.

J. G. stayed on, at both the Laurel Canyon house and managing the huge sums of money accruing to the Peggy-Jean Corporation. But he found a new outlet for his arrogant nature; he took over running the household, claiming that Mother did not know how to handle servants. He dictated each day's menu to the cook and hired and fired the help on a whim. Stripped of what little authority and control she had ever possessed over her life, Mother flew into an unprecedented rage and informed Father she was going to visit her grandmother Baxter in Lancaster. If things here didn't change, she was *never* coming back! While Mother kept him guessing about her decision during her monthlong visit in Lancaster, Father persuaded J. G. to find new lodgings elsewhere. The day Mother was due to return home, half a dozen florists arrived to get the house ready for the huge reception Father had planned. Elaborate floral decorations dominated every room. One, of overpoweringly fragrant gardenias, spelled out WELCOME HOME SHARKEY.* Another read I LOVE YOU: JACK.

I was surprised at his show of open adoration. I knew that his own strict British great-grandfather, who fought in the Crimea as a member of the Queen's Dragoons, had handed down to Father, and he in turn to his daughters, such militant admonitions as "Sit up straight!" "Chest out, shoulders back!" "Eat everything on your plate!" and, of course, "Don't cry!" As a consequence of his stiff-upper-lip philosophy I had learned not to be demonstrative, especially when it came to affection. I dutifully kissed my parents good morning and good night, but that was the end of any physical display. Father's uncharacteristic demonstrativeness signaled to me just how terrified he was.

---

*Sharkey was a nickname Jack gave Marian at the Grand Canyon. It was the name of a famous Mexican fighting bull in an Arizona-Mexican border town, and signified her feisty temper.

10

At about this time the independent producer Sol Lesser came into our lives. He was no novice, having made several films starring Jackie Coogan, but Lesser now had his sights set on three classics in which a little girl was the heroine: *Captain January*, *Heidi*, and *Helen's Babies*. He sounded Father out on the prospect of my making all three films in one year. The bait he held out was irresistible—a million and a half, plus a five-hundred-thousand-dollar bonus and a nationwide personal-appearance tour with each film. Father also got to split the box-office take fifty-fifty with each theater where I appeared. Profits from each picture were to be split evenly between Father and Lesser.

This fabulous deal was closed soon after Mother's show of independence and triumphant homecoming, at a time when Father was in need of some stunning achievement that would both win her back and recoup his own self-respect. It was difficult for a man to be forced to woo his wife by furthering his child's career, but that was the trap in which he had placed himself when he allowed me to become the family breadwinner. Whatever its wisdom, his ploy worked, and for a time our home was more peaceful than I had ever known it to be.

I left Universal for Lesser's Principal Pictures in September of 1922 and started work on *Captain January* immediately. I was supported by veteran stage and screen actor Hobart Bosworth and the popular actress Irene Rich. Most of the filming was done on location aboard a yacht anchored off scenic, sparsely populated Laguna Beach, sixty miles south of Los Angeles. Its *one* hotel, where we were put up, had no electricity, heat, or indoor plumbing.

Throughout my life, whenever movie buffs have seen this film, they've been sure to ask, "Surely you can't remember making that movie? You were much too young!" The truth is, every time I watch it, the same feeling sweeps over me that I experienced sharply on the first day of shooting—a feeling of being suddenly *very old*. This was a big production, an expensive one, and my part very demanding. I felt the weight of the load I was carrying. True, I was four and a half, but by now I had been working without letup for the past two and a half years, having made close to one hundred fifty comedies and three feature films. By the time I started *Captain January*, the day my fancied "stars" began pouring rain through the roof of Century's Barn seemed ages ago.

Father rewarded himself for the Lesser coup by purchasing a custom-made fire-engine-red Dusenberg, a phaeton with a powerful straight-eight engine, black wire wheels, white sidewalls, black leather upholstery, convertible top, dual windshields, and side-mounted spare tires. We drove home from location at the end of every week, burning up that deserted stretch of highway doing a hair-raising ninety miles an hour.

One weekend Mother and Louise were away visiting friends. Returning home, Father opened the front door and fell in a dead faint on the floor of the entry hall. Having been taught to memorize the phone number of my publicity man in case I was ever lost, or strayed, or was stolen, I dialed his home at once. As if it were a movie script, I told him Father was lying unconscious on the floor and asked him to come right away. He called a doctor and hurried to our house. Years before, while working as a cowboy in the San Joaquin Valley, Father contracted malaria. Every so often he suffered these deadly recurrences. Of course, he added my own straight-arrow handling of this emergency as one more proof that blind obedience pays off. In this case he was absolutely right.

* * *

The "In Person" tour that had followed all this in the late summer of 1924 proved grueling. Although I played every posh first-run house in the nation's largest cities, Father considered no town too isolated, as long as there was promise of a packed house. In Washington State I played small towns like Everett, Cedro Wooly, and Anacortes. I did a one-day and -night stand in an especially remote lumber camp where the men clumped down the aisle still wearing their spike-soled boots. The theater was packed, with standees in the aisle. When we went to pick up our half of the theater's take, the manager said it totaled almost two thousand dollars, but he hoped we would be willing to take it all *in silver dollars,* as that was the only currency in circulation there! We had to buy two leather satchels to carry off our ponderous and clanking loot.

In a bitter Missouri winter we traveled all night from Saint Louis, changing trains at three in the morning, Father carrying me wrapped in blankets from one warm Pullman car to the next, across a network of frosted tracks, to get up to the tiny village of Mountain View high in the Ozarks. The train pulled in at 5:00 A.M. on a misty frostbitten morning. There in the freezing dawn the town's combined Boy Scout and Girl Scout troops stood at attention on the small station platform while the town band played a welcoming tune.

Another fifty equally dedicated fans sent their breath steaming upward with the rest in the subzero temperature. At such times the rare chance to see and hear a "live" star, and the growing American passion to demonstrate devotion to a celebrity, evoked a heroism beyond the normal call of duty.

When we returned to California several unpleasant surprises awaited us. J. G., who had volunteered to keep an eye on the Laurel Canyon house during our extended absence, was nowhere to be found. Gradually it became apparent that Graham had lived in our home for an undisclosed period, but he too had disappeared. With father and son, all of Mother's best silver, china, linen, and crystal had also vanished. Worse lay ahead.

When Father went to the Peggy-Jean Corporation's office and then the bank, he discovered that its trusted vice president had withdrawn the entire account, a sum approaching one million dollars, including our half of the "In Person" money Father had been sending back every week. Checking with the Hollywood Hotel, Father learned that J. G. Montgomery had been courting an oil heiress from Texas who had spent the winter there. The week before our return they were married and had taken off for their honeymoon, future address unknown. It seemed to Father the gold-digging widow must have demanded—and got—matching funds!

11

Although we had played to standing room only nationwide, Lesser claimed the movie had not shown a profit. Lesser was a supremely skillful player at Hollywood's game of block booking. Theater managers were required to run his mediocre films in order to get *Captain January*. He then spread its profits to cover those that had lost money. This insured that Lesser came out ahead; 50 percent of nothing was left for us.

While at this time he suspected Lesser of keeping two sets of books, Father abided by the contract and I completed *Helen's Babies*. I made a second, not so extended tour, which Lesser crowned by having me named mascot of the Democratic Convention held in New York's Madison Square Garden the very same week the picture opened.

The convention was chaos contained by violence. While Father and I waited in a tentlike room for our signal to enter the arena, a horribly burned young woman was brought in and laid on a cot nearby. She had been carrying a festive gas-filled balloon when someone had touched it with a cigarette, instantly enveloping her in flames. She died before our eyes. I was badly shaken, but they called my name, and Father put me on his shoulders and strode out onto the convention floor, heading a sea of marching delegates.

Al Smith, a native New Yorker, was the party's nominee, and his partisans were wildly enthusiastic. Serving as my advance guard to clear the way, a dozen of Bryant Park's best marched ahead, powerful antiriot troopers all. As frenzied delegates surged in before us from both sides, these mostly six-foot Irish stalwarts wielded nightsticks with brutal force, cracking heads right and left like sappers clearing a trail. I watched amazed as one after another went down beneath their blows and the limp bodies were lightly tossed aside.

When we reached the speaker's platform where I was to have an honored place, a handsome man there warned Father not to let me up, saying it was overloaded and might collapse. But someone took me up anyway and sat me next to the man, who was very pleasant to me. It was not until he rose to address the crowd that I noticed he was crippled and wearing braces. A nearby politician told me his name was Franklin D. Roosevelt, and he had been stricken with polio.

While we were in New York, Father heard that Al Jolson was in a new play called *Big Boy*, famous for a scene where two live horses raced on a treadmill onstage. A journalist left two passes for us at the box office and we took a cab to the Al Jolson Theater. Although no one there could locate our passes, the manager graciously gave us seats in a front box. The curtain was already up, revealing a colorful stage full of handsome young men and buxom girls in a Bavarian tavern, singing lustily and hoisting hefty steins.

"When does Al Jolson come on?" I whispered. "Soon!" was Father's grumbled response. At last a good half hour into the show, Father asked an usher when Jolson would appear. The surprised usher responded, "Sir, this is *The Student Prince*. Jolson's playing over at the Winter Garden!" I longed to stay and see if the prince got the girl, but Father was afraid he would miss the horses, so he hailed a taxi and we raced across town. Arriving late, we were handed our passes, and as we entered the front box Jolson was in the middle of a blackface number. A ripple of whispers and a flurry of pointing fingers and fans attended our ill-timed entrance.

Suddenly Jolson interrupted his song and signaled the orchestra to stop. Stepping up to the footlights, he announced with scathing sarcasm, "Yes, ladies and gentlemen! That's Baby Peggy in the box up there. Now everybody take a good look at her, and then pay attention to *me*. Remember, I'm the one you *paid* to see!"

We returned to Hollywood after only a few weeks on the road, and Sol Lesser once again confronted Father with the lamentable news that, alas, my second film had *also* shown no profit on his books. After a stormy scene, filled with bitter mutual recriminations, Father canceled my contract.

With J. G. having stolen my fortune, Father tried to collect his half of the merchandise royalties only to find the companies had dissolved their Baby Peggy product divisions. There was no business entity left to sue.

For the first time I could remember, I was out of work. To compound our problems, my two front upper baby teeth fell out. Unlike the children of Our Gang comedies, I had not built my career by portraying the ordinary kid next door. I was instead a miniature version of the "personality star" which flourished in the silents' golden years. I could no more appear in a close-up flashing a toothless smile than could Gloria Swanson or Greta Garbo.

We sold the Laurel Canyon house at a loss and rented a bungalow on Hobart Avenue. Father even parted with his beloved Dusenberg. Anxious to mollify Mother and with at least *some* money in the bank, Father took her on a second honeymoon to the shores of Lake Louise in Banff, Canada.

For the next two weeks Louise and I were left in the care of Mrs. Cook, a spry and wiry sixty-year-old housekeeper. Her son was a casting director at First National Studio, but being more independent than a hog on ice, she insisted on earning her own living. A devout Irish Catholic, she had come from Ireland as a girl and prized her faith above rubies. She also danced a mean jig, had a brogue as thick as the old sod itself, carried around a cache of enough saints' medals to start her own religious-goods store, and sang hymns all day long while she worked.

Discovering that Louise and I were locked in a paganism deeper than that which Saint Patrick banished from the Emerald Isle, she set about saving our heathen souls. The three of us sat on the front steps each evening, gazing up at a large cross made of white lightbulbs, high on a hill above the Hollywood Bowl. *The Passion Play* was performed there nightly every summer, and with it as her opening wedge, she launched into the story of Christianity, from the serpent in Eden right up to and including the name of the reigning pope. When summer electrical storms raged, she laid a Saint Joseph medal on each windowsill for protection. As she predicted, the storms rolled harmlessly by. She was a likable old lady, but I couldn't make any sense of her at all.

Father gave her strict orders *not* to go to church the two Sundays they were away, because Louise and I must not be left alone. Crafty as she was pious, she promised, but with permissible mental reservations, knowing all along she would simply take us to church with her.

Come the first Sunday, she donned her silk flowered print dress and black straw hat with paste cherries (her summer Sunday best), and with Louise and me both dressed to kill, we took a trolley downtown and debarked before a soaring Victorian gothic church. I literally did not know what a church was, but once inside I saw it was simply a theater by another name—it had a stage, seats, and an audience. Before we took our seats, Mrs. Cook led us over to see what I assumed to be a miniature set of some kind. It featured a pretty little grotto, cleverly lit with hidden blue spots, and a stone lady in a long white robe standing on a rock from which gushed a stream of *real* water. A young peasant girl knelt nearby looking up at the lady. Impressed with all the realistic special effects, I asked Mrs. Cook what it was called. Busy lighting a votive candle, she whispered absently, "It's called Lourdes Grotto."

When Mother and Father returned and asked what we had done while they were gone, I chirped up knowingly, "Well, we went to see Sid Grauman's newest theater. It's fancily decorated as much as his Egyptian, but this one's done with blue rocks and running water. It's called 'Lourdes Grotto'!" Louise stepped on my foot to shut me up before I betrayed poor Mrs. Cook's pious treachery. Louise was old enough to understand that our parents were militantly anti-Catholic.

These proved to be grim times. Money was scarce. Our horses had been sold, so Louise and I threw our saddles over two sawhorses, pretending we were riding. Since I had rarely played at home, anything Louise suggested we do was all new to me. One day with Mother's help we made our own lemonade. I enjoyed that so much that next day we set up a stand in front of the house, and I had great fun selling it for a nickel a glass. When Father came home and saw me taking nickels from the neighbors, he was livid. "It isn't bad enough we're broke!" he upbraided me, after ordering us and our stand inside. "Do you want people to think Baby Peggy has to sell lemonade to keep us alive?"

With my teeth gone, Father realized my career was definitely on hold, and he set out to launch a career of his own. Certainly, he told himself, none of the leading cowboy stars had any better looks or riding credentials than his. Early in 1925 he got a job with director Henry King, who was making a big Western entitled *The Winning of Barbara Worth*, starring Vilma Banky and Ronald Colman, and a young newcomer named Gary Cooper. Father was given a small part and also doubled Colman in all his riding scenes. While making the film, he and Cooper became lifelong friends.

When this production was finished, Father had professional portraits taken of himself mounted on his favorite horse. There was no doubt the film had greatly restored his badly battered ego. But the money was pitiful compared to what both he and Mother had become accustomed to. When he heard that a Poverty Row producer at Chadwick Studio was looking for a small girl to play a role in a new film called *April Fool*, he took me down for an interview. I cringed at the prospect, ashamed to be back on Poverty Row.

In the office I sat quietly in a large carved armchair, Father having cautioned me *not* to smile, no matter what. As negotiations progressed, Mr. Chadwick made it plain that $150 a week was his best offer. Father accepted and the brief interview ended. I left my chair, curtsied to the man, and instinctively smiled.

"Good God!" Chadwick cried in alarm. "You'll have to do something about that hole in her face!" He acted as though losing baby teeth was a freak accident that had never befallen any other six-year-old in the history of mankind. But he did have the common sense to recommend a dentist he knew who made plates for adults. Maybe he could make uppers for a child? Fortunately the dentist worked the needed miracle for a bearable fee.

I was greatly relieved to be earning money again, even on Poverty Row. I had been feeling guilty over the terrible losses we had suffered at the hands of J. G. since returning from my last tour. Perked up by my upper plate and by seeing me do well in the rushes of Chadwick's potboiler, Father decided he could hire a cameraman and small crew and make a three-minute screen test of me, all on his own. He could then circulate it among Hollywood producers to prove that—even going on eight—Baby Peggy had lost none of her magic. He did not seem aware of the fact that his quarrels with Julius Stern, his abrupt leave-taking of Uncle Carl, and his stormy break with Lesser had earned him the reputation of being anti-Semitic. He was—and through him of course so was I—virtually blackballed in Hollywood.

After filming the screen test, we took off with friends for a week's vacation in Yosemite. On our second day there Father was seized with violent stomach cramps, but the park doctor assured him it was only "an old-fashioned bellyache" and told him to drink a bottle of castor oil. He did, and by midnight was in agony. Mother awakened a vacationing doctor in a nearby cabin who correctly diagnosed a ruptured appendix and its often fatal consequence, peritonitis. He advised us to get the patient back to Los Angeles posthaste. Our friends drove Louise and me back home while Marian put Jack in a baggage car on the first train out of the valley. The good doctor arranged to have the train met at every stop by a nurse to give the pain-maddened patient morphine. But the doctor who met them in Fresno told Marian, "Either he gets off here and I operate, or he's a dead man." They rushed him into the hospital and emergency surgery.

The Jack Montgomery who tottered through our front door six weeks later was a wraith, a shadow of the man who had thought himself a rising cowboy star two months before. The severity of his peritonitis and the length of his recovery coupled with the massive hospital bills plunged him into a deep depression. Day after day he lay motionless in his bed, and only rarely could we get him to walk as far as the front door and back.

Once, after making a house call, and as Mother walked him to the door, I heard the doctor say, "There's nothing more I can do. He's given up. He needs some real reason to go on living or he won't pull through."

That evening while the three of us were sitting around Father's bed trying to lift his spirits, the phone rang. Mother answered and after a pause inquired, "A collect call from Fort Worth?" She looked at Father and shook her head. "No, operator, we don't even *know* anyone in Texas!"

"Give me that phone!" Father said, a trace of the old authoritarianism in his tone. Taking the instrument, he listened a moment and then said magnanimously, "Why, yes, if it's from Earl Larson, I'll accept the charges."

Earl Larson was a familiar name in our household. I never did learn how they met, but until Father was forced to sell his Dusenberg, he used to let Earl smuggle gallons of bootleg whiskey across the Mexican border from Tijuana hidden inside its two ample spare side tires. Bootlegging was Earl's hobby and drinking his job. He repaid Father's generosity by sharing his precious contraband with my parents. Many a party in those otherwise dark days were enlivened by Earl's openhandedness with booze, quick wit, and blond, dandified presence.

From Father's answers I grasped the drift of the conversation. Earl was in Fort Worth smuggling liquor to a friend who was a theater manager. His star vaudevillian was ill, and he needed a big-name replacement. Knowing our plight, Earl said he could get Baby Peggy as easily as whiskey or gin.

"You mean, he'll pay her *that* much?" Father gasped. "But Earl, she doesn't have an act!" There was a pause. "Get one? By *when*?" Next Wednesday noon?" Father exploded. "Jesus H. Christ, Earl, that's only *five* days away!"

By now I was sitting helplessly on the edge of my chair, my future being bartered over long distance.

"Okay, Earl. Tell him she'll be there. And as of now, you're her advance man. Drum up some local publicity. Reserve a suite at a good hotel and meet us at the station!"

Father hung up and set the phone down. No one spoke. For the space of a heartbeat the silence was profound. Then, as the three of us watched in openmouthed wonder, Father threw back the bedcovers in a decisive gesture and swung his feet to the floor. "Well, don't just *sit* there!" he roared. "Somebody get my robe and slippers! For the next forty-eight hours we've all got to move like holy hell!"

PART 3

1925 – 1929

"CONTINUOUS
PERFORMANCE"

Babby Peggy in Person!
Six Big Acts!
Starts Wednesday
Continuous Performance!

1925 Fort Worth Theater Poster

12

---

ort Worth couldn't have seemed farther away. It was like closing my eyes, pointing randomly to a tiny spot on a globe, and declaring, *"Here* my future lies!"

That future, so far as we knew, was nothing more than one week's booking. Still, on those slim odds, we gambled the once-solid ground of Hollywood out from under us. We had no leisure weeks or months to ponder over which heirloom to take and which to leave. Earl had called Thursday night. We were due onstage Wednesday at noon. We had less than two days to pack the bare necessities and throw everything else in storage. The train would take three full days and nights to travel from Los Angeles to Fort Worth.

Saturday afternoon we arrived at the Southern Pacific station, having worked frantically around the clock, aided by two or three foul-weather friends. These were ordinary, nonmovie people much like Earl Larson, friends my parents had made during these last few difficult months. George

Day was a happy-go-lucky young LAPD policeman who enjoyed playing our grand piano (salvaged from the Laurel Canyon debacle) and winking at Prohibition as he downed Earl Larson's illicit booze. George played the policeman in my last screen test, filmed in the spring of 1925; it was now early October of that same year. The plan was to run this one-reel test as a two-minute teaser prior to the act, whatever *that* turned out to be! It gave me the right movie-star aura, and the reel's closing chase—in which Peggy rides off on George's motorcycle and he pursues her, Keystone style, on foot—provided a perfect segue into what would follow onstage. Father decided *he* would play the stage version of George Day's screen policeman, although he had never faced a footlight in his life, except to introduce Baby Peggy, In Person, trembling with stage fright all the while.

Hours before our departure, George found the necessary policeman's uniform for Father but was unable to lay hands on the equally essential Sam Brown belt. Then, just as we were boarding, George came racing into the station, stripped off his own belt and pistol, and handed them to Father. We would never see or hear from that generous man again. A half-dozen friends bade us farewell.

Rootless as we were, both Louise and I had long ago mastered the protocol of traveling by train. In an era when it took five days to go from Los Angeles to New York, those who could afford the fare had to know how to dress and comport themselves. (Mother saw to it we wore tailored navy blue or brown wool jersey dresses with snow-white detachable linen collars and cuffs, which we hand-laundered every night.) Without exception every passenger, child or adult, abided by a code of conduct clearly spelled out by the porter assigned to one's Pullman car. Every word of that stern black figure was law, and no civilized traveler ever challenged it. Children sat quietly in their seats by day, with no raucous laughter and—God forbid!—no shouting or running in the aisles. We filed quietly into the dining car, politely ate what was set before us, and at night entered our freshly made-up berths, all without a word of criticism or complaint. Travel was a delicately balanced business, and passengers had to work to maintain it. I was sure every porter had the right to put any uncouth or wisecracking kid bodily off the train and leave him there, anywhere along the roadbed. And rightly so!

While on all our former trips we had spent the hours quietly with games or puzzles, aboard this Texas-bound train there was no time for play. Somehow, these four inexperienced comedy writers had to come up with a first-rate vaudeville headliner's act from absolute scratch in a matter of hours! Louise had clipped some cartoon and funny-paper gags, while I salvaged a Joe Miller joke book that ex-vaudevillian Alf Goulding once gave me in jest. Father had cribbed a few successful sight gags from my two-reeler days.

On our compartment's lift-up table we spread these fragmented clues, and as California's Mojave Desert gave way to the flat mesquite-covered plains of Texas, the task of forging something from nothing continued at a desperate pace.

True to his word, Earl Larson was waiting at the station to greet us, a pink carnation in his buttonhole, a broad smile on his face, the faint cologne of bourbon on his breath. Earl was a welcome touch of home, and it was nice to find we knew somebody here in this far-off land of Texas.

"I've papered the town with posters," Earl boasted. "I've got Peg lined up for two or three newspaper interviews and a couple of good radio spots. The fire department's gonna name her Honorary Chief, and photographers will get shots of the mayor handing her the key to the city. How's that for my first four days as advance man?" he asked as he led us to a cab and we headed for the hotel.

As we passed along the streets of Fort Worth, one troubling poster kept appearing before my eyes:

BABY PEGGY IN PERSON!
Six Big Acts!
Starts Wednesday
CONTINUOUS PERFORMANCE!

That short announcement filled me with apprehension. For me it was a grim reminder of what lay ahead. Mother, Father, Louise, and now even Earl were betting everything they had on my pulling off what might easily prove impossible. What if I failed? This time the hurdle was as ruthlessly high as the stakes, and I was beginning to have serious doubts about being able to clear it.

On both my personal-appearance tours we had visited other theaters where I watched eminent vaudeville stars like Sophie Tucker, Al Jolson, the Duncan Sisters, Eddie Cantor, and Elsie Janie perform. It was crystal-clear to me that vaudevillians were a breed apart. They had to have brass, be able to sing, dance, do strong celebrity imitations, be masters of ad-lib, deliver rapid-fire jokes, and keep on firing even after one proved to be a dud. Above all they had to be emotionally *tough*. None of this was lost on me, especially when I witnessed the fearful experience of veteran Elsie Janis at a small-town "supper show," when a rowdy audience peppered her with vegetables! She had taken it in stride, picked that audience up by the scruff of its neck, and shaken it until the dissidents were shamed. Well, I thought, reflecting on that acid test, Elsie was made of much sterner stuff than I!

13

O nce the bellboy had ushered us into our two-bedroom suite, Earl left us, setting out to canvass the town for some special props which the now-finished act called for. We had barely doffed hats and coats, when Father and I began rehearsing our lines on an imaginary stage in the center of the spacious sitting room, each of us reading from a handwritten copy of the script.

Louise was seated on an upturned wastebasket in the make-believe wings, doubling as prompter and captive audience. A wilted copy of the act dangling from her hand, she wore an expression of immense weariness and dismay on her freckled face, as though she were telling herself, "If I'd been born anybody else's sister in the whole wide world, I wouldn't be living through this nightmare now."

Mother, pacing nervously, gave voice to such despairing utterances as "I *knew* we'd never get it done in time!" and "Oh, why in God's name did we ever let Earl talk us into this mess!"

While my films were all silents, I had always been required to memorize dialogue, since there had to be a reasonable synchronization between lip movements and accompanying titles. But in this fourteen-minute act I had to be absolutely letter-perfect, for with comedy, timing was everything. Because we kept cutting and adding lines, it was virtually impossible to commit this script to memory. Exhausted though we were, we continued to hammer away at it for the rest of the day.

Father's frayed temper kept snapping over my head. It must have been more scary for him than anyone, for never, since my first day's work, had he seen my spirit falter. "Come on, Peg," he prodded, "you're not even *trying*! Why, you could do better than this when you were three years old!"

To add to the confusion Earl kept coming and going, startling us with his conspiratorial, one-two-three speakeasy raps on the door. "Well, I finally found a derby, a fake white beard, the frock coat, and a set of handcuffs," he reported cheerfully. "But it sure as hell wasn't easy!"

"Do they even have costume shops here in Fort Worth?" Mother asked.

"Marian, they haven't even got a dime store worthy of the name in this burg," Earl quipped, rubbing lint off the derby with the sleeve of his coat. "I found all this stuff in different pawnshops. Sure does make you wonder, doesn't it? Just who would hock a Shylock beard, an old cane, and a pair of handcuffs in a whistle-stop like this?"

"We've also got to find a stuffed dog," Father reminded him. "I've decided the baby needs a dramatic scene where her dog's been killed by a hit-and-run driver. She'll deliver a short monologue and cry over him for an encore."

"I know just the pooch!" Earl chirped merrily. "I saw him downstairs in the hotel gift shop."

Ten minutes later he was back, carrying a life-size stuffed brown-and-white velour dog sitting on his haunches and wearing an enormous blue taffeta bow around his neck.

"But Earl," Father cried. "He's supposed to be limp-looking—you know, *dead*! She can't cry over a dog that's sitting there onstage staring back at her!"

"No problem," Earl responded. Whipping out his pocket knife, he sliced the dog's stomach seam and removed all of its excelsior stuffing.

"But now he's got no insides at all!" Louise protested. "He's only an empty skin!"

"Despair not!" Earl cried.

Minutes later he was back, a paper bag filled with the fine white sand the hotel used for cigarette disposal. "Okay, Louise," he said, after pouring the sand into the empty dog's skin. "He's all yours. Sew him up with good strong thread and he's as good as dead."

The following morning at ten o'clock we appeared at the Majestic to rehearse with the electricians, stagehands, and orchestra. The other five "big acts" on the bill were all on hand as well, but not a single vaudevillian made the slightest overture of friendliness. Open antagonism seemed the agreed-upon order of the day. It was evident from their closed ranks they regarded us as outsiders—Hollywood movie people who were trespassing on their own sacred turf. Each act had hoped it would be chosen to replace the headliner who was taken ill. As the one who stole their thunder, I was no doubt the object of their resentment.

Our universal unpopularity was finally put into words when Father handed the orchestra leader a simple piano part for the song "Baby Face," which we had chosen as my signature and bow music. The leader opened it as though expecting more pages to fall out. With exaggerated patience he remarked acidly, "I guess you movie people don't know much about vaudeville. There just happens to be seven other musicians in this pit besides the pianist. We sure as hell can't *all* play off this one lousy copy!"

Father flushed and apologized. One of the doll-faced girl dancers with frizzed blond hair who worked in the closing dance act giggled openly.

"Of course I *could* have my arranger make you the extra copies," the leader ventured grudgingly, "but it'll cost you something." Father gladly agreed to pay the going rate.

By Wednesday noon Father was frantically trying to borrow a sufficiently dark greasepaint for himself, as mine was so light that in a white spot he would come across to the audience as the Phantom of the Opera. Earl persuaded a swarthy Greek actor on the bill to loan Father a tube of his makeup. Unhappily, once Father got it on, he saw it was *so* dark he looked more like a Crow Indian scout than a Los Angeles policeman. But by now it was too late to change. I could already hear the strains of the "Merry Widow Waltz," which told me the opening act, "Al Gordon's Dogs," was already on, and two hardworking fox terriers, dressed in a tuxedo and a tulle ball gown respectively, were waltzing together on their hind legs.

As we reached the top of the iron stairs that led up from the basement dressing rooms to stage level, the two-spot, the man-and-wife team of "Rich and Cheri," was just going on. Larry Rich was six feet tall and close to three hundred pounds. With his dark suit, moon face, and tiny waxed mustache, he was a double for the well-known bandleader Paul Whiteman.

Their act began provocatively. "I love you with a passion that burns my very soul and buttons up the back!" Larry told a busty and flirtatious Cheri, temptingly dressed in a short, skintight skirt, a form-fitting black jersey top, and a saucy French beret. Father found their material shockingly risqué, but he needn't have worried on my account. It was all way over my head. The only thing I picked up on was that they were getting lots of laughs, and I wished we had their jokes instead of ours.

The third act was a full-stage comedy skit entitled "Adrift." Its star was the Dutch dialect comedian Gus Fay, who had recently graduated from burlesque. The audience was kept in convulsions of laughter from the time the curtain went up on a bearded Bolshevik terrorist throwing a bomb that sank a huge onstage ocean liner. The scene changed to seven survivors on a raft, drawing straws to see who would be thrown to the sharks. Finally only Fay remained on the raft with a water keg, at which point a yellow cab came driving to his rescue through heavy seas of heaving blue-green canvas waves. "Adrift" brought down the house. (Fay later told me he was paid three hundred a week for this riotously funny act, which required lots of props and a cast of five men and two women. I never did figure out how they all managed to live, let alone travel on so little!)

While the next act was on, I climbed into the barrel from which I would make my entrance. It had both the top and bottom knocked out, and handles installed inside so it could be picked up and carried. Shaking from head to foot with my first and worst case of stage fright, I sat hunched inside the barrel, watching as the scrim was lowered before me on the darkened stage, and BABY PEGGY—spelled backwards from where I was—was flashed on it. As I watched the one-reel play itself out, it dawned on me why I was shaking so. I was worried sick about how I was going to pull Father through this matinee! One night, introducing me at the Hippodrome, he had gotten entangled in the black velvet curtains and forgotten his lines, and even his memory of who and where he was! What if that happened? What would I do if it did?

The scene of George Day running after his stolen motorcycle faded, the scrim was lifted into the flies above, and the orchestra—happily, all eight musicians playing—struck up "Baby Face." The footlights came on full, revealing nothing more than a barrel at stage right and a couple of boxes of old clothes center stage, all placed in front of the Majestic's own painted canvas backdrop of a big-city street scene. The policeman hurried onstage, paused to ask the leader in the pit if he had seen a little girl, and then exited on the opposite side. At this point the spot focused on the barrel, which developed legs and started walking. Stopped in midstride by the police officer's sharp command, the barrel set itself down and I rose from inside, turning on the full battery of big-eyed surprise, a Baby Peggy trademark. Warm welcoming applause.

After an exchange of dialogue, filled with jokes, the policeman handcuffed the culprit and went offstage to phone for the Black Maria. In his absence the resourceful child went over to the box and found a white beard, dark glasses, a frock coat, and a cane. Upon his return the policeman saw not his prisoner but a white-bearded old man holding out a tin cup and begging in a quavering voice, "Please help the blind." Touched, the officer tossed a fifty-cent piece to the beggar, which (by design) rolled into the footlights. The blind man, hearing the silver hit, lowered his dark glasses, spotted the path of the coin, and made a beeline for it. After penetrating the culprit's disguise, the policeman and the little girl exchanged a few more minutes of humorous dialogue, then exited together.

While I was in the wings with Mother helping me strip off the frock coat and beard so I could return in my red-and-white-checked taffeta rompers for my dead-dog encore, Father stepped back to center stage, smiled ingratiatingly at the audience, and launched into his favorite three-minute speech on the virtues of obedience to parental rule. When he related how uncomplainingly I ate my spinach and drank my milk, every mother in the audience nudged her offspring triumphantly, and every discomfited child squirmed uneasily in its seat.

Meanwhile, in the wings, Mother and I were engaged in a desperate struggle. In his nervous state, Father had mistakenly locked one of the joined handcuffs on my wrist, and I could not get the coat sleeve off over the pair. Mother finally scissored the sleeve off my arm, and Louise handed me the sand-filled dog as the opening strains of "My Buddy"—my first choice for "cry music" ever since Universal—reached my ears. Kneeling center stage in a blue spot, the suitably limp velour dog before me, I shed a respectable amount of tears while delivering the monologue. All the while, a pair of handcuffs, dangling from my right wrist, glittered disconcertingly in the bright blue spot.

The blue spot was doused, the lights came up, and Father joined me onstage to take our final bow. At first I mistook the shouts, cheers, and whistles for boos, but gradually emerging from a five-day daze, I realized we were being repeatedly called back for bow after bow. The dreaded matinee was behind us at last and the impossible had happened—I had remembered every line and Father had come through without missing a single cue! Most of all, by some miracle which we were never to understand, our amateurish attempts at comedy writing had succeeded beyond our wildest hopes.

As we came offstage and headed for the iron stairs leading down to the dressing rooms, we were surrounded by a congratulatory crowd that included every other performer on the bill, excepting those now onstage in Danny Duggan's closing dance act. The same people who had been so hostile to us at Tuesday's rehearsal were vociferous in their praise.

"Great act you people have!"

"Who wrote your material?"

"Freshest stuff I've heard in years!"

Waiting at our dressing-room door was rotund and bombastic Larry Rich. "Maybe you could give us some pointers on sharpening up our act?" he asked. "And in return I'd like to teach Peggy here a Scottish song-and-dance number I cribbed from Sir Harry Lauder's latest farewell tour."

"Oh, but Peggy doesn't know how to sing or dance," Mother interjected accommodatingly.

"Say, lady, you just wait until tomorrow night's supper show. Give me a few hours to work with her and you'll see. She'll knock their socks off. Why, I'll bet you twenty to one there's *nothin'* this kid can't learn to do!"

I was alarmed by Larry's boundless enthusiasm. Such blind faith in my abilities always set off warning signals in my head. It usually meant someone was lining up another set of flaming hoops for me to jump through. But I was grateful that Larry and the others had accepted us as one of them. This, I later learned, was no small favor, since vaudevillians often had to travel on the same bill for months at a stretch.

In our dressing room the mood was jubilant. "Virtue deserves its own reward," announced a beaming Earl Larson as he hurried in and shut the door secretively behind him. From under his coat he drew a virgin fifth of bourbon. Holding it aloft like a trophy, he cried laughingly, "It's positively amazing the things you can find in a Fort Worth pawnshop!"

While he poured drinks for the three adults, Earl rattled on happily. "I was out front and you could hear every word, even in the last row, clear as a bell. Harry Weber was in the audience too, and he's coming backstage later. Says he wants to handle you."

"Who's Harry Weber?" I asked numbly, almost beyond caring.

"Why, honey," Earl said reverentially, "Harry Weber's just about the biggest vaudeville agent there is."

"But did you see your friend, the manager?" Father asked anxiously. "What did he think of the act?"

"Jack, you're in like Flynn!" Earl exclaimed. "He's crying for joy. He wants to hold you over a second week. That means it's in the bag."

"What's in the bag?" Mother asked dubiously, accepting her welcome drink from Earl.

"You get the rest of the booking the former headliner had, twenty-six weeks on the Interstate Circuit." He chanted a litany of the cities to be played: "Fort Worth, Dallas, Houston, Little Rock, New Orleans—the whole damn shootin' match. And all at a sweet fifteen hundred dollars a week!" He paused, no doubt to relish his own fifty-dollar-a-week salary that came with the package.

For a moment we stood there in stunned silence, the four of us trying to digest the fact that headlining a bill in Fort Worth was *not* a one-week stand. Vaudeville, not movies, was now our permanent way of life.

After handing Father his drink, Earl paused dramatically, lifted his own glass, and proposed a timely Larson toast, "Down with Prohibition! Long live vaudeville!"

14

To celebrate my birthday, which occurred during our second week in Fort Worth, Mother bought me a new dress to wear when the mayor presented me with the key to the city. That October when I turned seven, Louise was going on ten, and it was apparent to her, though not yet to me, that our lives were—and had always been—unbelievably abnormal. She was also old enough to see that, judging by the present view from Fort Worth, childhood as we knew it wasn't likely to change for the better in the foreseeable future.

Louise had observed the lives led by other children in more average, less neurotic families. A Los Angeles judge, who had briefly helped Father with some legal advice, had a boy and girl close to Louise's age. These were the only two children trusted enough to be allowed to come to our home and play with us. Louise was even granted the privilege of staying overnight with the girl. Louise had also visited the Burroughs children at Tarzana. Ed and Emma were of one mind in being concerned for their children. Ed emulated the movie elite by enrolling his two sons in the strict but fashionable Black Fox Military Academy.

What Louise had seen opened her eyes to what she aptly described as "the real world of normal people." In such normal homes both parents were adults. The fathers were mature, conscientious breadwinners, who worked hard to provide their children with food, shelter, clothing, recreation, and an education. Mothers saw to it they attended school every day and had friends their own age to play with. In that universe the children circled a fixed sun of dual parental protection, which was part of the process of being groomed for adulthood. In our lives the whole solar system was reversed. To a serious degree our parents were still temperamental and dependent children, while Baby Peggy had assumed the role of breadwinner, serving as the responsible adult head of the house. The younger child was the sun around which the older members of the family orbited.

In our Beverly Hills period, Louise had a tutor (the one who gave up on me!) and a piano teacher (to give the suitable panache to that address), and she attended Hollywood's best academy of dance. But serious schooling was a start-and-stop parody of the real thing. For a time at Laurel Canyon we had been blessed with Miss Coy, a dedicated teacher, who made heroic efforts to help both of us catch up to where we were supposed to be in a real school. A practitioner of phonetic reading, she had a way of teaching so it stuck. She even came to my *Captain January* set, fearlessly demanding I be given the legally required off-camera time for study.

By the time I was five she had me reading primers with ease. When I began work on my last Sol Lesser film, I was able to learn my lines almost on my own. Except for trying to grasp the times tables, I found learning a lark. What I enjoyed most was the luxury of being taught something *before* being asked to perform it. The adult I became owes that tenacious lady a tremendous debt, for in precious little time she laid a solid foundation on which, when forced by circumstances to become almost entirely self-taught, I was easily able to build.

After Miss Coy was dismissed, there was a great hiatus. Throughout 1924 and 1925 we received no schooling at all. We were too broke to afford either a tutor *or* a private school, and Father held himself proudly aloof from the matter. While Louise agreed with him it might be unwise to expose her celebrated baby sister to daily contact with "ordinary children" (who were also fanatical movie fans), she pleaded with him to at least let her attend public school, especially since it was absolutely free.

But years of easy wealth had added money-conscious snobbery to Father's strong dislike of educators. His girls would have nothing if not the best. So while he might be a poor man once again, he had become too elite to permit us to study with the rank and file; the only option his pride would choose was nothing.

However, now that I was embarked on my "comeback"—an unfamiliar term with which I would become much too well acquainted—someone must have raised the obvious question, "So how do the girls get their lessons?" Early in 1926 we engaged that rarity, a qualified teacher willing to practice her profession in a seemingly endless succession of hotel and dressing rooms, Pullman compartments, and train stations.

Lucille was an Anglo-Saxon spinster, pickle-relish plain, with horn-rim glasses, straight bobbed blond hair held back with pink barrettes, and a small, boxlike figure that required sensible oxfords to make it suitably navigable. I suspect she thought this life would be an exciting way to meet the collar-ad-handsome stage-door swain of her dreams. Well, if Lucille had Hollywood stars in her eyes when she signed up, they soon vanished. While most of the time we enjoyed one- and two-week bookings, there were enough harrowing split weeks and one-night stands to get her blood up. Cross-country travel in 1926 was only a cut above the rigorous stagecoach and swing-station jaunts of sixty years earlier.

We often arrived in a strange town at 4:00 or 5:00 A.M. and had to wait for a cab on exposed station platforms in cutting winds, snowstorms, or sub-zero weather. In very small towns there was the added dismay of discovering that the only hotel willing to take in such pariahs as vaudevillians was overrun with a resident host of bedbugs. The life proved too harsh for Lucille, who went back home after three months. No more Joan of Arcs came forward. Louise and I felt Lucille was luckier than we. She at least had a home to go back to.

But those first two weeks in Fort Worth were so crammed with newness, risk, and activity, I had no time to think about anything except survival. The Majestic's manager added a morning matinee and a Baby Peggy look-alike contest to my regular three shows a day, and Earl's packed publicity schedule kept me hopping between performances. Then Louise learned the Majestic was holding a Charleston contest onstage, the last Friday night of our run. A good dancer, she saw her chance to shine, for once, on her own. First prize was a solid booking on the same Interstate Circuit we would be touring anyway. A girl in the "Adrift" act helped her make a suitable costume, and Louise spent every free minute polishing her Charleston backstage.

But by the second week I was growing bored. Without even trying, I had now memorized every line of every act on the bill; I even knew by heart which of Al Gordon's dogs did which dance with whom in which colored spot. To my surprise, I found repeating the same fourteen-minute act three and four times a day mind-numbing and hypnotic. I was also tired of watching Father, Mother, and Earl play serial games of pinochle in our dressing room between shows, and afterward arguing bitterly over who won or lost.

By the beginning of the second week I was ready to heed the blandishments of Larry Rich, who had taken a shine to me that was little short of worship. I found he was still eager to teach me the Harry Lauder bit, and now I was ready to try anything that offered challenge and change. While everyone was otherwise occupied, Larry and I slipped away to the greenroom to rehearse the number he had in mind.

Sir Harry Lauder, the popular Scottish entertainer, was a living legend in vaudeville. He had made half a dozen purported farewell tours of the United States, but his Scots blood couldn't resist the astronomical increases in salary he was offered each time if he agreed to make one more. I had seen the great Sir Harry on one of these "final" junkets in New York in 1923, a lucky coincidence which made it easier for me to imitate his distinctive delivery now.

"I picked up this number when Lauder toured Australia, while I was courting Cheri, who's from Sydney," Larry confided. "The old boy wowed 'em with it over there. Elsie Janis does a takeoff on him in her act, but no kid your size is doing an imitation of him. You'll knock 'em dead!" While I wasn't all *that* sure, I was certainly willing to try.

"Okay, Peg, it goes like this," he said, singing in a heavy Scots brogue, " 'McPherson was a *Scots*-man, an' ai'm 'is bonnie *Laur*-r-rie!' "

There was a trick to capturing the accent and burrs, but Larry was a good mimic. I soon had the brogue and the bow-legged waddling strut and swagger all down pat. To my amazement, the song-and-dance part proved the easiest of all—short on effort but long on effect. In that rehearsal in the Majestic's greenroom, veteran vaudevillian Larry taught me that this was the hidden modus operandi, the carefully guarded secret behind most of those flashy windmilling finales. "The trick is," he said, "you simply make what's actually very easy *look extremely hard!*"

Larry had been right about needing only an hour or so to rehearse. By the supper show I was ready. When he told Mother and Father I was going to break in a new skit for the act, they were horrified. They accused Larry of pushing me, saying I couldn't sing a note and had only done one simple dance in *Carmen, Jr.* Larry winked at me and I kept my own counsel. (I rather enjoyed letting them think it was highly complicated.)

I broke in "McPherson" as my encore, with Larry in the pit to guide me through the number. I found "McPherson" garnered more applause than crying over a dead dog. Better still, it was ten times easier to imitate the bold, crotchety gestures and brogue of Sir Harry than it was to generate a flood of real tears. But that, I decided, would remain *my* secret.

15

Louise entered the Charleston contest with three dozen other contestants and beat out all but one, a fourteen-year-old Fort Worth girl named Virginia McGrath. Each got to repeat their routines one more time. Then, judged by audience applause as the manager held his hand over each girl's head, Louise lost by one or two decibels. She was devastated, but the first to rush over and console her was the winner's mother, a local drama critic and newspaper reporter named Lela Rogers.

"You danced real well, honey," she said encouragingly. "You just keep on practicing and your big break will come."

Miss McGrath won the coveted tour of the Interstate, accompanied by the extraordinary Lela, who served as combined stage mother, agent, coach, wardrobe woman, and publicity person. She also changed her talented daughter's stage name to Ginger Rogers. This unlikely introduction began our long association with Lela and Ginger, an acquaintance that continued well into their glory years in Hollywood.

Our next stop was Dallas. We arrived there at three in the morning amid a freak storm that blanketed the city with several inches of snow. Held over once more, we celebrated Christmas there. With no hint that there would be any real celebration, Louise and I went to bed in our room after the last show on Christmas Eve. Jack and Marian had rented a separate suite and spent the few days before the holiday secretly shopping for toys. They installed an eight-foot-tall Christmas tree in the second suite and buried its lower branches under a mountain of beautifully wrapped toys.

When we awoke they told us the manager had moved us into a different suite. When we opened the door, we were stunned to behold every child's dream of a Christmas morn, made even more welcome because the year before had been so lean they could not buy us any presents.

After opening my gifts, I only had a short time to play, because I had to give a special holiday radio interview before going to the theater. Also, it being Christmas Day, we gave four shows instead of the usual three. A few days later we entrained for Houston, and Louise and I had to leave all our new toys behind "for the chambermaid's children." This involuntary act of philanthropy was repeated often on the road. Being assigned as chambermaid to Baby Peggy's suite was the next best thing to winning the Irish Sweepstakes.

New Year's Eve inside Houston's Majestic Theater was a scene out of a "flaming youth" movie. During the special midnight show, the increasingly rowdy audience broke out paper hats, whistles, and party favors. Soon they were openly passing around silver flasks, filled with straight gin or bourbon. After finishing with my Lauder encore, I reentered almost immediately, carried onstage in a portable bathtub, wearing a flesh-colored velvet bathing suit (to look nude) and a wide ribbon across my chest that spelled out, HAPPY NEW YEAR, 1926. The outside of the bathtub bore a suggestive sign which read, PROPERTY OF EARL CARROLL, a witty reference to the Earl Carroll scandal of the time, in which police caught one of his showgirls in a bathtub filled with gin while tipsy gentlemen sipped the forbidden elixir from her high-heeled slipper. By the time I stepped out of the tub, silver slipper in hand, half the audience was incapable of even remembering who Earl Carroll was, for they were dancing in the aisles, drinking, and singing "Auld Lang Syne."

After the house was finally cleared, the manager served a complimentary banquet onstage for everyone on the bill. There Earl Larson, who was apparently as well connected in Houston as he was in Fort Worth, managed to turn more water into moonshine than was turned into wine at Cana. Earl was on a roll and so were we.

Our pilgrimage seemed destined never to arrive at any final destination. Not that vaudevillians, individually and as a group, did not have a definite goal in mind. They most decidedly did. From their repeated references to it, I soon learned that the shrine which every last man, woman, and child among them hoped and prayed to reach at the end of this often lifelong hegira was the holy place prized above rubies—the Palace Theater in New York. To vaudevillians, this last bastion of the revered two-a-day, which was built in 1913 at a cost of $850,000, was their Valhalla, Mecca, Jerusalem, and Rome all rolled into one. They all devoutly believed that talent and tenacity would eventually take them there.

The Palace, however, was not my goal, nor my family's. Survival was. We had been cold stone broke when the miracle of this reprieve from poverty occurred. But my comeback career quickly developed into a kind of treadmill: no matter how hard we worked, we never really got anywhere. However, after the first few weeks I did get more money.

Every Friday afternoon on my makeup bench a long fat white envelope appeared mysteriously. It contained two thousand dollars in fifty- and one-hundred-dollar bills. Vaudevillians were a leery tribe. Having been bilked many times, they did not consider any theater manager's check worth the paper it was written on. They may have been light-fingered gypsies when it came to lifting towels, spoons, and ashtrays from hotels, but they demanded to be treated honestly themselves.

Magnanimously, following our first matinee in Fort Worth, Father announced that, after each performance, he would give me *one* of the two nickels we used as a sight gag in the act. It was the first money I had ever been given as my very own. "This will teach you how to save money," he admonished me soberly, "and to spend it only after you've thought long and carefully."

I kept my nickels in a matchbox and was tighter with my hoard than Scrooge. Not even Louise could pry a penny out of me, until all $20 of it was stolen in Detroit's Book Cadillac Hotel. Of the $2,000 a week earned for three shows a day (twenty-one performances in all), my nickel-a-show reward totaled exactly $1.05! This was one more paradox in the upside-down life of a child star and her family.

But while many aspects of backstage life were monotonous and confining, I found my fellow travelers a fascinating lot. Many "Dutch" comedians and aerialists were refugees from chaotic postwar Germany. Backstage there was such a density of White Russians, Cossacks, and Russian gypsies who had fled the 1917 Communist takeover, they could have set up a nation of their own. (I listened spellbound to their tales of hairbreadth escapes over ice-packed rivers and snowy wastes.)

Some acts were composed of entire families, such as Italian acrobats and Japanese jugglers. One of the latter had seven children, every one ablaze in a gorgeous blue satin kimono. Brother-and-sister duets abounded, as did husband-and-wife comedy duos and dance teams. Portly Irish tenors, leaning on a baby grand, rendered everything from "Mother McCree," "The Road to Mandalay," and "Chloe" to a relic of bygone minstrel days with the opprobrious first line "Now, some folks say that a nigger won't steal—h-mmm!"

The bloodlines of not a few of these floating dynasties went back four and five generations. Of course there were also trained dogs and seals, hillbillies who played the saw, and men who swallowed fire. I vividly remember a family act in which one brother ate razor blades and broken glass three times a day. He confided that he routinely downed large amounts of spinach and some cotton before each show.

The word "vaudeville" derived from the French *vaudevire,* first used in the fifteenth century to describe the drinking songs written by a mill owner in the valley of Vire in Normandy. But its roots reached back to the jugglers and court jesters performing for Caesars, Gothic kings, and Oriental potentates. It was a point of honor among vaudevillians that the Byzantine empress Theodosia was a bearkeeper's daughter and a former exotic dancer. However, in the United States vaudeville dated back only to 1875.

Certainly they brought along every talisman, taboo, and superstitious belief they had picked up in every country and from every culture in the world. A bill traveling for weeks together was not unlike a sixteenth-century galleon, aboard which blasphemy was punished by marooning the offender. Vaudeville was an equally precarious voyage with little or no security. If one passenger carelessly displeased the deity, divine wrath fell upon everyone aboard. To circumvent such disaster there had to be rules. A hat tossed on a bed, an umbrella opened indoors, or, God forbid, a broken mirror, all spelled impending woe if not tragedy. Dressing-room numbers routinely jumped from 12 to 14, and no vaudevillian in his right mind would ever sleep in a berth numbered 13.

If Friday fell on the thirteenth, the mood backstage was cautious and grim. Acts such as knife-throwers and high-wire artists cut their more dangerous tricks from the act entirely on that day. The last line of an act or play must never be spoken in rehearsal or the whole production would fail. Among Russian gypsies backstage, poring over dream books, puzzling out tea leaves, telling fortunes with cards, reading palms, and discerning the future with Ouija boards were all regarded as serious professions. Mother became addicted to them all.

Salt was kept at the ready to toss over one's shoulder or to scatter on the spot where a mirror smashed. To insure good luck (and/or full-time bookings), cheek rouge must be scrubbed on, not with a brush, but with a rabbit's *left* hind foot, with the fur still on. You were judged severely if your makeup bench lacked this amulet. Before we left Fort Worth, we armed ourselves with the required rabbit's foot, which was thereafter kept in full view.

If vaudevillians felt themselves royalty, the buildings in which they spent their lives were truly palaces fit for kings. After 1918 the owners of theater circuits engaged in a decade-long orgy of building "dream palaces." By the time we entered this world, there were some twenty-five thousand vaudeville artists working part- or full-time in four thousand such theaters. Most of these vaudeville-cum-movie confections were as ornate as any castle in Spain. Architects such as the Lamb brothers, Rapp and Rapp, John Eberson, and half a dozen others specialized in designing and building resplendent replicas of everything from a Pharaoh's tomb to Versailles. Carpets were deep, draperies rich, pillars and stairways made of pure varicolored marble, ceilings coffered or, simulating a night sky, studded with glittering stars. As theater magnate Marcus Loew put it proudly, "We sell tickets to *theaters*, not movies."

While everything "out front" was unusually sumptuous, dressing rooms tended to be spartan and were most often buried in the basement. After the great flood in the spring of 1927, our dressing room in a theater in Galveston had high-water marks well above the five-foot level and was dank as a castle keep. Small wonder so many show people developed tuberculosis. Although we were always assigned the star dressing room, that did not mean it always came with its own private bath. But vaudevillians tended to be a hardy and enduring lot. If the change of water from one city to the next caused me to suffer from diarrhea, it sent the two Mosconi brothers reeling with pain and dizziness as they executed the fast turns and dance leaps in their "Blue Danube" finale, but nevertheless the show went on.

No dressing-room door was tight enough to keep all its secrets from the rest of the bill. Infighting between longtime partners, brothers, sister teams, or married couples was lively. Epithets were hurled, followed by the cold-cream jar. Black eyes were expertly camouflaged with makeup, and dance teams snarled smilingly at each other onstage as they glided through a dreamy tango or waltz. The mother of Gracella, one half of a dance act billed as Theodore and Gracella, told me that her daughter was slammed to the stage so violently in her French apache number, three times a day, that her female organs were all "out of place." But I never forgot Gracella's smashing finale when, dressed as an Indian princess, she climbed a high papier-mâché cliff and, to the beat of one of composer Edward McDowell's more thunderous Native American suites, did a swan dive into the waiting arms of "Chief" Theodore, magnificent in an all-white Sioux war bonnet that trailed to the floor.

In spite of the running battles and the threats to get a divorce, or worse still, to quit the act, vaudeville marriages were surprisingly enduring. Wives of acrobats made sure the rosin box in the wings was always filled; the patient spouses of magicians meekly submitted to being sawed in half three times a day for years. They bore children in the lower berths of Pullman cars and reared sons and daughters who rarely knew any bed other than a dresser drawer or the tray of a wardrobe trunk until they were six. By that time they were old enough to be in the act.

One other hardship with which they had to contend was the circuit's strict code prohibiting broad sexual innuendos. Larry Rich was to be thrown off the bill in Fort Worth until he agreed to cut the line "Lady, you're hotter than an oven and your biscuits are burning!" There was a standard list of off-color gems banned from the Keith-Orpheum Circuit. Girls were warned not to deliver such taboo chestnuts as "My boyfriend's in the automobile business. Last night he gave me an auto. Tonight he's going to give me the business!" Another forbidden bit was for a pretty girl to walk onstage with an oar over her shoulder and announce to the audience, "Well, folks, I just made the team!"

But I soon learned there were enough real tragedies backstage to warrant the vaudevillians' wholesale dependence on talismans. I would never forget a pert young wire-walker bearing a yellow parasol in a theater in Denver. In the middle of her act she tripped and fell astraddle the wire, seriously injuring herself. My father rushed forward and carried her offstage as the poor girl's mother kept asking me distractedly, "Oh, why did it have to be *my* Dorothy?"

In Indianapolis there was a petite Italian aerialist named Rosa who executed a dangerous but spectacular high-speed spin around a steel bar, almost thirty feet above the stage. Her husband, Arturo, usually stood at the foot of the steel rig, but Rosa insisted it detracted from her act, so this day he stayed in the wings. As her spin reached top speed, becoming a blur to the audience, a ribbon on one of her slippers came loose and threw her off balance.

From the side Father and I watched frozen in horror as she rocketed off the bar and slammed against the back curtain, which was weighted with a heavy wooden beam. Arturo could not move, but Father was onstage a split second after she fell, and carried her to a sagging sofa backstage. There she lay in an agony of pain while we stood beside her helplessly and Larry phoned the "house doctor" to come at once.

"This was our last week on the road!" Arturo sobbed. "We bought a chicken farm on Long Island, and our daughter was going to leave convent school and live with us at last!"

When the doctor came, he said Rosa had grave internal injuries and a broken pelvis. An ambulance whined up to the stage door, and a weeping Arturo carried Rosa out. Did she live? Did she die? We moved on to the next town and never saw or heard of that tragic couple again.

16

___

Working our way up through the South on the Interstate Circuit, we reached Little Rock, Arkansas. This proved to be a memorable booking, for here Father was taken off the train on a stretcher. Mother rode with him to the hospital while Earl took Louise and me to the hotel in a cab. She called us a short time later to say Father was having another malarial attack and would be hospitalized for several days.

"Okay, Marian, if you say so," Earl agreed reluctantly. Hanging up the receiver, he said glumly, "Well, so much for our week in Little Rock. Now I have to call the manager and tell him we've got to cancel."

Before he could dial the number I stopped him. "No, Earl, wait! Hospitals cost an awful lot. Now, of all times, we shouldn't cancel. Besides, there's no reason to. I can go on without Daddy. I can do the act as a single!"

Earl stared at me. "Oh, Peg, you know that's impossible!" Nervously he drew the ever-present flask from his breast pocket and fortified himself with a quick jolt of bourbon. "Not to mention," he added, "your mother would kill me if I let you try such a thing without telling her."

"There isn't time to tell her!" I protested. "Besides, the matinee's the *only* show I'd have to do alone. I'll break Larry Rich in as the policeman. He knows most of our lines and can be ready in time for the supper show tonight!"

Since my solution looked out for Earl's financial interests as well as our own, he finally agreed. He took us to the theater, and by the time Mother called from the hotel an hour later, it was a fait accompli. Louise was in the dressing room, unpacking wardrobe trunks and pressing costumes, while I was in the pit with the orchestra leader and Larry, working out special musical cues for my solo matinee.

Mother arrived at the theater, beside herself with anxiety, so my first concern was to convince her it could be done. "Mother, believe me," I assured her, "after seven weeks on the road I can deliver every line of this act backwards, *in my sleep*!" That was no exaggeration.

But, while this was true of the act itself, Larry and I had been working up a new encore and had secretly agreed Little Rock was the place to try it out. This was a satiric imitation of the grande dame of the American theater, Ethel Barrymore. Recently she had deigned to stoop to the uppermost tier of vaudeville by appearing at the Palace in a James Barrie piece called *The Twelve Pound Look*. Larry said *Variety* had panned the show, saying it was "Sir James Barrie moralizing, and our first actress Barrymoralizing." Due to this critic's barb, Ethel was now fair game for clever parodies.

I had visited her New York dressing room back in 1924 and been impressed by her husky voice and slow, overly dramatic delivery. Mother had asked Ethel that night if she wasn't proud of her brother John becoming a screen star. To which query Ethel, looking stricken, delivered a savagely disdainful opinion of her bibulous younger brother: "Oh, Lionel—*yes*! But—nawht—*Jawhn*!"

Larry came up with the idea of my doing the new post-Charleston dance rage, the Black Bottom. I would open the encore by telling the audience it was my impression of Ethel Barrymore doing it in slow motion. Cheri made me a high-necked, long-sleeved, floor-length black velvet gown with fluted chiffon collar and cuffs. I would wear my hair up, à la Barrymore, and flourish a long sheer handkerchief.

As soon as the curtain rose on that matinee, I stepped to the footlights and announced, "Ladies and gentlemen, my father is sick in the hospital. He usually plays the policeman, but today I'll explain his part as I go along, and I will also play myself, the way I always do."

That forthright speech, delivered by a serious seven-year-old, no doubt put the audience in my pocket. I probably could have sat down and chewed a straw for the next ten minutes and won applause. But I wasn't seeking audience sympathy. I knew the manager was out front, and would dock my salary if he thought I hadn't given him a complete show.

When it came time for the Barrymore skit, I addressed the audience again. "I need to change for my last encore, so please be patient. The orchestra will play for you in the one-minute interim." The conductor struck up a fast and hot rendition of "The Black Bottom."

Moments later a pink spot, focused on stage left, picked out an unmistakable Ethel Barrymore as the music's tempo slowed to a funereal pace. This was the old Century satires all over again, and I felt on solid ground. Miss Barrymore sang in a slow husky voice, head up, eyes closed. She licked each thumb, as the dance required, and tapped her derriere discreetly every time she repeated the title. Then, after holding a deep, exaggerated bow until the applause died down, I delivered Ethel's own famous "no more encores" speech: "That's all there is, there isn't—any—more!"

Pandemonium exploded out front, but by now I had learned no true professional *ever* milks an audience. Besides, with the manager watching and a full week's salary on the line, it was wise to leave them clamoring for more. After a second Barrymoresque bow, I stalked off, as imperiously as Ethel herself would have done. The audience cheered. Of far more importance to me was making sure the manager was pleased.

Earl's blond wife, Ada, joined us soon after Little Rock, a slim, cringing, spineless little creature. All her dresses had detachable lace collars and cuffs, and in every sink—train compartment, hotel, dressing room—one or two sets were eternally put to soak, to everyone's irritation.

In most cities, adult vaudevillians could get in a relaxing round of golf before the matinee, but vaudeville offered no such perquisites to children. The two most accessible to us were the privilege of watching the between-show movie out front for free or, if you had already seen that ten times over, using a special pass which spelled open sesame to any other vaudeville house in town.

In one city the Hilton Sisters were headlining the bill at a theater nearby, and Mother decided we should catch their act. The Hiltons were not an ordinary sister act. They were quite pretty eighteen-year-old twins who harmonized songs and played saxophones. Both affected long Mary Pickford–like curls, and while blond Daisy wore a daisy-flowered cotton print, brunette Violet wore a dress that was identical, except for being strewn with violets. The secret of their success and high pay (they also made two thousand dollars a week) lay in the fact that they were world-famous Siamese twins, inoperably joined at the lower spine.

Nothing would do but we had to go backstage and meet them. I found the experience depressing, for I sensed something was terribly wrong, over and above their tragic handicap. It turned out that their natural mother—a barmaid in Brighton, England—had sold them soon after birth to the midwife. She, in turn, trained them to sing and play instruments, exhibiting them as circus freaks for her own profit. At the time we met them, they were virtual prisoners of their midwife "owner," who was collecting and pocketing every penny of the sizable fortune they were earning. In all their years in sideshows and vaudeville, they never received a dime. Daisy managed to find (and hoard) *one* fifty-cent piece, Violet a *solitary* quarter. Compared to them, my nickel-a-show made me a vaudeville Rockefeller!

Another of vaudeville's premier stars we saw whenever we crossed paths was Elsie Janis. A visit to Elsie's dressing room anywhere was a full stage production all its own. Crammed with baskets of gladioli, redolent with French perfume, alive with star-caliber visitors, all striving to be heard above the song of half a dozen caged canaries whose thrown birdseed crunched underfoot, it was bedlam. While Elsie changed and chatted from behind her dressing screen, her mother, Jenny, darted about, bidding the ever-changing guard of guests hail and farewell, determined to be everywhere for everyone at once.

Jenny was the archetypal stage mother, who had pushed Elsie since she was old enough to recite poems at parties and carry wedding rings in church. Having divorced her husband, who forbade her to put Elsie on the stage, she took her nine-year-old prodigy to the White House, where she sang for President McKinley. It was clear sailing from there. If Lela was a snappish fox terrier who barked for Ginger, black-eyed Jenny was a steel juggernaut who flattened theater managers with her outrageous salary demands and special perks for Elsie.

Mother and daughter were inseparable. Jenny was also rarely parted from the two Pekingese dogs she carried inside the wide, hanging sleeves of her seal-fur coat. "Look," Jenny said to me as she lifted both arms to reveal two sets of shining round eyes staring out from the depths of her sleeves. "I take them with me to the movies just like this!" she explained. "And they really *do* enjoy the show!"

Elsie was no less a prisoner than Daisy and Violet. Every time she tried to quit vaudeville to take up the far less rigorous trade of screenwriting, Jenny slyly blocked her. After Elsie told her agent she would accept no more bookings, she celebrated her fortieth birthday, for which Jenny gave her an extravagantly expensive string of real pearls. Poor Elsie was forced to play the entire Orpheum Circuit one more time to pay for it.

Aside from breaking our own boredom, the deeper reason for these backstage forays was Mother's fascination with celebrities, however fleeting their notoriety. It baffled me, because I thought she, of all people, should know how nebulous fame was. During the late 1920s, several heroic aviators were striving to be first to fly over the South Pole, around the world, or across the Atlantic. Mother stayed hot on each contender's trail. If the governor honored one such pilot on the front steps of the state capitol, she was there, with me in tow, to meet him. I was embarrassed, but the worst part of her shameless fix on celebrities was that she always pretended I was the starstruck little girl who was dying to get their autograph!

When they heard that Charles Lindbergh had landed in Paris, my parents, like many other Americans, burst into tears of patriotic joy. They were ecstatic we were booked into Saint Louis the very week Lindbergh returned to Lambert Field and a hero's welcome. We had already met O. E. Scott, manager of the field, a very kind, white-haired aviator. He had believed in "Lindy," he said, and was proud he had taught the fatherless lad to fly. Pushing his way through the well-wishers, he embraced the man he loved like a son, crying, "Welcome home, Slim!" Taking offense at the use of his former nickname, in front of everyone Lindbergh told his mentor icily, "It's *Colonel* Lindbergh to you from now on!"

Scott returned to where we were waiting, sat down on the steps of his office, and sobbed like a child. My heart ached for him. The next day Scott took me up in his plane for my first flight and later apologized for not having been able to obtain Lindy's autograph for me.

Mother bought an expensive autograph book to hold what she termed "my" collection. She filled it with autographs she solicited (for me) from the other acts on every bill. Nearly all added a gratuitous bit of advice after their "Dear Baby Peggy" salutation. This enigmatic message was invariably the same: "And remember to always be grateful to your wonderful parents for all they are doing for you!"

Entering our Baltimore theater lobby one morning to rehearse with orchestra and crew, I was surprised to see another act had star billing on the marquee next to my own. "Who are these Yong Foys?" I asked Father. "And how does a Chinese juggling act get headline billing?"

Father was equally baffled, but once inside we discovered our mistake. Eddie Foy Sr., a renowned Irish comedian and soft-shoe artist, had been a vaudeville headliner for decades. Over the past few years he had been touring with seven of his own children. Now they had formed an act of their own, billing themselves as the Seven Young Foys. The marquee left out one essential letter.

The Foy Kids, as they were informally called, were absolute hellions. Aged between sixteen and thirty, the pack consisted of five boys and two girls. Their mother had died when they were small, and their doting father let them do whatever, whenever they pleased. Incredibly enough, they were likable, even lovable, in their deviltry. By the time we played those two great strongholds of bootleg liquor and gangster rule—Chicago and New York—the three oldest of these enfants terribles had become close after-dark friends of my parents. It was party time every night following the last show, for the Foy Kids knew the password to every clandestine saloon in Cicero, and—so it seemed—to every one of the more than twenty-one thousand speakeasies doing business in greater Chicago. They also found their way to every racy cabaret and socially "in" Harlem nightclub in New York. The tireless Mary, Madelaine, and Eddie Foy Jr. took Jack and Marian on the good-time joyride of their lives.

We had the dubious luck to reach Pittsburgh in time for what some folks believed was nothing less than the end of the world. The city was heavily polluted with coal dust and smog from its steel mills, and even the hotel curtains were gritty with soot. But at high noon on a clear day, as we were leaving for the theater, the skies turned black as night. Like everyone else in the hotel, we rushed out into the hall to find out what was happening. In the open doorway of the room directly across from ours, I saw a distinguished elderly man forcing entire packets of greenbacks upon a bewildered chambermaid, who was protesting against the generosity of his tip.

"But you must take it all, my good woman!" the distracted man pleaded with her. "Don't you understand? The 'three dark days' foretold in the Bible have begun. The end of the world is at hand. Surely you remember the camel not passing through the eye of the needle? Well, I'm a very rich man, and I need to make sure I'm saved!"

In Detroit, we had no sooner checked into the Statler Hotel than we received a call from an old acquaintance—Lela Rogers. The normally un-flappable Lela was sobbing hysterically over the phone, and begged us to come up to her suite right away. When she admitted Mother, Louise, and me to her room, it was apparent she had lost a precious treasure. "It's Gin-ger!" she wailed. "She's run off with a tap dancer, that no-good Jack Pep-per! He's nothing but a *lousy two-spot hoofer*!" She spat out Pepper's lowly billing as if it were bile.

"Has Ginger—married him?" Mother asked, half afraid to hear she had not.

"Oh, they're legally married all right!" Lela said, dabbing at her eyes. "But that's not the worst. Don't you understand? *She's joined his act!*" (I was se-cretly amused at what might be their curious billing, Ginger and Pepper: Spicy Dancers.)

After bemoaning all the sacrifices made for Ginger, the dancing lessons she had paid for, the costumes she had sewn, Lela got up and took a bel-ligerent stance before Louise and me, addressing us as accusingly as a dis-trict attorney. "So, let this be a lesson to you both! Don't you girls ever do to your poor mother what Ginger's just done to me—break her heart!"

I saw no connection, but from Mother's expression I guessed this was a cautionary tale she would not soon forget.

Eating on the road was a problem. Between-show meals usually had to be bolted hurriedly, and young fans would often gather outside a plate-glass window to stare at me while I ate. In that era before air-conditioning, sum-mers on the road could be sheer hell. When the natural ninety-eight-degree heat and humidity were augmented by footlights and spots, the stage became boiler room and steam bath combined. Dressing rooms were suffocating. Be-tween shows, stagehands in undershirts dark with sweat gathered around the light board in the wings, listening to summer baseball games on the radio.

"Push 'em up, Tony!" the stadium crowd roared as some favorite Italian pitcher stepped up to the mound. "Push 'em up, Tony!" the stagehands echoed, so lustily the audience could hear them clearly above the organ's soft accompaniment of a torrid love scene in the movie dominating the screen.

Despite Mother's telling reporters that I was like a fire horse in the wings, dying to get out on that stage, I was actually dying of boredom. Before al-most every show, as I sat in the barrel before the scrim was raised, I felt it was suspended over a great abyss where a web of railroad tracks led out in every direction. Not infrequently, in the close confines of that barrel, the only private place I now possessed, I thought about our lost Laurel Canyon home, our two collie dogs, our horses—and I cried.

*Marian and Jack
Montgomery on their
honeymoon, June 1915.*
AUTHOR'S COLLECTION

*Peggy-Jean Montgomery,
nineteen months old,
posed in front of
the Beaudry Arms
Apartments in downtown
Los Angeles, April 1920.*
AUTHOR'S COLLECTION

Baby Peggy in her first Century comedy, PLAYMATES, with its star, Brownie, The Wonder Dog, April 1920.
AUTHOR'S COLLECTION

In the same film with Florence Lee and an unidentified male comedian.
AUTHOR'S COLLECTION

*A view of "Poverty Row" studios, directly east of Gower Street
on the south side of Sunset Boulevard, circa 1921.*
COURTESY OF THE BRUCE TORRENCE HISTORICAL COLLECTION

This bungalow at 6100 Sunset Boulevard, on the southwest corner of Sunset and Gower, served as Century Studio's "front office" until fire destroyed the entire studio in the summer of 1926.

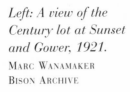

Right: TARZAN *author Edgar Rice Burroughs, visiting Century in 1920 to negotiate a deal for the first* TARZAN *movie, greets the studio's newest acquisition, Baby Peggy.*

A break on the set of SUCH IS LIFE. *From left to right (standing) Joe Bonner, former vaudeville star Johnny Belasco, cameraman Jerry Ash (in visor); (front row) Florence Lee, Jack Montgomery (in white hat), Baby Peggy, Alf Goulding, and Peggy's sister, Louise. Others not identified.*

Arriving for work at the studio with hand-tooled leather makeup case and chauffeur.
AUTHOR'S COLLECTION

*Above: A quiet moment with
Julius Stern. Note the broken
board sidewalk that wound
around the Century lot, and
the sun-rotted canvas
awning hanging from
the window.*
AUTHOR'S COLLECTION

*Baby Peggy reads her fan mail
(said to run a million and a
half letters a year) at her
Beverly Hills home.*
AUTHOR'S COLLECTION

On the set of HANSEL AND GRETEL, Julius Stern and a "sinless" Baby Peggy welcome movie morals czar Will Hays to an otherwise scandal-riven Hollywood. AUTHOR'S COLLECTION

Essaying the lustful expression of Rudolph Valentino while satirizing THE SHEIK, in the two-reel comedy PEG O' THE MOVIES. AUTHOR'S COLLECTION

*A family gathering at the San Fernando Valley Ranch.
Standing, left to right, Jack Montgomery, Stanley Hanna
(a former cowboy companion), Baby Peggy, Jack's mother and his
stepfather, J. G. Montgomery (who later headed the Peggy-Jean
Corporation). Seated, Marian Montgomery, daughter Louise, the
children and wife of Hanna.* AUTHOR'S COLLECTION

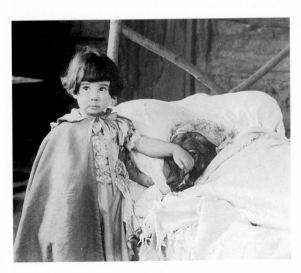

*A bewildered double-
take after delivering the
famous line, "What
big teeth you have,
Grandmother!" in
the same film.*
AUTHOR'S COLLECTION

*Peggy poses with director Arvid Gilstrom while filming WESTERN UNION
atop Hollywood's Japanese Gardens. Immediately left of the door is actress
Blanche Payson, to her left are Marian and Jack Montgomery, and Johnny
Belasco is in the striped shirt. Others not identified.* AUTHOR'S COLLECTION

*Former Los Angeles
policewoman Blanche
Payson dons her
uniform for a role in
THE KID REPORTER.
This scene was filmed
outside director Frank
Borzage's mansion, a
location type that
Poverty Row scenery
scouts labeled "classy
backgrounds."*
AUTHOR'S COLLECTION

As the Spanish spitfire.
AUTHOR'S COLLECTION

"With a rose in her teeth and a knife in her garter." AUTHOR'S COLLECTION

As the arrogant matador in
CARMEN, JR. AUTHOR'S COLLECTION

654-13

Baby Peggy satirizes a famous Pola Negri scene in
PEG O' THE MOVIES. AUTHOR'S COLLECTION

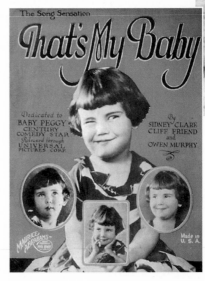

Jake Earle, the Century Giant, and the small but bold hero of JACK AND THE BEANSTALK. AUTHOR'S COLLECTION

Peggy riding Tim, her midget Mexican horse.
AUTHOR'S COLLECTION

The title sheet for PEG O' THE MOUNTED.
AUTHOR'S COLLECTION

Shooting around a crumbling adobe corner, on location at San Fernando Mission.
AUTHOR'S COLLECTION

While the ever-changing water and weather were a constant threat to everyone's health, I seemed to have been uniquely blessed with an almost cast-iron constitution. The hours I kept—never in bed before 2:00 A.M., up again at nine, and back at the theater by noon—were hardly a healthful regimen. We went from the humid heat of the South to Winnipeg's freezing snows. But about all that seemed to show the strain were a nervous stomach and badly infected tonsils.

Several doctors on the road said I was suffering from severe tonsillitis, which was causing my chronic sore throats. Father's preferred treatment was *not* to have them removed but to swab my throat daily with argyrol. With my salary at three hundred dollars a day, who could take time out for even a simple tonsillectomy?

In Indianapolis I opened the door to the bathroom and lifted a big toenail completely away from the quick. When Father tried to press it back, I fainted dead away from the pain. As soon as I was brought around with smelling salts, we figured out how I could still go on. Resourcefully we cut a hole in the toe of my left black Mary Jane and camouflaged the "window" with the cut-out toe of a black sock. Who out front would be the wiser? That was the easy part. Doing three shows a day until it healed was a tad more difficult.

In a major city in Wisconsin, Earl arranged to publicize my appearance by having me endorse the local dairy's milk. A big blowup of Baby Peggy was mounted on one of the dairy's trucks, and as it drove through the city, a loudspeaker proclaimed that while she was in town the child star was drinking only their brand of milk. Of course Earl commanded a steep price for the use of my name, but as the week wore on, the dairy kept putting off payment. Father was sure they were stalling until we left the state and could no longer legally sue them for the amount.

Ironically, it was here a tonsillitis attack made it impossible for me to speak. "Ladies and gentlemen," Father announced at the matinee, "I'm sorry to disappoint you, but Peggy is too sick to appear." He paused before intoning gravely, "The doctor's not sure what caused her illness, but he thinks it may very well be traced to the milk she's been drinking all this week."

Minutes later a representative of the dairy was beating on our dressing-room door. "For God's sake, Mr. Montgomery," the man cried, close to tears, "don't do this to us. Here's your fee in full. Please announce tonight that her illness was not caused by Green Valley milk!"

In Battle Creek, Michigan, which called itself the Health Capital of the World, I collapsed. For ten days I lay in a semicoma, suffering from what was diagnosed as a severe case of "black pneumonia." My parents were petrified. After all, in those days before antibiotics, people died even from the far less serious "white pneumonia." Mother had always worried herself sick about my health, constantly asking "How do you feel?" countered by my reassuring "I feel fine!" (often seconds before upchucking), which got to be a family joke. Now she was thoroughly frightened that my health was beginning to crack under the strain. I liked to think my parents loved me as their child, but I was also well aware that they worried more about what would happen to us all if the machine that made the money ever broke down. However, as usual I bounced back, and the wagons rolled on.

After Battle Creek a long-burning fuse finally reached flash point. Earl had become a hopeless alcoholic. His wife had left him because of his drinking, which had by now become virtually nonstop. His thirst was so overpowering that in one town, when he couldn't lay hands on any alcohol, he drank a whole bottle of Mother's best imported perfume. Father knew his fifty-dollar-a-week salary was now money lost, but it was painful for Father to fire Earl. After all, we were where we were thanks to him. It was like putting a bullet in the head of an old and faithful dog. But finally, after embarking on a series of lost weekends, Earl left us no choice. His leaving the act his call had initiated seemed to mark the end of an era.

In a very real sense it did. Making jumps by train was costly. Fifty dollars a week for Earl and his wife, plus all their expenses on the road, had come to a hefty sum. As a family we traveled in compartments, but with four of us the train fare, meals, and a two-bedroom hotel suite also added up. Father decided to buy two seven-passenger sedans and amortize their purchase price over time with what we would save on train travel.

Father found a new advance man in New Orleans, and in one of those rare spurts of parental thought for his daughters' adult futures, he picked up a tutor who said she was up to all the rigors of life on the road. A chauffeur was hired to drive her and the advance man in the MacFarlan while father drove us in the Lincoln. And so, after a year of barnstorming by train, we set out in our own two-car gypsy caravan, bound for who knew what challenging new horizons.

17

As our caravan rolled across the nation, it became increasingly difficult to remember what it had been like to be flat broke and out of work in Hollywood. Money was plentiful again and Harry Weber, still our agent, was asking and getting $2,500 to $3,000 a week for Baby Peggy's greatly embellished act, which was booked solid. Feeling like a prisoner, I resigned myself to vaudeville as a way of life. Without even a short-term goal, time seemed to have stopped, as it must if I was to remain a marketable golden egg forever. But, as all humans must do or go mad, we developed a pattern of behavior which gave the illusion of purpose to what was actually a pilgrimage with no destination, a perpetual quest for money.

The new tutor we hired quit after six weeks, so again schoolwork was no part of our daily regimen. In Hollywood Mother had read children's stories aloud to us. Now she never had time. Her taste had risen to the level of modern novels, serialized in *Cosmopolitan* and *Colliers'*. These she loved and fretted over until the new issues hit the stands, while Father polished off as many as four or five *Western Story* magazines a week. But these pastimes weren't all bad: at least the pinochle marathon had ended in a stalemate.

Louise spent every waking hour in hotels and dressing rooms, drawing marcelled flapper-age beauties with extra-long eyelashes and bee-stung lips. I loved to read but was put off with "Honey, you know books are too heavy for the road." Although Louise and I were dispatched out front between shows to watch, indiscriminately, the sexiest silent films the law allowed on-screen, Mother assured us her magazine stories were too grown-up for children.

One day Mother mentioned she had just read a new novel entitled *Bad Girl*, written by Viña del Mar, who was only sixteen. She marveled that one so young was already a best-selling author. It struck a nerve. Performance being the coin between my parents and myself, the message I received was that I was expected to top this phenomenon at once. That night I sat down and wrote my first five-page story. Then, by devoting all my between-shows time for a week to the task, I produced a book-length novel—ninety handwritten pages of very large scrawl on *very* small pages of hotel stationery. I told Mother I had become a first novelist too, even though I was eight years younger than Miss Del Mar. In the course of this tour de force, I discovered that I truly enjoyed writing: it was not a public performance but a private act, over which I exerted real control. Without books, writing proved the next best thing, and with time to kill between shows, I began devoting several hours a day backstage to writing stories.

Louise and I had added a "bear bag" to our limited luggage. This small gray case carried a road-show company of ninety miniature teddy bears about four or five inches high. I had always liked bears, perhaps because they were portable and unbreakable, like me. These bears were also actors whose large repertoire provided us diversion in the form of ongoing sagas dealing with embezzlement and financial ruin (one respectable white bear lost his jewelry store to a gold-digging chorus girl!). Their dramas also dealt with murder, love affairs, quarrels, divorces, even companionate marriage, that scandalous premarital experiment everyone was talking about. As a change of pace, the bears occasionally did musicals—lavish productions with fancy costumes and sets, which Louise and I staged under the lamp table between the twin beds in our hotel bedroom.

Our bruin soap operas were true-to-life. We were both experts on quarrels and threatened divorce. We had picked up some courtroom techniques from movies, but mostly from the mock trials our parents held regularly, trials in which we were called in to testify, under oath, repeating word for word exactly what Jack or Marian had said or done to the other on such and such a date, all too often events that had taken place years before.

Given this unhealthy means of trying to settle their marital dilemmas, it was ironic Father should find himself drawn into a mutually admiring friendship with Denver's renowned judge Ben Lindsey. Although he was the same judge who advocated the controversial companionate marriage, he was most famous for his innovative work in juvenile court. His idea of justice was to hold what he called the "delinquent parent" responsible for crimes committed by juveniles. Naturally, this approach appealed to Father, for it reflected his own view of himself as a responsible parent. Soon after their meeting backstage, Judge Lindsey invited Father to sit with him on the bench and offer informed comments on each case. Father attended several sessions, Lindsey introducing him to the court as "the father of Baby Peggy [that ideally reared child], who deserves the credit for his daughter's well-balanced home life and successful career."

It was here in Denver in 1928 that Father made a surprising and typically arbitrary decision. He announced we were going to take a summer-long vacation in nearby Wyoming. Up until now, either he or I had to be literally at death's door before he would consider canceling even *one* performance. Now I was thunderstruck to find he was blithely willing to sacrifice twelve thousand dollars for a full six-week layoff. I had never had a vacation in my life, except when my front teeth fell out and no one would give me a job. The thought of being out of work for such a stretch made me anxious and edgy. But there were no discussions on the matter. Father didn't make decisions. He issued decrees.

We spent the summer camping out in Wyoming's beautiful Snowy Range, adjacent to the summer camp of the University of Wyoming's Department of Geology. I found the freedom from work and the open space heady. But even more surprising were some of the people we met at what we now learned had been a well-planned family reunion all along. Here Louise and I were introduced to the long-hidden highly literate branch of Father's family. His mother's sister, our great-aunt Emma, was the wife of a renowned geologist, Dr. Wilbur Knight, head of the Department of Geology. Emma was herself college educated and a respected teacher and former dean of a private girl's school in the nearby university town of Laramie.

Her younger sister, Alice, who was here as well, was founder and head of the theater department at the University of Nebraska. I learned that Aunt Alice toured Europe nearly every summer and was an actress in her own right, in addition to teaching drama. Unlike most adults to whom we had been exposed, their conversation was not about movies, a friend's record calf-roping time, or how to smuggle good Scotch in from Canada or Mexico. These people talked about things I did not know existed—new discoveries in science, a graduate student's progress, a scholarly book, an archaeological dig in China, the wonders of a trip to Rome, and a new Wyoming oil field recently discovered by Dr. Knight.

Not only was I bowled over to discover I was actually kin to such highly educated people, they in turn were thoroughly shocked to learn the sorry state of my so-called education. Through all my years of child-star fame, they had naturally followed my movie career proudly but from afar. Knowing that my earnings were enormous, they made the perfectly logical assumption that my sister and I were being privately tutored by the best teachers money could buy.

What these perceptive blood relations now encountered were two extremely well behaved, emotionally jaded, and nearly road-foundered little girls, one going on nine, the other twelve, who had cracked about as many schoolbooks as two trained seals. By asking us a few leading questions, Aunt Emma discovered that our combined years of schooling didn't add up to even *one* third grade.

I later learned that she found our situation analogous to that of the children of migrant workers: having to travel to follow the crop, enduring long hours of work, exposed to ever-changing weather and other health risks, uprooted and deprived of normal home life, friends, and schooling. It was true we traveled in nice cars and lived in fine hotels, but in every other sense we were no better off than beet and berry pickers' kids. Granted, it was not easy to seek out and interview tutors in a strange town and find a willing candidate, but Father could have turned to his own relatives for help. What angered these academics most was that they could find no reasonable excuse for such extreme educational neglect.

Our ignorance and isolation slipped out in a thousand ways—while playing with second cousins our same age, or looking blank when adults around us discussed such things as the Ice Age, glaciers, the Civil War, or well-known classic books of which we had never heard. I knew Sophie Tucker from Belle Baker, Jolson from Jessel, and had even shaken hands with President Calvin Coolidge, but who had ever told me about Julius Caesar, William the Conqueror, or Napoleon? All our lives Father had kept us locked in and locked away from other children. It never occurred to him what might happen once we escaped his tight control and mixed with our peers.

Despite their sense of moral outrage, these relatives dared not openly challenge Father on the issue, for they could see he considered himself a model parent.

But he *was* challenged on a far different front that summer. His handsome young football-hero cousin Brick had come from his home in Lincoln, Nebraska, for the reunion. The moment Brick set eyes on Marian, he fell head over heels in love. They danced at evening get-togethers in the lodge and went on hikes, trail rides, and picnics together with the summer students. Brick singled out three popular love songs, playing them repeatedly on the lodge Victrola whenever he could get Marian to himself. Later, when Mother dreamily played one of them on our portable Victrola, it set the scene for another bitter battle over what Father called "your flagrant affair with Brick!" Mother claimed she had merely danced with the lovesick college youth and tried to avoid being rude. He accused her of leading poor Brick on, and worse.

Father's lifelong distrust of women was reflected in a particular cowboy song which he had taught me early on that began with the lines

> I have no use for the women,
> A true one may never be found,
> They'll stand by a man when he's winning,
> When he's broke they'll let him down.

There were many more verses, each one expatiating on what Father considered the universal treachery of women, a lethal female trait which I believe his beleaguered ego stressed in order to justify his irrational jealousy.

I began seeking some means of ending my parents' war. Making them happy became ever more important. Soon I put together the twin facts that vaudeville teams, like devoutly Catholic Jack Haley and Flo MacFadden, attended church every Sunday, no matter how many shows they had to do, and they also never quarreled. Believing that only I could reconcile them, I suggested to Mother and Father that if they went to church too, it might make them stop fighting. Finally, they agreed on something: attending any church, anytime, anywhere was *absolutely out*.

Soon after I lost that round, they took a week's vacation together and left me with Father's sister in Decatur, Illinois. When my aunt's small son took me to his Episcopal Sunday school class, I hadn't a clue what it was all about, but when the teacher asked me to stand up before the class, I curtsied, as I'd been taught to do. "So tell us, Peggy," she inquired, "what religion are *you?*"

"Scotch, Irish, and English!" I shot back, the pat answer I'd been drilled to give everyone who asked me what I was. Horrified, my cousin tearfully recounted my embarrassingly pagan response to his mother when we got home. She heard him out, then put her arm around me and said softly, "It's all right, honey. You just didn't understand the question."

Years before, when making *Captain January*, I had been impressed by the scene where the minister visits the lighthouse keeper to see if he is educating me properly. Hobart Bosworth pointed to the table and said, "Reverend, she gets all she needs to know from these three books I read her every night: *Webster's Dictionary*, the Bible, and Shakespeare!"

Recalling the great size and heft of the volumes used in that scene, I knew they were all "too heavy for the road." But in my innocent quest for some magic talisman of peace, I stole a Gideon Bible from my hotel room. Mother tut-tutted me about daring to lift the Good Book itself. "After all, stealing a Bible's not the same thing as taking hotel towels and spoons" was her indignant but ambiguous response. Still, she never offered to help me read or understand it, and to both Marian and Jack my pilfered white flag of truce was anathema.

But while striving to bring about the reconciliation of my real-life parents, even falling back on the same histrionics that had worked with my divorcing movie parents, I was treated to a demonstration of what the term "irreconcilable" really meant.

One day when we were playing Milwaukee, the desk clerk called on behalf of a lady in the lobby who wanted to visit our suite. Father, who answered, told the clerk to put the lady on. Following a brief, noncommittal conversation, he gave her the number of our suite.

After hanging up he turned to Mother and said hesitantly, "Sharkey, that call was from . . . your mother. She's in the lobby. I told her to come right up."

Mother turned pale, and then a look of deathless rage distorted her face. "You know damned well I have no mother!" she cried angrily. "I told you that years ago!"

"I think you should at least see her," he urged gently.

"No! Never! I won't even let her in the door!"

Father took me by the hand and led me out into the hall. Going back inside alone, he prevailed upon Mother to join us and greet the woman out there, on what he must have convinced her was neutral ground. Moments later a trim, gray-haired lady wearing a veiled hat, tweed suit, and small stylish fur piece came walking down the hall. Cautiously she pulled herself up short a little distance from where the three of us stood, like armed sentinels guarding a firmly closed door.

"What do you want with me?" Mother asked the woman in a cold, threatening voice.

A faint smile touched the woman's lips. "I only wanted to see my famous little granddaughter with my very own eyes," she said. Stepping forward gingerly, she knelt down beside me and clasped me to her bosom. "And what a perfect little darling she is!" she gushed, sounding like all the other Baby Peggy fans who were also total strangers to me. Ill at ease, I gave her the same uncertain smile I gave them. Releasing me, she rose slowly to her feet. Gazing a long moment into Mother's hard eyes, she remarked liltingly, "Well, Marian, I must say—you did a good job on her!"

Shocked, angry, and hurt that it was Baby Peggy the woman had come to see, and not her own flesh-and-blood daughter whom she had abandoned years before, Mother shouted at her, *"You're not my mother! My real mother's dead!"* Bursting into tears, she spun around and ran back into the suite. I stood rooted to the spot, stunned at the cruelty and rashness of Mother's rejection, afraid to show pity for my instant grandmother, and mortified by the whole terrible scene.

After a moment of embarrassed silence the woman dabbed at her eyes with a handkerchief, shrugged philosophically, and said, as if to herself, "Oh, well, at least I got to meet Baby Peggy." With that enigmatic aside, she turned and walked slowly down the seemingly endless hall, disappearing at last into an elevator that was going down. I never saw her again.

Oddly enough, that same week Marian's father and stepmother also appeared at the stage door, requesting admission to our dressing room. Mother adamantly refused to see them, so Father led me, in makeup and costume, outside to the alley where I met the silver-haired couple and talked with them for a few awkward moments. Mother, it seemed, had no capacity for reconciliation.

In an effort to attract increasingly capricious audiences soon to be seduced by "talkies," traditional eight-man pit orchestras were replaced in big-time theaters by resident presentation bands, with fifteen musicians in flashy costumes ensconced onstage.

Working in front of these distracting, glittering bands only served to increase Father's abiding stage fright. He was constantly forgetting his cues.

I had a different problem. Repeating the same lines three and four shows a day for two years, I was having almost daily mental blackouts onstage. I would emerge from these right on cue, but aware that I had not been wholly on that stage for a frighteningly long time.

A big change in our lives came in late 1928, when Harry Weber suggested we settle permanently in New York. It had hundreds of theaters—Brooklyn alone had fifty-three—and working out of a central address was a great savings in travel costs. He promised us solid bookings in the boroughs for two years, not counting New Jersey, New England, and across the border in Canada, without our ever having to change any part of the act.

This move coincided with one of the best things that had yet happened to Louise and me. Our great-aunt Emma was joining us in New York to serve as our live-in tutor! Apparently, she had seen enough of us at summer camp to know *someone* must come to our rescue. In the formidable Emma Knight, Father met his match. She possessed keen intellectual weapons he did not, had good reason to use them, and was one woman who refused to be intimidated by either Jack Montgomery's temper or his iron-fisted authoritarian rule.

18

V audevillians avoided mentioning the precipitous decline of the grand old two-a-day, but the mournful truth was that by 1927 New York's Palace was the last vaudeville-only two-dollar-a-seat house in the nation. Its near demise was caused by competition from theaters offering mixed bills featuring a first-run movie and six acts of big-time vaudeville for as little as eighty-five cents. Better still, their audiences were hopelessly addicted to the menu. Nation-wide, eighty million Americans patronized 20,500 such theaters at least once a week, shelling out $30 million annually for these popular mixed bills—and this at a time when unskilled workers were lucky to earn $500 a year, and most American families lived on as little as $800. (This figure also reveals the astonishing fact that my weekly salary was more than double the average household's annual income.)

With lavish theaters costing anywhere from $125,000 to $600,000 to build, it was not surprising that their palatial interiors were an intrinsic part of the show patrons paid to see. They made taking your girl to the movies an event to look forward to and remember. For thousands of homesick Italian immigrants these splendorous Venetian and Neapolitan interiors evoked memories of the ornate basilicas and villas they so dearly loved but would never see again.

From a purely business standpoint, these theaters constituted Hollywood's main arteries, for through them circulated film. Every major studio had to possess a circuit of its own if it was to prosper. And all the majors did— Paramount, Fox, First National, RKO, Universal, United Artists, Warner Brothers, and Loew's, the parent company of MGM. To fill these many screens studios kept increasing production until most of them were now cranking out as many as fifty or more pictures a year.

These studio circuits were also gobbling up the large privately owned chains of such tycoons as Alexander Pantages on the West Coast and F. F. Proctor in the East. At one time F. F. Proctor had as many as twenty vaudeville acts on one bill, shows running continuously from 11:00 A.M. to 11:00 P.M. His ad read: "After breakfast go to Proctor's. After Proctor's go to bed." Radio interests pumped much-needed money into the faltering Keith Orpheum Circuit, which then became Radio-Keith-Orpheum. As a child I was unaware of all the financial machinations of these great theater chains, but from Harry Weber I learned my name would now be appearing mostly on RKO, Loew's, and former Proctor house marquees.

The journey east to our new base in New York was interrupted by a rush booking into the Kansas City Orpheum, to replace seventy-year-old Eddie Foy, who had just suffered a heart attack and died backstage. Being close friends to the Foy Kids, we had often visited the family home in New Rochelle, and I had come to know and like this grand old gentleman. I saw him in his last poignant act, "The Fallen Star," in which he played a grizzled stage-door man who had once been a star. I found his monologue, recalling the glorious gay nineties, a touching daguerreotype in a pink spot that brought his beloved gilded era brilliantly alive. Now, sitting in the same dressing room in which he had breathed his last, I recalled the droll advice he once passed on to me: *"You don't need talent to get by in show business, YOU NEED COURAGE!"*

In Kansas City, as in many other towns we played, a child psychologist came knocking on our door, eager to test my IQ against my skill with numbers. This was genuine cause for alarm. Not only was my mind a fence post where math was concerned, but thanks to sketchy schooling it was a clean slate as well. The earnest analyst began by asking if a quarter was worth as much as five nickels. No way! I knew what I knew: five nickels were worth five times more than *one* quarter! After three hours of dogged argument he left in dire need of an analyst himself. It was noble of him to close his written report with "Peggy has some difficulty with numbers." That might be, but what the poor man didn't know was that he had taken on the greatest living authority on nickels. They were all I ever handled!

From Kansas City, Harry Weber booked us into Chicago's State-Lake for a second emergency—filling in for indisposed cowboy star Tom Mix, who had been headlining their bill. Father hoped to renew his old acquaintance with the cowboy star, but we were told Mix was too blindly inebriated to even find the stage door, let alone risk doing an act whose climax was throwing knives the full length of the stage to outline the body of his trusting human partner.

While in Chicago, Louise finally persuaded Father to let her work in the act. He not only paid for her first permanent wave but shelled out $125 for an original dance routine and another $125 to have a showy ruffled costume made. At last she could prove she was someone in her own right!

Always fearful Louise might detract from Baby Peggy if we were put onstage together, Father let her do her dance as a solo during my costume change. As bad luck would have it, Nature chose this hour to usher Louise into womanhood—a rite of passage no one had ever bothered to mention or warn her about. Radiantly happy, she high-kicked her way offstage to the sound of welcome applause, unaware that anything untoward had occurred. Father met her in the wings and, mortified that the stagehands had seen, hustled her into the dressing room and behind closed doors.

"That's a hell of a thing to let happen out there onstage for all the world to see! You'll never work in the act again!" he upbraided her savagely. Reaching in his pocket, he took out a coin, telling her to go to the drugstore to get whatever. Mother softly volunteered the product's name but offered no explanation either then or later. (Given Grandmother Baxter's lectures on sex, I'm sure Marian had no hard facts to pass along.) As for Louise, she now lived in mortal fear that she was slowly dying from some rare and fatal disease.

For the first time in his life Father was confronted with the problems of a girl entering womanhood. He had never thought ahead this far. What did a father do with a grown daughter? How did he warn her about men and all the other unspeakable details of adult sex? Well, the long and short of it was, he didn't. That was the safest course, that and keeping her sequestered from the younger stagehands and chorus boys. Long a prisoner of cell-like dressing rooms, Louise was now relegated to the backstage equivalent of solitary confinement.

Arrived at last in New York, we settled into a three-bedroom, one-thousand-dollar-a-month apartment at fashionable 12 East Eighty-sixth Street, adjacent to Central Park. Aunt Emma had her own private room and bath, along with all the cultural riches of the city at her fingertips. But I began to wonder if this tall, regal lady really understood what she was getting into with us. I was now fully awake to the fact that we were not at all what outsiders took us to be.

Our home atmosphere was highly charged with anger, anxiety, hostility, resentment, and guilt. Louise was marinating in a brine of resentment against me. I had not only replaced her in Father's affections, I was her eternal jailer, blocking all her efforts to forge an identity of her own. Worse still, as the acknowledged breadwinner, I was the one on whom both parents focused their full attention. She knew it wasn't my fault; at times she even felt sorry for me: this in turn curdled into self-hatred when she realized she was jealous and envious of her baby sister who was every bit as helpless as herself.

Mother was equally powerless. Caught between the demands of my work and Father's tyrannical domination, she had no access to money of any kind, with Jack doling out every dime, for which she had to beg. He kept bank balances or savings (if any) his own dark secret. Constant concern for my health sparked buried feelings of guilt for having launched my career in the first place. She was sorry for Louise, but what could be done? On one level she wanted to be free of Jack, on another, being his wife and the mother of his children was the only identity she possessed.

As for myself, I tried to parry Louise's envy by always asking for a second for her of any gift I was given at functions she did not attend. This she found condescending. Aware of Mother's concern for my health, I tried to stay well, but when I got sick I blamed myself.

Father had more wolves circling his camp than anyone. Proud, autocratic, unable to tolerate authority, he was forever being addressed or referred to as "Mr. Baby Peggy." With his ego beleaguered and undermined, he seemed consumed by a desperate need to "win back" Marian's love and respect. He became a compulsive buyer of extravagant gifts: fur coats, pearls, an emerald-and-diamond ring one year, a star sapphire the next, a solid platinum and diamond wedding band on their anniversary, and fancy atomizers of imported perfume almost every time he walked into a hotel gift shop.

With Aunt Emma's arrival, Jack and Marian soft-pedaled their rows at home, but once inside the dressing room they let fly. Two former tutors had told Louise they were leaving because of the constant fights.

Nevertheless, Aunt Emma single-mindedly pursued her goal of educating my sister and me. Out of her suitcase came such marvels as Beard and Bagley's history of the United States, two fat histories of the world, and one whole book devoted to learning the times tables! Precious mornings were no longer frittered away. By 10:00 A.M. on her second day in town, the three of us were touring the Ancient Roman section of the Metropolitan Museum. The next morning we did the Egyptian rooms and later in the week toured period furniture, costume, sculptures, and endless galleries of paintings. She purchased colored stamps of the museum's art masterpieces. No more fifth-time viewing of the movie out front between shows! We studied the artists' lives and paintings, glued stamps in an album, and wrote essays on them.

Until the advent of Aunt Emma, the only historic site we had seen in our travels was Andrew Jackson's Hermitage, thanks to the Nashville theater manager who, bursting with civic pride, drove us there and took us through. It affected me as profoundly as my visit to the San Fernando Mission when I was three. I was stunned to be inside anything so venerable. Jackson's long, gleaming walnut dining table, his imported Chinese wallpaper, and the carriage that took him to Washington were burned into memory.

On short out-of-town bookings Aunt Emma saw to it we toured the Smithsonian, Mount Vernon, Monticello, Revolutionary and Civil War battlefields, and the house in Frederickstown where Barbara Fritchie cried, "Shoot if you must this old gray head, but spare your country's flag!"

We hit world history running. Tracing early man through the Stone, Iron, and Bronze Ages, we hurried on to the Battle of Hastings, the Magna Carta, Napoleon's campaigns, and the American Civil War. Aunt Emma was inventive and interesting. She also bought us books as gifts. Luckily, her two students were both parched for knowledge and as eager to learn as she was to teach. But we had a formidable amount of ground to cover. By her reckoning Louise should be a seventh-grader by now. I ought to be in fourth grade, even with the IQ of Quasimodo! But where in fact *were* we? Lost in some textbook limbo between the sharp-mindedness of show business savants and cultural benightedness.

To make things harder, I still had a full-time job. At noon every day, we descended from our ivory tower in this posh part of town to enter a world like no other I had ever seen. It was a world of little sun and teeming streets jammed with pushcarts piled high with cut-rate clothing, yardage, watches, and costume jewelry. Vociferous vendors fought for space, screaming insults at each other in half a dozen foreign tongues. Housewives leaned over windowsills, hollering across at antagonists and friends while cranking in or out their share of a vast network of crisscrossed lines from which hung miles of dingy sheets, shirts, and long underwear.

Putty-faced, rickety children ran wild in the crowded streets or sat wrapped in quilts on scabrous fire escapes above, gazing down pensively at the chaotic scene below. The air was redolent with the smell of ripe fruit, charcoal smoke, and garlicky foods being cooked. So these were the slums from which so many immigrant Hollywood producers had risen, I thought. This was the *real* New York street where *The Darling of New York* ought to have been filmed!

Every day our chauffeur, James, fearfully maneuvered the aristocratic nose of the midnight-blue MacFarlan through this pandemonium. For my protection, I had to be met at the theater and escorted by three or more strapping policemen, who held back the waiting crowds of fans until I was safely through the stage door. There were a few theaters which had semiopaque skylights in certain dressing rooms, and around them groups of children gathered on the sidewalk above to stare down at me as I moved around below. It made me feel like some zoo animal on display in an underground cave.

In these predominantly Italian neighborhoods, presentation bands played mostly Italian street songs. Prologues featured a cardboard gondola being rowed down a canvas canal, with the gondolier baritone serenading "Angela Mia," or a full onstage chorus singing such Old Country favorites as "Torno a Sorrento," "Funiculi-Funicula!" and "Tarantella." The exuberant patrons usually stood up and sang along.

Such solidly immigrant audiences turned every show into an indoor picnic, women calling out to each other during the performance, boisterous children crossing aisles or climbing over seats to share sandwiches and gossip with relatives and friends. When Father clapped the handcuffs on me, a belligerent street kid in the balcony was sure to cry out something like "Let her go, ya big stiff!" at which Father lost his lines until I threw him a cue.

In these poor tenement areas of the Lower East Side we worked in such scabby brick relics as Kenny's and the old Delancey Street Theater. The children got to know our car, and as soon as we approached, set off at a run after us. On hot, humid summer days, half-naked youths gave up splashing in the cool jets of open fire hydrants to pile all over our car. Some jeered, stuck out their tongues at me, or made obscene gestures they had picked up in the streets. Others simply stared in silence, gazing greedily at the car's interior, my clothing, and even the large teddy bear I carried.

Suffocating though the summer heat was, we ran up the windows and locked the doors when they started banging their fists on the car's top and windows. Soon they were rocking the MacFarlan from side to side. The first time this happened, Mother and I feared they would tip the car over. But after a while, we found it was a daring street ritual and became inured to it.

One day as James was creeping through these teeming mean streets, being cursed by every handcart vendor forced to move out of his way, a five-year-old girl ran directly in front of the car. James slammed on the brakes and she retreated to her mother on the curb, who pushed her back out shouting, "Go back, Rachel, *go back! Let them hit you! We can sue!*"

Small wonder I grew up afraid of children. They always seemed to run in packs. If I wasn't holding two hundred of them at bay with balloons and autographed pictures during Baby Peggy look-alike contests or morning matinees, they seemed ready to tear the clothes off my back or drag me out of the car.

Aunt Emma soon found there were more demands on my time than she had dreamed. Not only did we do four shows on Saturday and Sunday, we did *five* on such holidays as Thanksgiving and Christmas. In New York it was also de rigueur that every headliner appear gratis at all of half a dozen National Vaudeville Association benefits staged there every year. Such fundraisers charged patrons fifty dollars a ticket but supported the NVA's tuberculosis sanitarium at Lake Saranac, New York, and assisted sick, injured, or stranded performers. These all-star marathons, featuring a million dollars' worth of headline talent, started at midnight, after the stars had finished their own last shows, and usually ran all night.

At one such NVA event, having driven all the way from Brooklyn, we arrived at 2:00 A.M. Al Jolson who, as I well knew, was no fan of mine, was waiting in the wings to go on next after Georgie Jessel exited. Both men had fought their way up from Hell's Kitchen, one of New York's toughest neighborhoods, and were famous for milking audiences for encores at these benefits. As usual, Jessel hogged the stage for more than thirty minutes. When he finished, Father asked Mr. Jolson if I could go on ahead of him because "it's so late and she's only a little girl."

"Sorry," Jolson snapped, his black-corked face making his exaggerated white lips and eyes grotesque. "I was a kid once myself! That's show business!" With that he dashed onstage, where he sang every minstrel number in his large repertoire, asking for and basking in repeated waves of warm applause for the next forty-five minutes. I did not go on until nearly 4:00 A.M.

My late hours appalled Aunt Emma. The night Eddie Foy Jr. turned twenty-one, the Foy Kids invited us to a big birthday bash on the hotel mezzanine. Aunt Emma accompanied me to the party, but at nine o'clock she said it was my bedtime. "But I feel fine!" I protested. "Besides, I'm up much later than this every night when I'm working!"

"Such overwork and late hours aren't normal for a child your age," she said soberly as she shepherded me to my room. "You don't feel it now, but it will catch up with you later on in life when you're about thirty." Years later I remembered her cautionary words when her sage prophecy came true.

To New York's Gerry Society—an organization dedicated to rescuing children from sweatshops, coal mines, and dressing rooms—I was about the juiciest theatrical quarry to come along since Elsie Janis and the last of the Young Foys turned sixteen. They had put through a law making it illegal for anyone under that age to work on a New York stage. But it was common knowledge among vaudeville families that the society winked at two-year-old Japanese children walking high wires three times a day or other small fry doing one-night stands or split weeks on the small time. Instead they set their sights on such high-ticket headliners as Mitzi Green, Baby Rose Marie, and Baby Peggy. The Gerry Society's fines were stiff, they were relentless pursuers, and whenever feasible, they took the child permanently from its offending parents and placed it in the custody of the court.

To keep the society at bay, Mayor Jimmy Walker armed me with a special New York City work permit. Nevertheless, two Gerry Society vigilantes caught me red-handed, working on a forbidden Sunday in Queens, a borough where Gentleman Jim's permits cut no ice. "We'll see to it the court takes over custody of this child!" the buxom spokeswoman proclaimed from under her wide, overhanging hat brim. A brisk little man in a derby stepped out from under her shadow and served us with a summons to appear in court, and then the two disappeared.

"But what if they declare us unfit parents?" Mother cried frantically. "Can they take her from us legally and put her in a juvenile home?" Not even Father could come up with an answer to that.

After a long, tense wait in a crowded courtroom, the dignified white-haired judge took me into his chambers alone. Now it was Father's turn to worry. Not since I started in pictures had I *ever* been interviewed by *any* stranger outside his presence. What would I answer to loaded questions? Would I reveal damaging family secrets and quarrels? Instead the judge asked such questions as, did I suffer from overwork and late hours, and did

my parents starve or beat me. Gathering that he harbored little love for the
Gerry Society himself, I carefully edited my answers to point up parental care
for my health and downplayed the frightful lateness of the hours. When we
emerged from his chambers half an hour later, he announced he was throwing the case out of court for lack of evidence. The society had been wounded,
but was all the more dangerous for that. Now they were determined to remain on my trail for the next seven years, or until I turned sixteen!

Our close call with the Gerry Society was only one more worrisome
straw in the winds of change. At nine I was growing alarmingly fast. In my
recent lobby stills, I was posed hugging my knees or curled up in a chair,
artfully trying to resemble cuddly four-year-old Baby Peggy as much as possible.

Then there was the matter of my health. I often overheard my parents dis-
cussing their fears that I might come down with tuberculosis if we continued on the road. They had good reason to worry. Although I was conscientious and willing, my tonsillitis was chronic and becoming increasingly
severe. Colds and flu went automatically into acute bronchitis. On several
occasions I went onstage so yellow-dog sick they had to put buckets in both
wings: I threw up in one before I made my entrance, and in the second when
I exited, before changing and going back out for my encore.

I had often thought the only way I could escape vaudeville would be to
die young, like Beth in *Little Women* or those frail movie heroines whose
death from the White Plague was delicately attributed to their own fatal
beauty. Now, amid growing rumors that talkies just *might* hurt the big time
the way mixed bills had the two-a-days, I saw the first glimmer of hope that
I might actually outlive vaudeville.

For the first time since Forth Worth three years earlier, Father spoke about
our finding an alternative livelihood. He said he had a plan in mind but gave
not the slightest hint of what it might be.

19

T he storm that had been brewing ever since Warner Brothers released *The Jazz Singer* nearly two years earlier broke at last. The talkies were not only coming, they were here. Musical movie shorts, in full sound, many featuring veteran vaudevillians' dancing, singing, and comedy acts, were being filmed in New York and Hollywood studios, living proof that vaudeville could be canned and shipped anywhere, as handily as spinach or beans.

From Western Electric, Warner Brothers got an exclusive license for the sound process known as Vitaphone. In return Warner committed itself to selling twenty-four hundred of the new systems over the next four years, on which they would receive an 8 percent royalty. Spyros Skouras, a Greek waiter who had founded a great private theater empire on the monies he received from diner's tips, was told by Harry Warner he could convert his entire circuit for less than thirty thousand dollars a house. Skouras weighed the risks and took the plunge. At the staggering cost of one and a half million dollars, he equipped every one of his forty gilded odeons with Vitaphone. It proved a wise and timely investment. Soon, crowning every Skouras marquee was a sign that magnetized moviegoers: THIS THEATER WIRED FOR SOUND! By early 1929 the conversion to talkies had been so sweeping that out of 20,500 movie theaters in the United States, a mere 400 lacked sound. The year silent film turned twenty-five, it was struck down.

Our vaudeville friends reacted to the overthrow of American entertainment's ancien régime in a variety of ways. Fleeing for their professional lives, many headliners sought refuge in radio. Others made a beeline for Hollywood to join what they could not lick. As more and more circuits phased out six-act bills, the best cabarets offered big-name comics plum spots as resident emcees. Top-flight torch singers and svelte dance teams enjoyed successful second careers headlining floor shows in sophisticated hotel restaurant–ballrooms such as the Sherman's College Inn and the Marine Room at the Edgewater Beach.

Nevertheless, among troupers like Larry Rich, confidence still ran high. When we caught up with him in New York, he had formed a new act with Cheri and a twelve-piece band, pulling down fifteen hundred dollars a week, a far cry from the two hundred dollars they had earned at Fort Worth's Majestic.

"Talkies?" Larry scoffed. "Why, they're just a flash in the pan. Remember the fella with the dog who could sing? He put him in the act, but all that dog could warble was 'Ira—Ira!' Nobody paid to hear it twice. Same thing with sound." He paused long enough to keep up his side of a pinochle game. "Look at the Victrola," he continued. "Has it killed vaudeville? Not on your life!"

Those bright blue-and-white cardboard icicles, dripping from marquees promising 20 DEGREES COOLER INSIDE! were to have spelled blessed relief to vaudevillians from the brutal backstage heat, but precious few of us ever got to enjoy it. By then most theaters had a bigger sign above the icicles announcing ALL SINGING, ALL DANCING, ALL TALKING FILMS!

Because comics like Larry cracked jokes to the bitter end, vaudeville died laughing. But die it most certainly did. By the spring of 1929 only fifteen hundred out of six thousand acts which had played the big time for decades could find bookings. But what I was too young to understand, and the adults around me too close to events to see, was the revolution taking place all across America: far more than vaudeville was changing.

Overnight Lindbergh's flight had brought Europe closer than it had ever been. In the hinterlands, the miracle of radio was breaking down old barriers of time and space. On occasion even Baby Peggy's fans could hear her without leaving home. An unprecedented era of prosperity and spending led to a phenomenal proliferation of motorcars. Many newly mobile families chose to take to the road instead of attending the most splendorous of air-conditioned theaters.

When we returned from a week's booking in Canada, Father reflected this prevailing mood of change by quitting the act. He hired a team of comedy writers to write a new skit based on a sequence in Universal's *The Family Secret* in which Baby Peggy outwits her governess. (I was growing weary of being a sequel to myself.) Father persuaded his cousin to come out from Omaha and work with me. Cousin Helen, handsome and about thirty, stood six feet three and weighed all of three hundred pounds. Her governess's uniform took enough black serge to make two army tents.

Taking a page from Fred Fishbach's script, Father paired me with this mountainous partner in an effort to further bonzai what was an undeniably spindly nine-year-old he still referred to as "the baby." I was sure no audience would swallow either this poor excuse for an act or the syrupy ballad that Billy Frisch and Larry Rich had written as my new theme song: "Sweet Baby Peggy, I'm in love with you. . . ." It was pure treacle. Writing songs myself by then, both music and lyrics, I protested.

"Oh, Peg, you're just a child!" Mother said. "What do you know about writing acts or songs? These people we've hired are paid professionals!"

After all these years I thought I was a paid professional too! As for the implied "what did I know about show business?" a few hot retorts sprang to my lips, but I prudently held my tongue.

My first rehearsal of the finished skit convinced me it qualified as cruel and unusual punishment for everyone, especially the audience. But rack-and-rope time was already upon us: we were booked into theaters in Connecticut and Ontario. As I feared, the concept was so dated it proved to be a god-awful albatross of an act, a dead weight around my neck. Adding to my dismay, I discovered I was yoked to a partner who, though well intentioned, was three hundred pounds of quaking stage fright. Compared to Cousin Helen, Father had been John Wilkes Booth.

After a ghastly three weeks on the old Proctor Circuit, Helen's nerve finally cracked, and she could not bring herself to face an audience. (I was close to being in the same condition, but for quite different reasons.) We canceled the tour and returned to New York, where we were confronted with another family crisis. Aunt Emma was calling it quits.

Just after we returned, Father let slip that he had involved Mother, Louise, and me in a smuggling scheme to conceal liquor flasks on our persons when we came back across the Canadian border. He made the serious miscalculation of hilariously describing in her presence how he had suspended a flat flask of crème de cacao around Peggy's neck from one of his neckties. "You should have seen her clutch her teddy bear tightly to her chest to keep the stuff from gurgling and giving us away in customs!" Aunt Emma wasn't prudish about liquor, but she was appalled that Father would enlist his own children to help pull off such a heist.

Chagrined, Father offered to drive her back to Laramie, and Aunt Emma was quick to cut a deal. Louise must go along and enroll in the private boarding school which Emma had headed for years. I was my family's meal ticket; if she couldn't get us both out, she could at least save Louise.

In a delirious whirl of preparation Louise changed her name to Jackie and sewed it on name tags in all her new clothes. The initials "J.L.M." were stamped in gold on her brand-new set of matched luggage. No expense was spared in helping her create a new identity. If she had her way, no one at tony Ivanson Hall would ever know she had been part of anything so tacky as vaudeville. At long last she was free of Baby Peggy and bound for her idealized "real world of normal people"!

We moved out of the apartment, and until Father's return, Mother and I rented a small upstairs studio apartment in the Tavern on Forty-second Street, a favorite vaudevillians' haunt. Old friends Flo MacFadden and Jack Haley, recently married, lived across the hall. Jack was weathering the circuits' troubles by switching to Broadway musicals. Veteran comedian Fred Allen and his wife and partner, Portland, lived downstairs. They were going through a time of double crisis, he not able to find bookings and she suffering from a serious mastoid infection. Realists, they thought vaudeville was mortally wounded and told us they were toying with the notion of getting into radio.

Mother and I made the rounds of New York's Tin Pan Alley. This constituted my spring training for a possible new act or a foray into radio. Visiting Irving Berlin's cluster of glassed-in, soundproof cubicles, each with its own piano, I learned and rehearsed such current hits as "Mean to Me" and "You're the Cream in My Coffee." Song pluggers accompanied singers there, giving tips on how to sell their numbers. Introduced to Mr. Berlin, I told him I was writing songs myself, although I couldn't read music. He confessed he couldn't either, and offered some curious advice about songwriting. "Always steal the first four bars from a well-known song. People pick it up quicker and that makes it a hit!"

With Father gone, Mother became as giddy as a kid out of school. Except for my occasional rehearsals, life was one long romp. She slept late, but every afternoon without fail we took in a double feature. Every evening we were taken to dinner and a Broadway play by a very remarkable couple.

Rose Olson was president of the Baby Peggy Fan Club and met my train on my first visit to New York when I was five. She had married Frank Olson, a thirty-year-old millionaire stockbroker known as the "boy wonder" of Wall Street. Rich, carefree, fun-loving, and generous to a fault, they were also hopelessly star-struck. We introduced them to the Haleys, and the two disparate couples became lifelong friends.

Our six-week theater spree ended at the Palace, where our old friends the Duncan Sisters were headlining in their shortened version of their popular play *Topsy and Eva*. As wild a pair as all seven hell-raising Foy Kids combined, they too had been pursued by the Gerry Society's bloodhounds. When we greeted them backstage, Vivian and Rosetta concocted a spur-of-the-moment scheme that was both their own sweet revenge against the society and a fitting swan song for me. Vivian was wearing the long curls, short skirts, and Mary Janes of Little Eva. Rosetta, in black cork, was dressed as Topsy. Each sister grabbed a hand and cried, "For once you're going to play the Palace! We'll show those Gerry Society bats what we think of them!"

The heavily muscled Montini Brothers were winding up their act with a precarious human pyramid as the Duncan Sisters and I raced onstage. We hit them dead center, toppling their pyramid and sending all six brothers stalking off in a high Italian huff. Rosetta presented me to the audience by boldly announcing, "We're proud to introduce our friend Baby Peggy! But did you people out there know that there's a ridiculous child labor law that makes it illegal for her to play the Palace until she's sixteen? That's not fair and we think it's a lousy way for the blue-nosed busybodies of the Gerry Society to treat a star!"

The audience gave us a standing ovation. But later that night, as I was drifting off to sleep, I thought how ironic it was that I—who had not shared other vaudevillians' lifelong pilgrimage to this holy shrine—should get to "play the Palace" after only four years! Still, it felt great to take a swipe at the much disliked Gerry Society.

The following night a snowstorm kept Mother and me at home, and Father called long distance. "Well, Sharkey," he cried exultantly, "I've done it!"

"Done what?" Mother countered cautiously.

"I just bought the sweetest little spread this side of paradise. Tall grass and timber and a river running through."

Father always shouted on long distance, as though he didn't trust the wire, so I was able to hear every word. He sounded like the lyrics of one of those "Western Nest and You, Dear" ballads of his youth. But Mother was wary. She had spent months trying to persuade him that if vaudeville foundered, we would go back to Hollywood. Her plan called for a modestly financed waiting period until I turned sixteen. By then I would have blossomed into a beautiful willowy brunette, be able to sing and dance flawlessly, and, it went without saying, would have also developed into the greatest actress since Bernhardt and Duse. Mother was not about to toss out this rose-colored script without a fight. But Jack invoked my health and her resolve dissolved.

His words must have evoked a mental image of me lying pale and motionless in the National Vaudeville Association's TB ward at Lake Saranac.

Just as one long-distance phone call had launched my comeback four years earlier, this one brought it to a close. Our troubador life ended and delivered us to Chicago, where Father had set up an office. It seemed our ranch was to replace me as our breadwinner.

20

O n the door of Suite 810 in gold letters was written:

J. FLAG RANCH AND RECREATION CENTER, INC.

JACK TRAVERS MONTGOMERY, PROPRIETOR

Entering the waiting room, we found a second door marked PRIVATE which stood half-open, and through it we beheld the new executive image of Jack Montgomery. Tipped back in a leather desk chair, steep-heel boots resting on a gleaming mahogany desk, a lighted maduro in his hand, he looked for all the world like a Wall Street tycoon gone Western.

When the excitement of reunion subsided, Father introduced us to a thin, deeply tanned gentleman in an adjoining office, Mr. Slim Garnett.

"Slim has a dude outfit in Roswell, New Mexico," Father explained, "and we'll be working together, using his desert place in winter until I get my own winter sports and game-hunting programs going in Wyoming."

I noticed Mother glancing about suspiciously, dollar signs in her eyes. "Naturally I couldn't tell you everything on the phone," Father continued. As it turned out, there was a great deal to tell. The office was cluttered with freshly opened boxes of elegant tan stationery bearing the logo of a bucking horse and rider in brown ink. Brochures, printed on rich, heavy-coated stock, showed photographs of dudes trail-riding or relaxing in rustically furnished log cabins.

"Is this one of our guest cabins?" Mother asked, flicking through a brochure.

"Well, no," Father hedged. "I had to put something together for this summer, so I used pictures from other outfits, but they show what we'll have." After Slim left, Mother asked more probing questions and got more elusive answers. No, the ranch wasn't quite ready yet, lots of remodeling lay ahead, and almost as many "developments" as there were acres. "Slim and I have some big investors lined up, and I've incorporated so I can sell stock in the ranch. Those who buy shares become charter members, and that furnishes the capital needed to put up the nine lakeshore cabins we'll be—"

"Oh, there's a lake on the property?" Mother brightened perceptibly.

"No, not *yet*," he parried. "I'll have to flood a hay meadow for that, and freeze it in winter for ice-skating." He paused and then, deciding it was easier to buy time than explain everything now, he said, "But hell, we've got until June to go into all the details."

Mother's intuition had proved remarkably prescient with several of my money managers who later proved larcenous, and she felt no different about Slim. She considered it a charmed weapon that implied she had powerful psychic forces at her behest. But in everyday terms it served her mostly to keep Father off balance and unsure.

We spent from February until early June in Chicago "going into the details." Mother was horrified at the money Father had spent making his dream ranch a reality. It did no good for him to defend his expenses by saying three wealthy investors had already promised to put a total of seventy-five thousand dollars into the club by October.

Over the next few weeks, while Father dealt with ranch affairs, Mother tried to fan into flame the few live coals left in the cooling ashes of Baby Peggy's fame. Two ladies living at the Sherman Hotel, where we were staying, had invented a surefire cure for falling hair and total baldness. They called their tonic Hair-Again and sponsored a radio program which was broadcast from the hotel penthouse. Amazingly enough, Mother sold them on the notion that if Baby Peggy sang "There's a Rainbow 'round My Shoulder" on their program and acted as spokesperson, she would put their new product on the map. I marveled that she thought any ten-year-old girl with an abundant head of hair was a natural for pitching a snake-oil cure for baldness. But then Mother's skewed notions of show business had always baffled me.

The ranch was a new cause of quarrels, and when the Sherman's assistant manager sent a dozen roses to Marian when we arrived, Father went into a fresh frenzy of suspicion and jealousy. In a way he had good reason. At thirty-one Mother had reached the peak of her beauty and charm, and knew how to enhance it with flattering gowns, coiffures, and makeup. There was a sort of feverishness about her too, as she saw herself facing the loneliness of life on a remote ranch, all of thirty-five miles from the nearest town, and a mighty small town at that!

Father was thirty-eight, and both seemed to fling themselves with genuine desperation into their final months of big-city night life in the Roaring Twenties. Perhaps it was good they did, for soon the Roaring Twenties themselves would vanish overnight.

We dined regularly at the Sherman's popular College Inn, enjoying its fine food and floor shows. Jimmy Wade, a footloose and witty young bachelor who seemed to be orbiting the outer peripheries of show business, one night attached himself to us there. Finding him amusing, my parents gladly let him share our table. For three whole months Father picked up the tab for Jimmy's dinner without a murmur. For my part, the short, chubby, and self-deprecating Jimmy provided me with a welcome neutral party in the war zone that life with Mother and Father had become. He also provided the much-needed comic relief that often quelled open combat before it began.

Jimmy was just the right height to dance with me, so every evening he led me out onto the Inn's dance floor until I had mastered the fox trot and waltz. One night a youthful stranger tapped him on the shoulder and asked to cut in. Jimmy acceded and I found myself looking into the luminous brown eyes of Jackie Coogan, grown into a handsome young man. He said he was on holiday from his private school and on an Easter vacation trip with his father. I was flustered, flattered, and nearly mute. Having dealt only with adults, conversing with anyone near my own age was unfamiliar and awkward for me. I had no idea what children or young people talked about to each other. Jackie was shy too, and I got the impression he had only asked me to dance because his father told him to.

Soon, the white spotlight found and followed us, and all the other dancers voluntarily left the floor to stand and watch. When the music ended, the entire room burst into sustained applause. Jackie escorted me to my table, both of us scarlet with embarrassment. That was our last public appearance as child stars, together or alone. Jackie Coogan was fifteen, Baby Peggy ten, and the decade which had brought us both to the zenith of stardom was drawing to its close. At my table the light flicked off at last. It would be a long time before a white spot warmed either of us again.

It quickly became obvious to me that Mother was trying to use me as a way to give ranch life the slip. If, by June, she could land me some kind of job, she would have the perfect excuse to remain "in civilization," as she put it. As part of this desperate strategy she sought out an old friend and trusted advisor, Lela Rogers.

Ginger, now a pert and pretty eighteen, was headlining Chicago's Oriental Theater, doing a squeaky-clean skit with emcee Paul Ash while baby-talking an invisible pet flea named Alexander. With her ill-starred marriage to Jack Pepper ended, her mother was back in charge of her career. Wisecracking movie roles and a man named Fred Astaire were still frozen inside some fortune-teller's crystal ball.

The relentlessly managerial Lela was full of the sort of advice I hated for Mother to hear. "Keep an eye out for radio work for Peggy," she pontificated backstage. "It's ideal for girls her age, 'cause the audience can't see them!" Lela was openhanded in sharing the tricks she had learned from Ginger's steady triumphs. "And mark my words, Marian, talkies are opening up a whole new world for troupers like Ginger and Peg!" Talk like this made me increasingly desperate to make my escape. Mother may have wanted the cheese, I only wanted out of the trap!

I was also trying frantically to escape from Baby Peggy. People saw the two of us as one, but we were more like Siamese twins, not joined by flesh and bone like Violet and Daisy Hilton, but by an invented persona. I began to suspect the only way to free myself from this other self was to cut her away, and if necessary even destroy her.

If Baby Peggy had been a jailer to Louise, she held me captive too. I had never fully admitted how much I hated the monotony and confinement of vaudeville: now I was ready to say a firm "No!" to anyone trying to draw me back inside its prison. But Baby Peggy was incapable of refusing a command. Her synapses were programmed to obey, and all she knew how to do was perform and placate in response to every crisis. Yoked to her, I could never have a life of my own. City mayors, fire chiefs, psychologists, and my parents saw me only as a golden egg. Its shell reflected back to them whatever image they held up to it. But inside that shell a new being was struggling to get out. The day my real self hatched, their golden egg would be shattered forever.

Out of the blue, Aunt Alice and Father's cousin Brick, of unhappy Snowy Range memories, paid us an unexpected one-day visit in Chicago. Brick used the opportunity to take Mother aside and ask her to run away with him. She turned him down, but after he and Aunt Alice left, she indulged in a bit of wistful dreaming of what might have been by playing the two songs he had sung to her that summer in the mountains. When the strains of "Girl of My Dreams" drifted through the suite, I braced myself for trouble. "The Pagan Love Song" started up just as Father returned home from his office. Trembling with rage, he swept the Victrola from the table and smashed the hated record to smithereens.

After a solid hour of screaming insults at each other, Father declared he was finished. "I know how to put myself out of my misery!" he announced melodramatically, retreating into the bathroom and locking the door behind him. There was the tinkle of what sounded like a razor blade hitting the floor. Taking the bait, Mother screamed, pounded the door, and begged him not to kill himself.

I had been through many such climactic screamers before. Every few months, in a different city, Father would pull out the trunk and start packing, shouting he was going to leave us. Louise usually watched knowingly from the sidelines, but I was psychologically wired to pull out all the dramatic stops from every movie I had ever made. "Please don't leave us here in Detroit!"—or Philadelphia, Minneapolis, or Boston—I would plead, genuinely terrified at the prospect of being left alone in Mother's care, for she was more helpless than a child. Almost on cue he would relent, saying he "could not bear to hurt you children." A tearful reconciliation always followed.

But here in Chicago I was all alone and emotionally overwhelmed by the burden of being responsible for saving them from each other. I finally coaxed Father out of the bathroom, and things quieted down while they dressed for dinner in the College Inn. Her feathers still ruffled, Mother went on ahead. I hung back, and when Father did not come out of the bedroom, I went in and found him standing before the tall, low-silled window, the sash thrown up high. "It's better this way, Sharkey!" he exclaimed in his best Othellian style, and threw himself over the sill.

With a scream I lunged across the room and grabbed hold of his suit coat. What he may have intended as a grandstand play for sympathy now took a deadly turn. He lost his balance and would surely have plunged down all nineteen floors had I not somehow managed to summon the superhuman strength born of adrenaline and terror that finally hauled him in. White as a ghost, he recovered quickly enough. Downstairs we found Mother and Jimmy Wade in fine form, and soon Father too was laughing at Jimmy's jokes. Although I was still badly shaken, I was careful not to show it. It was no different from being onstage.

Chicago, then in its prime years as gangster turf, was an uneasy kingdom, with three strong kingpins and their henchmen contending for power. Al Capone and "Bugsy" Moran were each trying to destroy the other and gain control of Chicago's lucrative bootleg liquor trade. The third man was "Big Bill" Thompson, the city's corpulent and politically powerful mayor. Although put in office legally, Thompson played with marked cards, and his trusted underworld go-between was a bald middle-aged man who looked as meek as a diamond cutter. He answered to the name of "Doc" Meyer.

When Mayor Thompson presented me with the key to Chicago, Father met Meyer and they became friends. While Meyer looked harmless, he knew where all the bodies were buried—literally. When the notorious Saint Valentine's Day Massacre took place in the Clark Street Garage, a few blocks from our hotel, Meyer told Father he knew exactly who had planned it.

A few nights later, I was walking with my parents and Jimmy Wade. When we passed McVicker's Theater, two men were out in front arguing loudly. Jimmy accused them of using foul language in front of a lady and a child. One of the two, a handsome and swarthy young man, made a courtly apology, but Jimmy kept haranguing him. Finally the man ripped open his camel's-hair coat, revealing a veritable arsenal of handguns. "Okay, shorty, I said I was sorry!" he snarled. Jimmy backed down.

The next day Father told Doc Meyer about the incident. "Holy Jesus!" Meyer cried. "That was Capone's right-hand man, Jack McGurn! He's the twenty-six-year-old who masterminded the Valentine Day's Massacre!"

At last the day drew near when we were to leave for Wyoming. While Mother and I were at the hotel packing, Father was at a golf club in Oak Park, where he and Slim Garnett were trying to sell ranch shares to a couple of wealthy society doctors on the green *and* the nineteenth hole. By the time they reached the Sherman Hotel's Clark Street entrance, Father was the proverbial three sheets to the wind.

Traffic was jammed, and an open touring car with five male passengers, directly in front of Father's Lincoln, failed to move. When leaning on the horn did no good, Father gave the wheel to Garnett and, with his golf bag over his shoulder, got out and confronted the driver of the car ahead.

"Why the hell don't you move it?" he demanded angrily.

"Who you think you're tellin' to move what?" the driver shouted back. The car's front door opened, and a man's leg shot out and kicked the offending stranger alongside the head.

Blood running down his face, Father swung his loaded golf bag against the car's windshield. Shattered glass spewed into the street, traffic started moving, and Father dodged among the cars and disappeared into the hotel's lobby.

Striding into our suite, blood still streaming down his cheek, Father answered our puzzled questions with, "Oh, some klutz on the last tee swung his club too close and clipped me under the eye. It's only a nick." With that he lurched unsteadily into the bathroom to wash up and shave. A moment later Slim arrived and joined him in there, the two of them laughing hilariously over what seemed to be a private joke.

Suddenly the door to our suite was noisily kicked open and five burly men stormed in as one. I was shocked to recognize their leader. He was the same man Jimmy had accosted on the street—Jack McGurn.

"I've come for the son of a bitch who just smashed in my windshield!" McGurn demanded furiously, his handsome face dark with rage. One of his men walked over to a window and threw it open. "When I get my hands on him," McGurn continued, "I'm personally gonna throw him out that window, see?"

"I'm afraid you gentlemen have the wrong room," Mother said, utterly fearless in her innocence. "We're all theater people here! This is the suite of child star Baby Peggy. I'm her mother, and we're packing to leave the city."

McGurn shot a long, hard look at me. I smiled my best uncertain smile. Suddenly he jerked his thumb toward the open window in a silent signal to a hunker who went over and pulled it down. "Could be I was mistaken, lady," McGurn said softly. "The guy I'm lookin' for acted more like Golf Bag Hunt,* and was probably packin' something more lethal than clubs." He

---

*A notorious local mobster of the time, who always carried a machine gun in his golf bag.

touched the brim of his fedora with two fingers and said gallantly, "Sorry if we bothered you, ma'am."

Once they were safely gone, Mother called to Father in the bathroom and told him what had happened. He came out swinging. "Where's the punk who tried to kick my face in!"

Two days later—with a black eye as big as a saucer, but grateful to be alive—Father sat behind the wheel of the Lincoln driving west. Sitting in the back seat, I braced myself for one more leap of faith.

PART 4

1929 – 1932

TALL
GRASS
AND
TIMBER
AND A
RIVER
RUNNING
THROUGH

21

Aunt Emma had told us Wyoming was the sixth-largest state in the Union, boasting 97,890 square miles: our ranch seemed every bit as big as all that to me. The 1,500-acre property translated roughly into 240,000 square feet, which was about 10,000 times more elbow room than the most spacious dressing room I'd ever known.

My first glimpse of this vast realm of mountain, meadow, forest, river, and plain was from atop a high ridge by the side of the Lincoln Highway. To the east lay cloud-shadowed Jelm Mountain. West of the highway rose the steep, timber-dark sides of Sheep Mountain, named for the wild mountain sheep still roaming there. An ancient seafloor of grouse-blue sage, now known as the Great Laramie Plains, surrounded both sentinels. I found it hard to believe this wild, wonderful domain actually belonged to me.

After this brief foretaste, Father turned the Lincoln onto a narrow dirt lane which wound about a mile down into a sheltered parklike area shaded by noble cottonwoods. In their midst the two-story log ranch house stood. While the name J. Flag Ranch and Recreation Center had a country-club ring to it, it was set down in a bona fide wilderness. From our front door it was six miles to the nearest neighbor, thirty-five to the nearest town of Laramie, a hundred to Cheyenne. All three were accessible via the Lincoln Highway. That too had a civilized ring, but it was a primitive two-lane dirt road over whose washboard surface it was foolhardy to try and drive more than forty-five miles an hour.

Jake Lund, a Bunyanesque Norwegian from the old country, got a quit-claim deed to this property from its first homesteader in 1880. That was a mere six years after nomadic Cheyenne and Arapaho Indians, the original lords of this region, were placed on distant reservations. It was only four years after Sioux and Cheyenne warriors wiped out Custer's command on the Little Big Horn. It took courage for Norwegian-born Jake and Lenna Lund to drive an ox-drawn wagon across these plains fifty years ago and park it on the very spot where I stood that June morning in 1929.

Father's description had been accurate—tall grass, plenty of timber, and a good river running through. Thanks to Jake it even had an apple orchard numbering sixty trees, the only one in Albany County and, old-timers claimed, the only one ever to thrive at an altitude of 8,500 feet. The Big Laramie River, running directly behind the three big ranch corrals, was a large, swift-flowing stream, abounding in trout, and about 150 feet across at its widest point. But this spring, due to exceptionally heavy winter snows, it had overflowed its banks and had risen until it formed a lake in the very dooryard of the house.

Rotten apples, beets, and potatoes, brought up from flooded underground root cellars, bobbed on the tide. The bloated carcasses of drowned cats, mice, chickens, and lambs floated everywhere. Glancing at Mother, I found her face a study in disappointment and dismay.

"My crew of workmen will have all this cleaned up in a few days," Father offered cheerfully. Later we learned what a genuine act of faith this purchase had been. In early January, while I was breaking in the new act back in Connecticut, he had arrived in Laramie with Aunt Emma and Louise, and heard the old Lund Ranch was for sale. In 1924, after decades of improving the homestead and mortgaging it repeatedly, old Jake Lund had finally lost the place when the bank repossessed it. The ranch had been up for sale ever since, but in the interim had been rented out to various sheep outfits.

On the stormy day Father drove out to see it, lambing season was at its peak and so was a blizzard, forcing the shepherds to take shelter indoors.

Bleating ewes in every stage of pregnancy and postdelivery, with their off-spring, filled every one of the building's fourteen rooms, upstairs and down. Snowdrifts from two to thirty feet deep covered everything. But love is blind. Neither sheep, which he loathed, nor bad weather could keep Father from buying the ranch he'd dreamed of owning ever since his cowboy days.

Very gingerly, one bit of bad news at a time, Father let Mother know the house had no inside plumbing, no running water, no electricity, no furnace, and no fireplace. As for a telephone, it would soon be installed. But there *was* a good pump and well a few steps from the back door, and a slab-walled outhouse *only* two hundred yards from the house!

Pitching a wooden-floored tent in the dry apple orchard, we settled in. For the next six weeks a crew of men worked at clearing the grounds and remodeling the house. In 1888 Jake and his sons had built the solid log house. Every squared log had been peeled and hewed by hand, each one dovetailed to the other. To the workmen's amazement, they found not a single nail had been used in the building. Jake's eight tiny bedrooms upstairs quickly became four, the six downstairs rooms expanded into a large sitting room and dining room. We added a kitchen, a large back porch, and a ve-randa, screened against mosquitoes, along the full length of the house.

In August we moved in and a large moving van arrived from California bringing all the possessions we had put in storage when we left Hollywood for Fort Worth. Our formal Beverly Hills furniture, Chinese rugs, and Max-field Parrish prints were a bit out of tune with Navajo rugs, panther hides, and rustic log walls, but Mother was happy to have her own things again. Among them was Father's small library of Zane Grey, James Oliver Cur-wood, and Harold Bell Wright Western novels, which Louise and I de-voured. I was also glad to have my long-unread set of *My Book House*, and caught up on the classic fairy stories I had missed. The van also brought four trunks full of Baby Peggy clippings, stills from my comedies and features, and unopened fan mail dating back to 1924.

Just as we were regarded as interlopers by vaudevillians, we now found ourselves outsiders again in this cliquish mountain community. Everyone up and down the river for twenty miles was either Norwegian or Swedish and they all ran sheep. Being fresh from show business, we were already alien enough, but what further ostracized us from our neighbors was that we ran horses and were engaged in what they viewed as the useless business of dude ranching.

In another problem peculiar to the region, Swedes and Norwegians had feuded with each other for centuries in the Old World. Now, after several decades of living as neighbors on the Big Laramie, they had racked up lots of fresh disputes over water-weirs, stray milk cows, misbranded colts, and hard-knuckle Saturday-night brawls over liquor and girls in the dance hall at Wood's Landing. Wood's was three miles upstream from us and fascinated me. The only bridge across the river for miles was built there, and I thought it symbolized the place where warring factions should come together, which intrigued the perennial peacemaker in me.

There was yet one more social obstacle for outsiders to overcome. If one was cordial to an Erickson (Swedish), one gave up hope of making friends with the Wickstroms, the Sodagreens, and Hansens (Norwegians). Not surprisingly, the first neighbor Father dared approach was a jovial cattleman bearing the noncontentious name of Charlie Thompson.

Although Father assured Mother the seventy-five thousand dollars coming from his investors this fall would completely modernize the ranch, for now we had to settle for a nineteenth-century frontier lifestyle. Except for a Victrola, and our so-called portable radio (a hundred-pound black box!), the ranch held not *one* convenience more than it had when Jake Lund put down his ax.

We spent the summer adapting to our primitive living conditions. Father installed a hand pump over the kitchen sink and taught Louise and me how to milk a cow. Our back porch was lined with wide shelves where covered crocks of strained raw milk were set out for the cream to rise. Skimming the crocks daily, we gave the chickens the excess milk and made the heavy cream into butter in a hand-cranked glass churn. (My best speed was twenty minutes.) I also learned how to skin and clean rabbits and hang and clean the carcass of a deer or elk. Of course both Louise and I began polishing our riding skills by living in the saddle. Now Mother transferred her lifelong obsession with my health to the haunting fear I would be crippled or killed in a riding accident. She fought to keep us off horses, Father fought to keep us on.

This was the third time in my ten years I had been thrust into a new environment where everything was alien to what had gone before. This time the challenge was not only regional and social but chronological, for we had stepped back in time. At least the performance skills learned in making movies had served me well in vaudeville. But what good was a time step or an imitation of Harry Lauder out here? Who had even heard of him? Even Baby Peggy "in person" didn't carry much weight out here. This milieu required mastering an entirely different set of skills, mostly those on which one's very life depended. It had its own talismans and taboos.

If backstage gypsies read the future in tea leaves, river folk discerned it in phases of the moon, the river's height, ground hogs, and even the common horse fly. "A hard winter coming!" old-timers warned that September, when the region was beset by a biblical plague of flies. The savage winter that followed made a true believer of me.

My parents struck up several friendships with Anglos in Laramie—a dentist, a physician, a butcher, and a World War I veteran who ran the local haberdashery and told hair-raising stories of soldiering in Chateau Thierry and Belleau Wood. Mountain Dew was the preferred brand of bootleg booze, mostly because it was distilled locally, but judging from its kick, it should have been called White Mule. Weekend parties began with such bucolic amusements as tossing firecrackers under ladies' chairs on the veranda and went downhill from there. After three or four drinks, most guests passed out on a couch or bed quite painlessly, but from what I observed, Mountain Dew hangovers were a foretaste of hell.

As the summer passed I spent most of my time riding along the river or up on Jelm Mountain. I loved the lonely trails, the tangy air laced with pine and sage, the soothing murmur of the river. Most of all I treasured solitude, the rare opportunity to be alone and free of the oppressive shipboard-tight backstage society. For the first time in memory I experienced a total absence of fans and audiences, and blessed surcease from "continuous performance."

"Why don't you come back to the house and help Mother and me with the washing," Louise would complain as she came upon me sitting on the bank watching the river roll by.

"I'm tired of working," I told her one day, with an honesty that surprised me. "This is my time to *rest!*"

I needed the rest more than I or anyone in my family realized, psychologically far more than physically. I relished every minute in which I was asked to do nothing. I lay in hay meadows watching the clouds drift across the blue-black Wyoming sky. I passed hours reading "graveyard poetry" in a book Aunt Emma had given me. My interest in the subject sprang from an urgent need to deal with a mortality problem uniquely my own.

One day under a Douglas fir high on Jelm Mountain, with a view that stretched for a hundred miles, I mentally buried Baby Peggy. It was a simple, private ceremony at which I was the sole witness. I sat by her imaginary grave a long time and felt at peace knowing she was safely put away. In doing so I also felt I had secured a final resting place for myself at her side, when my own time came. Nearing the ripe old age of eleven, I knew that Baby Peggy's career was over forever. I was also convinced that this was the country where I would spend the rest of my life. That odd ceremony gave me a wonderful sense of completion and certainty.

I who had spent most of my life on wheels had stopped rolling at last. For the first time, Peggy, the plant that had been deliberately bonsaied for years, put down deep roots in a portion of earth my hard work and earnings had made my own.

Falling hopelessly in love with those fifteen hundred acres of wilderness was just about the riskiest thing I had ever done.

22

While I was ceremonially burying the part of myself I wanted safely dead, another part that would shape my future as an adult was beginning to germinate. I had listened spellbound to vaudevillians' life stories backstage: now I persuaded Scandinavian neighbors to tell me theirs. Finding well-made flint arrowheads on Jelm Mountain, I asked an old trapper why they were so plentiful.

"This was all Arapaho country, before the 1870s," he explained. Mr. Crissmore was a bona fide old-timer, being around sixty and having lived, hunted, and trapped along the Big Laramie since boyhood. Father let him live gratis in a one-room cabin next to the ranch in exchange for trapping the pesky beaver that kept damming the ditches irrigating our hay meadows.

"Lots of Indian trails still to be seen in these hills," he said. "Arapahoes hunted elk and deer on Jelm, buffalo and antelope on the Laramie Plains yonder under Sheep Mountain. They preferred using arrows to hunt game, 'cause they were silent and didn't give their presence away to enemies."

Being able to touch the heart of living history sparked what had always been more than a passing interest in Indian lore. Back in 1923, Tim McCoy had brought a band of Arapahoes out from their Wyoming reservation to appear in a prologue for the epic Western film *The Covered Wagon*. McCoy and Father were longtime cowboy friends, so he invited me to visit their real-life Indian camp atop Cahuenga Pass. There I met two middle-aged members of the tribe who lived as Indians but were actually white. Both had been captured as small children from an immigrant wagon train crossing Wyoming, not far from our own ranch.

That same day the Arapaho chief initiated me into the tribe by pricking my forefinger and his with his own hunting knife, then pressing the wounds together to let our blood mingle. "You are now one of us, the People," he had said. That ceremony made a profound impression on the four-year-old I was then.

After talking to Mr. Crissmore, I read every book about Arapahoes I could lay hands on in the libraries of various rancher friends. By the time I was twelve, I knew I wanted to be a historian, as well as a writer, and Western history was the trail that beckoned. But given my parents' determination to make me an actress, I knew that pursuing a career of my own choosing would not be easy.

The Thompson family became our willing guides to homestead living. We shared hayrides, picnics, and berry-picking jaunts across the river where clusters of wild chokecherries were turning black under a late summer sun. From the Thompsons, Mother learned to make chokecherry jelly and to cold pack deer and elk meat for winter, regional survival skills. We had a cook, a hired man, and a hired girl to help with the chores, so Louise and I were free to enjoy the excitement of haying season, the high point of the ranchers' year. All the equipment that came with the ranch was horse-drawn and rusty, but Father borrowed extra hay rakes and workhorses from neighbors, hired a small haying crew, and went to work with ten men in the field. Father himself was an expert at "topping off" a field stack, lightly thatching the final layer to seal it against rain, snow, and the mildew that could ruin two or three tons of valuable hay.

In his new role of ranch owner, head of the house, and provider, Father was his own man at last. Here he could put to use his wide knowledge of horses, livestock, and ranching in general. But the ranch's isolation also enabled him to keep sequestered and maintain iron-clad control over the three females in his life. Not one of us could get to Laramie for a real tub bath, to shop, or to see a movie unless Father agreed to drive us in. Coaxing him to take us to town became a cagily played, four-sided game which he most often won by simply saying no. We were even more his captives now than we had been in hotels and dressing rooms.

Still, only Louise had reason to be deeply unhappy. Her first venture into her "real world of normal people" had proven an unmitigated disaster. Like most boarding schools, the one in Laramie had its fair share of spoiled and cruel teenage girls. She fell afoul of their petty plots and machinations. But her classroom experiences were worse. On her first day the teacher asked her to go to the blackboard and write the answer to a simple seventh-grade equation. Having never even heard of the problem, let alone its solution, Louise froze in front of the whole class, unable to speak or move. Finding the new girl hopelessly unprepared for the seventh grade, the teacher sent her back to the fifth.

There Louise sat, a wretched thirteen-year-old, overflowing her child-size desk seat while beady-eyed fifth-graders lifted a forest of eager hands to answer questions utterly beyond her ken. Summer vacation presented her with an even more devastating crisis. Lonely, and with her already low self-esteem severely battered by six months in school, she developed a young girl's crush on a member of the hay crew.

Buddy Jones and his father were drifting Oklahoma sharecroppers who hired out by the week as a team. A shy sixteen-year-old country boy, Buddy returned Louise's affection in puppy-love fashion. Our cook, observing them stealing a furtive kiss on the back porch, reported it to Father. His response was a frightful example of overkill, born of his ignorance and distrust of womankind.

In the best tradition of a tent-show melodrama, Father ordered Louise and Buddy into the living room where he and Mother presided over their familiar home-style court. I was dragged in as an unwilling witness to the "affair." First he dressed Louise down; then, turning savagely on Buddy, he fired the flabbergasted youth *and* his father, demanding the boy see to it they were both off the property by sundown "or else."

As soon as Buddy slunk out of the room, Mother burst into histrionic tears of rage and turned on Louise. "Well, I hope you're satisfied! Now he's going to spread it all over Oklahoma that he made Baby Peggy's sister!" I was appalled. Was Baby Peggy all they ever cared about? There was obviously *no* connection, and I felt they were being brutally unfair to Louise. I watched her age ten years during that traumatic hourlong scene which left her scarred for life.

On a bright sunny day in mid-October Father climbed into the Lincoln and headed east to confer with his three key investors and collect the seventy-five thousand dollars which I now understood was badly needed money. We all thought Father had paid cash for the ranch. Gradually he admitted that he only had twenty thousand dollars left of the more than half a million I had earned in vaudeville. Soon after we arrived in June he had to take out a first mortgage for ten thousand dollars.

My eleventh birthday fell on October 29, while Father was away, a date that marked four memorable events. I combed back my Baby Peggy bangs and prepared to grow up as somebody else, we had our first snow of the season, and Ole Erickson rode into the yard leading a pretty bay mare named Silver, my birthday present from Father. The fourth unforgettable event did not take place locally but was nevertheless felt even way out here: the crash of the New York Stock Market reverberated like a thunderclap across the great Laramie Plains.

WALL STREET LAYS AN EGG! screamed the headline in *Variety*, the trade paper to which Mother continued to subscribe. "Drop in stocks ropes showmen. . . . Legit shows hit." The paper estimated "twenty million people were in the market. Tragedy, despair, and ruination spell the story of countless thousands of marginal stock traders. Many will remain broke for the rest of their lives." Among those who would remain broke for the rest of their lives was our friend Frank Olson, the boy wonder of Wall Street who lost everything.

The local *Laramie Boomerang* told the story from a vastly different perspective. Here in sheep and cattle country, where hay was a priority crop, land values were the solid foundation on which the ranching economy was built. Good pastureland and hay meadows had been selling for ten dollars an acre before the crash. Following that catastrophe land wasn't going at any price. Wyoming ranchers had been dealt a stunning blow.

Two weeks later, with Louise back in boarding school (I was still not in school), Mother, a hired man, and I were in the orchard picking the last of the apples and packing them in barrels for winter storage in the root cellar. Her apron filled with apples, Mother glanced up as a shiny new Model A Ford came bumping down the lane, trailing a long plume of dust. "How strange," she remarked. "That car doesn't belong to any of the neighbors, and it's too late in the season for dudes. Who can it be?"

When the Ford stopped in the dooryard, the front passenger-side door opened and out bounded a spectacular burnished-gold German shepherd. Then from the driver's seat there slowly emerged a haggard and weary Jack Montgomery.

"Why, it's you, dear!" Mother cried, letting the apples fall to the ground. "I didn't recognize the car. What happened to the Lincoln?"

The Lincoln having been traded in for the far cheaper Model A and some much-needed cash was only the opening chapter of the frightful story Father had to tell. But before he could even bring himself to speak, he broke into tears.

23

A wealthy Chicago heiress, who had often clasped me to her gem-encrusted bosom in my Beverly Hills days, had married an executive with a fortune of his own. When Father had approached this couple in March, they had promised to invest twenty-five thousand dollars in the ranch come autumn. But when he visited them days after the crash, he was told that the husband, a heavy loser in the market, had been found dead in his bathtub, a shotgun by his side. His grieving widow explained she was now penniless.

Slim Garnett, whom Father had trusted to run the Chicago office, had vanished, taking with him the joint bank account Father had set up for their partnership. Moving on to New York, he discovered the second investor who had pledged twenty-five thousand dollars had also been bankrupted by stock losses and had jumped to his death from an office building. Also in New York the millionaire president of a nationwide chain of stores dropped dead of a heart attack when hearing he was wiped out.

As Father recounted this incredible litany of ruin and suicides, he stammered often and occasionally paused to brush away tears. Even the magnificent golden German shepherd, he said, was the parting gift of another Chicago friend who had lost his home in the wake of the crash and no longer had a large enough yard for his prize dog.

Slowly the grim truth sank in on all of us. The ranch was never going to be modernized—we were now doomed to live in this time warp forever. Fortunately, mountain and plain abounded with wild grouse, rabbits, antelope, elk, and deer, and the river teemed with trout. None of us fancied fish, but Father was a crack shot with both his forty-five and 30-30, and ammunition was cheap.

While we confronted this upheaval in our lives, the president of the Albany County School Board, Ole Erickson, rode into our place to announce that school would soon be held in a small log cabin on his property. The shack had been built sixty-five years earlier as a schoolhouse for the children of immigrants on the nearby Overland Trail. Unable to afford it, Father had taken Louise out of private school, but he flatly refused to let us attend a "fallen-down one-room country school." Erickson said school would begin there in January and coldly threatened legal action if Father did not cooperate.

Stung by this defeat at the hands of a hardheaded Swedish sheepman, come January Father sent us to school with strict orders not to speak to *any* of the other children. "You're not to associate with those backwoods kids in any way, do you understand? Eat your lunch apart from them."

Mother echoed his elitist sentiments. "God knows it's bad enough you have to be in the same room," she sighed. "Next thing you'll be picking up their bad grammar—those awful 'ain'ts,' 'we seens,' 'he dones,' and all the rest!"

Upon arrival Louise and I agreed that, even cleaned up, this old cabin was a wall-to-wall ruin and looked like something Lewis and Clark would have hesitated to winter in. It measured twenty feet wide by forty feet long, with three windows on the left wall, where a row of five bench-and-desk units took advantage of the light. These were old enough to have seen service when Lincoln was a boy. A Franklin stove stood in the center of the room, the teacher's desk at the far end facing both students and stove. To her left a well-filled bookcase sagged against a corner for support. These readers and histories, illustrated with quaint steel engravings, were our textbooks. Their publication dates hovered between 1821 and 1869.

Our teacher, middle-aged Mrs. McClaran, boarded at Erickson's ranch, the school board paying him twenty dollars a month for her room and board. Completely adaptable and unflappable, she kept such good order she managed to teach five separate grades simultaneously in this one small room. Louise and a boy named Jack Gilroy from the nearby hamlet of Jelm were in ninth grade; the teacher's little girl was in fifth; two Swedish boys from upriver were in first and fourth grade respectively. Father arbitrarily ordered Mrs. McClaran, in writing, that I was exceptional and must finish the sixth, seventh, and eighth grades this year! Why waste time, when I could get school out of the way once and for all? He had no doubt I could do the work. Wasn't that what high "Eye Cues" were all about? This being my first day in any school, I had no idea what he was asking. The teacher knew, and I soon found out.

Louise and I rode horseback the four miles to school and back each day, feeding our horses from nose bags during our lunch hour and watering them at the river. Fifteen-year-old Jack Gilroy hauled our drinking water from the river in a bucket to the schoolhouse every morning and split firewood for the stove to keep us from freezing when temperatures dropped to thirty below zero during winter storms.

Mrs. McClaran assured me it was impossible for anyone to take three grades at once. There simply wasn't time. But she suggested I listen to the recitations of those in the lower grades to help me catch up. Later, while watching a second-grader cut an apple into four parts, I got my first glimmer of what fractions might be all about. But the brutal truth was, math was a hydra-headed dragon I seemed doomed never to slay. In English, composition, and history I earned straight A's.

I also learned a number of other things which have made striking up conversations in farm country with total strangers a breeze. I'm an expert on the conformation of horses, hogs, dairy cows, beef cattle, sheep, and chickens: I know all the breeds, their histories, their diseases and cures. I learned to measure the tonnage in a stack of hay and the probable tonnage per acre of timothy and clover growing in the field.

We invented a recess game in which one person played Eliza, while the rest were "bloodhounds" pursuing her through the snow. It polished our game-tracking skills. In spring we carved boats, propelled by rubber-band paddles, and raced them in the creek near the school. Come May we engaged in the high-minded business of drowning out gophers who ravaged spring crops: two of us flooding the hole with buckets of water, a third polishing off the villain with a hammer blow when he came up for air.

The ghosts of the Overland Trail seemed as close as the arrowheads on the ground, and my love of history kept tugging at my sleeve. The teacher took care to cultivate it. Each weekend in Laramie she picked up several library books, boy's stories about frontier history. After the books had made the rounds, she took them back and returned with a new lot.

In our second October on the ranch Father suffered a serious fall. Racing with Mother and a hired man over the open prairie, his horse plunged both front feet into a badger hole concealed by sage, and he was thrown thirty feet, knocking him unconscious. With the help of a passing motorist on the nearby Lincoln Highway, Mother and the hired man managed to get him back down to the ranch house and onto a sofa.

In response to a frantic phone call a doctor drove out from Laramie, but all he could do was set two or three ribs with no more anesthetic than a shot of the moonshine he had brought along in a cream-colored ceramic jug and which he sampled generously himself as he worked. When he was done, Father was still unconscious, and the doctor opined the patient was probably suffering from both a fractured skull and a brain concussion, but he couldn't really tell. "Just keep him snubbed up close the next few days and hope for the best," was his sage advice.

Father did not see a doctor again, never visited a hospital or had his skull x-rayed. There was no money for such frills. As he had often said, "On the open range horse falls were common and doctors rare as rosebushes. Out west a man either died or got well." He remained either unconscious or delirious for the next ten days, and then one morning he woke up sane. Two weeks later he sat upright on the sofa for the first time and asked Mother to bring him his boots.

"What in God's name do you want with your boots?"

"I'm going out to the corral and catch up Ginger and take a ride along the river. It'll do me good." To Mother's astonishment he returned an hour later a well man.

That winter was the coldest ever recorded since Wyoming became a state in 1890. From a warm spell of thirty-five below zero the thermometer plummeted to a Klondike low of fifty-nine. In those days no one spoke about the wind-chill factor, but the wind never stopped out here on the great Laramie Plains. We started to ride to school, but our horses' breath froze in their nostrils and we turned back.

Approaching the back porch, I noticed the last of my many keys to American cities, which hung on the outside log wall of the house. It was the key to Buffalo, New York, and had a real thermometer attached, which made it useful where all the others were purely decorative. Drawing closer, I was astounded to see it registered an ungodly *sixty-two below zero,* and even as I watched, the mercury hit bottom, shattering the glass! This strange occurrence struck me as symbolic, signifying that things had gone as far down as they could possibly go. I was wrong.

24

The price of being transported back into nineteenth-century frontier life was a never-ending round of manual labor: butter to churn, windows to wash, rugs to beat, the wooden floors of ten rooms to be mopped weekly and treated with linseed oil, bed linens to launder. Our wash-day methods harked back to the Middle Ages: gallons of water, heated and hauled to the back porch and poured into two huge tin tubs where each piece was scrubbed on corrugated-metal washboards. By the time we finally hung out the week's wash, the three of us had expended enough energy washing, rinsing, and hand-wringing everything to have climbed the Matterhorn. Winter brought the added challenge of making sure we brought in the sheets before they all froze stiff on the line.

In the fall Father ingeniously hooked up a circle saw to a jury rig, driven by our Ford car's engine. While I hand-fed a steady flow of cottonwood logs down a long tin chute, the fast-whirring saw sliced them in twelve-inch lengths which Father tossed to one side. Later he stood each chunk on the flat stump of a giant cottonwood he had felled for firewood and split it into several pieces with his ax. Louise and I carried and stacked the finished stove wood on the back porch against the coming of winter.

During what we euphemistically called "dude season," it fell to me to carry to the distant outhouse and dispose of the contents of our own and the guests' bedroom chamber pots. After Louise and I helped Mother prepare breakfast, we waited table, made the beds, cleaned the guest rooms daily, and served as trail guides to the few dudes venturing our way. At night we sang cowboy ballads around an outdoor fire or, on cooler evenings, performed our tap routines after dinner in the dining room to entertain guests or neighbors.

Our third spring on the Big Laramie River had none of the euphoric expectations of the first. The Swenson Lumber Company slapped a five-hundred-dollar lien against the ranch for bills long overdue. Our charge accounts were mounting with the grocer, the feed store, and even the sporting goods store where Father bought his badly needed ammunition for hunting game. The patience of all these hard-hit retailers was growing thin. We had to find a way to earn money fast or go under.

In June we started up a second business as a wayside restaurant, serving chicken dinners every Sunday. Father advertised in the *Laramie Boomerang,* inviting families and civic groups to hold their banquets there. Hiring help being beyond our means, this was 100 percent family-run operation. While the number of diners who responded was not overwhelming, it was admittedly all we could handle. People came from as far away as Cheyenne for the food and convivial charm of their witty host and hostess, which my chameleonlike parents instantly became in the presence of attentive strangers.

The dinner itself was a steal: all the fried chicken (or chicken and dumplings) you could eat, a vegetable, mashed potatoes, biscuits, sage honey, individual salad, homemade dessert, and coffee for $1.50. Granted, our costs were low, but even so it was like skinning a gnat for its tallow to clear seventy cents on every meal served.

The process moved along on a homespun assembly line. Sundays at sunrise Father killed two dozen hens from our flock of white leghorns. Once Louise and I had picked, singed, and scalded the birds, he cleavered them for cooking. After Mother plunked the various parts in stew pot or skillet, I began stoking the 1876 Centennial stove with firewood. Using a fitted tool resembling the crank on a Model T Ford, I shook the ashes down into the cinderbox below to keep the fire roaring. That side of the oven got cherry-red, the other stayed cold. Constantly turning the biscuits to compensate was like spinning a hand-propelled country carousel.

Louise waited on four long rustic tables seating twelve each, while I, when not turning biscuits, whipping potatoes, shelling peas, and slicing pie, helped Mother move caldrons like chessmen on the black stovetop. Once diners started arriving at noon, I began washing, scalding, and drying dishes until long after sundown. It was "continuous performance" all over again—only this time with feathers!

Our restaurant enterprise peaked in early autumn, when the Laramie Boosters asked to hold their annual membership-drive dinner at the ranch. There would be thirty-five men at $10 each, $350 for the night. Father had business that night in Laramie, so he hired a cook and butler for the evening. The tall, fiercely handsome butler was a full-blood Sioux Indian who said his name was Chief.

For this signal occasion Mother brought out her best silver and the large set of gold-edged Haviland china, complete with consommé cups and finger bowls, which had replaced the set purloined by J. G. in 1924. Exquisite smoked-glass goblets and dessert dishes, presented to Baby Peggy by a famous glass factory in Pennsylvania, made a rare appearance. Under white linen tablecloths, our rustic tables looked elegant. Wild Indian paintbrushes and scarlet buglers formed each table's colorful centerpiece, massed around a forest of twenty-four-inch contrasting blue and gold tapers, the Boosters' club colors, which Mother thought a nice touch.

Louise and I donned rarely worn dresses and silk hose, while Mother looked radiant in a scarlet lace gown from her cabaret days. Chief was regal in an immaculate white jacket which set off his deep bronze color, olive-black eyes, and thick raven hair. Casting a last prideful glance around the dining room, we all agreed everything looked first-rate.

In the luminous twilight, with a full moon rising, our guests began arriving in several cars. However, as we greeted them it became apparent the Boosters had in tow far more than a dozen potential new members. Most seemed to have already consumed half the bootleg booze in town that wasn't under lock and key. During a thirty-minute "club business" meeting, held in our large living room, they went from slightly looped to blind-pig drunk.

When they finally weaved into the dining room, their president took an instant shine to the centerpiece candles. Snatching one from the table, he brandished it like a rapier, challenging a fellow member to a duel. Within seconds all thirty-five men were armed with flaming tapers and dueling with each other, executing the daring thrusts and bench-leaping swordplay of a Douglas Fairbanks epic. Blue and gold wax was spattered over tablecloths, benches, and floor.

Confronted with a dining room full of small-town businessmen gone stark staring mad on rot-gut alcohol, Mother ran into the office and began cranking the wall phone frantically, trying to reach Father in town. A reveler crept in behind her and playfully closed the door. "Well, they didn't tell me we were gonna have a pretty Red Riding Hood like you here tonight!" he breathed. "How come I didn't see you before?"

"Please," Mother said, backing away, "I'm making an urgent call!"

Lurching forward, he placed both hands on the wall behind her and held her caged. "So how's about a kiss, sweetie?"

Trapped, Mother's composure left her. "Chief!" she cried at the top of her lungs. "Help me!"

Seconds later Chief burst into the office, brandishing the biggest, sharpest meat cleaver he owned. *"Let her go!"* he ordered, his eyes ablaze, his expression savage. "Let her go *or I kill you*!"

"Oh, my Gawd!" the drunk gasped, turning chalk white at the sight of this angry Indian warrior with a cleaver at his throat.

"No, Chief, not *that*!" Mother pleaded. "Just get him out of here and away from me!"

Chief dragged the man out to the front veranda and threw him down the stairs. Once released, the terrified Booster lit out running and climbed the nearest cottonwood. Returning to the dining room, Mother found the banquet more ruined than consumed. Most of the Boosters had gone outside, apparently to get more liquor from their cars. Most of them ended up perched high in the cottonwoods, draining flasks or bottles and howling at the moon. It was three in the morning before the more sober Boosters coaxed the last brother down from his tree and the last car rattled away.

The first snowfall spelled the end of our Sunday dinners and our future looked bleak. Creditors had our backs to the wall and winter was closing in. Because our last "work-for-board-and-room" hired man had long since drifted on, Louise and I were helping Father by milking the two cows, stacking firewood, and doing as much else as we could before and after school. Then one fall day I walked out front with Father to greet a stranger striding down our lane.

The man looked to be about forty, a lantern-jawed giant, wearing plow boots, twill trousers, hair to his shoulders, a hand-sewn rawhide shirt, and, slung in a scabbard at his hip, a long hunting knife with a deer-horn handle.

He put down his small pack by his feet and stood hip shot and haughty, appraising our spread with the lordly air of a prospective buyer. Finally, as if addressing the log house itself, he said, "I'm willing to work for room and board."

His name was Henry Booth, and he explained only that he had lost his upriver ranch and had to sell his horse and saddle. Like all his many predecessors, he said he was a hard worker and only needed three squares a day and a dry place to sleep. He asked if he could trap beaver on our stretch of river and sell the pelts for extra cash: they brought five dollars each. Since Mr. Crissmore had moved on long before and controlling the destructive beaver population had become an endless and onerous chore, Father agreed.

Judging from all the stories I'd been reading, Henry was a mountain man born out of time. He spoke of living by his wits and his faithful Green River knife. My proudest possession for years thereafter was Henry's gift to me of a smaller version of his knife, with a deer-horn handle and a blade he made from a saw. Oddly enough, he didn't own a rifle, and the first time the two men went hunting for meat, Father had to loan him one of his.

By mid-December of 1930 an eight-foot Douglas fir tree stood in a corner of our living room, snaked down behind a saddlehorse from Jelm Mountain and hung with expensive ornaments from our Laurel Canyon days. The few packages under it were gifts of warm clothes from our parents, and presents from us to them of wooden letter openers and bookends handmade at school. I looked back painfully on our lavish 1928 Christmas in New York. Every one since then had grown slimmer and this was the poorest of all. Father was deeply depressed this season, for the sporting goods store had refused to extend him credit to buy even a single box of 30-30 shells. Without ammunition he was unable to provide the fresh venison roast which had always brightened Christmas Day dinners at the ranch.

At sunup on the day before Christmas, having built the cookstove fire and milked both cows, Henry rode up to the back door on the big bay Father had cut him for his own use. "I'm goin' downriver to check my traps," he announced with his usual thrift for words. "Be back by milkin' time."

Twelve inches of fresh snow lay on the ground, and the cold was so intense Henry's breath all but froze as he spoke. I stared after him admiringly as he rode away. It was like watching whang-leather tough Bill Williams or the young Kit Carson back in 1831, heading fearlessly into deadly Blackfoot country in search of rich beaver plews!

A little before sundown Mother was in the kitchen, glumly preparing three stringy laying hens for tomorrow's dinner. I was curled up on the couch, engrossed as usual in a library book about some real-life frontier hero's derring-do. I glanced out the window and saw Henry walking toward the house from the corral, leading the bay. At first I thought his horse had gone lame, but as he drew near I saw the bay was carrying a load, which explained why Henry was on foot. When I ran out to greet him, he tossed back the tarp covering the load. Across the saddle, its throat cut and the carcass duly bled, lay a two-point buck deer, steam from the still-warm animal rising in the below-zero cold.

"How in holy hell did you manage to bring him down without a rifle?" Father asked incredulously as I stood in the horse barn watching them attach the carcass to a wagon's singletree hoisted by a rope from the roof beam so they could clean it.

"Easy," Henry said dryly. "They was at a salt lick, this buck and four doe. I was up on a ridge directly overhead. I just dropped straight down, landed on his back, and stayed aboard him when he reared." Patting the knife at his side, he added, "My old Green River here did the rest."

Father had never heard of such a Bunyanesque feat, at least not in modern times, but examination showed the deer *had* died of knife wounds in the heart and lungs.

New Year's Day Father and I came downstairs to find the cookstove cold and the cows lowing from the barn. On the table lay a note, scrawled in pencil on yellow lined paper. Father picked it up and read its message aloud:

> Sorry to leave without sayin' good-bye, but I always get a hankerin' to move on, come start of a new year. I sold all the pelts I took on your place and it give me a little grubstake. But I figured you can use some small percent of what I got paid for the lot. After all, they *was* your beaver!"

Nearby in an oilskin pouch was a packet of five-dollar bills. Father counted them out slowly—a hundred and twenty-five dollars.

"But what will you do now without Henry to help you with the milking and other chores?" I asked Father worriedly.

He walked to the door and looked up the snowy lane down which Henry had come striding three months earlier. "I don't know," he mused, "but I'll tell you this—we sure had one helluva hired man for Christmas!"

25

By now I could read the regional signs of nature as well as any old-timer on the river. I knew the worst storms usually came out of the north and west, for no real reason anyone could explain. At school I wrote a column headed "Warnings for Ranchers" in a local weekly called *The J. Flag Journal,* of which I was the editor. Such vague but alarming admonitions as "keep your best saddle stock and milk cows in the shelter of your barn this coming week or you'll be sorry" were cribbed from the *Farmer's Almanac* and the same brave guesswork of many more widely circulated forecasters than I. But such prescience made us river dwellers feel that our fragile selves and livestock were not entirely helpless victims of random nature's whims: we were at least in partial charge of our own destiny. Similarly I liked to think I could read the signals portending killer storms between Jack and Marian.

Early in 1932 the temporary truce that was in force when we moved to the ranch fell apart. While they had never really stopped skirmishing, what came now was deadly serious. The all-pervasive pressure of the depression and their crushing personal financial worries were taking a toll. The economy was a shambles, the outlook for recovery bleak. We were mired in debt, the ranch buried under two mortgages, and tempers were short. Once again Mother accused Father of "going through all the baby's money," but now his failure at ranching gave her fresh fuel to throw on the fire. Frantic with worry and never knowing what our actual bank balance was, Mother vowed repeatedly, "I'll open a hamburger stand in Reno so I can pay for my own divorce!"

Late one night Louise and I gave up trying to make peace and went upstairs to bed. The fight raged on past midnight, when Father took out his pistol and tried to kill himself. Mother got the gun and the shot went wild, but the bullet ripped through the floor of our bedroom, burying itself in the dovetailed log corner, three feet above my head. Every morning Louise and I rode off to school sick with worry that when we came home we would find one of them gone, or both of them dead.

I had now developed a schoolgirl crush on Jack Gilroy, the sixteen-year-old lad from Jelm. Fed by a fervid imagination, it had grown out of all proportion to my twelve and a half years. Now I feared I would not only lose the ranch but also be torn from Jack's side and the romantic future life together here in the mountains I had spun for the two of us.

From Father I had picked up on the frightening if unspoken impression that if a boy even touched a girl she was "ruined" for life, but I couldn't fathom exactly how or why. One day when he saw us playing Eliza and the Hounds together during recess, Father warned me darkly, "Remember, boys only want one thing." Well, whatever other boys did, Jack was different. He was kind and sang his favorite hillbilly songs for me—the mournful "I Wish I Had Died in My Cradle, Before I Grew Up to Love You!" and "Red River Valley." But most poignant of all was the day we sat alone together on the creek bank and he wrote "I Love You" in the sand while he sang:

> On a day like today
> We passed the time away,
> Writing love letters in the sand.
>
> Now my poor heart aches
> With every wave that breaks
> Over love letters in the sand.

In the fall of 1931 our family took a memorable trip to Denver. There Father pawned my Add-a-Pearl necklace, a costly gift from the New York jew-

eler who had photographed me with the million dollars' worth of jewels.
Mother had been hoping to pawn these pearls later to cover the cost of having my badly bucked front teeth straightened. My upper plate may have saved
the day back in 1925, but wearing it onstage for almost two years had worked
havoc with my bite. To keep us eating, Father also pawned Mother's emerald ring, her star sapphire, and the solid diamond-encrusted wedding band.

While in Denver we shared a strained reunion with a greatly preoccupied
Judge Ben Lindsey, whose controversial political career was in serious dis-
array. Gangly and gawky, I felt uncomfortable balancing myself on his knee
like a child, for a publicity photo someone wanted to take. Lindsey seemed
equally miserable having me do so.

In a surprising coincidence, we discovered Larry Rich and Cheri were
headlining at the Tabor, one of the few wired-for-sound theaters still showing big-time vaudeville. When we went backstage to see them, Larry insisted
on dragging me onstage to take an unexpected bow. All freckles and front
teeth, elbows, knees, and feet, I felt as awkward as a Percheron in a corps de
ballet. But however different I may have looked from the Baby Peggy of
yore, the audience retained its former warm affection and gave her a standing ovation.

"What did I tell you?" Larry crowed as we came offstage. "She can still
bring down the house!"

"Maybe you could write a new act for her?" Mother asked.

"Just say the word!" Larry replied with his usual enthusiasm. "Like I told
you, vaudeville's not dead. With fewer acts competing for bookings, a big
headliner has a better chance now than ever."

I shuddered at this news. A possible return to vaudeville was the most
hideous solution to our money problems I could think of, but the following
day it was topped by another suggestion which was equally dismaying.

John Hay was the banker Father had come to Denver to see, hoping he
would act as guarantor for what was now our double mortgage with the Bank
of Laramie. Unlike the wicked landlords in road-show melodramas, Mr. Hay
was an understanding, indeed, even a compassionate villain.

"Much as I would like to, I don't see any way I can help you any further,
Mr. Montgomery," he said soberly as he sat facing us across his desk. "A dude
ranch in these times is not only a desperate gamble, it's—well, in my opinion, a truly suicidal investment for a banker." He shook his head sadly and
then opened a desk drawer and withdrew a sealed envelope. "But having said
all that, I do want to help you in some small way."

He pushed the envelope across to Father before continuing. "Inside is three hundred dollars, but it's my wish that it will help you take your famous little girl back to Hollywood. She was a big star once. No reason she couldn't be again, is there? After she succeeds in pictures, you can always buy another ranch—when times are better."

I was crushed. There would never be another ranch for me! After we returned to the ranch, I doggedly refused to accept the awful truth. At this low point I received a letter from George Bye, the New York journalist I had met at my fifth birthday party, the man who wrote Baby Peggy's biography. Now he was asking that I write a brief autobiography which he would try to place for me in the *New Yorker*.

My hopes soared. Visions of earning enough money (and best of all as a writer!) to pay the mortgage and save the ranch danced before my eyes. I took Father's portable typewriter out to the orchard, set it on a small orange crate, and determinedly taught myself to type. In a week's time I had turned out a brief, forthright, and unpretentious summing-up of my twelve years of life.

When Father read it, he declared, "Peg, this isn't the kind of thing Mr. Bye wants."

He rewrote it completely, holding forth for twenty pages on his pat vaudeville speech, praising the virtues of obedience. His stilted piece was titled "The Life of Baby Peggy Montgomery, As Told to Her Daddy." I felt betrayed. For the first time in my life I was secretly furious at him. He had stolen from me the opportunity to write and sell something entirely on my own. A very tactful Mr. Bye wrote back that "Peggy's finished piece lacks a certain spontaneity. Perhaps it would be better to wait until she is a little older." Instinct told me that however juvenile it may have been, my version was closer to what he had in mind. But, alas, that door was closed to me forever.

Mrs. McClaran decided to hold a pie social one evening at school. Jack Gilroy's Norwegian uncle brought along a jug of moonshine and his ancient feud with Erickson. The women, including Mother, brought favorite homemade pies. Father attended with great reluctance, while my adored Jack appeared, scrubbed and handsome but miserably uncomfortable not wearing his familiar logger's garb. The pants and sleeves of his hand-me-down black suit were several inches too short.

After Louise recited Hamlet's "To be, or not to be?" (an ironic choice) and Jack had agonized through "Alas, poor Yorick" without the required prop skull, I rose to deliver Antony's Address, which I was proud to have memorized in its entirety. Since I loved the cadence and ring of the language,

I gave the immortal "Friends, Romans, countrymen" plenty of fire and feeling. I was also anxious, as always, that my performance please my parents.

On the drive home Father said he thought my speech was a terrible waste of time. "If it has to be delivered by a man, how are you ever going to use it in either vaudeville or pictures?" Crushed and angry, I made no response. I wondered if he even knew who Shakespeare was.

Eugene Smith, sheriff of Albany County, paid us an ominous visit in early March. I watched from a distance but within earshot as he talked with Father by the corral gate.

"The only thing I can do to soften the blow for you folks," the sheriff said, "is to post the required public foreclosure notice near your own corral, instead of on your J. Flag sign up on the Lincoln Highway. No one's likely to see it here." With that he tacked the grim poster to the log wall of our chicken house.

I was stunned. We were actually going to go the same way after only three years of struggle that poor Jake and Lena Lund went after a full forty-five! It was bad enough we had to leave. But virtually everything we owned and cherished had to go first—furniture, rugs, books, all the livestock, saddles, harnesses, and tools. I felt like Marie Antoinette in the tumbrel on her way to the guillotine, her eyes taking in every familiar sight for the very last time. But our agony of humiliation, separation, and loss was destined to drag on for two whole months.

One day Louise and I came in from a ride to find Father and a stranger waiting in the corral. As soon as we dismounted, the stranger bought both our favorite mounts out from under us. (Before each one went, I clipped a lock of hair from its mane, which I kept in a secret jewel box for the next ten years.) One by one our pet sled dogs were sold or given away. The four trunks of Baby Peggy memorabilia were shipped back to the same Lyon Van and Storage in Hollywood where they had languished throughout our vaudeville years.

In the midst of all this, Louise and I were taking final examinations, she to finish the ninth grade, I the eighth. I was handed a report card and diploma, proving that by some miracle I had actually gotten through all eight grades in only three school years. In spite of the emotional turmoil of family dissension and losing the ranch, we had both maintained an A average in every subject except mathematics. Mrs. McClaran was indeed a wise and wizardly teacher.

The day before we were to leave, we helped Jack Gilroy lower the school flag from its pole and fold it away. Although I felt my heart was already broken, it broke again when I shook hands with him for the very last time and through my tears forced myself to say good-bye with a smile.

On the morning of May 15, 1932, we loaded what few belongings we could fit into the Model A Ford and a small trailer. In utter silence we headed up our private road to the Lincoln Highway, our golden German shepherd riding on top of the trailer behind.

Behind my parents and Louise lay a shattered dream; behind me, the only place on the face of the earth where I thought I had put down permanent roots. Ahead—for ill or well—lay Hollywood, where the motion-picture industry was caught between the rock of depression and the hard place it had created for itself with its revolutionary conversion to sound.

PART 5
1932 – 1933

BACK TO
COMEBACK
COUNTRY

26

From a small town of 36,000 in 1925, the Hollywood to which we returned after a six-and-a-half-year absence had become a haphazard sprawl of 235,000 inhabitants. The only unchanged factor in its growth was that the percentage of residents hailing from somewhere else remained the same.

Our first impression was that land sharks were running amok: For Sale signs dominated every other front lawn, vacant lot, and unoccupied foot of ground. It also seemed that every other corner lot had been converted into a miniature golf course. Mary Pickford was said to own the most courses, with the Jackie Coogan Corporation her nearest rival. These centers of family diversion ran the full gamut of styles, from diminutive Japanese pagodas and fairy-tale castles, to midget Dutch villages, complete with windmills and fake tulips. Open all day and garishly lit at night, they were always crowded and some had patrons waiting in line. No wonder: adults played for a quarter, kids for only a dime.

Hollywood Boulevard, while not yet in decline, had clearly slipped several rungs down the ladder of fashion. Robertson's upscale department store near Cahuenga had decamped, high-toned Mitchell-Innes Shoes had moved out to the more desirable Wilshire district, and the Montmartre Café was out of business. While several first-run movie houses and the Treasure Chest (rare Chinese imports) remained, the intrusion of trendy frock shops and chain shoe stores made the street déclassé. Studio "stock girls,"* female dress extras, and aspiring starlets (mostly ex-chorines or former shopgirls themselves) shopped these stores for bargains, snapping up a dozen flashy gowns and ten pairs of "baby doll" pumps at a time.

Despite the depression the turreted hulk of the old Hollywood Hotel was still fully occupied by permanent residents, mostly devout movie fans to whom it offered an incomparable view of paradise. On the dark hillside behind it, the tipsy Hollywood sign flashed its everlasting promise.

Despite the boulevard's undeniable slide, a few new quality establishments had moved in. The Brown Derby's Hollywood and Vine branch was thriving, having become the in place to be seen for both silent and sound movie stars hoping to survive. Max Factor had built a swan-white art deco salon that catered to women dead set on having something other than the face God gave them.

On Sunset Boulevard the lawn in front of white-pillared Warner Brothers Studio was now defaced by two Eiffel Tower–like spires, each topped with its radio station letters, KFWB. The fan palms of my earliest memories still lined Sunset, but how tall they had grown! At Gower and Sunset, we were surprised to find an empty block where Century had stood. We were told a fire broke out one night in 1926 and burned the studio to the ground, including the few Baby Peggy comedies not already intentionally melted down for their silver nitrate. Julius Stern had been in New York at the time, so Abe had wired him to send instructions. With typical acerbity Julius wired back: "Fire the night watchman!"

Hollywood's economic situation was chaotic, everything in the process of change. Many seemingly indestructible studio heads had been toppled. The soaring careers of such visually strong but vocally weak stars as Mary Pickford, Douglas Fairbanks, Clara Bow, and Charlie Chaplin were either

---

*Put under contract by a studio, with yearly options, these so-called stock girls were paid an average sixty dollars a week and formed an economical stock company for walk-ons and bits. They were also on call to serve as "hostesses" or party favors for visiting exhibitors for whom the studios often served banquets. There were also "stock boys" who were required to do movie work only.

guttering or had already been snuffed out by the unforgiving technicalities of sound.

Many once-prominent studios had gone under or been taken over by others. First National belonged to Warner Brothers, and DeMille had sold his Culver City lot to RKO-Pathé, putting his productions under Paramount's umbrella. Carl Laemmle Jr. had sold Universal's theater chain to finance an ambitious program of costly quality films. Uncle Carl still ran the lot, but the "Bottomless Pit" was awash in red ink.

Fred Fishbach had died of cancer at the youthful age of thirty-six. Universal's cowboy star Art Accord had been killed in a knife fight in a Mexican saloon. Father's good friend Western star Neal Hart had gambled and lost his entire movie fortune in a posh dude ranch in Alberta, Canada. Neal was now back working as a "riding extra."

But while the fortunes of many had plummeted during this sea change, other once-lowly talents were now ascendant. Lewis Milestone, once my twenty-five-dollar-a-week gagman at Century, was the Academy Award–winning director of Universal's 1931 classic *All Quiet on the Western Front*. Another who had prospered almost beyond reckoning was Edgar Rice Burroughs. Readers, radio listeners, comic-strip addicts, and talking-picture fans alike could not get enough of Tarzan. Ed now worked at the business of making his money make money. Emma and the boys divided their leisure time between Tarzana, their imposing Bel Air estate, and a beach house at Malibu.

Hollywood had also seen a wholesale invasion of veteran vaudevillians. Jack and Flo Haley were recent arrivals, with a new arrival of their own in year-old Jack Haley Jr. Other instant Californians included the Duncan Sisters, Mitzi Green, Al Jolson, Elsie Janis, Ginger and Lela Rogers, Ruby Keeler, Frank Fay, Harry Richmond, and Barbara Stanwyck. Bryan Foy became a unit producer at Warner Brothers and the other six Foys had followed their eldest brother west. LeRoy Prinz, the dance instructor who had taught Louise and me routines in Chicago, was now working as DeMille's choreographer for exotic dance sequences. The Mosconi Brothers, with whom we had toured, headed their own dance studio on Franklin Avenue. Most surprising of all, Larry Rich and Cheri had also resettled here. Cheri worked as a saleslady in an elegant department store, but Larry still had the act with his brother and was booking his tours from here. Even Harry Weber, who was Larry's agent, now worked out of a new West Coast office in Loew's State theater building in downtown Los Angeles.

Hollywood resembled an immense emergency shelter, and in a very real sense it was; vaudeville's precipitous decline had wreaked havoc among

those who tried to hang on. With a sob in his voice Larry told us the powerful NVA had gone bankrupt, canceled all insurance policies and aid to
members, and closed its legendary TB sanitarium at Lake Saranac.

The one hopeful sign on the near horizon that summer was that the 1932
Olympic Games would be held in Los Angeles. The Hollywood Chamber
of Commerce was praying that large infusions of tourist money might help
revive the local economy.

During my first few days back in Hollywood I was in a near-catatonic
state. I was incapable of accepting as fact the catastrophe that had befallen
us. We were now crowded into a small furnished apartment. After luxuri-
ating in more than a thousand acres of open space, I became claustrophobic
and withdrawn, repeatedly losing all conscious awareness of my new sur-
roundings and blacking out just as I had done onstage. Confining walls vanished like struck sets when daydreams overcame reality. At such times no
one could have convinced me I was not actually riding my favorite Indian
trails on cloud-shadowed Jelm.

We had been in town only three days when Father took me with him to
visit Douglas Fairbanks at United Artists' studio. Fairbanks was still enor-
mously wealthy, and Father's hidden purpose behind our visit was to try and
persuade his old friend to invest in "the ranch," a term which at this stage
referred vaguely to some ranch, somewhere, someday.

Fairbanks, who maintained his own dressing room, gymnasium, and indoor pool at the studio, welcomed us graciously. (He and Mary Pickford
were secretly separated, and he was actually living here.) Just as graciously
he parried Father's financial feelers, explaining that all his resources were
invested in producing documentary films on Africa and Asia.

Whether by choice or chance, he deftly turned the topic of discussion to
Baby Peggy's future. "Well, now, if Peggy's going to make a comeback in
talkies," he said with typical Fairbanks enthusiasm, "she needs an opening
blast of publicity." He turned to his friend and publicist, Eddie Sutherland.
"Eddie, will you round up the studio photographer and have him take some
shots of us together?"

I was wearing a cheap blue silk dress from J.C. Penney's in Laramie, pat-
terned mesh hose, and a pair of badly worn tap shoes with wilted black
bows. I preferred drowning myself in Fairbanks's pool to facing a camera
dressed as I was, but Father was beaming. When the photographer had finished, Fairbanks turned to me, his smile a dazzling white in his mahogany-
tanned face. "Tomorrow these pictures will be in all the papers, and every

studio in town will know you're available!" I realized he was being kind, but his generosity only served to tighten the vise closing in on me.

As Fairbanks had promised, the pictures made a celebrity splash in every local newspaper. The photo caption invoked a question that had become a popular but ironic joke about the ephemeral nature of both time and fame recently making the rounds in Hollywood, "What ever happened to Baby Peggy?"

"So, only yesterday you were asking 'What ever happened to Baby Peggy?' Well, ask that famous question no longer! She's back from vacationing on her Wyoming ranch and ready to return to films as a grown-up actress."

It was hard for me to face the bitter truth that Baby Peggy was still alive and well. Her name still had the power to generate headlines, while I had no power at all. The old hostility against her now became a fight for survival, for this time she was taking over my own adult identity and making it her own. Still, I could not ignore the fact that my family had never needed her help more desperately than now. In these stormy times, even the wreckage of my childhood fame was something for all of us to cling to, until other rescue came.

Reporters called to ask for interviews. A publicity woman and an agent both asked to handle me. Most important of all, a producer called to say he had a part in an upcoming series for which he wished to interview me. Father was radiant, Mother overjoyed. I felt no emotion at all, thinking only that a job would put food on the table again. I moved toward a second movie career as inexorably as some mad scientist's electrically run robot.

My direst necessity was clothes. I could not be interviewed dressed as shabbily as a hired girl, but we had no money. Pocketing her pride, Mother called Katherine Goodrich, a longtime Hollywood friend and heiress to the Goodrich tire fortune, who had also vacationed at the ranch the summer before. Would Katherine play godmother to my Cinderella? She agreed, took me to the new Bullocks Wilshire, and bought me a complete debutante's wardrobe worth several hundred dollars, which she charged to her own account. I now had a white polo coat, fashionable brimmed hat, turtleneck sweaters, tailored slacks, several smart dresses, sheer silk hose, and high-heeled pumps. Baby Peggy's former barber styled my shoulder-length hair. With my physical image remade, I invented a persona to match—a chic, independently wealthy, going-on-eighteen miss, based on an entirely fabricated self.

The producer who interviewed me said his proposed series would star James and Lucille Gleason, a veteran film and vaudeville family who had recently written and starred in the highly successful play *The Shannons of Broadway*. They were capitalizing on the Olympic sports craze by making a dozen comedy shorts featuring themselves as typical American parents. I was being considered to play the girl next door who is in love with their son, Russell. What transported Mother was the news that a feature film with all the same characters would follow, and after that a Broadway play! This was the sort of deal Lela Rogers had told Mother to keep an eye out for, because it would carry me through the turbulent white waters of adolescence and into the safe lagoon of adult stardom.

This interview was held in the front office of the same studio where I had made both *Captain January* and *Helen's Babies* for Sol Lesser. I took it as a favorable sign, for although we did not meet the Gleasons at this time, Father and I returned from the interview with a contract. Well, not a signed contract, but Father and independent producer Normal Speer had shaken hands on it, and Father considered that just as binding. I was set for twelve pictures, at $150 a week, the shorts to be filmed consecutively until all were completed. The feature film and play would require a separate contract.

It was a promising, almost miraculous comeback opportunity, the second in my still young life. I was in unexplored territory now. No one had penetrated this post-child-star wilderness before me without money, map, mentor, or guide. Blocking out bittersweet ranch memories, I braced myself to meet the challenge of such frightening innovations as quilt-shrouded cameras, hidden mikes, soundproof stages, "mixers," dollies, and booms. It was no secret to me that sound was a ruthless, man-eating dragon which had already slain a host of adult and far more experienced actors than I. But I was game to do anything that could pull the four of us up from ruin. Besides, what choice did I have?

27

For two weeks before we began shooting, Russell Gleason picked me up each morning and took me to the studio, *not* to rehearse our lines, but to teach me how to play softball and tennis. When they said my "girl next door" was sports crazy, they didn't mean she rode horseback, something at which I excelled, they meant any game where I had to keep my eye on a ball. For me, that posed a grave problem.

First, I had never played any sort of ball game in my life; second, I had trouble even seeing a ball coming my way. I had not been given an eye examination since I was five, and only then because it was required by the California Child Labor Law. Although I was unaware of why, I knew I had an increasingly hard time seeing anything at a distance of more than three or four yards. I noticed it first at country school, because when playing outdoor games, I had trouble making out my classmates at a distance. Whenever this inexplicably poor vision had interfered with my ability to meet some challenge at the ranch, Father would shake his head and look down at the ground.

"It's really sad," I overheard him tell Mother one day after I'd failed to rope a calf, "but I'm afraid Peg's got serious mental problems. She doesn't seem to see what's right in front of her. And have you noticed how she falls over her own feet all the time?" He sighed. "Remember those psychologists who said some gifted children like her proved to be 'burned-out geniuses' by the time they're twelve? By the looks of her, I think that may be what's happened."

His remarks shocked me. At first I was terrified: was I *really* going crazy? I asked myself. But the sure answer came back "No!" Deep down I knew I was sane. Granted, I often felt as if I had three left feet, but that was because I was growing so fast, not because my mind was gone. I was coping with life pretty well. I had passed easily, if ignorantly, into womanhood, because Louise took care of that. Mother's sole advice was "Remember, *never* ride a horse, wash your hair, or go swimming at that time, or you'll get tuberculosis and die!" Noting that our female guests did all of these forbidden things, I figured out her warning was absurd. I got around it by never letting her know the days when my resistance to TB was at its lowest.

Neither parent ever asked us what we were learning at school, only that we be sure to get "All A's!" As a result we were unable to show off any specific knowledge we had acquired. Mrs. McClaran, whose judgment I trusted, had assured me I was an exceptionally bright student who had been badly shortchanged on education. Luckily for my mental well-being, I chose to believe her instead of an eighth-grade dropout, even if he was my own father.

I was gradually losing my worshipful awe of Jack Montgomery. Although I admired his horsemanship and ranching skills, I no longer believed he had created the universe. But I remained obedient, unable to break the psychic bond imposed upon me as an infant. Defying his will was not yet possible for me, nor would it be for some years to come.

However, now that I was once again a hot movie property, Father's concern over my retarded mental state went into instant remission. He was back in the heady business of setting up my new career. Only three weeks back in Hollywood and all the celebrity drums were beating. A leading photographer had taken a series of excellent portrait stills. My PR person had planted a comeback picture and story about me in seventeen of the twenty-three monthly movie magazines. I was the guest of honor at a Louella Parsons afternoon cocktail party in Beverly Hills, and columnists talked up the new Gleason series and my role in it. Russell had finally taught me how to hit an oncoming ball with both racquet and bat, and shooting was to begin the following Monday.

Friday evening we looked out the front window of our second-floor apartment to see Father driving up in a glossy black Packard phaeton convertible with gleaming silver trim. The top was down, revealing opulent scarlet leather upholstery. "Oh, my God," Mother groaned, "what has your father done now?"

He explained he had bought this chariot secondhand, for the incredibly low price of five hundred dollars. "Things are not the same out here as they used to be," he opined. "Now stars drive their own cars down Sunset, and slowly enough to be recognized by their fans. I saw Gary Cooper the other day in his chartreuse Dusenberg, cruising along under thirty, with the top down. It's time for Peg to be seen the same way."

"But her salary for the first picture may not even come to five hundred dollars!"

"Don't worry, Sharkey, I have other irons in the fire," he assured her. "I'm having Chris specially schooled by an animal expert with hand signals so he can star in Western talkies. The trainer says he's never seen such a magnificent red-gold German shepherd. He'll be the next Rin-Tin-Tin! Just imagine him sitting all by himself in the backseat, shining like a new penny in the sun, framed against this knockout red leather upholstery!" So, I marveled, our dog was his ace in the hole in case Baby Peggy didn't fly. In a sense I found that curious fact almost consoling.

Because he was daunted by the prospect of making me up in the new Hollywood of specialists, Father drove me to Max Factor's Makeup Salon early on the morning *Off His Base* was to begin shooting. I arrived wearing my "girl next door" outfit of crisp white tennis shorts, shirt, and shoes. Once inside I was whisked into a booth where three experts studied what they called my "camera problems" and closed in to cure them. The bridge of my nose was narrowed by shading each side and highlighting the center. My cheeks were Garbo-ized (sunken), brows were lifted, eyes enlarged, lids tinted, a forest of lashes added, and a generous Joan Crawford mouth painted on. I had entered the salon a gangly thirteen-year-old girl. I emerged a thirteen-year-old girl fitted with the head of Medusa. Father drove me to location and stood around but made no move to direct me. Given the situation on this set, that was wise.

Jimmy Gleason was easygoing, a typical comedy-patter vaudevillian with flawless timing. Russell was meek. But Lucille Gleason was a moving crate of temperamental dynamite. Possessed of a boxlike build and a square jaw, she had long ago cowed both husband and son; now she brought the entire cast and crew to heel.

I had memorized every line in the script; no one could fault me there. But Lucille rewrote it to her own satisfaction, insisted on directing, and gave no one time to learn lines. Veteran comedian Eugene Palette heaved a martyr's sigh, gazed heavenward, and waited for her to run out of adrenaline. Every one of the ten days of shooting began with wrangling and ended in anarchy. Seeing *Off His Base* previewed at the studio later, I was appalled at the confused nature of the film itself. Even more horrifying was how I looked and sounded. I had improved upon Max Factor's extreme version of me by doing my own makeup, but I had to admit I would need help to master the depth and range of voice required for talkies.

Because no one registered well on early sound equipment, virtually every actor in town was taking voice lessons—from a studio coach if under contract, or if not from an independent teacher. I studied with freelancer Edgecomb Pinchot, a fascinating British gentleman (and author of *Viva Zapata!*) who had lived many years in Mexico. His diction was flawless, his vocabulary enviable, and his knowledge of English language and literature awesome. He read aloud to me, mostly Shakespeare, Coleridge, and Poe, choosing selections rich with vowels and lilting alliterations. He required that I memorize them and recite them to him for correction and improvement of accent, tone, and feeling. Most wondrous of all, he explained who the authors were, and why they chose certain words to make the language resound and ring.

Downstairs, with his vivacious French wife, Madame Du Four, I studied bodily carriage and poise, every movement to the measured music of Bach. Madame taught her pupils how to comport themselves like ladies. "You float down into a chair, and arise from it in a single graceful upward flight." I learned how to walk without bouncing and how to "g-l-i-d-e down a staircase with the motionless grace of a cloud descending." These lessons, ten dollars for two hours, seemed expensive at the time, but they opened up my mind and gave me vocal techniques and bodily controls which proved invaluable. When I returned from these exhilarating sessions—feeling graceful as a swan and my head filled with the music of the English tongue—Father was quick to express his disapproval.

"Who the hell do you think you are, Lady Astor? Cut out all the big words and that stuck-up British-accent crap and just be yourself." It was becoming increasingly difficult to deal with Father's contempt for the special skills

I needed to master for my career, simply because they exposed his own educational and cultural shortcomings.

Two weeks passed with no word from either producer Norman Sperr or the Gleasons as to when the second short would go before the cameras. At last Father drove over to the studio to check. He found they were already shooting, but with another girl playing my part! She was being paid only $75 a week, against my $150. When Father confronted Sperr, he was told the company couldn't afford my higher salary. When Father reminded him I was under contract for the series, Sperr refreshed his memory. "Nothing was *signed* between us."

I felt the roller coaster begin to head down the first sickening big dip when Father came home the following day and announced he had engaged a lawyer and was filing suit for five hundred thousand dollars against the Sperr/Gleason firm for breach of contract and defamation of my character and career. I knew his reputation for being disputatious was only too well known here in Hollywood. But if there was one thing studio heads disliked even more than a contentious parent, it was a litigious one, dragging lawyers into what movie moguls discreetly referred to as "family quarrels." However, I had no say in this fight, no matter how vital it was to me.

Despite the pending lawsuit, the momentum of the initial publicity kept me riding the crest of celebrity. I appeared (gratis) in a *Hollywood on Parade* publicity short, featuring the first generation of Our Gang stars, all of whom were now in their teens and had been replaced by a new, younger Gang.

It was a schoolroom set, with boys and girls paired off to kiss as they left their seats and marched up the aisle toward the camera. I was teamed with serial star Frankie Darro. It was my first kiss, offscreen or on, and I nearly died of embarrassment, as did he. I developed a secret crush on the handsome, dark-eyed sixteen-year-old actor, who I discovered had been the plucky meal ticket for his parents ever since he was a toddler. This was my first real encounter with other performing children who had been lifelong family breadwinners like myself, and they made an indelible impression on me. Naturally, I felt a strong bond with them.

As the summer wore on, and I was pushed increasingly into the limelight, I was required to pull off the biggest public hoax in Hollywood history, namely to pretend I was the heiress to my own long-gone childhood earnings. I was pursuing a film career only to prove myself a fine actress and not—God forbid!—for any financial need or gain. I had to summon what little nerve I possessed to fake my way through the maze of half-truths and outright lies this charade required. And worse still, to do it on an empty stomach!

I appeared at the Culver City Auto Races, awarding a silver cup to the winner. I was called upon to judge a dance marathon at Ocean Park. Marathon judging was nearly as grueling as marathon dancing, but after staying awake a brutal number of hours, I was duly photographed presenting a tacky prize to the poor, dead-on-their-feet couple who won. These nonevents sustained my celebrity status, but by August we were stone broke, unable to buy food, let alone pay the rent. Nevertheless, I was still braving the role of Lady Bountiful at Motion Picture Relief benefit teas (helping raise funds for the poor!).

Ironically, the lady who organized these teas was secretly providing my family with Motion Picture Relief food coupons which were good at certain markets in exchange for groceries. At the same time a basket of food was also being delivered to our door once a week by the Makeup Men's Association. Grateful as I was to all of them for keeping us alive, the pain of hurt pride was almost greater than the worst hunger pangs.

By autumn we were served with our first three-day notice. A landlord's legal document, it meant the next move was the sheriff armed with an eviction notice that would land us in the street. In those days Hollywood abounded with furnished apartments, so no renter needed bother with furniture. For $37.50 a month you could move into a single-bedroom apartment with a pull-down bed in the front room and find everything supplied, right down to pictures on the wall, sheets, towels, silverware, dishes, and cooking ware. The only formality required was checking this complete inventory with the landlord before moving in, and once again before moving out.

Confronted with our first three-day notice, I recalled the hilarious experience dance director LeRoy Prinz had once recounted: namely, how he had "shoe-boxed" his way out of a swank Parisian hotel to which he owed a huge sum he was too broke to pay. Now I suggested we emulate his escape. As soon as darkness fell, each of us singly and unobtrusively carried most of our belongings in a shoe box to the car. After midnight we broke out the suitcases and made our final getaway. Father had already talked another apartment-house manager, several blocks away, into renting to us with only *half* a month's rent down.

This daring procedure was repeated several times over the next few months. Furthermore, by that time Louise and I had perfected certain vitally important delaying tactics. In order for a three-day notice to be valid, the landlord had to serve it on the head of the household, in person. By keeping safety chains on doors, by saying, "I'm sorry, my father is out of town," and ultimately, by pretending not to understand or speak a word of English, we were able to buy considerable lead time before being reduced to a full-scale shoe-box flight in the night.

The worst part of our plight was that my agent absolutely forbade me to accept work as an extra. That, he said, would blast any future movie career as certainly as the stroke of midnight shattered Cinderella's spell. With all our hopes riding on my comeback, we dared not risk rubbing off what little luster was left on the golden egg. But at last, in desperation, the four of us accepted jobs as extras for $3.20 a day each, a rich haul of $12.80 a day for the lot, and a run of two weeks.

When that run ended, we had both rent money and food on the table for the first time in months. It was at this point that our case against the Gleasons went to court. The trial garnered more nationally syndicated publicity than a gold digger's breach-of-promise suit against a millionaire playboy. Photographers snapped pictures of me looking sad, outraged, disbelieving (but *never* poor). Despite my impassioned testimony on the stand and my performance as outraged heiress before reporters and photographers, the judge dismissed the case because, as a minor, I did not have the legal right to enter into such a contract.

It was a terrible blow to Father, who had convinced himself my five hundred thousand dollars was in the bag. So much for handshakes in Hollywood. We not only lost our lawsuit, but a few days later I opened our apartment door to a surly stranger and found myself face-to-face with a Los Angeles School Board truant officer. This man informed Father that it was already December and neither of his school-age children was lawfully enrolled in any public school. Furious at being entrapped, Father told the man to go to hell. The officer coolly told Father where his two daughters had better be by January 1 of 1933, or else: nearby Fairfax High School.

After the man left, Father exploded. "So we've paid the rent and stayed at one address for three whole months—and what did it get us? It gave the public school people time to run us to ground and force you to go to some goddamned filthy public school!"

PART 6

1933 – 1938

"WHAT EVER HAPPENED TO BABY PEGGY?"

28

In early 1933 some thirty-five hundred students, predominantly white, were enrolled in Fairfax High School. Built some twenty years earlier, it had a semi-Spanish façade, tile roofs, and a lofty Italianate rotunda. Inside the rotunda's dome and over various arches and doors, the sayings of great philosophers and statesmen on the subject of learning were spelled out in letters of gold. The entire edifice was a monument to the worth of education.

I was both impressed and intimidated. After a one-room schoolhouse with only five other students, this massive assembly-line learning edifice simply overwhelmed me.

For me ninth-grade algebra proved an unendurable form of torture. After valiantly going all the way back to first-grade arithmetic, my distracted teacher despaired and sent me over to a Miss Brown's "General Mathematics" class. Several days later, sitting mutely in this room with only a dozen other students, it finally dawned on me what kind of class I was in. Every student except myself was either spastic, severely crippled, a stutterer, deaf, mentally retarded, or blind.

When one of my epic poems won first prize and was printed in the school paper, Miss Brown kept me after class. "That's a splendid poem you wrote," she told me, somewhat bewildered. "It most certainly proved to me that you aren't mentally or physically handicapped like all my other poor students. Why in heaven's name are you in my class?"

"I can't learn algebra," I confessed helplessly.

"Then leave it until later," she advised. "But you must get out of this class. All you'll do here is tread water."

In Spanish class, which involved a lot of blackboard copying, I moved from the back row to the front, trying to get close enough to see the texts, but I was still unable to make out anything written there. Ashamed to tell my teacher, afraid to mention it at home, I cut that class every day until I got a failing grade. Finally, after six torturous weeks, an unexpected event solved my problem. A school nurse visited Fairfax to test everyone's eyesight and hearing. When we returned home, Louise broke the awful news to my parents which I was too distraught to even mention.

"An eye test at school today showed that Peg can hardly see across this room," she announced bravely. "She's terribly nearsighted and will have to be fitted for glasses."

"Glasses!" Jack and Marian exclaimed in unison. Then Mother sprang to her feet. "But Baby Peggy can't go around wearing horn-rimmed glasses!"

"I absolutely forbid it!" Father thundered, Joshua freezing the sun over Jericho. "You know damned well glasses would *ruin* your career," he added accusingly, as though I had invented this handicap to destroy it.

I stood mutely in the middle of the room, crushed under the double burden of having bad eyes and needing expensive glasses which I knew we could not afford. I seemed to be guilty on both counts but felt I had done nothing to bring these twin misfortunes down upon myself and my family.

"I warned you a million times at the ranch *never* to read by Coleman lantern," Mother said. "I told you it would ruin your eyes. But no, you had to go ahead and do it anyway. I hope you're satisfied." (So it was my fault after all.)

"I can go without glasses on the set, I'm sure," I risked at last, trying to restore a semblance of peace. I obtained the glasses, solely because the school authorities insisted, and marveled to find that the stars overhead were not big fuzzy blobs but sharp pinpoints of light. A tree was no longer a green furry mass but was composed of thousands of individual well-defined leaves. But I was prudent enough to keep my amazement to myself. My glasses became a taboo subject, unmentionable at home.

Like a fool, I chose sewing for Home Economics, although I had never even sewn on a button in my life. Each student ran a foot-pedaled sewing machine and was engaged in the salutary task of making dresses for the poor. All the others were doing precisely that, but my rogue needle chewed up and damaged every piece of yardage I fed it. The teacher demanded I drop her class before she ran out of cloth and money.

I kept aloof from my fellow students, being incapable of making small talk about the interests "normal" girls shared: boys, dates, clothes. They were baffled by or miffed at this uppity freshman, not suspecting that all her life she had conversed entirely with adults. I could only discuss heavy subjects such as history, poetry, Indians, and immortality. I was also hopelessly entangled in a web of guilty lies and denials, which I was constantly spinning to conceal my identity, my family's shameful destitution, and my failure which had brought us all to this sorry pass.

"No, I'm not *that* Peggy Montgomery," I parried several times a day with a smile. "I know it's the same name, but I was never in movies." (Once in a while this tack backfired when a student had seen my picture in the papers.)

These ceaseless repudiations and disavowals served to cancel out the identities of both my warring selves—the aspirant along with the has-been—leaving an all but invisible fourteen-year-old nonperson walking around inside the skin the other two shared.

We were living on the second floor of a modest apartment house near Fairfax, and Louise and I always did our homework on the dinner table in the small dinette. One evening in early March I finished an essay for my English class and got up to go into the living room. Suddenly the lights went out, the floor began to pitch, and the sharp rat-a-tat of machine-gun fire seemed to explode all around me, as every pull-down blind in the place snapped straight up to the top of its proper window sash. With the floor angling under us, I looked out the window to see the telephone and high tension lines turning slowly like giant jump ropes while the street below was a slowly rolling wave making for shore.

Father ordered us down the stairs into the street, where all the tenants were gathering in frightened knots on the small front lawn. A series of hard aftershocks followed the initial earthquake, and although night was falling, no one dared reenter the building. While we were not affluent enough to boast a radio of our own, the apartment manager had a small Zenith which she plugged in to an outside socket. Everyone listened spellbound as news of the county-wide devastation came flooding across the airwaves. However, despite the force of the quake, nothing in our apartment was broken. Fairfax High was not so lucky. Some of its stucco walls cracked like eggshells and several buildings were condemned. For the rest of the semester we attended classes in makeshift tents set up outdoors.

Throughout the following week the four of us worked on behalf of the Motion Picture Relief Association. (We owed them many favors.) We took up posts at key intersections, holding out tin cans and collecting donations from passing motorists for victims of the calamity.

About a week after the great earthquake of 1933, with aftershocks causing insomnia and making a chronically high-strung family more jittery still, there was a knock on our door. I opened to find a small dapper man carrying a black briefcase. "I'm looking for a Mr. Jack Travers Montgomery," he announced in a faintly British accent. "Is he in?"

If I hadn't known the rent was paid, I would have thought he was serving a three-day notice. As it was, I invited him in. All efficiency, he sat down, opened his briefcase, took out some papers, and got right down to business, informing us that Father was the heir next in line to inherit his great-grandfather's estate of Oldtrim in Tipperary, Ireland.

We all knew this legendary estate had belonged to the old captain of the Queen's Dragoons. After his death, Oldtrim had been taken from his son and heir by the old man's greedy second wife. As a consequence the young heir migrated to Canada. Later his son (my grandfather) moved on to the United States, where he married and started a family in Nebraska.

I was ecstatic at the idea of having the old captain's romantic Irish mansion as our very own. Now I could leave Hollywood and Baby Peggy behind forever. Perhaps we could even sell off some small portion of Oldtrim's valuable property—not much, of course—but just enough to buy back the ranch in Wyoming.

"There are no strings at all," the precise, mustachioed gentleman continued in the now completely hushed room. "Of course, I'm sure you know, times have been hard in England, just as over here, so I'm told there's been some small neglect of the buildings, namely the roof on the main house. But, except for such minor repairs, and of course paying the three hundred thousand U.S. dollars due the British government for unpaid back taxes, Oldtrim is yours!"

I could almost hear the tinkle of broken dreams.

*   *   *

Local newspapers told us Cecil B. DeMille was casting a cautionary tale about American youth, entitled *This Day and Age*. I was granted an interview in the great man's wood-paneled Spanish Gothic office. After briefly balking at my being under sixteen (requiring the presence of a paid teacher on the set), he mellowed, recalling that several other players my same age had already been hired. "And, since you *were* Baby Peggy," he observed, bestowing a wintry smile upon me over tapering tented fingers, "I'll ask my assistant to try and find a few lines or a bit for you to do." The charitable smile faded, the tent folded, and he dismissed me with a quick but regal wave of his hand. "That will be all!"

I worked for DeMille for two weeks, at $7.50 a day. The money was welcome, but I never did get the promised line. Worse still, for every day of school I missed I was given a demerit slip, necessitating my serving a penitential hour in a raucous detention hall. Here were gathered all of Fairfax's surprisingly large contingent of rebellious boys and impudent girls. I could see it would be impossible for me to ever graduate from this school as long as I had to work in pictures at the same time. All my good grades would be canceled out by steadily rising demerits.

However, on the DeMille set I met sixteen-year-old George Offerman, who told me he attended Lawlor's Professional School, operated specifically for movie kids. Students working in films went to school only from 8:00 A.M. to noon, and one could spend weeks on a picture and make up the lost schoolwork later. It was now summer vacation, but I was determined to find some way to get enrolled at Lawlor's Professional School in the coming fall.

George also tipped me off about an upcoming reading for a play called *Growing Pains*, being held at the prestigious Pasadena Playhouse. It offered several good parts for male and female juveniles. The only catch was that we would not receive a salary, or any compensation for the long commute and meals during weeks of rehearsal or the run of the play. Still, all movie children had been raised to believe that "being seen" was the key to success. There was always the chance that one's performance would be caught by a studio talent scout, and we all knew full well the Playhouse was a showcase for nascent stars. For the three of us who landed good roles in *Growing Pains*, that traditional act of faith was to pay off handsomely.

29

G*rowing Pains*, a play dealing with adolescents coming of age, was timely—perhaps even ahead of its time. Three years later MGM would film a similar story by the same author, Auriana Rouveral, and launch the remarkably successful "Hardy family" series, which shot Mickey Rooney to stardom.

The author's daughter, seventeen-year-old Jean Rouveral, played the ingenue lead, while a twenty-year-old New York stage star, Junior Durkin, held down what was the precursor of the Andy Hardy role. Fourteen-year-old Dawn O'Day and I had feature parts. Leon Holmes, a red-haired, freckled Jewish youth who had worked with me in *April Fool* back in 1925 on Poverty Row, also had a role, as did George Offerman, who had led me to this job.

The play and everyone in it got great reviews. The second week a Paramount talent scout plucked Jean Rouveral from our ranks to play the lead in the film *Eight Girls in a Boat*. Jean was replaced by eighteen-year-old Charlotte Henry, whom Paramount promptly snapped up as the perfect Alice for their upcoming film version of *Alice in Wonderland*. The same talent scout hired me to play a featured role as one of the *Eight Girls in a Boat*.

My salary was fifty-five dollars a week, and all expenses paid for Mother and myself on location at the posh Big Bear Lake Tavern. While this was hardly a memorable film, it was notable for the fact that their fear of the heroine's climactic dive into the deep lake forced both Jean and her successor to withdraw from the picture. Six weeks of worthless film and a small fortune in production costs were lost before it finally occurred to someone at Paramount to hire a stuntgirl for the controversial dive before the *third* leading lady resigned. But those of us in the cast earned eight weeks' location time instead of two, plus another month of shooting at the studio.

While I received a great deal of publicity during the making of the picture, most of it led nowhere. But early in 1934 my agent, George Ullman, managed to sign me up for a test at Universal. To prepare for this, Mother insisted I enlist Lela Rogers's professional advice. Having studied with Mr. Pinchot, I did not share Mother's blind faith in Lela, but she had carved out a reputation for herself in Hollywood as a drama coach and head of her own Hollytown Theater. I waited in Ginger's living room for my turn, along with two other nervous aspirants, Phyllis Fraser and Betty Furness.

Lela was closeted in her dining room with newcomer Dick Powell, advising him on how to force Warner Brothers to pay him more than the seventy-five-dollar-a-week starting contract he had signed as an unknown: he was now the hottest musical star in town. Before Ginger gained screen recognition as a wisecracking chorus girl in *42nd Street*, she had played small parts in fourteen program films. Naturally, Hollywood newcomers felt they should listen to Lela. I listened obediently to her tips on acting techniques, then quietly went my way.

At Universal I was given a choice of two tests—one in which a girl and her date deliver insipid dialogue over a gift box of candy, or my choice of any scene from Universal's own shooting scripts. Anxious to show Uncle Carl I was capable of passion, fire, and real tears, I chose the tense highlight of Margaret Sullavan's recent hit, *Only Yesterday*. In it the secretly pregnant heroine welcomes her lover home from war, only to be told he is marrying another. A young stock actor was assigned to play the soldier, and as we rehearsed alone together in a studio bungalow, he tried to help me find ways to display my full dramatic potential.

"I think you need to identify more with this woman's anguish," he ventured. "I mean, you understand all that's transpired between the two of them—don't you?"

"Well—ah—it's terrible he won't marry her," stammered his fifteen-year-old partner who, despite her clear diction, matronly mien, and Madame DuFour-ized carriage, knew nothing about sex. To my utter mortification, this twenty-five-year-old male stranger sat me down on the couch beside him and proceeded to lay out the facts of life. Objectively, but in detail, he described exactly *how* my character had gotten into her tragic predicament: who had done what to whom, and with what inevitable natural results. When he was finished, he took a deep breath and asked lightly, "Now shall we try the scene again with these—*deeper* insights?"

Psychologically paralyzed from the combined overload of appalling information and emotional chagrin, I was bereft of speech. Grabbing the script, I ran for the door.

Attracted by its utter simplicity of line, I had chosen from Universal's wardrobe an art deco evening gown, made entirely of layers of white silk fringe, shimmering from neck to floor. Unfortunately, it had the effect of making me look like a thirty-five-year-old walking lamp shade. But when the big day dawned, I was on the set made up and in costume by the required 6:30 A.M. My erstwhile sex instructor had the painful task of playing opposite a dozen girls who were also taking tests that day, so we barely made eye contact.

Following Lela's advice, I went off in a quiet corner of the set, as she said Ginger always did, rehearsed my lines "with feeling," shed the necessary tears, and then returned to my chair, where I waited to be called. The wait lasted until five-thirty that evening, for mine was the last test of the day. By then Lela's technique had backfired. After weeping off and on all day long, I didn't have a tear left, but I gave the dry version the best I had.

My agent called me a few days later to tell me how my test had been received at Universal. He said he was at the screening with Uncle Carl, who had personally viewed my test. As the two men emerged together from the projection room Uncle Carl looked stricken. Shaking his head, he told Ullman gravely, "George, it's not good, 'the baby' being an unwed mother—and good God, with her not yet fifteen."

If I was having identity problems with my former self, Father had become the dependent shadow of an increasingly shadowy Baby Peggy. During the eighteen months we had been in Hollywood, he had spent almost every day telephoning producers, directors, and stars at virtually every studio in town. When I was home, I winced each time I heard him dial a number and deliver the familiar preamble to what all too often turned out to be no conversation at all.

"Yes, I'd like to speak to Millie Milestone" (or whoever else it was he was trying to run to ground). "This is Jack Montgomery calling." A pause. "That's right. Jack Montgomery." Another pause. "Well, just tell him it's Baby Peggy's father calling."

If he managed to reach his quarry by phone, he tried to make a firm appointment. If things got that far, he took along a portfolio of his nonexistent ranch and laid out the great financial potentials of the property, hoping to pry a sizable investment out of them. Of course, everything conspired against his being successful in this.

The depression still lay heavily over Hollywood. A great many movie people were destitute and begging for help. Money was tight, low-cost drawing-room comedies with small casts were in—big-budget movies delayed or trimmed. Many directors, actors, and even big-name stars had been forced to take sizable salary cuts. Financial ruin from stock-market losses or career failure in talkies had decimated the ranks of former silent stars. Suicides by gunshot, walking into the Pacific, opening gas jets, or confinement in a carbon monoxide-filled garage had become so commonplace, the tragic deaths of once-famous stars were relegated to the back pages of local dailies. Silent stars, now braving talkies, lived in dread of being displaced by stentorian-toned Broadway actors, or by one of the growing colony of formidable British thespains now collecting major roles as handily as they had taken over the polo field at the bon ton Uplifter's Club.

Those few producers, stars, and agents who were riding high spent their money gambling at the Clover Club, playing the ponies at Agua Caliente, or building their own stable of thoroughbreds. Ed Burroughs, who had grown tired of aging and overweight Emma, was now squiring a svelte young blond about town. If Ed spent any of his fortune, it would be on a Hawaiian honeymoon cottage with sunny tennis courts to keep him tanned and young-looking for his new lady love, not on a "dream ranch" in some far western state.

Mother, Louise, and I were now getting extra work on a fairly steady basis, all of our earnings going into the family purse. But Father still scorned extra work for himself. He railed against Louise when she landed an eighteen-dollar-a-week job as a chorine in a third-rate Hollywood musical, *The Shim-Sham Revue*. One night, as she was about to leave for the theater, he forbade her to go. When she left anyway, he went into a temperamental seizure, screaming wild threats and begging someone to tell him "Who am I?" With that he threw himself on the bed in a catatonic fit, eyes rolled back and apparently unable to breathe. Mother became hysterical, and after casting about wildly, I remembered seeing a simple cure for such fits of madness in a movie. Dashing into the kitchen, I came back with a pitcher of cold water and poured it slowly over his head. Father returned to sanity with a vengeance, cursing me roundly for my impertinence but fully aware of who he was.

When the *Shim-Sham*'s lead singer, Winnie Shaw, got a movie break, I boldly auditioned for her part, which paid seventy-five dollars a week. In cocktail gown, picture hat, and black elbow-length gloves, I looked like a jaded forty-year-old soubrette. Entering the crowded, noisy rehearsal hall, my young accompanist in tow, I found Mort Gould in charge. "Okay, kid, give out!" he ordered, chomping on his already frayed cigar. My pianist opened with a keyboard flourish. "Cut the Stokowski!" Gould snarled. I closed my eyes and began my sultriest rendition of "I walk along the street of sorrow, the boulevard of broken dreams—"

"Okay," Gould interrupted, "so you can sing. Now let's see your gam!" He pointed his cigar at my hemline.

I'd played this game before with casting directors. Sometimes it led to a lively chase around the office and, if you were lucky, out the door. Other times it got you the job without a struggle. I lifted my skirts. "Higher!" he ordered. "Yeah!" he breathed, fixing me with a lecherous gaze. Then his mood changed sharply. "You eighteen?"

I nodded, visions of seventy-five dollars a week dancing before my eyes. "Of course I am!" I said in a throaty, Kay Francis voice. His eyes bored right through me. Quick as a cat he threw his cigar to the floor. "Like hell you are. You're San Quentin quail. I don't waste my time on jail bait. Beat it!"

In February of 1934, Louise and I enrolled at Lawlor's Professional School, which most of the cast of *Growing Pains* attended. Tuition was $25 a month each. We paid for the first two months by trading Mrs. Lawlor a six-volume set of Presidential Papers, priced $125, which some fast-talking pitchman had sold Father back in our Beverly Hills days. At Lawlor's my interest in performing children was reawakened, particularly by the presence of Frankie Darro, the young serial star who had brushed my lips with his in that schoolroom two short years before. In all seriousness I told him I was an author and I wanted to write his life story. He agreed, and during several sessions he poured out the tale of his harrowing childhood as the only child of circus aerialists, forced to learn his parents' trade, although terrified of heights.

His parents were divorced, and he lived with and supported his father. His mother lived in the apartment building directly across the street from Lawlor's. Every day when he left school for work or home, the curtains of her window parted and his mother's face appeared, her black eyes following the fleeting figure of the son she adored.

Lawlor's occupied the second floor of a five-story building on Hollywood Boulevard near Western Avenue. Appropriately enough, Central Casting was located in the building next door. Viola Lawlor was a plain, large-boned, dyed-in-the-wool Vermont Yankee schoolmarm. She had succumbed to a lifelong yen to come to Hollywood and mingle with the stars. Her dream came true, after a fashion, for many of her students were either former child stars or aspiring youngsters destined for fame. A prime example was seventeen-year-old Lawlor graduate Betty Grable, who was already singing with a popular band. Fourteen-year-old Gower Champion, my helpful classmate who got me through algebra, was a marvelously creative dancer who showed promise of becoming a star.

"Don't think you're going to lord it over anybody here just because you were Baby Peggy!" Mrs. Lawlor greeted me gruffly over her desk on my very first day. I didn't know why she thought I was haughty, but decided her wrath was preferable to Fairfax's detention hall. In time I learned "Mom" Lawlor was all bark and no bite. What she really wanted was to be entertained and be able to drop famous names.

The longer I was at Lawlor's the more I learned about terrible childhoods. Frankie Darro was not the exception but the rule. Eleven-year-old golden-voiced Edith Fellows had been dragged to Hollywood from Atlanta by her ambitious grandmother. A fake talent scout who saw tiny Edith perform in Atlanta got a sizable cash advance from Mrs. Fellows, gave her a card with his Hollywood office address, and promised her a contract if she came west. His office turned out to be a vacant lot. Barbara Perry's parents had come west seeking to cure her father's TB. He died. Her widowed mother, once a Metropolitan Opera chorister, opened a dance studio on Highland Avenue, so Barbara could study with world-renowned dancers teaching there and become famous herself. Barbara had studied under all the greats of classical, Japanese, and modern dance, but so far fame had eluded her.

Jean Darling of Our Gang was breathtakingly beautiful but considered washed up at thirteen. Dawn O'Day and I had become close friends during the run of *Growing Pains*. She had been her mother's sole support since infancy. Minutes after Mitzi Green's mother walked off the set of *Anne of Green Gables* demanding more money for Mitzi, RKO called Dawn. While I waited breathlessly outside the public telephone in Lawlor's lobby, RKO made her a star and changed her name to that of the film's heroine, Anne Shirley. Because she and her harridan mother lived in a mean apartment above a dime store, the studio quickly rented and moved them into a Cinderella cottage. Here movie magazines could interview Anne without reporting on the grim poverty in which she lived.

Jane Withers had been "Dixie's Dainty DewDrop" back on the Georgia airwaves. At nine she vied with Shirley Temple for top child-star honors at Fox. Mickey Rooney had supported his mother, Nell Carter, ever since she left his burlesque-clown father and came to Hollywood. I first met him when he was palling around with Junior Durkin at the Pasadena Playhouse. Durkin's close buddy Jackie Coogan also visited us backstage during the long run of *Growing Pains*. Mickey was crazy for showgirls taller, and often much older, than his own sixteen years. Right now his career was soaring, under the guiding hand of my old vaudeville agent, Harry Weber.

Mrs. Lawlor favored both Mickey and Frankie. If there was an uproar reported in the study hall, she marched off like a one-woman posse to collar the culprit. But once she found it was Mickey, standing on a long table, convulsing everyone with his impressions of Lionel Barrymore and Clark Gable, or Frankie doing nip-ups and back flips, she folded her arms, smiled contentedly, and took in the show.

One day she came into study hall to tell us that Frances Gumm, a brand-new student from the desert town of Lancaster, was going to sing for us. When I saw this plain eleven-year-old girl hoist herself up onto the baby grand in an overlong dress and tap shoes with wilted black taffeta bows, I was ready to cry. How could Mrs. Lawlor let a small-town amateur face this audience of sharp professional kids? Then she began to sing.

No one in that room would ever forget the powerful, mature, riveting voice that came welling out of that forlorn-looking child. When she finished, her new classmates nearly tore down the study hall. At Lawlor's annual Christmas shows, Mickey Rooney always served as emcee, and Frances Gumm (Judy Garland) sang encores until well past midnight. Even then audiences never seemed to get enough of her.

I was also amazed at the operatic potential of a seventeen-year-old Italian student with a glorious tenor voice whom I overheard rehearsing for the Christmas show. He was introducing a new ballad I felt sure was headed for instant fame. After unloading my schoolbooks on the dinette table when I got home, I raved about the new song to Mother. "I don't know who wrote it," I enthused, "but mark my words, it's bound to become number one on the Hit Parade!"

"Oh?" Mother remarked idly as she cut up onions for our usual spaghetti dinner. "What's it called?"

" 'Silent Night.' "

In May of 1935, Jackie Coogan, his father, Junior Durkin, and two others were driving home to Jack Coogan's Pine Valley Ranch near San Diego after a day of dove-hunting across the Mexican border. Reported by witnesses to be traveling at excessive speed, the elder Coogan failed to make a hairpin curve and sent the coupe hurtling down into a boulder-strewn canyon. Jack Coogan, Junior Durkin, and two other passengers were killed. Only Jackie survived.

Lawlor's was plunged into mourning. Junior Durkin was an orphan who supported his two sisters by his acting. It was he—the only one of us who owned a car—who generously picked up almost every member of the *Growing Pains* cast on various Hollywood street corners every day and got us to Pasadena and back. I attended two funerals in one day: Durkin's, with a large Lawlor contingent, and Jack Coogan's, with my parents. The latter was the grimmer of the two, and clouded by dark emotional overtones.

The Coogans, who were Catholics, had been living apart since the wife of Arthur Bernstein, Jackie's business manager, sued Lillian Coogan for alienation of her husband's affections. In 1928, Mrs. Bernstein had been amply compensated for her irreparable loss with a large chunk of Jackie's money, but Bernstein remained in charge of the Jackie Coogan Corporation. Now the weeping widow leaned heavily on the arm of a troubled-looking Bernstein. Eighteen months later the two were married.

While I had known Jackie since childhood, we remained mere acquaintances. The competitive careers of adolescent professionals forced most of us to be loners. While Mickey and Frankie were Lawlor's recognized leaders, Jackie headed a band of idle rich youths from private schools. His followers spent their time on such elite pursuits as playing badminton at Malibu, driving fancy cars, dating starlets, and attending Santa Anita races. We also knew Jackie would inherit $4 million of his own childhood earnings when he turned twenty-one next year. Jackie had it made, while the need to feed our families kept the rest of us fighting with each other over what few crumbs might fall from the movie industry's table.

Hard on the heels of Jackie's loss, my Baby Peggy self underwent a painful near-death experience. Lyon's Van and Storage notified us we were so far in arrears with storage fees on the trunks we had stored there, they would now be sold at auction simply for their intrinsic value as trunks, the contents going sight unseen. These trunks contained most of my Century and feature production stills and everything that was left in the way of clippings, scrapbooks, and publicity photos. In an industry that discarded its patrimony like Dixie cups, the historian in me was outraged to think this chunk of my life and movie history might now be lost forever.

Although we lacked the money to bid for the trunks ourselves, Mother and I begged Father to learn the names of those who purchased them. After the auction we could approach the buyers and request the contents, which most likely would have been of no interest to them. Virtually no one in 1930s Hollywood would have given any silent movie star's collection of stills so much as a second look.

But Father refused to risk such embarrassment to himself, or even allow us to contact the buyers. On a windy winter's twilight, while Father sat safely barricaded behind his newspaper, Mother told me the deed was done. Knowing that the record of Baby Peggy's childhood labors would tomorrow end up ashes in one of Hollywood's ubiquitous backyard incinerators, I went outside, gazed up at the storm-tossed fan palms lining nearby Sunset Boulevard, and wept.

But later in that same year of 1935, Father received a small yet unexpected windfall. Out of the blue, Sol Lesser called and invited him to his office. Once there, Lesser explained he had heard we were having tough sledding financially and he wanted to help out. It had "just occurred" to him he could buy Father's half of the screen rights to *Captain January* and *Heidi* (the latter film I had never made because of the falling-out between the two men). Unprepared to find the milk of human kindness flowing in Sol Lesser's veins, Father was grateful but also stunned and mystified when his former nemesis handed over six hundred dollars for both properties!

The mystery was solved when Louella Parsons wrote in her column that Fox had just paid a "very sizable sum" to buy the film rights to two childrens' classics. Shirley Temple would go before the cameras soon, starring in the first of these, a musical remake of *Captain January*. She would star in *Heidi* later. So much for the milk of human kindness.

A view of the courtyard entrance to Universal Studio in the early 1920s. The original stone fountain and fish pond can be seen in the upper center.
COURTESY OF THE BRUCE TORRENCE HISTORICAL COLLECTION

As the immigrant Italian child in THE DARLING OF NEW YORK.
AUTHOR'S COLLECTION

A dramatic scene in THE FAMILY SECRET when Peggy's grandfather (Frank Currier) unwittingly shoots her father (Edward Earle), whom he has mistaken for a burglar.

Captain January tries to comfort actor Hobart Bosworth, who portrays the lighthouse keeper suffering from heart trouble.

*An optical
illusion created
by cameraman
Glenn McWilliams
on location at sparsely
settled Laguna Beach
for the Sol Lesser film
CAPTAIN JANUARY.*
AUTHOR'S COLLECTION

*Jack, Marian, and
Peggy with friends,
enjoying the sights of
Yosemite National Park
in the fire engine red,
custom-made
Dusenberg.*
AUTHOR'S COLLECTION

The unforgettable meeting with Left Hand, the old Arapaho warrior, who is wearing the uniform he took from a dead trooper on the Custer battlefield.
AUTHOR'S COLLECTION

Cutting a layer of her giant birthday cake at the New York Foundling Home, while sister Louise (seated) and delighted orphans and nuns look on.
AUTHOR'S COLLECTION

Selling the new composition Baby Peggy doll, in Gimbel's New York department store, November 1923.
AUTHOR'S COLLECTION

The costume worn in the two-reel Century comedy THE FLOWER GIRL was the model for the new doll's dress.
AUTHOR'S COLLECTION

The "million dollar baby" displays a million dollars'
worth of bejeweled bracelets to advertise the wares of a
prominent New York jeweler. AUTHOR'S COLLECTION

Members of the "six big acts" touring the interstate circuit in the spring of 1926. Back row, second from left, Gus Fay; next row, Larry Rich (with cap); third row center, Cheri Rich (in beret); front and center, Peggy and Marian Montgomery. All others unidentified.

*On the platform at the Democratic National Convention that
reintroduced Franklin Delano Roosevelt to politics.* AUTHOR'S COLLECTION

Peggy in the Scotch outfit for her Harry Lauder encore. AUTHOR'S COLLECTION

*Above: Eddie
Sutherland, Douglas
Fairbanks,
a nervous thirteen-
year-old Peggy,
and Jack and Marian
Montgomery at the
United Artists studio
in June 1932.*
AUTHOR'S COLLECTION

*Marian Montgomery,
St. Louis, Missouri,
1927.*
AUTHOR'S COLLECTION

The golden German shepherd "Chris" and Peggy, in the summer of 1932, when she was entering talkies and he was being trained to replace Rin Tin Tin as Hollywood's top dog star. AUTHOR'S COLLECTION

The cast of THE CAPTAIN HATES THE SEA. *Back row, third from left, Arthur Treacher, Leon Errol, John Gilbert, director Lewis Milestone, Wallace Smith, Victor McLaglan, Akim Tamiroff, Walter Catlett, and Claude Gillingwater. Seated, left to right, Larry Fine, Curly and Moe Howard (the Three Stooges); Allison Skipworth, Walter Connolly, Wynne Gibson, Emily Taylor, and Donald Meek.* AUTHOR'S COLLECTION

Peggy playing a turn-of-the-century high school graduate in MGM's AH! WILDERNESS, autumn of 1935.
AUTHOR'S COLLECTION

Former child stars Wesley Barry, Mary Jane Irving, Baby Marie Osborne, and Baby Peggy, on the set of RKO's HAVING A WONDERFUL TIME, in the spring of 1937. Ginger Rogers starred and Marie Osborne was under contract as her stand-in; the rest of us were merely extras.
COURTESY OF RICHARD LAMPARSKI

Eleven-year-old Frances Gumm before she became Judy Garland, as she appeared when she first sang for the students of Lawlor's Professional School in early 1934.

COURTESY OF BARRY KEHOE

Starting a new life in Carmel, California, after filing for divorce from first husband Gordon Ayres in 1948.
PHOTO BY MORLEY BAER

Bob Cary and his bride after their wedding at Santa Inez Mission, Solvang, California, May 15, 1954.
Author's Collection

A recent photo of the author with a rare collection of Baby Peggy dolls. Author's Collection

*Former child stars Jackie Coogan and Baby Peggy,
photographed together for the first time since 1923, taken at
a Hollywood convention of film buffs in 1983, where she
hosted a panel of former child stars.*

30

Throughout those rock-bottom depression years, one abiding presence saved desperate families like my own from despair—the studio system. This driving force, quiet and well oiled, generated the energy, order, and promise that not only ran each studio from front office to back lot but ran almost everything else in Hollywood as well. The system spawned thousands of jobs, and its steady purr assured us that if not today, a job would be out there tomorrow. Since the entire world was addicted to movies, we knew the market for our product was as inexhaustible and enduring as the machine that produced it.

That is not to say the studio system was entirely without flaws. Many stars hated the straitjacket of typecasting and weak stories. Directors railed against the rigid production schedules and strict budgets set by fiscal nitpickers who they said savaged all artistic creativity in the name of the system. But with all its limitations and restraints, it was a unique cooperative effort with totally intermeshed teams of ultraprofessionals working in a variety of fields, experts able to gear up for action with astonishing speed and work together seamlessly. Without the system a production as complex as *Gone with the Wind* could never have been realized on such an imposing scale with so small a budget. For almost forty years it sustained both highly paid stars' careers and a steady wage for workers while churning out a thousand films a year for its insatiable global market.

Of course, Hollywood was not a union town, nor its wages union pay, but Hollywood was strike free. Workers had a certain reverence for the product, so that extras, crewmen, and even temperamental stars could be persuaded in a pinch to work overtime without commensurate pay to wrap up a difficult sequence. "Get Frankenstein off the wall!" a chief electrician would shout to his crew when a shadow appeared on a set where it shouldn't be. But for producers and directors the "Frankenstein on the wall" was the fear that one day Hollywood would be unionized from top to bottom with carpenters, crewmen, and extras demanding wages that would make big productions too costly to film. (For all their vigilance, in time that dreaded day would come.)

Like everything else in town, local newspapers were locked into the studio system, publishing twice-a-week production schedules. These listed every upcoming film by title, studio, starting date, stars, director, and assistant director. Planned films requiring large contingents of dancers, children, horsemen, midgets, or other specialized talent got written up as feature stories, so those who qualified knew when and where to apply.

Gone were the days when extras "got on" by meeting a director through a friend. Gone too was the cowboys' holding tank at Universal. In 1932 the enormous task of putting studios in daily contact with the approximately seventeen thousand available extras was institutionalized by the innovative Bert Hampton, himself a former extra. His Central Casting occupied one entire floor of an office building on the corner of Hollywood and Western. In order to work as an extra, one was supposed to first register at Central. The studios picked up the tab for Hampton's salary, his five full-time assistant interviewers, and the payroll for a sizable crew of operators who manned what was the busiest manual switchboard in the Los Angeles area, processing three thousand calls an hour.

But with an average of only three thousand extra jobs a month spread among what in the mid-1930s had grown to nearly thirty thousand applicants, competition was brutal. Those seeking work dialed Central *at three-minute intervals* between 3:00 and 7:00 P.M., receiving a disheartening number of

"Try later!" replies. When jobs were assigned, operators gave them such movie shorthand labels as "rain or shine," "small-town street clothes," or "weather permitting." If it was a period film, extras were told to report to Wardrobe by 5:00 A.M. for costumes, and to Makeup for hairpieces, beards, and braids.

One of the four of us had to monitor the phone at all times or risk missing a lifesaving job from Central. We even hung the washing out in shifts so the phone was never left alone. Perhaps due to this restriction on his freedom, Father had a dream. In it he was shown, down to the smallest detail, a device that automatically recorded telephone messages which could be played back later. The next morning he made a careful drawing of this amazing "message machine." Convinced he had hit upon a million-dollar invention, he hurried off to the downtown Bell Telephone office to sell it. Officials there laughed at him, turning down flatly what they called his "worthless Rube Goldberg invention."

Disappointments in those black years were the order of the day. Father had finally abandoned all hope of financing a ranch. Swallowing his pride, he returned full circle to his pre–Baby Peggy days, entering the ranks of riding extras. The camaraderie of the cowboys provided a sense of community and gave him a respected place in it.

As for pride, I had long ago pocketed mine. I now played strictly by the unspoken "upstairs-downstairs" protocol prevailing on studio sets. Stars and principal actors sat together, grouped about the director's chair. Between scenes, most male stars played cards with their peers or prowled the set in search of carnal prey. The women knitted or crocheted.

Extras formed their own group apart. Among them were several fallen greats of the silent era, evoking memories of the disparaged art of silent films.

The younger extra men, a uniquely purposeless group, had their own off-camera ritual: dropping sexual innuendos, pursuing young women, and treating those they caught to a slow and sensual neck and shoulder massage. Because several tried recruiting me, I knew many moonlighted as pimps. More than a few were paid paramours of wealthy older women outside the industry.

The cowboys were unfailingly chivalrous toward young women they considered ladies. I often sought them out and put myself directly under their protection, volunteering as their passenger if they were driving a stagecoach or wagon. The older male extras, many of them silent-era actors, killed their time by perusing racing forms, hoping to God their diligence might be rewarded by picking a fifty-to-one winner at Santa Anita or Del Mar. Extra women of all ages traded job rumors, read Louella's column religiously, and rehashed any old or new scandals involving the stars sitting over yonder.

Whether a job placed me inside the clique with the principals or apart with the extras, I spent my time reading. I found that on a movie set a scholarly book drove predatory males off quicker than a cloud of mustard gas. Sometimes, puzzled by the fact that no one else cared enough to ask, I quizzed extras who as silent stars had pioneered the industry, asking them what life had been like in the early days. Florence Turner, once famous as "the Vitagraph Girl," admitted she had sewn her own costumes and helped paint flats, in addition to acting.

But like most old-timers she always belittled her role in motion-picture history and disparaged the industry as well. "It was all very unimportant, really," she said, dismissing both past and present with a wave of her hand. "Making pictures has always been such a flimsy fly-by-night business, no one should ever feel proud about working in them!"

Fellow extras in the same apartment house devised ways of solving each others' money woes. If our phone was disconnected for lack of payment (as it often was), a generous neighbor let us call Central on theirs. If their gas was turned off, we let them use our stovetop and oven until they could pay the bill. Electricity, water, and home-delivered ice and milk were other trade-offs, making the possible combinations of these interfamilial charities endless.

Resourcefulness was the golden key to survival. Although I could never execute even one pirouette without staggering, I invariably accompanied Louise on every audition for a dance job, just to collect the fifty cents in carfare the studios paid any would-be chorine with nerve enough to do a turn before LeRoy Prinz or Busby Berkley. The round trip on the red car cost ten cents each, so between us we cleared eighty cents. With hamburger nineteen cents a pound, carrots a penny a bunch, and a loaf of bread a dime, more than once the carfare from a dance tryout bought the entire family dinner.

Since we all wore the same dress size, Mother, Louise, and I built up between us enough of a formal wardrobe to enable at least one of us at a time to work as a dress extra, earning $16.00 a day instead of $7.50. The most lucrative and long-running such job any of us ever landed was in the spring of 1934 when my old gagman from Century, director Lewis Milestone, hired Mother as one of thirty-five dress extras placed under contract for the Columbia film *The Captain Hates the Sea*. All played well-dressed upper-class passengers on a luxury liner, and Mother had to commandeer our entire communal wardrobe to meet her part's demands.

Milestone admired John Gilbert, once MGM's greatest matinee idol but recently released from his contract by Louis B. Mayer. In 1926, after secretly living together for a year, Greta Garbo stood Gilbert up on what was to have been their wedding day. When Mayer wisecracked, "What do you have to marry her for?" the enraged groom banged the mogul's head against the wall. "You're finished, Gilbert," Mayer hissed. "I'll destroy you if it costs me a million dollars!"

Mayer cast Gilbert in a string of bad films which his contract obliged him to make. Not even his success opposite Garbo in *Queen Christina* saved him. Now, eight years later, Milestone hoped to restore his friend's career by giving him the leading role in this film. It also gave Milestone's boss, Harry Cohn, a chance to needle his rival, Mayer. The only wild card was the troubled star's heavy drinking.

After staying sober for the first week, the insecure actor hit the bottle. Confident he could control Gilbert's access to liquor at sea, Milestone took the company on location, aboard a rented ship cruising the Los Angeles harbor and Catalina Island. But his cast boasted a pride of inveterate drinkers, including the Three Stooges, who found ingenious ways to keep Gilbert's party going. The sun refused to shine, the wind blew, and the frantic director found most of his all-star cast too drunk to deliver intelligible dialogue.

Six weeks later, with production costs spiraling, Cohn cabled Milestone at sea. "Hurry up. The cost is staggering." Milestone cabled back: "So is the cast." (The unfortunate John Gilbert died of a heart attack two years later.)

The Captain Hates the Sea left an indelible mark in my memory for more personal reasons. Hearing the storm of rumors that the film's location was a floating orgy, Father was possessed by jealous visions of Marian lying blind drunk in another man's arms.

Mother had been at sea for over a month, and her sixty-dollar-a-week salary remained unpaid until the ship docked. As a consequence Louise and I found ourselves alone at home on the Fourth of July weekend without a dime and nothing to eat except a can of plum pudding left over from a Christmas charity basket. "It's the wrong holiday, but at least it's food," Louise remarked dryly as we cleaned our plates in otherwise stony silence. When Father returned on Monday, he solemnly ordered us into the living room, where he announced that he had spent the weekend in the arms of beauteous Florence Lee, one of my movie mothers in my Century days. Their affair, he explained gravely, was all Mother's fault. This self-righteous confession coming from a man who all his life had preached moral rectitude left us both absolutely stunned.

But while these crises came and went, my parents never lost sight of my comeback. I dutifully followed every lead for promising parts. However, I was beset by a host of unsolved health problems. I had still not had my tonsils out, so I suffered chronic sore throats and was easy prey for the flu.

So nearsighted without my glasses that I was unable to recognize my own sister twenty feet away, I had real trouble finding my way around a set where wearing them was taboo. The dentist I consulted about straightening my teeth took X rays and informed me I had four badly impacted wisdom teeth that must come out before I could consider braces. That was such an insurmountable financial obstacle I had to abandon the project. Fortunately, the studios were pioneering the use of porcelain caps as an instant correction of their more important stars' flawed smiles. I decided to invest my meager earnings in this more affordable miracle cure.

The improvement in my appearance was striking. I had a set of professional portraits made by a leading Hollywood photographer and was finally beginning to feel really good about myself. But when I went to the photographer's studio to pick up the final prints, the clerk who took my money leaned across the counter and asked me in sepulchral tones, "Tell me, how does it feel to be a has-been at sixteen?"

With my parents at a holiday party and Louise off visiting a school friend, I sat alone in our apartment on New Year's Eve and made a solemn vow to myself which I duly entered in my diary.

"Because I am only fifteen, I have made up my mind *not* to fall in love or marry for the next fifteen years. Instead, I will devote myself to becoming a truly fine actress. When I've earned my second fortune, I will buy Father a ranch out west, and Mother a house in Hollywood, making both of them happy." After a thoughtful moment I added, "Then, at thirty, I will finally begin living *my own life!*"

Thirty was actually early to begin a second career, I thought. Eva Le Gallienne was only thirty-six, Helen Hayes thirty-seven, and both were at the peak of their powers. Because I had never really been a child, I had no fixation on staying young forever. I was undaunted by youth's evanescence. My sole intent was to master—long before the need arose—the art of growing old. Mother's example in this regard was a negative one. She not only hated being older but seemed incapable of gathering the slightest moss of maturity or wisdom after four decades of living. I did not wish to emulate either her wistfulness for youth or Father's childish rebellion against authority. I was also determined to avoid the common but tragic pitfall of many older stars who mistook their juvenescent screen image for their true identity. Having cultivated no sustaining private self, they were destroyed by the aging process of the public self, as was that forever-young girl in *Lost Horizon* who turned into a crone when she left Shangri-la.

Bizarre as my fifteen-year plan might seem, at the time it gave me direction and enabled me to devote myself wholeheartedly to the acting career I did not desire but was yoked to anyway. It gave me the courage to pick up the spent arrow of Baby Peggy. Meanwhile, I would continue to read, study, and prepare myself for my "after-thirty" life as a writer.

I played ingenues in several plays at little theaters all over town. In the summer of 1935, I was rushed into the leading role of a play opening at the Uplifter's Club Theater. Under killing pressure, I got up in a part of eighty sides (pages) in two days. The play ran a week and I received excellent reviews. After that successful run, my new adult self-image blossomed under the praise of fellow actors. My director said, "I've worked with some great stars in my time who had the rare quality of charisma onstage. You have it too, and you'll go far in the legitimate theater." Well, I told myself proudly, my life plan is really paying off.

At this juncture a chance encounter with a well-remembered figure of my childhood reinforced my rising faith in my next fifteen years. I met Peter the Hermit stalking down Sunset Boulevard, twisted staff in hand, his five tireless greyhounds panting at his heels. Tanned and lean with long white hair and beard, and wearing the clean but faded shirt and shorts of some island castaway, he had long been Hollywood's self-appointed prophet of blessing and doom.

While the town was awash in preachers and gurus, Peter was unique in that he claimed his sole mission was the salvation of movie greats. As far back as I could recall, my nonreligious parents had given Peter's ad hoc prophecies as much credence as if he were Jehovah himself. I had last seen Peter in 1923 at the gates of Universal, lying in wait for the limousines of such black-sheep members of Uncle Carl's fold as Tom Mix and Art Accord. When their cars rolled slowly by, he pounded his staff on the pavement and thundered about God's impending wrath. No one knew whence this solitary Jeremiah hailed. He belonged to no religious sect and never preached from any other pulpit than the road.

Oddly enough, Peter had never told me what the fates had in mind for

Baby Peggy. Now he surprised me by saying he had been expecting me, and had "a message" concerning my future. "Ah, yes," he murmured, blue eyes closed, hand on my head. "Your life moves in cycles of seven. Seven years of fame, then seven of obscurity. You're now beginning seven more years of fame!" Given my profound religious ignorance, Peter might as well have been a backstage gypsy or a river-wise oracle, but who would *not* choose to believe such an upbeat prophecy?

I attacked my senior year at Lawlor's with renewed energy and purpose. My English teacher was an inspiring recent college graduate, a young woman for whom I would willingly have walked barefoot over red-hot coals. Frustrated by the unavoidable absenteeism of so many Lawlor students, she heaped on me the largesse of college-level work.

At the same time I felt sorry for classmates like fifteen-year-old Helen Robey. Her ribald language shocked me, but I knew she had picked it up working in rowdy beer joints for five dollars a night to support her aged and invalid parents. She was homely but had a wealth of blond curly hair, and her comedic act was a female takeoff on Harpo Marx. She came to school each morning dead for lack of sleep and with the attention span of a zombie. I took it upon myself to forge her name and that of two or three other night workers on the required essays they were themselves too exhausted to write. "Why don't you hand in Helen's essay as your own?" quipped my teacher, who was not easily fooled. "By the *fifth* rewrite you start getting really good."

Our chief escape from work and worry was going to the movies. Louise and I had an endless supply of passes to neighborhood theaters, courtesy of a real-estate agent who was our friend. Managers of these small theaters advertised their weekly programs on small billboards that stood in the vacant lots this realtor had for sale. In lieu of cash they paid her off with passes. Thanks to her we had been viewing double features four and five nights a week ever since our return to Hollywood. This movie marathon not only got us out of the house and saved our sanity, it formed the cinematic side of an education which was to a large degree self-instruction.

We also haunted public libraries, and I devoured biographies of historical figures. I once made the mistake of bubbling over to Father about brain surgeon Paul Broca, and how much he had learned about the human brain.

"Why fill your head with such garbage?" he exploded over the evening paper. "You're a woman, for God's sake! You're *never* going to be a brain surgeon. You're going to work in pictures the rest of your life!"

Encouraged by my teacher's praise for a collection of my sonnets, I sent it to my great-aunt Alice at the University of Nebraska asking her opinion. She and a literature professor said my work was very promising. At this response Father wrote back immediately asking her how to go about selling the collection to a publisher.

"Jack, do *not* push her too soon!" was her cautious reply. "A failure now could discourage future tries. *Protect* her work from public exposure until it has time to mature." I was grateful for her wisdom, but Father was furious. "Why won't she cooperate? There should be a helluva lot of money in a book of Baby Peggy's poems."

I longed to remind him that Baby Peggy had not written this poetry, *I had*. But I lacked the nerve to cross him. I continued writing popular songs and lyrics, but my newest ambition was to compose symphonic music, something to which school and radio had recently exposed me. But a piano was out of the question. We were living in a one-bedroom rented apartment, Louise and I sharing a pull-down bed in the living room. To find the privacy to write at all, I had to closet myself in our one bathroom. Well, someday . . .

But that remote someday seemed knocked out of the box when Larry Rich surfaced with a new act he said he had written especially for me. I tried every possible ruse to avoid drinking this poisoned wine, but Larry sold my parents on the mad notion that vaudeville was coming back and this was the witching hour. Every day for a week Father drove me downtown to the Orpheum where Larry was headlining, to rehearse with him backstage between shows, a grim flashback to my three years of hell on the road.

One day while Larry was onstage, a Mexican singer on the bill asked me if I spoke Spanish. Having flunked the class at Fairfax, I confessed I didn't understand a word. Despite that, he offered to give me an original set of lyrics he'd written for "La Cucaracha," even coaching me for proper accents. He said he'd used it in his own nightclub act, audiences loved it, and it would make a surefire encore for my act. He rehearsed me and I thanked him for his generosity.

The act Larry had dreamed up, and which we were to break in at the Long Beach Strand theater, was beyond ghastly. I was to portray a faded film star emerging from a theater while Louise played a fan seeking my autograph. At sixty it would have been humiliating; at fifteen it cut to the bone. Next I recalled at great length, aloud, how I had fallen from fame. Then, changing into an eye-popping floor-length red satin gown and rhinestone earrings, I would close with my secret weapon—the flashy surefire "Cucaracha" finale.

Helen Robey went out front to prime audience applause. The tension backstage was Fort Worth all over again. Harry Weber's man was to be out front.

Once onstage I confronted an icy Long Beach audience which, after watching four other acts, still refused to thaw. Not even my stylish Mexican encore struck any sparks.

Helen joined us in our dressing room to be present when Harry Weber's man came to deliver his verdict.

"I caught your act," he said glumly, standing in the doorway. "Honest to God, folks, it's not good!" Then, looking straight at me, he fixed me with a baleful eye and added, "But if you ever go onstage with this act again, for Christ's sake, cut out that filthy Mexican ditty at the end!"

" 'La Cucaracha'?" I blinked in astonishment. "Filthy?"

"No manager in his right mind would let any woman, let alone a girl your age, sing lyrics that lewd and obscene."

As Father drove us home, I tried to figure out how Weber's man knew the words. He didn't look Mexican. I also cursed that Mexican singer for his deliberate treachery. But then, I also owed him thanks. His blue and bawdy nightclub lyrics had scuttled any chance of my return to vaudeville.

Helen Robey, beside me in the backseat, leaned over and whispered, "To hell with the act, Peg. It was dogshit anyway." Then, with her usual rough candor, she added, "You've simply got to give me the words to that fuckin' filthy version of 'Cucaracha.' I know a Cuban drummer who can put it into English. My boozed-out beer-hall crowd will eat it up."

31

W hile sex may have been the stock-in-trade of casting directors, flesh peddlers, and such aficionados of virginal pulchritude as Charlie Chaplin and Errol Flynn, the rank and file of Hollywood's younger generation were unabashed romantics. Most of us were so thoroughly segregated from each other by our competitive careers and overzealous parents, we knew less than nothing about dating, dances, and the innocent overtures to real-life sex.

The emotional responses of youthful stars like Lana Turner, Elizabeth Taylor, Judy Garland, and Mickey Rooney were much less realistic than their counterparts' in Kalamazoo and Peoria. Hollywood youngsters' ideas of love were dominated by the larger-than-life fade-out kiss they saw onscreen. While later castigated for multimarriages by critics and fans, more often than not these celebrities were driven into matrimony by hidden but powerful social forces that were unique to Hollywood.

During the run of several plays, I had myself discovered how simulating love for a handsome leading man could, in a few days' time, ignite passion between two virtual strangers. Falling in love—in an industry where propinquity was *the* major occupational hazard—triggered an almost Pavlovian rush to the altar. Because they were regarded as studio "properties," young stars had to placate such ruthless manipulators of their personal lives as the publicly puritanical (but privately womanizing) Louis B. Mayer. Many romances were often the direct result of the calculated pairing of two "hot properties" on the part of the publicity department to promote an upcoming film. To keep their screen images pure, stars hastened to sanctify what, given time, they would have recognized was no more than a passing infatuation. They were also deeply influenced by Hollywood's highly idealized version of the American dream.

My own emotional makeup had been cast in the same sentimental studio mold, made even firmer by massive doses of nineteenth-century literature and such richly costumed historical films as *Wuthering Heights* and *The Barretts of Wimpole Street,* the latter a supremely romantic movie recounting the towering love story of my two favorite poets, Elizabeth Barrett and Robert Browning.

Conversely, whatever love had existed between my once-romantic parents had apparently vanished. After twenty years of merely sparring, they seemed to have settled down to the serious business of destroying each other. Now earning her own paycheck, Marian became cockily independent, doing as she pleased and going around with her own friends whom she had met on the set. In the process she further honed an already razor-sharp tongue, whose main function seemed to be cutting Jack down to size.

Goaded by her cocksure attitude, which she openly flaunted, Jack's volcanic temper exploded with increasing frequency and his rages now escalated into physical violence. The mock trials ground on, resifting the scores of long-past card games and the sordid secrets of alleged love affairs. During one dinner-table donnybrook, Marian threatened divorce and Jack replied, "You do that and I'll air all the dirty linen between us in a sensational divorce suit against you that will rock this town to its foundations. I'll tell the world once and for all who spent Peggy's money."

"You aren't even thinking about what such a scandal would do to Peg and her future!" Louise cried furiously. "All you two ever care about is getting even with each other!"

Stung to the core, Father sprang at her across the table and would have succeeded in strangling her if Mother and I had not torn them apart. Louise and I were now terrified to leave home even for the movies, for fear we would come back and find our parents the victims of murder, suicide, or both.

At nineteen Louise was free to leave home, but I was only sixteen and knew Father could—and would—exert his legal authority over me until I was eighteen. Louise refused to go and leave me alone. After one all-day row with Marian, Jack moved out and checked into the Padre Hotel. Despairing of ever making them happy as long as they remained together, we counseled Mother to get a quiet divorce. But at this eminently sane suggestion she only wept harder, wailing, "But how *can* I! He's the father of my children!" They were hopelessly bound together, psychologically and emotionally, and each of them was too neurotic and insecure to function without the other.

After a miserable week, Marian asked Jack to return home. He did, and once having made up, they presented a solid accusatory front against the two of us.

"You know damn well your father and I would never fight with each other if it weren't for you kids," Mother informed us archly.

"Your mother's right," Father said in rare agreement. "You two have always been the cause of all our trouble."

Louise and I were by now nervous wrecks. Sick with worry and battle fatigue, our nerves were so completely shot we had the shakes worse than two confirmed winos.

My parents' stormy mismating had instilled in me a fierce determination never to settle for anything short of the perfect marriage. With my lifelong penchant for total commitment, I intended to marry for life, for love, for true intellectual companionship, and for all the other ninety-nine right reasons. But, as I reminded myself in the late summer of 1935, I had a good fourteen years left to go on my fifteen-year plan. Wrong.

In September, Eugene O'Neill's *Ah, Wilderness* went before the cameras at MGM. I landed a small part as a member of a turn-of-the-century graduating class and choir. Not only did Mickey Rooney have a leading role, but a dozen other veteran child actors worked as extras or had a line or two in the film. The studio went to great lengths to publicize our presence, handing out daily news releases and photos of us singly or together, with false claims that all of us were playing important roles.

My long white organdy choir dress and a high coronet braid were very flattering, so I did not really mind that the front office was shamelessly exploiting us to plug the picture. We all still believed that being seen was Hollywood's magic key to being rediscovered, so we gladly went along.

More than that, I always enjoyed working on costume films because I could study firsthand what people living in other times wore. The carriages on the street, the interior sets, the men's dress, and my own gowns all made me feel I had been set down bodily in some distant time and place.

Between scenes on this set the other girls smoked cigarettes, hitched up their floor-length skirts, and crossed their legs in a bold manner that rudely shattered the chaste mood of the film. I told myself I was being unfairly judgmental. Just because I didn't smoke and wanted to conserve the movie's historical mood, why should I expect everyone else on the set to stay "in period" between takes? Still, it bothered me.

Only one young auburn-haired, green-eyed extra man behaved as if he too had just stepped out of a 1900 parlor. Unlike most relentlessly on-the-make male extras, he was turn-of-the-century gallant, bringing me a glass from the watercooler and choosing me as his partner in the dance scenes. I was so impressed when he asked to take me to lunch at the tiny Dill Pickle Cafe across the street from MGM, I completely overlooked the fact that it was I who finally had to pick up the check. When the picture ended, he phoned to ask if he could visit me at home.

Although I agreed, I was uneasy. I had only had one date in my life. Red-haired, freckle-faced Leon Holmes had asked me out on a double date with Frankie Darro. (I was still fond of Frankie, but by now I knew he was a heavy drinker, preferred his women on the wild side, and could have stepped over my dead body without giving me a second glance.) He and Leon had not arrived that night to pick me up until after nine o'clock.

"When I was young I was bringing girls home at this hour," Father thundered. His parting shot at Leon was a threat to kill him if he got me home a second after midnight, assuring the quaking youth he had the gun to do it with. Word of Father's wrath must have gotten around, for no one else at Lawlor's ever asked me out again.

I was prepared for similar parental objections to this young man's visit. But Gordon Ayres was respectful and well mannered, and on his third visit he wisely invited Louise to go along with us to the drugstore for a Coke and to see *The Informer,* a movie in which he had a small part. After walking home from the theater with us, Louise went inside immediately while Gordon pulled me back. Taking me in his arms, he gave me a lingering good-night kiss. Having kissed his date at the door, as was expected, he released me and went on his way.

Standing on the front steps alone, I could feel the planet pitch beneath my feet and saw the firmament begin to wheel overhead. If I had been struck by lightning the effect could not have been more stunning, convinced as I was that I had found the one true love of my life.

32

Since infancy I had been told in a thousand different ways that *I* alone held the key to my parents' security and happiness. As a consequence, I now had a capacity for whole-souled dedication to a single cause that ranked right up there with flagpole sitters and dance marathon contestants. Haunted by constant dread and ruthlessly reminded that every act or inaction of mine could either help or harm my family, I had been running for years on a rich mix of fuel that was equal parts duty, guilt, and fear. Now I would devote my single-minded nature to undying love.

For other sixteen-year-old girls, falling in love might be a normal rite of passage from child to woman. For me it was threat, surprise roadblock, and moral ambush all in one. Breaking the chains of duty to my family in order to make a selfish commitment to my own future happiness seemed a treacherous betrayal that required doing violence to myself.

But the magnitude of my reaction to a simple good-night kiss hinted that something essential to sound emotional balance was missing in my character. Although unable to put my finger on it at the time, years later I understood more clearly what it was. Being my family's protector had always been part of my compulsive drive to make them happy. But it had also caused me to blind myself to the fact that they had been exploiting me all these years. In the 1930s "exploit" was not the well-worn term it has since become, but when it *was* used it carried the same opprobrious connotation.

Ever since our return to Hollywood I had been reading scathing articles in newspapers and magazines which directly or by transparent implication accused my parents of having exploited me shamelessly throughout my childhood career. These writers ticked off all the fancy cars, the cloud of relatives, the mansions, and the mind-boggling sums of money I had earned which they had so blithely spent. True as I knew these cruel accusations to be, they cut me most deeply because they hurt my parents, who had no defense against them. Perhaps most of all I was determined *not* to believe that they could have deliberately used the willing and trusting child I had always been for their own selfish ends.

From as far back as I could remember I had kept my worries and problems to myself—even sickness when possible to conceal—so as not to trouble anyone. Not even to Louise did I ever confide my exhaustion, loneliness, and homesickness on the road. When I symbolically "buried" Baby Peggy under the fir tree in Wyoming, it was a private and no doubt a psychologically necessary act to heal a hidden wound within. Neither Louise nor my parents ever heard a word of it from me. Nearly all the frightening mysteries and confusions of early puberty I had dealt with on my own. This sense of isolation was part of my protective attitude toward my family, and in a sense myself, for I was not sure they could deal with my problems. This willful denial in the face of all the evidence of exploitation enabled me to maintain the love and respect I wanted desperately to feel toward them.

For all my strong ego and self-esteem, I had never believed I was genuinely loved for myself alone. I had worked hard all my life, convinced I must *earn* the love which other parents gave unconditionally. Through continuous performance I paid for my family's affection but was never certain if what I gave was enough to get me anything in return. Consequently, by sixteen I was literally famished for love.

When Gordon phoned me the next morning, I told him I simply had to see him. He agreed to come at once but I'm sure was totally unprepared for the scene that followed.

I greeted him at the door, dressed in a floor-length, high-necked long-sleeved wine-red damask hostess gown which Father had given me for Christmas. Mother and Louise were both at work, so we were alone, but it never occurred to me to take sexual advantage of the opportunity. The prevailing mood I had created in the room was part psychiatrist's office, part second-act curtain.

Not having slept all night and now putting into words what had been bottled up inside me left me feeling weak. I sank down on a chair across from him. "What I'm saying is that if you don't mean it—if you're not prepared to love me forever, as I love you, tell me now. I must know, because for me there can be only one great love in my life!" No one had told me that in this day and age even resolute virgins like myself regarded a chaste good-night kiss as a social grace, not a pledge of deathless love. But I was no more capable of recreational sex than I was of recreational Russian roulette.

Perhaps it was a tribute to Gordon's own acting credentials that he was able to keep a straight face. But as I would discover much later, there was a wild card in Gordon's own past which prompted him to take my histrionics seriously. My value system was no more upside down than his. His Iowa-born Baptist mother fell under the thrall of a clever, self-styled "Ascended Master" when she first came to Hollywood. This master assured her that Gordon was set apart by God "to achieve great heights in the spiritual life." That promise had been made shortly before federal agents arrested this false prophet on charges of defrauding the U.S. mails and sent him up to serve time in San Quentin.

Bereft of her trusted guru, poor Mrs. Ayres—herself a fine needlework seamstress in MGM's vast wardrobe department—had tapped only a portion of Gordon's promised potential, landing him a few small parts in Our Gang comedies. He parleyed this bit of luck into later claims that he was the Gang's original Freckles. While a less confused soul than Gordon would have no doubt sized me up at once as being one brick shy of a load, he wanted to believe that an honest-to-God world-famous movie star might be the missing piece in the jigsaw puzzle of his life. Drawn to both spirituality and celebrity, he did not seem to notice the luster had long since worn off Baby Peggy's fame.

Myself being innocent of Gordon's background at the time, I was pleased to have him all but swear in the name of all the Ascended Masters that his love for me was indeed forever. If other romantic girls practice a small degree of self-deception, those reared in show business become masters of the art without even knowing it.

*   *   *

Despite all the melodramatic complications true love brought in its wake, I continued pursuing my comeback at the studios and refereeing parental quarrels at home, all the while being eaten alive with guilt because my intense love for Gordon hampered my fifteen-year plan. I was also killing myself with schoolwork so I could graduate from high school in the three years Father had ordained, instead of the customary four. Through protean efforts I had managed to telescope twelve years of schooling into six and, although working in films almost three quarters of the time, had racked up mostly As in the bargain. I had hoped Father would be proud of my accomplishment. It turned out he was only interested in getting school behind me so I could devote all my time to picture work.

Soon after graduation I received a surprisingly generous offer from my great-aunt Alice—a scholarship to the University of Nebraska and the hospitality of her own home throughout four years of college. I was ecstatic. This was the turning point of my life. Oh, to be around educated people all day and not have to cope with handsy male extras on the set. Also, deep down I was beginning to have some misgivings about Gordon, and I thought the separation might give me a better perspective on things. Emotionally dependent as I had become, I could not shake off the nagging fact that despite his good manners and sensitivity, he was a male movie extra with the same feckless nature and lack of goals that characterized the breed. But college for me was not to be. Father considered his aunt's offer ridiculous and wrote her his refusal, pointing out that Peggy had "better things to do than waste her time in school when she should be building a new career in films." I was crushed.

Father moved back to the Padre Hotel, and Mother, Louise, and I moved into a nicely furnished apartment in the comparatively elegant Fountain Manor, financed with our pooled earnings.

At this time a wealthy acquaintance from our Chicago and New York years resurfaced in Hollywood. Far removed from show business, Maude Hall was a statuesque redheaded fortyish merry widow. Her late husband (over whom she often wept by the third Manhattan) had left her a chewing-gum fortune whose long-lasting flavor had come through the depression intact.

Maude had sailed around the world several times, and voyaging was a trade she worked at the way other people hold down a steady job. Whenever we had bumped into her back east, we always found three steamer trunks standing open in the middle of her suite, for she was forever just returning from one cruise and about to embark on another.

Although she was now headquartered in Hollywood, nothing had changed. A career drinker, Maude was still celebrating the endless party that was her life. She was lonely (if she remarried, she forfeited her inheritance), had round heels and a special weakness for gigolos, and was a devout Christian Scientist who faithfully got her lesson every morning, hung over or not. Whatever else Maude Hall may have been, she exerted a baleful influence on Marian.

With Father gone, watching over Mother when Maude was on shore leave was like trying to control a headstrong teenager. Marian loved parties but couldn't tell a gigolo from the cop on the beat. She also couldn't down more than two glasses of anything containing alcohol without completely losing her bearings. Her hangovers were monumental but quickly forgotten, so the lesson never stuck. (I would never forget that awful night in 1928 when Father burst into our bedroom at 3:00 A.M. to tell us Maude and Mother were disgracing themselves on the dance floor of Harlem's "wicked" Cotton Club. "Now I want you both to solemnly swear you'll never take a drink *as long as you live*!" Groggy with sleep, Louise and I both swore. It was a subliminal promise I was unable to break until well after twenty-five.)

For a poor Hollywood extra, Gordon proved financially resourceful. Courting a girl by trolley from Venice to Hollywood was proving difficult, so he enlisted a former school friend who managed a family-owned appliance store in Venice. Jack Keller was twenty-three, clean-cut, single, did not drink, and owned that rarest of possessions, his own car. Gordon set up a blind date for Jack with Louise in the early spring of 1936, hoping for the best. Jack being right out of Louise's "real world of normal people," the two hit it off nicely.

Soon we were double-dating every weekend, a circumstance which both parents condoned because we were chaperoning each other. Except for a little discreet petting at Santa Monica's Castle Rock (which had been a location spot for me on *Captain January*), these weekend dates were as chaste as a nun's picnic. A Saturday-night movie, then Sunday-morning Religious Science church services (a Christian Science splinter group that preached success, serenity, and supply, all badly needed in the Montgomery household). A quiet after-church stroll through Forest Lawn's cemetery to view the statuary, then on to Sunday dinner at a nice restaurant and a first-run movie. That was about as racy as it got.

I met Gordon's mother and learned that she was now a follower of what was known as the Ballards' "I AM Movement," a group who believed in Saint Germain and other Ascended Masters, but I had trouble swallowing Ballard claims that the Astral Bodies of Ascended Masters gathered for seasonal conventions inside a miraculously hollowed-out Mount Shasta. However, as bad luck would have it, about this time the male Ballards, father and son, were picked up by federal agents for defrauding the mails. Fleet-footed Mrs. Ballard decamped to New Mexico, and poor Mrs. Ayres, once more bereft, continued her search for a nonfraudulent cult to follow.

While it was understood marriage was our ultimate goal, I explained to Gordon my long-range plan to make my parents happy. He surprised me by confiding he had a goal too. He might only be working as an extra, but he intended to be a star. He was wild about show business. I was fed up with it. In fact, the older I got the more I wondered if I had the stomach for even one more year in movies or the theater.

Although I was addicted to Gordon's physical presence and emotional support, I risked losing both by setting out to convince him how terribly unreliable show business was. He flatly refused to listen or believe. In June, he stunned me by announcing he was leaving to take New York and Broadway by storm. Not even my tears could dissuade him.

The next few months were grim ones for Louise and me. There was no one to turn to for either comfort or guidance. Maude was back in port and she and Mother were barhopping again. One cold and foggy March morning I awoke as Mother took off for the studio. I lay in bed a long while, thinking. Very well, if no one else could help us then I would! Throwing back the covers, I made a once-in-a-lifetime decision which I knew would be a point of no return.

I told Louise that eighteen or not—though only six months shy—the two of us had to pack up everything we owned and leave home. For Louise, to whom even a minor decision was an agony, my radical decree was terrifying. But, having been reduced to a chain-smoking bundle of nerves by the conflicts of the past few years, even she was willing to risk it.

I telephoned the new husband of a close school friend of ours from Fairfax. He worked for a rug-cleaning company and drove a closed van. Next, I composed a carefully worded note to Mother, telling her we had left for good but assuring her we had ample funds to see us through for several months (a lie). Knowing we were the cause of their problems, we were not going to let either Mother or Father know where to reach us. Perhaps our absence would give them time to rethink their own differences. The note was entirely without rancor or blame, but even so I knew it would wound her deeply. That was a consequence I had to hazard.

Our undetected exit proved we had not shoe-boxed our way out of a dozen apartments for nothing. At ten o'clock the rug cleaner's van pulled up in front of the Fountain Manor. While the Filipino houseboy absentmindedly vacuumed the hall, Louise and I casually strolled past him several times. I was carrying my few books, a small chest of drawers, a couple of suitcases, and a small cardboard carton containing the three hundred Baby Peggy production stills remaining from my Century days. Louise lugged a brand-new Church toilet seat that Jack Keller had won as a prize at a plumbers' trade convention. He and Louise were now engaged to be married, and she was not about to leave such a valued hope chest item behind.

When Marian read that note, I knew her first reaction would be to burst into tears and telephone Jack at the Padre Hotel. According to a mutual friend whom we trusted not to reveal our whereabouts (the lady real-estate agent who supplied us with movie passes), it worked out precisely as I had planned it. Father came rushing to her side to comfort her, and the following day the two were back living together again.

Now the urgent question before us was, how would Louise and I survive without a roof over our heads and only twenty-five dollars between us?

33

Louise and I rented a room in a turreted Victorian mansion near West-lake Park. The elderly landlady said she was the widow of a former state governor and had turned her home into a rooming house. She was cadaverously thin, as was her equally emaciated spinster daughter. When she led us upstairs, we glimpsed a painting of Saint Germain, the High Priest of Ascended Masters. It soon became apparent mother and daughter never sat down to a real meal but nibbled piñon nuts all day, the "astral diet" decreed by Ballard "I Am-ers" to purify their devotees' auras. It was obvious these were two more spiritual orphans of the Ballards' mail-fraud fiasco.

But we faced more mundane problems. Unable to meet our second week's rent, and not quite as ready to meet the saints as our anorexic concierge appeared to be, Louise and I accepted a surprisingly timely offer of Southern hospitality. Although I had knocked about with gypsies, acrobats, Swedish sheepherders, and shady male extras, nothing had prepared me for life with the Shirley family. It was as close as one could come to joining Jeeter Lester's clan on Tobacco Road.

April Shirley and Louise had been classmates at Fairfax High. Over the years we had also become friends with April's older sister, Viv, an aspiring writer like me. That was back in 1933. Now both April and Viv were married, and four generations of this Georgia cracker clan were seeking shelter under a single roof which they offered to share with the homeless Montgomery girls.

Working on the lean commission of a corner real-estate shack's sales, old Mr. Shirley knew how many homes had been repossessed and were standing empty. Some banks rented out these houses for a pittance rather than let them fall into ruin. Three generations of Shirleys were now living in three such separate dwellings, but to form a more economical single household they needed something almost institutional.

Mr. Shirley found it in an enormous wooden sprawl, painted barn red, the empty shell of the 1898 Venice Military Academy, all ninety-three rooms of it. But until the long-abandoned academy could be made habitable, Louise and I were invited to stay with the elder Shirleys in a ramshackle old beach home where both Viv and April spent their days.

The family had admittedly fallen from its antebellum glory, but as things stood now, if any Shirley project could not literally run itself, it was doomed. April's parents spoke of and addressed each other formally as "Mr. Shirley" and "Mrs. Shirley," and the fine art of "visitin'" was the entire family's all-consuming interest. Time meant nothing, money scarcely mattered, and housework piled up unnoticed: talk was their meat and drink. The tea cozy had a tea cozy, and over endless cups of strong breakfast tea, the feats of heroic Confederate forebears were recounted, the flirtations and scandals of long-dead Southern belles brought alive again. These marathon talk fests meant the breakfast table was seldom cleared until well after time for lunch.

As she talked, Mrs. Shirley kept her strong hands busy industriously braiding into mud-colored throw rugs scores of pairs of worn-out lisle hose. These she had squirreled away in several cardboard cartons which she always kept stacked by her chair. As each lisle-stocking rug was completed, it found a waiting bare floor, and another just like it was begun.

Each morning Mr. Shirley took his place in his rocking chair, the Zenith table-radio by his side. Equally near at hand was his bottle of Southern Comfort, magically replenished daily. This he sipped steadily through the day, "to ease the pain of these bad teeth of mine," he explained. His wife naïvely pointed to a half-filled Ben Hur coffee-can spittoon at his feet as living proof that "Mr. Shirley never swallows any!" She may have been blind, but others could plainly see why the old gent felt no pain.

The military academy was ours all right, but it was up to us to swamp it out. A generation earlier the grounds had boasted lawns, flourishing date palms, oleanders, and flowering magnolia trees. Now devil grass was rampant and everything with roots was on the verge of going feral. Scores of grimed, hard-eyed windows stared out reproachfully, as though the building sought someone to blame for its woeful decline. Everyone concerned tackled the formidable task in the celebratory spirit of a frontier barn-raising, but after two weeks we had barely reached the window-washing stage. As I leaned out of a third-story dormer, I saw Father drive up and alight from his car. When Mrs. Shirley appeared at another window, Father pointed up at me and shouted reproachfully, "Well, Mrs. Shirley, I suppose you think it gives your place added prestige to have Baby Peggy living here!"

Being away from my parents even a few weeks had helped me get a lot of things about them in focus. I had worked several years with Father's cowboy friends on movie sets, and thanks to them I was able to view him from a perspective far removed from his "Mr. Baby Peggy" image. I had found the typical open range cowboy was happiest when he was footloose and single. Father should never have married. From everything I had seen, good cowboys usually made rotten husbands and tyrannical fathers.

The needs of wife and family fenced them in and cut them off from the company of their own kind. It wasn't so much that Jack Montgomery was a perennially angry man; he was angry because, as one twice-divorced cowboy put it, "marriage ties a man down worse than an Oregon boot." Marian wasn't fighting with a jealous husband, she was fighting a losing battle with a born drifter who was still trying his damnedest to run away from home, wife, children—and himself.

I stopped my window-washing, came downstairs, and joined Father in his car. As we talked, he seemed resigned to the splintered condition of our family. He said he and Mother had already split up again and he was on his way to Wyoming's Wind River Range to work out a partnership with the Mormon owner of a dude ranch there. He invited me to come along and spend the summer working as his secretary for my room and board. I doubted Father could function yoked to a Mormon elder, but I was so homesick for Wyoming and so dismayed over my present situation, I was glad to get away. Louise opted to keep on mucking out the academy.

As I had feared, no partnership was possible between two such opposite men, so my "summer" was only three weeks long. But it gave me time to feel free again, to steal some badly needed solitude and get my emotional bearings. On our return Father dropped me off at the academy after dark, and I groped my way through the unlocked front door. I found Mrs. Shirley seated alone in what had been the school refectory. She was happily braiding stockings into rugs, the ubiquitous cartons at her feet, the unblinking eye of the Zenith casting its eerie green light over everything.

"Oh, I'm sorry you missed our moving-in picnic," she exclaimed softly. "We had hot dogs and watermelon out in the yard under the magnolia trees, just like back in Georgia." I glanced around the cavernous interior, my eyes slowly growing accustomed to the dark. Plates of dead watermelon rinds were scattered everywhere, long columns of black ants marching upon them determinedly from all sides.

That familiar Shirley clutter aside, the place looked more like a disaster center than a home. Huge packing cartons had been used to create walls. In one partitioned section Mr. Shirley was asleep on a mattress on the floor. In the next, a considerably larger quadrant, slept a very pregnant April and her husband (the one who drove the carpet cleaner's van). In yet another cubicle slept Viv, her husband, and her small son, also on the floor.

At the far end, in her own cartoned-off suite, snoozed Grandma Jackson, Mrs. Shirley's indestructible, half-blind eighty-five-year-old mother. Grandma Jackson's forbidden but hearty breakfasts of grits and sausage drowned in fat were living testimony to an unreconstructed Rebel's triumph over diabetes and bad cholesterol. I counted eight Shirley clan members, ten residents in all, including Louise and me.

"Would you believe," Mrs. Shirley ran on in a whisper, "the other day in a far wing of this huge building, I found a very old French lady and her daughter living in a suite that was furnished and velvet-window-draped as lavishly as Empress Josephine's parlor. She said she's been living here rent free for twenty-five years. So," she continued happily, "I guess we needn't worry about our ever being thrown out. Oh, yes, and we now have a real boarder who can actually pay." (There was no rancor intended, for she was wholly without guile.) "He's a quiet man who works nights at a good steady job."

"What does he do?"

Her lined but childlike face lit up as she replied, "He pretties up the corpses for the local undertaker."

The next evening at dinner I met the mortician's Max Factor. Bland, balding, and with the typical night-worker's pallor, he talked of nothing but his lugubrious job. He also said his boss was looking for a receptionist.

Feeling guilty about not being able to contribute our share of rent to the Shirley commune, I had already decided to try and get a steady job. Surely, I thought, there must be something I could do outside a studio. As the mortuary was only two blocks away, I set out the next morning, as if I were going on a dress extra call, in suit, hat, veil, and gloves.

"Do you have any experience dealing with—well, upset or troubled people?" the unctuous undertaker asked.

"Oh, yes," I volunteered eagerly. "My parents have led very troubled lives and I've had lots of practice at—well, calming them down."

He rubbed his chin dubiously. "Do you know double-entry bookkeeping?"

Thinking he meant keeping two sets of books like Sol Lesser on *Captain January*, I nodded and said I'd had some "secondhand experience" with it. At this point he suggested I go across the street to a doctor who also needed a receptionist but didn't require bookkeeping. "He and I often work hand in glove," he added obliquely, which should have told me in what condition a doctor sends patients to be embalmed.

The doctor hired me on the spot, seven dollars a week full-time, Monday through Friday. The pay was awful, I thought. I got more than that per day at the studio. But maybe pay for "steady work" increased with time? The first day I arrived while he was pumping out a patient's sinuses. He handed me a bowl that quickly filled with blood. I fainted dead away. The next day he took me in a dark room to show me how to examine X rays. It turned out *I* was the one being examined. When I objected, he slipped his hand under my skirt and said, "You told me you wanted to be a writer. Well, you can't write about life if you don't experience it!"

I raced him to the door, rushed past four startled patients in the waiting room, and ran all the way home to the academy. Once there I began dialing Central Casting frantically. Obviously, I wasn't cut out for work in the real world of normal people.

A few days later Mrs. Shirley told me I had a call. Thinking it might be a job from Central, I rushed in and snatched up the phone. "It's Gordon!" said the caller.

I was thunderstruck. By this time I had all but made up my mind to put "the great love of my life" behind me as a mistake.

As the months apart had passed, I found I missed Gordon less and less. I was also humiliated and miffed to learn from Louise that on all those weekend double dates he had blithely let Jack Keller pick up our tabs. I had begun to hope Gordon would continue trouping through Texas as a member of

Harley Sadler's tent show for the rest of his life. Now we had to come to terms.

The following day, with as much dignity as I could muster, I led Gordon past endless corridors of giant Rinso, Campbell's soup, and Kotex cartons to the neat little room with a real bed, a window with curtains, and even a door, which I had fixed up as my own. As the somewhat chastened Gordon told it, he had not won a single joust in his year of charging Broadway windmills. His arduous weeks of barnstorming as a member of Harley Sadler's shabby repertoire company had in fact been the high point of the whole experience. But, exuding charm, he swore he still loved me deeply, and most of all, he had a dream. What he really wanted to do now was be a producer. He knew I had long wanted to establish a new identity as a writer and composer and had talked of someday writing and staging a musical.

Try though I might to dodge, I found the lure he tossed out irresistible. On my summer trip to Wyoming I had written a new song entitled "The Land That God Remembers." He asked me to sing it for him. The next time he called, he brought along the rough draft of a musical whose story was built around the title and the song. Tempted by the new horizons that a successful musical might open up for me, I was easily hoist on my own petard.

Over the next few months we hammered out the book, a play within a play set on a Wyoming dude ranch. The cast of New York urbanites is transported to imbibe the proper Western ambiance for their upcoming musical. I wrote five new songs. We hired a gifted, out-of-work arranger and cast a former child actress with a pleasing soprano in the female lead. I played the second girl lead and singer, while Gordon was cast as the producer. The work was painfully slow, for neither of us had the cash to cover the costly union wages demanded by musicians, stagehands, and actors. Then we hit upon the idea of staging it as a benefit for the Religious Science youth group to which we belonged. As a nonprofit operation the play acquired a host of monetary advantages.

During all that summer, I survived on nothing more than half a tuna sandwich and half a chocolate malt a day, split with Gordon, while we rehearsed relentlessly from morning to night. I also tried desperately to "demonstrate supply," the way Lela and Ginger Rogers had done with Christian Science.

I did everything the experts advised—even rigging up an indoor clothesline, pinning green ten-dollar bills to it, and staring at them until I began to "think green," the way the "supply people" said to do, even though I felt like a fool doing it. But nothing worked for me. I seemed to have a black thumb where money was concerned. Finally Gordon's older brother found an abandoned car and gave it to him. That must be it, I thought: I had finally "demonstrated" wheels! Of course the car was a wreck whose brakes were completely shot, but Gordon quickly mastered the art of turning right at every red light when he couldn't stop, a trick that saved our lives on more than one occasion.

Sometimes I wondered how I had ever gotten myself involved in such a wild and perilous scheme. But when I heard the orchestra rehearsing the beautifully arranged overture featuring my own half-dozen highly singable tunes, I knew it was worth all the grief. It was a damn good musical.

Propinquity and a shared goal soon bridged the gulf that distance had put between us, and in August of 1938, Gordon surprised me with a diamond engagement ring. I burst into tears, not tears of joy, but of anger and anxiety. "Every dime we can lay our hands on has to go into staging this show," I cried as we sat together in the front seat of his car. "I won't let you spend two hundred and twenty dollars on something so—so useless as a ring!"

Although I made him take the ring back to the jeweler, he leaked news of our engagement to reporters. I had to rush out and buy a fifty-cent lookalike in the nearest dime store with which to deceive photographers who turned up for the story.

Gordon insisted that the publicity generated by our engagement would help publicize the show. He was right. Like so many Hollywood celebrity stories, this one hit all the local papers, and because Baby Peggy's name provided an added dollop of nostalgia, it got widespread national coverage as well. Finding myself trapped, I was forced to make a public commitment I had not yet made privately. I felt the slope growing slippery beneath me, but we had sold hundreds of dollars' worth of tickets and I knew there was simply no turning back now.

34

Recalling now how superstitious I was at nineteen, I marvel that I managed to convince myself 1938 would be the lucky breakthrough year for my adult career. Certainly my blind optimism was severely dampened by a train of lawsuits taking place in the Los Angeles courts that spring, summer, and fall. These trials not only exposed the rank injustice done to trusting minors in the name of parental love, they also brought tragic endings to several child-star careers. Baby Peggy's early success having served as a false beacon to some of the greedy parents involved, I felt responsible for much of what these famous innocents were going through, but was powerless to help. As opening night approached—and with it my *third* comeback try—it seemed to me some evil gypsy witch must have cast a blanket curse upon our kind.

Over the years Hollywood was home to a large number of talented, hard-working screen children—Junior Coghlan, Muriel McCormick, Baby Marie Osborne, and a popular second generation of Our Gang. However, the first child to challenge the immense popularity of Jackie Coogan and Baby Peggy did not appear until 1931, when ten-year-old Jackie Cooper soared to stardom in *The Champ*. Around the same time six-year-old Dickie Moore rose from the Gang's ranks to star in a remake of Coogan's silent hit *Oliver Twist*. Still, a child-star mania of the magnitude and intensity that had surrounded Jackie and me in the twenties did not occur again until 1934, when Shirley Temple burst upon the screen. With her arrival public adoration of child stars once again became a worldwide phenomenon, and every major studio had to have one.

MGM had an entire stable of them in Mickey, Judy, Freddie Bartholomew, and Jackie Cooper. Fox had Shirley Temple and Jane Withers, Paramount boasted Virginia Weidler, Edith Fellows starred at Columbia, and Deanna Durbin's box-office magic was bringing Universal back from the brink of bankruptcy. But 1938 also proved to be the year when movie parents, not content with fame's reflected glory, began laying claim to their famous childrens' fortunes as well.

On April 11, 1938, twenty-three-year-old Jackie Coogan, not having inherited his fortune from himself as promised when he turned twenty-one, stunned a Los Angeles superior court by bringing a landmark lawsuit against his mother and business manager–stepfather, Arthur Bernstein, to recover his $4 million in childhood earnings. This was one of the most sensational, and bizarre, legal battles in Hollywood's long litigious history.

Jackie was goaded on by his new bride, Betty Grable, who gushed to the press, "Gee, I thought I'd married a millionaire. But the 'Millionaire Kid' didn't have enough to take me out dancing, let alone get married."

So, while the young newlyweds scraped to make ends meet, the Bernsteins lived lavishly in the mansion Jackie's millions had built, with two Rolls-Royces in the garage. Jackie said Bernstein bet heavily on the ponies and routinely charged his losses to "the corporation." He also accused his stepfather of appropriating (and still wearing) a twenty-five-hundred-dollar wristwatch given the young star by an admirer.

"Jackie has all that he is entitled to, and more," Bernstein snapped to reporters, citing the old common law in force in England *and* California. "He's been given food, shelter, clothes, private schooling, and college over the years, but he will not get one cent of . . . his past earnings. Lawyers tell [us] every dollar a kid earns before he's twenty-one . . . belongs to his parents." Jackie was still receiving from the Coogan Corporation a $6.50-a-week allowance begun when he was a child. On his twenty-first birthday Bernstein handed him a check for $1,000, and advised him his weekly pittance was being cut off! The press was aghast.

It came to light that the late Jack Coogan had been every bit as cavalier as Bernstein where Jackie was concerned. He bought himself a ranch near San Diego and lived well while his son had neither money nor an ounce of training on how to handle it. Totally dependent on the manager of the Jackie Coogan Corporation, all his life Jackie had clung to the belief that because his father loved him so, he had established a secret trust fund not yet found. The bombshell of the trial was the revelation that Jack Senior had not put away a penny for Jackie but had willed everything to his flighty wife instead.

The elder Coogan, while publicly touting his son's "boy genius" status on-screen, had gone out of his way to tell reporters what a dolt he was when it came to money. Long before the trial, I had often wondered if the elder Coogan's public statements were not simply red herrings intended for later use in discrediting Jackie's right to be given his own money.

I had never forgotten the night the Coogans were visiting us at our Laurel Canyon home and Jack Coogan, standing by the fireplace, drink in hand, announced to my father, "By the way, Jack, Arthur Bernstein told me another of his wonderful Jewish stories today."

I had been allowed to stay up for their before-dinner cocktails and sat on the stairs in my Doctor Denton pajamas. I liked it when my parents had guests and everyone was laughing and telling jokes. At least they weren't fighting.

"There's this Jewish merchant, see," Coogan began, "and his little four-year-old son, Abie. 'Abie,' he tells the kid, 'I want you should be a sharp businessman when you grow up. So for your first lesson you stand up here on the mantel and jump into my arms.' 'But Papa,' says Abie, getting scared, 'what if I fall?' " At this point Coogan picked up an invisible child and stood him on the mantelpiece. " 'You won't fall, Abie. Trust me, I'm your father; I'll catch you!' "

Dramatically Coogan held out his arms for the catch, crying, " 'Jump, Abie!' " at which point he stepped back abruptly. "So the kid jumps and smashes on the floor, screaming and crying. 'But Papa,' Abie wails, 'you promised to catch me!' 'Aha!' says his old man. 'That's the first lesson! In business don't even trust your own father!' "

The memory of that story came back to me sharply, and knowing all the parties involved in this trial made it doubly painful for me to follow. I knew Lillian Coogan was hardly the spartan mother she painted herself in court, willing to go through fire for her son. Snatched from her former obscure role of self-abnegating vaudeville wife and mother, she had found spending Jackie's earnings as delectable as spending the day in bed with a box of chocolates.

As for Bernstein, he was an opportunist, a dapper gent who had come out of New York's garment district. He had a way with vain, imperceptive women. One night at a large dinner party at the Coconut Grove in 1923, before being hired as Jackie's manager, he maneuvered my own mother onto the dance floor and asked her to let him manage Baby Peggy's career. I had not yet signed with Sol Lesser, and Mother, dazzled by Arthur's charm and Midas touch, tried to persuade Father to hire him. Jealous as always, Father felt Arthur was only trying to seduce her and so refused. Arthur went by default to the Coogans.

Back in 1928 Bernstein and Mrs. Coogan had earned unsavory headlines when Arthur's wife demanded and got $750,000 of Jackie's money as compensation for losing her husband to Lillian. However, it must be said to his credit, Arthur had invested shrewdly in real estate and steered the Jackie Coogan Corporation safely through the treacherous shoals of the depression. Given the doubtful fiscal acumen of vaudevillians Lillian and Jack, without Arthur I'm sure there would have been no more of a Jackie Coogan fortune to fight over than there was a Baby Peggy one.

Jackie finally settled his case out of court for a paltry $126,000, one half of all that was left of his $4 million. For me that seemed a king's ransom, but to Jackie, accustomed to thinking of himself as a multimillionaire, it spelled financial ruin. He suffered a sudden loss of adult identity from which he never quite recovered.

Years later, when Jackie appeared in the television documentary *Hollywood's Children*, based on my book of the same name, he divulged to a reporter for the first time a behind-the-scenes incident that had taken place during that trial. Louis B. Mayer, who had paid Jackie twenty thousand dollars a week as a child, called him into his office in 1938 and offered to give him a new contract at twenty-five hundred dollars a week. Desperate for both work and money, Jackie accepted.

"But there's one stipulation," Mayer added sternly. "You must drop this shameful lawsuit against your mother. No red-blooded American boy ever sues his own mother!"

"But that's impossible, sir," Jackie explained. "My lawyers are handling it on a contingency basis."

Mayer rose from his desk like a wrathful Jehovah. "Get out of my office, you little son of a bitch!" he thundered, throwing open his office door. "I'll see to it you never work at any studio in this town ever again!" His curse held good for decades, or until Mayer himself was no longer a universally feared figure in the industry.

While the Coogan trial was still in the headlines, Mother telephoned me at the Shirleys'. I had not heard from either of my parents for some time and wondered what prompted her call. "Well, I suppose you've been following the Coogan case?" Mother asked with undisguised sarcasm.

"Well, yes I have," I replied cautiously. "I think it's terribly sad—for everyone concerned."

"I suppose the next thing your father and I know, you'll be bringing a similar suit against us. Is that what you have in the back of your mind?"

I was more hurt than shocked. Louise had never held her tongue with them when coming to my defense, but not once in my life had I ever made a disparaging remark to either of them about my money. In fact, during a *New York Times* interview earlier that year, I had invented a spur-of-the-moment lie when asked if they had wantonly misspent my millions. I covered for them by telling the reporter Father had invested all my earnings in the stock market and we were wiped out by the crash. Although Father had distrusted stocks and wisely refused to risk a penny in the market, the moment he and Mother read that alibi in print they made it their own and quoted it as gospel for the rest of their lives.

In early summer, fourteen-year-old Freddie Bartholomew appeared in court before the same judge who had just presided over the Coogan trial. Freddie was asking relief from a battery of "commissions" he was being made to pay his family out of his weekly salary. His aunt Cassie had brought him to Hollywood from his native England in 1934 when he was ten. He won instant acclaim for his work in the title role of MGM's *David Copperfield*. But money being a great lure, his parents *and* grandparents followed him to Hollywood, seeking what they felt was their piece of the pie. All four relatives sued Freddie, his aunt, and each other, each laying claim to huge portions of the diligent child's earnings. His two older sisters, whom their father claimed were "way ahead of him [Freddie] in looks," also sued their famous brother for moneys they claimed he owed them and had never paid.

Freddie told the judge he had been in court an average of twice a month ever since 1934 and that an ungodly twenty-seven separate lawsuits had been filed against him. By 1938 he was spending half of every day in court: MGM suspended him for "nonperformance" and replaced him in several major films. His family's naked avarice, combined with lawyers' fees, demolished his brilliant career and consumed the million-dollar fortune he had earned in his four years at MGM.

During this same season of courtroom dramas, my old friend from Lawlor's, Edith Fellows, was dragged into court by yet another loving parent, her mother, the woman who had abandoned her in infancy. Edith's paternal grandmother had raised her and started her in movies at the age of four. Now in her teens she was a star, earning a substantial one thousand dollars a week. The mother appeared unannounced at Edith's door, asking for custody of "my own flesh and blood" and charging Edith's grandmother with the federal crime of kidnapping. Like Freddie, Edith spent her mornings at the studio, her afternoons in court. Although the mother failed to win either custody of Edith or revenge against her grandmother, Edith never recovered from the emotional trauma; the court costs and lawyers' fees wiped out her savings.

Opening night of *The Land That God Remembers* at the Wilshire-Ebell Theater was positively harrowing. Due to a critical lack of money, crisis piled upon crisis, and minutes before curtain time we still had not come up with the $125 the manager was demanding for one night's rental of his theater. I was near despair. At 8:15 we were still holding the curtain. At the last minute of the eleventh hour Gordon's older brother rushed through the stage door with the rental fee, which he had raised by selling off his stock in a gold mine somewhere out by Victorville. It looked for all the world like the finale of one of Mickey and Judy's MGM musicals in which they "put on the show!" but in real life it was not amusing.

At last the twenty-piece orchestra struck up the overture, and the full melodic strains of my own compositions, beautifully arranged, filled the theater. I was so giddy from anxiety, hunger, and excitement, I seemed to float rather than walk. Among many Lawlor schoolmates out front were Mickey Rooney, who was celebrating his eighteenth birthday by buying an entire block of tickets for himself and his friends. Elsie Janis was also present, and had already sent a touching opening-night telegram: "Peggy dear, love to you and the boy and great success tonight."

Gordon and I had visited Elsie the week before in her Beverly Hills home to tell her about the play. Having read about our engagement, she openly encouraged our marriage plans. It was a show-business legend that Elsie had fallen in love with her leading man in London during the First World War, but Jenny persuaded her not to marry until war's end. In 1917 this young man was killed in France and Elsie never got over his loss. A movie entitled *Mother Knows Best* was based on Elsie's stormy spinster life with Jenny.

The play was well received by a packed house opening night, and morning-after reviews were equally favorable.

"Musical drama contains many excellent songs," was *Variety*'s unexpected praise. "Peggy Montgomery, the Baby Peggy of yesterday's screen, conveyed a natural performance as the girl of the West. . . . Play is studded with five singable tunes. Title song stands out."

To the degree that I could feel anything after the weeks of near-starvation and emotional cliff-hanging we had just been through, such fine reviews by tough critics in the leading trade papers seemed heaven-sent. But what we needed most was money. Gordon had spent all the revenue from ticket sales on production costs, gasoline, and other necessities. As we were unable to raise another night's rent for a second performance, opening night proved to be closing night as well.

We had stalled off inquiring reporters by saying October 19 would be our wedding day. Gordon kept assuring me we would be able to go through with it, but as that day neared he couldn't afford a sprig of parsley, let alone a wedding bouquet. Maybe, I thought uneasily, whatever gods there might be were trying to tell me something. Maybe I wasn't supposed to marry Gordon after all. I had never been all that sure. And I was terrified of making the same mistakes my parents had made.

When our so-called wedding day finally dawned, I realized Gordon's publicity stunt had backfired. Fortunately for him, he was safely inside his parents' home: I was the one having to deal with the reporters who had my phone number, and I was the world's least convincing liar. Three charter pilots called to advise me they were warming up their planes to "fly you to Las Vegas or Yuma at a minute's notice!" Jimmy Fidler wanted a radio interview. Louella Parsons wanted a quote. Emotionally confused and physically exhausted, I came down with a severe case of bronchial pneumonia and collapsed.

The following day Father came to call. He and Mother had seen the show on opening night and liked it. But as usual they both took it grandly for granted that I could write the music and most of the book, and cast, produce, direct, rehearse, stage, and star in a musical with no one to show me how! But seeing how genuinely ill I was, Father began persuading me to come back home.

Despite the Shirleys' best intentions and their boundless charity to me, living with them was like being trapped inside an enormous unmade bed. Mother had always been a neat-as-a-pin housekeeper and trained us to be as well. After a year of occupancy by the Shirleys, the once spruced-up academy was reverting to its former state of ruin. Louise and I had staged seasonal housecleaning safaris, washing windows and floors and driving herds of giant dust mice before us. But Louise had married Jack in the spring, and I didn't have the strength to tackle such a daunting task alone.

That wedding had produced a major crisis. After serving as maid of honor, I had gone up to Hollywood to spend the rest of the day with my parents, trying to make peace between them and Louise. Their reaction to her marriage reached truly Wagnerian heights. Mother wept and raged, claiming Louise had "married beneath her." Father ranted against Louise for having committed the unforgivable sin of marrying a "Catholic plumber!" They vowed they would never speak to her again as long as they lived, and for the next six months they kept their word. I certainly knew what was in store for me if I ever married Gordon—or any other man for that matter. The only way to do it would be against their will.

But sick as I was, I once again thought fate was taking a hand in my life to save me from marrying in haste. I knew I needed rest and a quiet time to think. Father explained that he and Mother were back together again and had moved into a nice, new apartment. He said they wanted a second chance "to make a real home" for me, and doing so would make them both very happy.

I was touched. I had always tried to do everything to secure their happiness. Upon reflection, I decided I probably hadn't been the best daughter in the world and perhaps I really did owe them—and myself—a second try.

PART 7

1938 – 1953

REAL
TEARS

35

I n the front upper bedroom of a multiroomed 1920s California bungalow on Orchid Avenue, just two blocks north of Hollywood Boulevard, I prepared our one meal of the day. Rooming-house tenants were forbidden to cook in their rooms, but the landlady bent the rule for me because I was collaborating on a musical comedy with Greg Fisher, her teenage son, who was a gifted pianist and composer. My dinner of creamed canned tuna almost never varied, not only because I wasn't much of a cook but because it was cheap and, served over toast, went a long way. It could also be cooked in a skillet set on a square-topped electric toaster, which did double duty as the stove I did not have.

Glancing at the calendar on the wall, I saw it was March of 1941. My thoughts went back over the past three years—years of constant hunger, penury, and living on the jagged edge of survival in a marriage that ran the gamut from unstable to harrowing. My thoughts began moving in circles until I was back at the beginning of everything again.

After I accepted Father's offer and returned to live with my parents in the late fall of 1938, the truce held for two months, primarily because I knuckled under to the regimen Father immediately imposed upon me in exchange for this modicum of security. While all three of us worked extra and my earnings went into the common purse, his word remained law. "As long as you're living under my roof . . ." went the familiar preamble to his firmly autocratic code. I was forbidden to see or date Gordon and was to use this time to meet other young men. While that was an arbitrary rule to impose on a twenty-year-old woman, I was willing to accept it to keep the peace. Whenever we talked on the telephone, Gordon kept insisting he wanted us to marry as soon as he was able to find steady work, but I still felt that being apart and thinking things through might be time well spent.

Father pressed me to date stalwart, handsome, square-jawed Tom Hart, his hands-down choice for me, despite a shipwrecked marriage that had just ended in divorce. Tom worked as a carpenter at Republic Studio, but since he had grown up on a ranch, knew how to ride, and was Neal Hart's son, Father naturally gave him high marks. Besides, Father insisted all the other young men in Hollywood were either "gutless extras or flaming fags!"

On our first date I discovered Tom was badly scarred by his upbringing at the hands of a famous, very likable man who happened to be a despotic father, living out a wretched marriage. Although I sympathized with Tom's problems, there was no mental or sexual chemistry between us. But overriding our own feelings, both willful fathers (failed husbands themselves) knew what was best for two bolty colts whose congenital wrongheadedness demanded they be broken.

In early December I visited Louise in Venice to shop for Christmas gifts. At day's end, too loaded down to return by bus in the dark, I called Gordon at his parents' Venice home to ask if he would drive me back up to Hollywood. He was pleased to hear from me, and since we had not seen each other for nearly three months, the long drive would give us a chance to catch up on our separate lives. I was careful to phone Father first, explaining that Gordon was bringing me home as a courtesy, not as a date. He said he understood.

But when we drove up to the apartment house, Father was waiting at the curb, his emotions out of control, his temper at flash point. Our violent confrontation, lit by the bright spot of a streetlight, was classic melodrama.

Father challenged Gordon to fisticuffs, and when Gordon declined, he began hurling thunderbolts at me. "All right," he intoned, "promise me right here and now you'll *never* see this man again!"

"Don't push me too far, Father," I warned him boldly, although I was shaking from head to foot. All at once I realized I had to stand my ground: I was locked in a long-delayed battle of wills. Suddenly I saw my father as a badly spoiled, insanely jealous manipulator who was maddened by the prospect of losing control. For him, this match was to mark the ultimate triumph of his hypnotic power over me, irrefutable proof he could still bring even a rebellious Baby Peggy to heel. For me it was a last-ditch stand, a life-and-death battle to reclaim the separate self I had forfeited to him without conscious fiat in my earliest days at Century.

"Don't force my hand," I told him steadily, "because you'll regret it. If I go this time, I'll never come back!"

"You'll do as I say!" he commanded. "Either you stay with me or go off with him. Make up your mind between us."

I piled my stack of gaily wrapped holiday packages on the curb. "You can take these upstairs to Mother," I said tonelessly. Turning on my heel, I walked back to the car. Years later I learned from Mother that he told her nothing about our confrontation, so she lay awake all that night thinking I had been in a car crash. It was not until the next morning that he confessed what he had done.

As we drove away, Gordon fixed me with a bewildered questioning expression. "So, what do we do now?" he asked shakily.

Eyes straight ahead, I said, "We'll do what you've been saying we should do all along—get married!" Then, smiling bravely, the way Myrna Loy always did in those depression movies, I added resolutely, "And don't worry about money. We'll live on love." Bemused and heady with the realization that I had broken Father's psychic grip on me, I mistakenly thought I had also finally turned the spigot on Lela and Ginger's golden pipeline to limitless supply.

Gordon's mother, who had always been fond of me, even when we disagreed about Mount Shasta being a hollow hall for Ascended Master rallies, gave me sanctuary in her home. Gordon and I applied for a marriage license in Santa Monica and were met by a crowd of photographers who appeared from out of nowhere. When the pictures hit the papers, Father began a barrage of phone calls. His rage intensified with my steadfast refusal to obey his orders not to marry and to return home at once.

Gordon's family gave us enough money to get married. A Christian minister Mrs. Shirley knew performed the ceremony in his living room. No one stood up with us, not even Louise. The minister's wife, in bathrobe, slippers, and curlers, was our only witness. I was clammy with dread, thoroughly convinced Father would arrive any minute with a police escort and a lawyer carrying some kind of legal paper that would nullify the marriage before we said "I do."

I had good reason to be fearful, for earlier that morning he had called me, incandescent with rage, and this time his fury turned venomous. Trying to defuse his apoplectic anger, I finally asked tremulously, "But Father, don't you have some wedding-day wish for me?"

"Yes I do!" he shouted. *"I hope you give birth to blind quintuplets!"*

It was a miserable day, and a worrisome night, in a vacant cabin in Calabasas which Mr. Shirley had ferreted out at the last minute as a kind of wedding gift. As I should have known, with poor Mr. Shirley having had a hand in it, this ramshackle so-called honeymoon cottage turned out to be as bare and cold as a line-rider's camp, with a small kerosene stove to cook dinner on and a springless pull-down bed with only three legs.

The long-awaited bliss of the marriage bed, promised a bride who had steadfastly remained a virgin against considerable odds, was completely overshadowed by the awful fear that I might get pregnant right away and Father would swear we had been living together all along. Upon awaking next morning to face making breakfast over weak kerosene flames, I was given a preview of the future with my new husband.

"We'll have to leave right away for the long drive to Fresno," he announced matter-of-factly over coffee.

"Fresno?" (God, I thought, isn't Calabasas bad enough!) I managed a chuckle. "So what's your joke about Fresno?"

"Oh, it's not a joke. I guess I forgot to tell you. I've booked us into a DeMolay pre-Christmas Tin Can Drive in the big Fresno High School Auditorium there." He rolled the school's name off as if it were Madison Square Garden.

"Fresno! On our honeymoon?" I cried in disbelief. "Without even asking me?" Then, attempting a more conciliatory tone, I ventured, "And we'll be doing . . . what for an act?"

"Anything." He shrugged. "Who cares? Just so they can run ads in the paper and headline the benefit with 'Baby Peggy, In Person!' " He took a deep breath. "Besides, we'll get paid ten bucks each for just one show."

We ended up doing an unrehearsed and embarrassingly slipshod version of the Lambeth Walk, a current dance craze. Having always striven to be strictly professional, I suffered this indignity in silence. But when reporters from the school paper and the local press appeared backstage, I cringed.

"You used to be so cute!" the girl reporter breathed. "My, how you've changed!" The student cub asked what happened to my career, where my money went, and did I plan to appear in more plays "written by your famous playwright husband?"

I choked down the terrible rage I felt toward Gordon for exposing the very self he knew I was trying to bury, and for a lousy ten dollars at that. How dare he conjure up Baby Peggy's ghost just to get himself mentioned in the papers? By taking my husband's name I thought I had become a new person, but now it seemed he intended to keep the other "me" around forever to use whenever he needed a cheap headline-grabber. God, I thought despairingly, will I have to go through life as "Mrs. Baby Peggy"?

Now don't lose your temper, I lectured myself. Most of all, never argue or utter an angry word. That was what you just escaped, remember? You promised yourself there would be no fighting if you ever got a home of your own.

For twenty-eight dollars a month we rented a minuscule bungalow court set in a bean field in West Hollywood. Gordon got hired as a bartender in one of the best key clubs on La Cienega's posh Restaurant Row. Bartending suited him: it was a trade he regarded as an offscreen extension of show business. Here he could hobnob with famous stars over drinks, on what he considered an equal footing. This job unveiled another difference between us. I was a day person: Gordon bloomed at night. He left home in the mornings at nine and, due to his convivial nocturnal nature, rarely got home before 3:00 or 4:00 A.M.

I finally tried getting up at two, dressing festively, and meeting him at the door with soft lights burning and a pot of hot Ovaltine. This way we could spend at least half an hour together out of the twenty-four. Not surprisingly this tack baffled him. ("Hot Ovaltine at three in the morning?" he must have asked himself. "After three martinis? She's got to be kidding.")

In the spring of 1939, Gordon became night manager of a swank Beverly Hills bar with a raise in pay. We rented a brand-new unfurnished apartment in Westwood. A fellow barman could no longer meet the payments on his houseful of cheap furniture, so we bought it simply by agreeing to pay off the remaining installments. This windfall included a beautiful floor Magnavox radio with a marvelous tone. Now at last I could listen to symphonies to my heart's content.

To my further delight I rented a used upright piano for only $10 a month, the rental payments going toward the purchase price of $125. The day the movers brought it I was ecstatic. Through Gordon's mother I located a piano teacher and cut every possible corner to pay for my lessons, three times a week. By practicing ten and twelve hours a day I was soon able to pick out my own melodies on the keyboard. Composing my first symphony could not be far off.

With my circumstances improved I invited my parents over to dinner and they came several times. It was made easier since Gordon was never home. At first Father was somewhat stiff and formal, but he gradually grew more mellow. Mother often invited me to go shopping with her and to a movie. After all these years, they were still her favorite pastimes.

Then, without warning, Gordon lost his job. He never told me why. Now we could no longer afford our apartment or meet the furniture payments. I gave all the furniture to the Shirleys, except for my treasured lifeline to sanity, the Magnavox. But the most painful loss I had endured since the sheriff's sale of the ranch was having two burly movers repossess my piano when I was only a few installments short of making it mine.

"What will you do now?" Father asked.

"Move into a rooming house for a while until things get better," I replied stoically.

"You'd better come home with us until Gordon can keep a decent roof over your head and put food on the table."

I looked at him unflinchingly. "If I were a woman willing to desert her husband when he's down, you wouldn't want me for a daughter."

He dropped his gaze.

36

Gordon and I had been married a little over a year when we moved into our eighteen-dollar-a-month single room, sharing a communal telephone and a hall bath with three other tenants. The room's single luxury was a large balcony, but the view to the south overlooked the rear of Grauman's Chinese Theater and the Hollywood Hotel, while on the dark hills to the north stood the Hollywood sign. I found both views grimly depressing, but I tried to look at the sunny side. My landlady was pushing her teenage son's musical career, and since I now knew I would probably never become a composer myself, I enjoyed working with Greg at his baby grand downstairs.

One morning at sunup, shortly after we moved in, someone began pounding on our door. I jumped out of bed, threw on a robe, and admitted two strangers, agents from some credit bureau, who stormed in. They glanced around the room until their eyes lit upon my treasured Magnavox. Over my tearful pleas, they carried it off between them. I was desolate.

Gordon found work in a cheap neighborhood bar called the Arabian Room. There, over a tumbler of watered bar whiskey, a slick entrepreneur told him he'd invented a magic skin cream with a turtle oil base which made wrinkles vanish on contact. Over his second drink the man said he was displaying his product in sharp-looking cosmetic jars in a show window on Santa Monica Boulevard, but sales were slow.

"You know what I need? I need promotion. I need a scriptwriter to come up with a radio serial idea I can sponsor. A *Helen Trent* sort of thing, aimed at women listeners who buy cosmetics, but you know—different." Growing more loquacious over his third drink, he continued. "I need a writer who's willing to work cheap."

When Gordon came home that night, he told me about the man, simply as a good example of local color. But like a bolt from on high I realized that my interest in historical biographies was about to pay off. "He needs a series featuring women heroines through the ages!" I cried. "Joan of Arc, Empress Josephine, Charlotte Corday—I know them all!"

Although I was twenty-one, I looked sixteen and was still a dead ringer for myself as a child. The moment I was introduced as Peggy anything, every stranger I met responded with, "Why, *you're* Baby Peggy!' " Now, preparing to write a series of radio dramas under the general title *Cavalcade of Women*, I thought the name Peggy ranked with Mitzi as being better suited to a chorus girl than a serious writer. I decided Diana had a true air of dignity about it.

When Gordon introduced me to the turtle oil man as Diana Ayres, he never showed a flicker of recognition. I liked that! The man liked my idea too and promised to pay $150 for every script he used. I set to work at my portable typewriter with a vengeance. Later he said I could star in the series for another $75 a script. I had handed in my fifth episode, on the cuff, and was waiting for his acceptance and my pay when Gordon came home from work with terrible news. The Santa Monica Boulevard show window was for rent, the cream jars were gone, and the turtle oil man had flown, taking with him all my not-yet-paid-for episodes of *Cavalcade of Women*.

The same way vultures can spot a dying man in the desert, so out-of-pocket actors always seemed able to find someone in Hollywood who, no matter how down on their luck, was faring a shade better than themselves. Once word got around that Diana ran a clandestine one-dish eatery in her room, starving actors who found creamed tuna haute cuisine started turning up for dinner.

One of these was an out-of-work young man named Gerry, whom Gordon had met back in New York. One day he dropped by unexpectedly when Gordon was at work.

"Diana, how can you bear to live in such terrible financial straits and still keep love alive?" he asked.

"Oh, it won't always be like this," I said, loyally running up my ever-ready battle flag in Gordon's defense. "I'm hoping one day I can convince Gordon to take a steady job at one of these new aircraft factories springing up all around L.A. . . ." This was an attractive alternative to chronic hunger which I was beginning to press for strongly.

"Actually, Peggy—I mean Diana—I need your help," he said, changing the subject abruptly. "You see, I've got a chance to get a big splash in Winchell's column but I need an angle. Why, a mention there could land me my big break. You know, change my whole life!"

"I don't know Walter Winchell," I replied cagily, mentally backing off from what I smelled as trouble.

"Oh, you don't need to know him. I met his legman today and he told me if I could link myself to someone with a big name, he'd get me in. For example, I *could* say I was an old New York buddy of Gordon Ayres, who is now married to former child star Baby Peggy. That's all I'd need. And dropping your name there might even help you and Gordon get a break."

I felt sorry for Gerry. He had taken us out for dinner a few nights before, a five-cent bowl of half-moldy chili and beans each at the Owl Drugstore on the Boulevard. It may have been his last fifteen cents. "Oh, I have no real objection, Gerry, if it will help you. But be careful not to mention where or—well, *how* we're living right now. I know columnists. They make their living finding juicy stories."

"Oh, I understand, Diana. Jeez, you know I wouldn't hurt you for the world."

Two days later LaVerne, who lived across the hall and earned an honest living doubling as a freelance typist and call girl, knocked on my door when I was alone. I welcomed her in. "Look, kid, I don't think you're going to like this," she said, handing me the evening paper, "but you'd better see it anyway." LaVerne was the original good-hearted whore and didn't need to have anyone tell her we were having a struggle staying alive. She often brought me free groceries whenever she'd had a good night with a generous high roller. "You're in Winchell's column," she said flatly.

Glancing down the folded page, I read to myself aloud: "Two former child stars, now husband and wife, have been living in a small furnished room with only doughnuts to eat. They are Peggy Montgomery, once the famous Baby

Peggy, and Gordon Ayres, one of the original members of Our Gang. An actor friend recently hitchhiked to Hollywood and bought the couple breakfast with his last dollar. Mr. Ayres has landed a bartender job . . . while their young actor friend [he mentioned Gerry here, his full name, in caps!] and Peggy look for screen jobs. Surely the Hollywood casters will do something about these people?????"

One look at my face and LaVerne discreetly disappeared. I was aghast at Gerry's deliberate treachery and only wished to God I had Helen Robey's rich store of obscenities to help express my rage. Furious, hurt, and humiliated to the very marrow of my bones, I strode around the room like a charging bull, repeatedly stalking over and across both beds.

Always the peacemaker, I absolutely never gave vent to anger, afraid of what it might do to an already rocky marriage. Unable to direct anger at anyone else, I now turned it inward, not against myself but against the one who was ultimately the cause of all my problems—Baby Peggy. *She* had started it all, *she* was the one who kept it going! Not Father or Gordon or the traitorous turtle oil man, only my other self was the cause of all my woes. For those few moments she became actually tangible to me. Oh, how I longed to get rid of that child, murder her if need be, somehow drive her out of my life.

After years of living on charity baskets and the handouts of friends, both in and out of the industry, two years of eating stale day-old bread at the Shirleys' (only two cents at the bakery instead of ten), and having the Religious Science group leave a "holiday basket" at our door the first Christmas Gordon and I were married, my pride was raw and bleeding, and being in the public spotlight as an object of pity only made it worse. The private pain was bad enough.

Mother and Emma Burroughs often went out together these days for drinks, luncheon, and shopping in Emma's chauffeured limousine. Emma was heartbroken and lonely after being discarded by Ed for a younger wife, even though he settled a mint of money on her. One day when I wasn't at home, the two of them found my door unlocked (a common trustful practice in those days) and left six pretty, brand-new dresses with a card from Emma saying they were a gift from her. Knowing she must have heard my sad story from Mother over cocktails, I sent them back, with thanks and a note saying my husband was quite able to provide my clothes. (He wasn't, of course, which made returning the dresses twice as hard to do.)

For years the only gift I could afford to give anyone for Christmas or birthdays were two gift-wrapped bars of Lux Soap. In return for my posing for a big Lux ad back in 1932, Lux had deposited gratis a carton of twelve bars on my doorstep every month for years without fail, no matter how often I moved. To me the sharp perfume of Lux was the very scent of poverty. For all these reasons, fresh exposure to pity hit an already badly hammered nerve.

The next morning LaVerne appeared at my door with the morning paper, folded to reveal a bold headline. I took it from her gingerly. RKO PRODUCER GIVES FORMER CHILD STAR A BREAK. In smaller print I learned that "kindhearted Gene Towne, producer of *Tom Brown's School Days*," had read Winchell's column and was giving me a part in his film.

Suddenly I was inundated with calls. Mother offered to pay up my back dues at the Screen Actor's Guild so I could accept the job at RKO. Apparently she and Father had been mortified before their extra friends and the entire industry. Everyone knew they were prospering and wondered how they could let me starve in an attic while doing so well themselves. Actually, neither had any inkling how bad things were with me, since they never came by to see me, and I was too proud to breathe a word about my circumstances to anyone.

Gene Towne's publicity man called and asked me to report to him at 11:30 the next morning at the studio. In that night's column Winchell threw "Orchids to RKO's Gene Towne," saying it was folks like him who made Hollywood the greathearted place it was, and other words to the same tune.

I arrived at RKO neatly turned out in one of those timeless New Yorker suits I had managed to keep pristine. Before keeping my appointment, I made a point of dropping in on an old friend who was head of casting at RKO. He volunteered some information vital to my coming interview. Reporting to the publicity office, I was welcomed by a Mr. Unkifer, who escorted me across the lot to the commissary, where he said we could discuss our "pleasant business over lunch."

Waiting at our table were two other men. Both said they had already eaten and Unkifer pleaded ulcers. But he signaled a waitress and ordered the sixty-five-cent blue plate special for me with all the fanfare of the biblical father ordering the fatted calf for his prodigal son.

"Now, about the part for me?" I inquired demurely.

As I took my first bite, one of the newsmen asked brusquely, "Could you tell me when you ate last?"

"How long have you been starving in that attic?" the other man inquired, pad and pencil ready.

"Just what has this got to do with my being interviewed for a part?" I asked, trying to remain outwardly calm.

"Now, Peggy, I'll be honest," Unkifer interrupted. "These gentlemen are from UPI and Associated Press and have nothing to do with the studio. I invited them to hear firsthand what an ordeal you've been through and how Mr. Towne is going to—well, make it all up to you."

I shoved the plate of greasy veal cutlets away from me and said in honeyed tones, "All right, then, let's all be honest. I found out before I even came in here that this is the last day of shooting on *Tom Brown's School Days,* with the much-touted 'big part' for me. Well, there is no part and there never was. This whole thing is a publicity stunt staged to garner headlines for your producer and his picture."

The two pressmen melted away like fog, and the formerly effusive Unkifer became glacial as he steered me toward the front gate. "Now, Peggy, you know how we do things in the picture business. After all, honey, you were raised in it. I agree, there is no part for you. But I've arranged for the cashier to give you seven-fifty for your trouble, as a special token of our appreciation." Then he added cheerily, "As you know, that's a full day's pay for an extra, and you've only been on the lot half an hour."

I was livid when I reached home and called my former agent, George Ullman, who was now in casting at MGM. After I told him my story, he was more indignant than I. "Hang on. I'm going to try and land you the part of Tondeleyo in *White Cargo,* which is coming up soon here at MGM," he volunteered. "I'll check with RKO and see what they say."

When he called me back later, he dashed any hopes I might have had. Unkifer at RKO told him Gene Towne had made a screen test of me, but I had proved to be such an "impossibly bad actress" they had to scratch me from the very promising part they had lined up for me.

"This 'screen test' story blacklists you with every studio in town," Ullman told me angrily, "because not even I can convince anyone at MGM that RKO never made a test of you at all and they're simply lying to cover their own ass."

That would have been the end of it, except Father rushed out, got a lawyer, and filed suit against RKO for five hundred thousand dollars (that magic number!). A few days later he called to tell me RKO had just offered to settle out of court for five hundred.

I thought it was wonderful. It wasn't much, but dear God, it was enough to buy back my piano and maybe even afford something else for dinner besides tuna.

"Wonderful, hell!" Father retorted. "Their lousy offer simply means we've got the bastards on the run. I'm holding out for the full five hundred thousand and we're taking them to court!" Needless to say, that courtroom drama was never played out.

There was one last unpleasant aftershock from the Winchell piece. Maurice Kosloff, a former dance director for DeMille and now owner of his own ballet academy on Hollywood Boulevard, called and asked me to come down to his studio. When I arrived, the aristocratic, silver-haired Russian émigré greeted me warmly and seated me before his imposing desk, talking across it to me in a very businesslike manner.

"I'm planning to add a children's acting school to my ballet academy," he said in his heavy Russian accent, carefully kept and cultivated over his many years in Hollywood. "I've seen a good bit in the papers about you lately"—he bent his benevolent gaze on me and allowed himself a thoughtful pause before continuing—"and I'll pay you a hundred dollars a week to serve as my head drama coach, with the right to use your name in all my advertising."

I was staggered by his generous offer. Four hundred dollars a month was a positively munificent salary in 1941.

"All you have to do is simply audition each young applicant who enrolls and then make sure you tell every mother that her kid is—well, you know . . ."—he rolled his expressive eyes grandly and spread his hands—"what else? Another Baby Peggy! A second Shirley Temple!"

I wanted and needed the money desperately, but a deep-seated compassion for people like Edith Fellows and her grandmother welled up inside of me. I simply could not turn myself into a bona fide, feather-perfect decoy and deliberately lure such hopeful innocents into what was just one more cruel Hollywood blind.

"I'm sorry, Mr. Kosloff," I said, rising to my feet, "but I simply can't bring myself to do that. I guess I'm just not hungry enough."

"Very well, then," he said coldly, his convivial mood doused, a new conniving look in his fierce black eyes. "I have other options. I can always get Jackie Coogan. I hear he's hungry too."

37

fter Hitler invaded Poland in the fall of 1939, everyone in Hollywood was filled with a sense of foreboding, convinced the United States would be drawn inevitably into the war. And yet, precisely because of that fear, Hollywood beat the drums of peace more loudly than ever. There were antiwar demonstrations and peace-in-our-time broadcasts on every hand. When France fell in June of 1940 and the Battle of Britain began, the large colony of British actors mobilized to help their embattled homeland, organizing Bundles for Britain drives and staging benefits.

Swept up in the emotion of the times, Greg Fisher and I composed a wartime ballad that we felt had as much chance to be a hit as "The Last Time I Saw Paris." Our big opportunity came when we learned a huge Bundles for Britain rally was to be staged at the Shrine Auditorium, headed by Basil Rathbone and Ronald Colman. Greg and I went down, music in hand, to audition bravely for the event which was to be broadcast overseas to the gallant Brits themselves. Mr. Colman ushered us to the piano, where Greg set the mood with a dramatic sweep of the keyboard and I lifted my voice in song.

> "Lost in the dark of London
> Under a starless sky
> The world we loved in left me
> The night you said good-bye.
> Lost in the dark of London
> Wandering here and there
> Without a light to lead me
> Along Trafalgar Square—"

At this point Ronald Colman signaled me to stop. "I'm really quite sorry," he said in his clipped British accent and heart-melting baritone. "It really is a hauntingly beautiful ballad, but you see the whole idea of this broadcast is to cheer up the poor chaps over there, especially the civilians in bomb shelters. I'm afraid this song would—well, may I say, tempt them to throw in the towel!"

One sure sign of impending war was the proliferation of aircraft factories in Southern California. Thin as a rail, weak from years of constant hunger, and desperate for some kind of security, I began pleading with Gordon to give up bartending and apply for one of the good-paying jobs with McDonnell-Douglas. He was as adamant as I was insistent. It might have ended in a stalemate if Father had not entered into a partnership with a Mr. Hampton, a local radio entertainer, to lease a dude ranch in Montana for the summer. Hampton put up the lease money and Father the ranching know-how. Aware of my financial plight, and himself anxious to cut costs, Father offered summer jobs to both Gordon and myself: room, board, and fifty dollars a month each. It was our chance to escape the rooming house on Orchid Avenue. Caught between what he regarded as the grim alternative of factory work and what amounted to a paid vacation, Gordon agreed.

Except for the bitter war waged between the Hamptons—husband, wife, sulky grown daughter—and my parents over how to run the place, it was a wonderful summer. As usual, Jack and Marian rose to the occasion as ideal hosts, turning on the charm, telling their favorite stories to a whole new audience. I found it hard to believe this was the same couple who had called black curses down upon me on my wedding day. I served as reservation secretary, trail guide, and resident entertainer. Tucking into three ranch meals a day, I regained my weight, health, and strength. Along about August, Father bought out his quarrelsome partner and the Hamptons returned to Los Angeles. Father made a fair grubstake on the deal, and Gordon and I returned with a five-hundred-dollar nest egg.

We rented a small bungalow court on Ogden Drive, and Gordon took a job as floorwalker at Bullock's Los Angeles department store. We'd had many long talks about his leaving show business over the years, but his career compass seemed fixed on it. I was hopeful a regular weekly paycheck would not only free my mind for my self-study history program and music but might even become something Gordon would learn to live with and enjoy.

A gradual change was sweeping through the studios. Male extras were disappearing into the aircraft factories, lured there by full-time work at good wages, maybe the first steady work in their lives. After the bombing of Pearl Harbor, the few remaining male extras were drafted. But it was at the top that major studios suffered most. There was a hemorrhage of such irreplaceable stars as Clark Gable, Tyrone Power, and Jimmy Stewart at their peak of box-office popularity. Former child actors Jackie Cooper and "Junior" Coghlan joined the navy, Jackie Coogan became a glider pilot, and Mickey Rooney went into the army. I held my breath waiting for Gordon's draft notice to appear in the mail. I thought he might do better by enlisting in the Coast Guard or navy, but he was confident of a deferral for flat feet.

Among the many vaudevillians who had moved west were the Duncan Sisters; they planned to open a nightclub called the Pirate's Den, a far cry from *Topsy and Eva*. They talked glowingly about staging musical comedies. Encouraged by their ambitious plans and in the patriotic spirit of the times, Greg and I turned out an entire musical entitled *Laugh It Off!* It was filled with stirring wartime songs and production numbers: "I Promise to Remember" (war-parted lovers), "The Capital Guy on Capitol Hill!" (FDR), "Swinging on the Swing Shift" (home-front fare), and a flag-waving finale worthy of Irving Berlin himself, "It Won't Be Over, 'Til Someone Hollers Uncle, and It Won't Be Uncle Sam!"

Given some of the published songs of the era, ours might conceivably have made the Hit Parade, but the Pirate's Den never opened. The city revoked the Duncan Sisters' liquor license because the club's Sunset Boulevard address was too close to the Blessed Sacrament Catholic Church.

At this point Greg and I were contacted by a drama teacher on Highland Avenue who wanted us to write what he claimed was the crown jewel of all wartime songs, for which he had "an incredible title." When we met with him, he locked the door behind us and whispered, "I don't want a word of this title to leak out until we introduce it."

"What is your title?" I asked, prepared to be properly awed. He glanced around suspiciously and then recited softly:

> We're gonna drop a pearl in your harbor
> And you'll remember it when we do
> Mister Tok-y-o-ka-hama!

It is a tribute to our good taste—or possibly our limitations as songwriters—that we refused to set this bomb to music, having no stomach for the title or the vindictive spirit behind it.

Perhaps what had changed most with the war was Hollywood Boulevard. Soldiers and sailors on leave roamed its length day and night. Until Pearl Harbor, the Melody Lane Restaurant had been a quiet retreat. With the new piped-in romantic music, it was a place where lovers could gaze into each other's eyes across a neatly set table in a sheltered booth while listening to such dreamy ballads as "Deep Purple" and "I Don't Want to Set the World on Fire." Now, it was jammed with raucous, bustling military personnel. A long counter for quick lunches had been installed, and the jukebox never stopped blaring out such morale boosters as "Praise the Lord and Pass the Ammunition" and "Coming in on a Wing and a Prayer."

Hit-and-run clothing and novelty vendors moved into many recently vacated stores, hanging temporary hand-lettered paper banners over the entrances in lieu of signs. Bars proliferated, one of which displayed a neon sign featuring a top hat, a derby, and a cap, with 25 CENTS, 10 CENTS, and 5 CENTS flashing beside each appropriate topper.

Most of the younger cowboys had enlisted, some in the Air Corps, but many applying for the Coast Guard's Mounted Coastal Patrol. It was dangerous work, riding horseback alone while patrolling miles of deserted West Coast beaches in California, Washington, and Oregon. Although armed, each man carried a flashlight which risked giving their presence away, and they were often limned with the phosphorescent glow from the spindrift, which made them perilously visible to enemy submarines suspected of lurking offshore.

The older cowboys—Father, "Buck" Bucko, Handlebar Hank, and Neal Hart among them—were already on Los Angeles sheriff Eugene Bizcalouz's list of auxiliary deputies, men whom over the years he had called upon to help with rescues during floods and other local disasters. Now each was named a block warden in his own neighborhood. Armed with a pistol and a small whistle on a cord around his neck, Father walked his beat every night, ordering all blackout curtains in place and all lights off.

One evening the air-raid siren started screaming and the radio reported enemy planes over the area. Antiaircraft guns began a terrifying barrage while arc lights probed the night sky. Everyone rushed out of their homes and apartment houses to stand in the street and take in the spectacle. *"Go back inside!"* Father yelled through a megaphone. "This is not a Grauman's Chinese premiere! This is war! This is real!" But still they stood transfixed. Their street had suddenly become the back lot for some epic war film, and they had been hired for the night as extras.

Many female extras were recruited or volunteered to instruct citizens in the art of defense procedures, going from door to door explaining what to do in case of an air raid or gas attack. A siren dominated one rooftop in every two or three blocks. A small metal gong, like the one that opened Arthur Rank's films, was set up in every block, on the grass between sidewalk and curb, a felt-covered balled stick attached. With this wand some local Paul Revere was expected to run out and strike a resounding blow, announcing a gas attack as the lethal stuff engulfed him.

Two doll-faced blond extra women, former stock girls at Fox, arrived at my door one night, dressed in pastel-colored sharkskin slack suits and wearing as much makeup and long black eyelashes as Hedy Lamar's stand-in.

"We're the defense wardens in your district," they announced, each drawing a long checklist out of her handbag and glancing around my small place officiously.

"Well, I must say, you lack absolutely everything," the one called Flo scolded.

"What am I supposed to have?" I asked guiltily.

"Well," she rattled off, "a bucket of sand outside your door and a shovel, to put out fires from incendiary bombs. Ten gallons of boiled water in case of typhoid, three bars of Fels Naphtha soap, and at least one blanket per person, folded just inside the door, so rescue crews have something to carry your body out in. If you *don't* have a blanket"—she shrugged and batted her false lashes knowingly—"well, that's worse than having no callback for tomorrow."

"Now about air raids," her companion, Gloria, broke in eagerly. "The minute you hear the siren, check the sand in your bucket, 'cause kids steal it all the time for their sandboxes. Then immediately get under a bed or couch until the all clear!—assuming nothing worse happens. . . ." I got the feeling

Flo and Gloria were really padding their parts. "But if you smell gas, run out and ring the gong nearest you, then come back in and fill your bathtub with water, put on a gas mask—that is, if you can find one—"

"Yeah, they're hard as hell to come by!" Flo offered. "I finally found mine at Western Costumers, left over from *The Big Parade*."

"Anyway, get in the tub," Gloria pressed on, "and wash all over with Fels Naphtha soap to keep the mustard or chlorine or whatever gas it is from burning your skin."

I knew these two had never been very bright. They worked days at the studio and the usual nights when they were tapped for studio parties. I wondered what member of the military had entrusted them with this far more exacting job. But with starlets volunteering to serve the city as night lookouts and former chorus boys manning antiaircraft guns, they were not the exception but the rule.

"We've all got to do everything right," Flo insisted. "Remember what General MacArthur said to us in his heroic wire from Corregidor?" Then, assuming a patriotic stance, she delivered her big line in the studio drama coach's best Theater Guild accent. " 'If you can hold the West Coast for three more months, I can send you reinforcements.' "

"But," I asked, "what if both an air raid and a gas attack happen at the same time?"

Puzzled, Gloria consulted her reference sheet, her long lashes sweeping her cheeks. "Gee, honey, it don't say here. But maybe you'd better just get in the tub anyway, and then put the couch on top to keep the bombs off!" Our defense instruction was in safe hands.

On Christmas Day 1941, the Motion Picture Relief Association asked me and other volunteers to take a complete home-cooked dinner to a small unit of soldiers guarding an isolated stretch of coast. None of us had any notion where we were (we weren't supposed to know or tell), but the cold and lonely soldiers welcomed us as angels of mercy. One of the men was a young cowboy I knew, and after the soldiers had polished off the turkey and trimmings, he escorted me through the deepening twilight across the sand and back to our car.

Glancing down a long stretch of cold deserted beach, I felt my heart leap with a sudden feeling of pride and reassurance. Half hidden under camouflage cunningly painted by members of some studio's art department, I saw the long dark barrels of a dozen cannons pointing defiantly out to sea.

"Well, Japanese submarines better look to it before they try to land here," I whispered to my friend. "Those cannons will blow them out of the water!"

I ran my fingers along the smooth surface of one. I was stunned. It wasn't cold metal—it was rough wood.

Seeing my astonishment, he laughed softly. "I guess as long as the Japs don't know they're only telephone poles we can hold out till MacArthur comes."

For me the darker side of the war was dealing with what was a deep and disturbing psychological connection between myself and thousands of Europeans and Japanese. They had all known me on the screen and had written me letters, and I felt bonded to them in that odd one-sided relationship. I had constant nightmares in which I found myself roaming through bombed-out cities seeking to rescue these unknown "friends" and lead them to safety.

38

As 1943 closed, my family and most Hollywood friends chided me for allowing "negative thinking" to drag me into my present reality of tanks, troops, and tears, while they—obviously thanks to some intrinsic virtue of their own—had remained untouched by the war.

Louise's husband, now a father, was deferred. My youthful collaborator, Greg, with one sightless eye and chronic mastoiditis (incurable until penicillin came along) was rated 4-F. Father's friends were too old for the draft, so all were fortuitously immune. Those like me, caught in the vortex of war, did not enjoy the luxury of denial. We had to face it on its own brutal terms. And by now I had consoled enough emotionally shattered wives of drafted, wounded, slain, or missing husbands to know firsthand its reality.

In my dogged search for some transcendent credo to live by, I had investigated every "think right" religion in Hollywood—Christian Science, Unity, Religious Science, and for a time, Vedanta. But no creed had prepared me to deal with sorrow the way I had been doing at Sutton Place ever since I joined Gordon at Fort Ord in Northern California in the fall of 1943. When it came to coping with real human tragedy I found I owed a lot more to vaudeville than Vedanta.

As I dashed over to the Sutton Place dining room, I thought back on how quickly my whole world had changed.

Only ten months earlier Gordon was still working at Bullock's and I was writing songs with Greg. Father worked full-time riding and doing stunts in Westerns. But one winter day while on a Republic Western's location at Vasquez Rocks, heading a posse thundering through a narrow defile, his mount went down under him, throwing him under the oncoming hooves of half a dozen horses going as fast as they could run.

Remarkably, given the fact his own horse rolled on him twice and six others ran over him, Father suffered only a broken arm and smashed ankle. While mending, enjoying the unprecedented luxury of worker's compensation, he hit upon a system which would prevent such needless accidents and also provide him with a far less risky livelihood. His fall had been caused because the chase horse he drew was "rocker-footed," a cowboy euphemism for a horse that has not been shod in so long his hooves have overgrown his shoes. Father noticed it when he led the horse from the picketline, but declined to quibble over what movie cowboys stoically accepted as "the luck of the draw."

For decades studios had their horses, mules, wagons, coaches, and carriages supplied by two or three professional barns. The largest and best-known was run by "Fat" Jones out in San Fernando Valley. Jones's own tack men and wranglers were responsible for saddling, harnessing, and delivering animals and equipment to studios and location sites. But with the industry shooting a full venue of Westerns and historical epics, each picture with its own full quota of wagons, mounts, and teams, the barn crew was hard-pressed even to keep their stock fed and shod. As a result, when hames' straps broke, reins snapped, and cinches rotted, these vital components often went unmended.

This is where Father's system came in. He wanted to form two or three teams of veteran cowboy extras who would work as equipment inspectors. The studio would pay their salaries, just as they did Central Casting's personnel. The men would check the barns on a regular basis, seeing to it faulty equipment and lame animals did not get as far as the studio or location picket line. Their vigilance would save both riders and valuable chase horses from crippling or fatal falls. They would also protect the studios from bodily-injury lawsuits charging criminal negligence due to equipment failure. With the coming of the Screen Actor's Guild and a new and growing union presence in Hollywood, worker's compensation had become an expensive fact of life, but one the front office steadfastly refused to acknowledge.

Although Father spent months canvassing studio heads, shortsighted producers said the cost of inspectors' salaries would be too great. He was bitterly disappointed to see his noble scheme scrapped. But simultaneously he received a welcome cash settlement from Republic for his own recent fall. With it he was able to buy the dude ranch near Grand Lake, Colorado, for which he had been negotiating with the retiring owner, whose fair price and easy terms were irresistible.

Father asked Gordon and me if we would help him on the ranch. Despite Father's volatile temperament, we both preferred Colorado, hands down, over wartime Hollywood. When Gordon's draft notice arrived, he appealed his 1-A status on the basis that the West had been picked clean of manpower and he would be needed to help harvest hay on the family ranch in Colorado.

The day before we were to leave for Grand Lake, Gordon reported to the Los Angeles induction center. At noon he called to tell me they had turned down his request for deferment, he had passed his physical, and he was this very minute on his way to boot camp for basic training.

The following morning Father pointed the nose of a wooden-bodied Pontiac station wagon northeast. With him rode Mother, myself, and Louise with her two-year-old son. (His birth had served to heal the long parental rift with Louise. To my amazement they couldn't wait to get their hands on him, insisting only that he never call them Grandpa or Grandma, but Pancho and Sharkey instead.) It seemed ironic we were once again placing our destinies in Father's hands, following him blindly to yet another unknown destination not even he had set eyes on before.

We found the Sun Valley Ranch was beautifully situated and in good condition. I felt at once it would make up for the loss of our Wyoming ranch a dozen years before. With Gordon's military fate unknown, I was determined to invest all my energies into making this ranch succeed.

As for me, Gordon and my entire family were of one mind—I was physically and mentally incapable of earning a living outside a studio. My eyesight was too poor; my health was bad (I still owned my tonsils); I had no trade or profession; I couldn't drive a car; I had never been to college (!)—the obstacles to self-determination were legion. Being rejected as a has-been in my teens coupled with my total lack of job skills seemed to justify rele-

gating me to the rank of senior citizen at twenty-five. But here on the ranch
I could at least be useful doing work I knew. I would save my fifty dollars
a month from Father and my stipend as a serviceman's wife, and invest in a
herd of Hereford cattle. In the longer view I would be establishing a landed
estate which—unlike our lost Wyoming ranch and Oldtrim back in Tipperary—could one day be passed on to generations unborn.

The task of running a four-hundred-acre dude ranch was formidable, for
despite wartime restrictions on travel, we averaged twenty-five guests a
week all summer long. They donated their own ration stamps, but most of
the time only Father's 30-30 kept enough meat on the table. During haying
season I doubled as trail guide and member of the hay crew, working beside
Mexican *braceros* to get that precious crop in.

Among our last guests of that first season was a silver-haired angler
named Malcolm Wyer with the profile and manners of an English lord. He
proved to be head librarian of the Denver Public Library and founder of its
famed Western History Room. When I told him of my avid interest in Indian lore and Western Americana, he invited me to come to Denver and
spend two weeks with him in the library. It was like being welcomed into
paradise.

Over Father's objections I spent two weeks in Denver, working with Dr.
Wyer. I could hardly believe I was actually sitting at the same library table
with such a truly learned man, one who seemed to value my intelligence
enough to teach me the basics of serious historical research. I told him that
if Gordon went overseas, I was planning to take a correspondence course
from a state university, and asked his advice.

"Perhaps it would be more pertinent to your special goals if you permitted me to direct your studies. I'll treat you like my own private graduate student," he said, blue eyes sparkling and patrician features lit by a wonderful
smile. "I'll provide you with the same bibliography as for a graduate course
in Western Americana, and more than that, I'll loan you the books themselves."

That fall Gordon was given a permanent assignment at Fort Ord, being
attached to Special Services, which provided entertainment for the troops.
Now he wrote asking me to join him and rent our own place in nearby
Carmel. Although I promised to return to the ranch to work through the following summer, my decision to live near an army base sent both parents into
their usual histrionics. Nevertheless, I was adamant. My only regret was having to tell Dr. Wyer I would be unable to accept his offer to supply me with
books.

"But that poses no problem at all, my dear," he said warmly. "As soon as you're settled, send me your address. Books can be shipped to Carmel as easily as Grand Lake."

Perched anxiously on the front seat of the shuttle bus that ran from the Salinas train station to Fort Ord, I was awestruck when it made its first stop inside that enormous army post. I found myself among rows of identical wooden barracks, the wide streets between them filled, as far as the eye could see, with square, olive-drab islands of helmeted, uniformed, armed, and heavily booted men, all marching to the same hypnotic chant of "Hup-two-three-four! Hup-two-three-four!"

Disoriented, I felt all my false bravado leave me. "Where do I start to look for my husband?" I asked the haggard bus driver frantically. "He's a private, first class, in the Seventh Infantry, if that helps." The driver shot me a positively murderous glance just as Gordon dashed toward the bus from the curb.

Our meeting was not the World War II version of Ashley and Melanie's reunion at Tara. Instead, Gordon led me to a small guest house where only soldiers' wives or close relatives were permitted to spend one night before finding quarters in town. Once my suitcases were safe inside the room, Gordon explained he had a late show to do at the officers club. With a hasty kiss he was off, promising to be back later. It reminded me of our last year of Sundays in Hollywood, when he would go out about noon to buy a pack of cigarettes and not return until three the next morning. "Oh, I ran into Katherine Dunham and her troupe," was a typical explanation. "Knowing how you hate big parties, I didn't call. The time just got away from me."

As I sat down gingerly on the bed in this small cubicle with beaverboard walls, I heard the door of the next room burst open and a couple hurry in. I could hear everything transpiring and, being extremely modest and shy, was in an agony of embarrassment at what I heard. Nevertheless, I was happy for this couple who were obviously making love for the first time after a long wartime separation. There was a merciful silence and then the man suddenly broke into uncontrollable laughter. When he was finally able to speak, he cried gleefully, "Boy, oh boy, Darlene baby! Imagine what my old lady back in Cleveland would say if she knew I'd passed you off as my wife for this all-night toss in the hay."

Apartments, houses—even rooms—were at a premium in the over-crowded vacation village of Carmel. After several vain tries I found a large rooming house a short walk from the beach, called Sutton Place. They had no vacancy either, but Mrs. Sutton kindly offered to call around and find a place for me. While I waited, she complained that it was impossible to keep help nowadays. "Every soldier's wife I hire to cook and clean turns out to be pregnant. The last one left this morning!"

"Do you need a . . . hired girl?"

We struck a deal. She showed me into a bright, completely furnished bed-sitting room, kitchen, and bath, our home for as long as I was willing to work. When Gordon, who had no idea how difficult it was to find shelter in Carmel, came home to Sutton Place that night, he seemed deeply disturbed over the ingenious bargain I had struck. But why was he nitpicking, I wondered, when I was willing to do any kind of menial job in order for us to be together?

"But I've already told all my friends at the fort and the local USO that you were coming to join me," he said.

"What difference does that make? I'm here now."

"I know that, but how can I tell them you're a chambermaid, when they're all expecting *a star*?"

At Sutton Place, in addition to performing as chambermaid and second cook, I served as sympathetic confidant to a dozen displaced boarders: single soldiers, Special Service entertainers, and frantic young wives of soldiers and pilots destined for, or already fighting in, the bloody Pacific war zone.

Since Malcolm Wyer kept me supplied with several rare books each month, I read and transcribed my notes on my free afternoons. If there was time, I visited nearby Carmel Mission, a place I found as calming as Mission San Fernando Rey had been when I was three. At midnight mass on Christmas Eve I sang in its choir loft with a group of army carolers I had joined. For the first time, this holiday took on a deep spiritual meaning for me.

Most nights I took my turn dancing and visiting with servicemen at our Carmel USO, the small homelike Sierra Club, with a dance floor and stage for shows. Because it was run by dignified older women and circumspect wives and single women, we attracted lonely writers, composers, artists, musicians, and actors, who were like fish out of water in the military. They preferred stimulating conversation and playing symphonic records to getting drunk in the rowdy wartime bars of nearby Monterey and Seaside.

When traveling USO shows were scarce, I took the stage myself, singing seldom-heard nineteenth-century trail songs I had learned from old-time cowboy and Wild West Show veteran "Powder River" Jack who visited us in Colorado. I also performed in comedy blackout skits for Fort Ord audiences, where I had the disconcerting experience of playing to all-white soldiers on the right side of center aisle and all-black troops on the left, neither uneasy group venturing to laugh at or applaud the same jokes.

The USO entertainment director was one of those whom Gordon had alerted to my being a movie star. We became good friends and she decided to stage a Baby Peggy Night with everyone dressing up as children. She had obtained a rare print of the original *Captain January* to screen as part of the event. After some hesitation I agreed. It would be fun for the servicemen, and it also occurred to me Gordon had never seen Baby Peggy on the screen. Suddenly I wanted him to be proud of her performance, and maybe even learn to tell the two of us apart. This was my first tenuous, half-frightened attempt at merging my adult and childhood selves.

The evening was a great success, and for the first time in my life I had the déjà vu experience of sensing just how *old* that little four-year-old girl gazing out at me felt when she made this film. Gordon promised to attend but failed to show up until the film was over, saying he'd forgotten. Although hurt and angry, I was, as always, unable to utter a word of reproach.

Since Fort Ord's sole function was training and shipping troops to combat zones, hundreds of men were always facing their last night on home soil, and keeping up morale was our first priority. Gordon saved many talented performers from being shipped out, but Andre Singer, a young Austrian Jewish composer, was sent into combat despite such efforts. Andre had fled Vienna's opera house ahead of the Nazis, leaving the score of his unfinished symphony behind. In France he rewrote his opus but lost it when Paris fell. Escaping to America, he arrived at Fort Ord, bound for the Pacific. I wept as I parted from this gifted man, and begged him to write his opus one more time. I thought about him for years thereafter but never learned if he lived or died. My war years resembled vaudeville in more ways than one.

I did not see much of Gordon. We left Sutton Place after a few months and moved into our own apartment. Once or twice he took me out to dinner, but most of the time he was performing as an emcee or stand-up comedian, to the thunderous applause of GIs, most of whom had never seen live entertainment before. I cautioned him their applause was not an accurate gauge of any show's merits. But there was no lack of female admirers who assured him he was "a true golden boy."

Although I kept a busy study schedule under Dr. Wyer, I was lonely, in need of attention and love. Then one night a consoling thought came into my head. I shook Gordon gently to waken him. "Dear," I said softly, "maybe we should try to have a baby, now that we're settled here . . . ?" Like many confused young wives, I thought babies were the mortar that put shaky marriages back together. His reply astounded me.

"My God, no! Having a child would destroy you!" He was as vehement as though I'd threatened to cut off an arm. "If you ever became a mother, you'd stop being Baby Peggy!"

I spent every summer for the next two years working at the ranch. Father, now in his midfifties, was concerned about his age. A coincidental series of family deaths convinced him he also would die at sixty-one. He became restless and bored with the work of ranching, avoiding the dudes when he wasn't in a mood to be amusing. With increasing frequency I took over for him as wrangler-guide, racking up hundreds of miles on daylong trail rides. Yet when he shot a two-prong buck at dawn (illegally, but we needed meat for the table), I was the one he counted on to spring out of bed at the crack of his rifle, help him load the carcass in the station wagon, and secretly help him hang and clean it in the barn.

I made up guest cabins daily, helped Mother prepare and serve breakfast, lunch, and dinner, did the dishes, and sang Western ballads around the campfire at night. Once a week Mother and I laundered eighty sheets and scores of other linens in a small, gasoline-driven washer with a hand-turned wringer. When Louise was visiting she pitched in, but she now had two children to care for.

Whenever Father and I went riding alone together, I tried to pave over the tortuous road leading back to Baby Peggy by inventing a companionable "rancher's daughter" he could "ride the river with" and who would put him at ease. Being conversant with a great deal of Western lore, I mistakenly assumed it offered a common ground. But while he had lived the twilight years of the cowboy era, and loved telling his own tall tales, it turned out he was not at all interested in the West as history.

One midsummer day in my second year at the ranch, Father became depressed. With his usual penchant for the dramatic, he lunged for his fortyfive, hanging in a holster by a door, vowing to end it all. I grabbed the pistol first, then sat down beside him and tried talking up life's sunny side, a task in which I'd had plenty of practice. "The war will be over soon," I chirped, "and with restrictions on travel lifted, next summer the ranch will make a killing. It's almost paid for, so you can have all the hired men you need and all the dudes we can handle. We just have to persevere."

It turned out he was concerned with one pressing problem: not having a hired man to clean the barns and break out the beaver dams in the upper meadow. When Mother appeared with a tranquilizing pill, I slipped away. Summoning superhuman strength, I set to work with a vengeance, cleaning out the horse and cow barns first, a task that took three hours of wielding a pitchfork and singing "Buffalo Gal" to help keep up the pace. Next I rode up to the flooded meadow and attacked the interwoven willow dams with a shovel, Herculean work for someone weighing in at a hundred and twenty pounds, but I made enough of a dent to get the creeks flowing again.

I stood there a long moment, watching the water twinkling over the rocks. Then, lifting my eyes, I gazed up at the snowy white cone of towering Mount Baker and the dark forest of second-growth pines covering its flanks. I had ridden over every inch of that range. Just gazing up at that lovely mountain made me feel rested.

A week later Japan surrendered. The war was over.

In April of 1946, Gordon was discharged from the army. Now we had to confront our postwar future, and he and I saw it through entirely different eyes. I was beginning to understand that the man I married was pretty much a figment of my imagination. He was incurably in love with show business. He was not in love with me but with an abstract cinematic bargaining chip named Baby Peggy (whose market value he had badly overrated). That I was not ready to face.

Gordon saw himself in the same league with Sinatra and Dean Martin, earning big bucks in some glittering hotel in booming Las Vegas. But what about starting out as a two-hundred-dollar-a-month newscaster in a Monterey radio station? One position was even then being advertised in the want ads. While I did not envision its magnitude, I knew television was coming, and as a personable, well-spoken announcer he would be successful.

My advice fell on deaf ears. He and the Special Service crew he had worked with so long—pianist, comic, dancer, singer—had thrown together a musical about ex-GIs, appropriately called *Where Do We Go from Here?* "We're taking it on the road," Gordon crowed, "where our talents can be seen. We'll each draw down two hundred a week—"

"But who will come to see it?" I interrupted.

"Every 'Ruptured Duck' in America who's asking the same question. It's hotter than Irving Berlin's *This Is the Army!*"

The compulsion to postpone the frightening leap from unencumbered army rec room freedom to fatal entrapment in some dead-end peacetime job had seized Gordon and his companions. They drove off like carefree gypsies, loaded down with props.

As I prepared to sublease our small apartment for the summer and head for the ranch in June, I received what proved to be another of Father's fateful long-distance calls.

"Well, Peg, I've got some great news for you," he began enthusiastically. "Your mother and I are heading your way. A wealthy young investor from Maryland came by in February and expressed interest in the place. It's been a helluva long winter for an old man, and it's still spittin' snow. He called back, made me a good offer—and, well, I've just sold the ranch!"

He rambled on about how he and Mother were buying a house in Tarzana with the money, and how he was looking forward to "riding with Neal and the boys" again. I wasn't listening. For the second time in my life the bottom had fallen out of my dream of a landed future. At war's end, on the threshold of the biggest travel decades in history, without a word of apology to Mother, Louise, or myself, he had sold four years of blood, sweat, and tears out from under us.

Six weeks later I received a jumbo postcard from Gordon featuring a photo of the Mormon Tabernacle. On it were scrawled a few short lines. With no audiences, no money, and no salaries, the show had folded in Provo, Utah, each of its "stars" going his own way. "I'm heading back to Broadway!" was his enigmatic farewell to me.

I tried to deny the truth, but I had been deserted. Blinded by tears, I went outside into the quiet night, threw my arms around one of Carmel's noble pine trees, and was overwhelmed by a storm of grief and fear.

That was the last I would hear from my husband for the next nineteen months. I was now faced with near starvation: my army wife's allowance was terminated, and I had no way to eat or pay the rent. So I screwed up my courage and applied for a job as a manual switchboard operator at the Carmel phone company. To my astonishment I was hired at twenty-eight dollars a week; the first two weeks I was paid for being trained.

The job not only supported me, it restored my nonexistent self-esteem. So I wasn't too blind, too dumb, too sick, or too unskilled for the marketplace after all! I was soon promoted to the long-distance board, which was always lit up like a Christmas tree, requiring such rapid coordination among hand, eye, and brain only top operators got to work there.

My army friends moved on. The USO closed. I worked the switchboard nights, plus extra shifts and holidays for double and triple time. I opened a checking account and put away savings, both unprecedented in my adult lifetime. I bought a nice wardrobe with my own money and even paid off the private debts Gordon left behind.

During those nineteen months I also took instructions in the Catholic faith, and was baptized and confirmed in Carmel Mission, taking Serra as my confirmation name. I had finally found the emotional and spiritual home I had been seeking. So when Gordon telephoned at last from New Jersey after a silent interval of almost two years, I was prepared to forget, forgive, and approach our marriage as the true sacrament my new faith held it to be.

There was not a word about being sorry. He told me he had been very ill with a ruptured appendix and owed a hospital bill. I paid it and even sent him the airfare he said he also needed to come home, withdrawing the money from my savings.

On the third day following his return, and after we had resumed living together, he said he had something of great importance to tell me. "I really didn't plan to stay," he began offhandedly as we strolled the cypress-edged sea cliffs of Carmel. Suddenly he stopped in midstride. "I only came back to get a divorce."

I was speechless, aghast at his nerve.

"You see, I met this wonderful girl at an Arthur Murray Studio in New York. We formed a dance team and booked our act into the best hotels in the Catskills—"

"*You played the Borscht Circuit?*" I shrilled, my long-bottled-up anger at him uncorked at last by his having committed the unforgivable professional sin of touring the *one* circuit big-time vaudevillians scorned as the bottom of the theatrical barrel. "Don't you have *any* pride!"

"Of course! We wowed audiences for two seasons there, and we fell in love. So all I want now is to get a quick divorce from you in Vegas, so I can go back and marry her."

"*You* intend to divorce *me?*" I asked, my sense of outrage rising to unprecedented heights. "On what grounds?"

"Incompatibility, of course. You know—not being a real wife. What else?"

39

W hen I found myself back in Hollywood in January of 1948, I was surprised to see the studios themselves showed so few signs of change, despite the fact that the war had turned the rest of the world upside down. Strangers now headed Universal. Uncle Carl had died in 1939. I was told Julius and Abe Stern were also both gone.

But most of the industry's original immigrant titans remained on their respective thrones, hurling thunderbolts at one another's bastions of power by day, and at night testing their adversaries' nerve by playing cutthroat poker for sky-high stakes in a secret game room at the Trocadero. Such playgrounds as the Clover Club and Agua Caliente were casualties of the ever-shifting social and political subsoil underlying both Hollywood and Mexico. But Hollywood Park, the movie moguls' triumphant answer to Santa Anita Race Track (whose WASP bylaws barred Jews from membership), was still their special turf and thriving.

A bowling alley had been built on the site of Century Studio. Columbia was still booming, although Harry Cohn had been bloodied by Red-baiting Joe McCarthy and the House Committee on Un-American Activities. In spite of that, he was an even greater despot than before. Darryl Zanuck was in command of Fox, applying the grease of new technologies to the studio system's ever more efficiently whirring wheels. Conversely, David Selznick had embarked on a veritable orgy of grandiose films, and his unorthodox production methods were said to be destroying that same revered machine at his studio.

Louis B. Mayer continued as the patriarchal ruler of the most prestigious studio in Hollywood. "More stars than there are in heaven" still orbited in his contractual galaxy. The only innovation at MGM was Mayer naming Dore Schary production head. (Three years later Schary would replace him when Nicholas Schenk, still the gray eminence of the Eastern money establishment that financed Hollywood studios, deposed the West Coast's most powerful king by backing his younger rival. Denied production money, Mayer was finished.)

On a visit to old friends at 20th Century–Fox, I recalled my 1936 role in *Girls' Dormitory*. With forty other girls, I reharsed eight hours a day, six weeks straight, for a key fencing sequence. Our fencing master warned the producers that novices like ourselves would crack under such relentless drilling. But when muscles stretched too far and hips gave way, they sent in a masseuse to get us back on our feet. Finally on the set in full costume, foils in hand, we were told to hold an extended "lunge" a full ten minutes while a still man made a publicity shot through the tunnel of our legs. Slowly, one by one, all forty of us pitched over with the precision of Radio City Rockettes. Typically, the so-called key fencing sequence was cut from the finished film, but I would carry a trick hip for the rest of my days.

While the studios chugged along pretty much as before, I noted drastic changes in the fabric of Hollywood itself. All the old trolley tracks were being ripped up, so clean-running streetcars could be replaced by exhaust-spewing buses and, most of all, private transportation. By now the word "smog" had been coined and was linked to fuel exhaust. Nevertheless, the automobile industry, retooling from military to peacetime production, was poised for a postwar explosion of car sales, and Southern California, rich in increasingly long commutes, was their most coveted market.

The entire Hollywood–Los Angeles area was awash with ex-GIs who had been stationed in California during the war and were now returning en masse with their families to settle here. It only took one dollar down to move the entire family into a ready-and-waiting FHA home.

Hollywood was the very last place on earth where I would have chosen to ride out my own postwar ordeal, and I was hardly in a mood to pay close attention to even such revolutionary changes as these. Necessity, not choice, had landed me back here—that and the hospitality of a young woman journalist who had become my closest friend.

Kay Hardy and I had met in Carmel two years before, while she was recovering from demanding wartime work with paraplegic soldiers in a San Francisco hospital. Like me, she hailed from Hollywood, where before the war she had worked as a reporter for *Modern Screen*, interviewing stars on the set, doing home layouts, and writing the magazine's popular "Chatterbox" gossip column. She was an only child and an orphan whose parents had both died young but had left her comfortably well off and with a home of her own just above Ciro's on Sunset. A cradle Catholic, she was reassessing her faith and, with me, studying Church history and theology.

Kay had served as my godmother when I was baptized, and because she was a journalist and I an aspiring writer, we had much in common. While I was going through the trauma of Gordon's desertion in Carmel, she was facing her own time of personal uncertainty, being attracted to the religious life, but unsure. Shortly before Gordon's return she had moved back to her home in Hollywood, resuming her prewar job at *Modern Screen* and settling her mother's estate while trying to plan the rest of her life.

My penchant for deathless commitment, which I had counted a virtue, proved itself a lethal weapon when directed against myself. I had turned Gordon out of my bed, and flatly refused to let him divorce me on such fallacious grounds, but having invested nearly a decade in a pointless marriage, I felt called upon to throw good years after bad in a last-ditch effort to save it. What I was really trying to do (and could not admit) was save myself from facing the final demise of this major mistake of my life. Inside of this cleverly disguised perfect marriage, I had hidden, even from myself, all of my other failures as myself and as Baby Peggy. I dared not release those demons.

A healthy, white-hot rage at Gordon might have cauterized the wound. Instead, anger smoldered in the form of unquenchable, self-destructive guilt. By the time I finally called it quits and filed for divorce in January of 1948 on the grounds of desertion, I was an emotional wreck. Everything caught up with me at once, and I was unable to cope with it alone in Carmel. In this critical hour, Kay called and asked if I would come to Hollywood and share her home while we put our respective lives in order. I accepted. It was my ninth major move in nine years of marriage.

Coached by Kay and spurred on by the publication of my first freelance article, I began selling to major magazines. My only other income was a twenty-five-dollar monthly check doled out from a bequest of one thousand dollars which my great-aunt Alice kindly left me when she died. It didn't even pay for my food, so I began looking for a steady job. While my Carmel supervisor recommended me highly to the local telephone company, I was tired of staring at a switchboard eight hours a day. But, emboldened by that experience, I found a position as head of the sizable book department in a Catholic religious-goods store in downtown Los Angeles. By this time I was widely read in psychology, history, philosophy, literature, poetry, Catholic Church history, and the works of the early Church fathers; the job was not quite the wild card my parents claimed it to be. Still recovering from the shock of my conversion to their least favorite religion, they weren't able to make much sense of whatever I did now.

At this same time I applied to the local chancery office for a Pauline Privilege: neither Gordon nor I had ever been baptized or reared in any religion, and I hoped to someday marry in the Church. When they sent a priest out to interview my parents and verify my claim, Mother and Father both swore I had been raised a devout Espiscopalian, and attended church services with them from infancy. Despite this pious lie, I was granted ecclesiastical annulment of the marriage.

My divorce from Gordon was final, but not the one from Baby Peggy, it seemed.

"There's a good job out at Republic that could get you a lot farther than pushing rosaries," Father said to me one day.

"A movie job?" I asked suspiciously.

"No, but just being on that lot could damned well lead to something big. The other day Roy Rogers told me he needs someone to answer his fan mail. You're always talking about wanting to be a writer. Well—that's writing!"

His ludicrous suggestion hit me with a force out of all proportion to its importance. If I had not been a nervous breakdown waiting to happen, I probably would have been amused. As it was, I was suffering from severe claustrophobia. While I enjoyed bookselling, a trade that seemed tailor-made for me, I felt buried alive in Hollywood.

I also found I was extremely sensitive to the troubles of movie children, both young and old, and in this town their public woes were always in the news. (I didn't learn about their private sufferings until much later.) It was clear that many of the child-star problems I had faced when growing up were now being visited on the generation that succeeded me.

Jackie Cooper and Mickey Rooney, back from the war, were trying to make comebacks as adult actors, but the industry showed little interest. Cooper, with half a million dollars in the bank, was better able to wait: his mother had saved his earnings. Mickey Rooney was having a tough time trying to break out of his cast-iron Andy Hardy shell.

When Dickie Moore turned seventeen, his mother told him he would have to start paying rent for his room, despite the fact that his money had built the house. When he went to war, he worked as a reporter on *Stars and Stripes* and later became a journalist and business executive. Roddy McDowall was doing stage work in New York. Pretty and gifted Gloria Jean was now being told by the same Joe Pasternak who had discovered her, "I have no place for you here. We have enough singers."

Deanna Durbin's second marriage ended and she fled to Paris. A failure? Possibly, I thought, but she retained her fortune. Gossip had it that even Shirley Temple's marriage was on the rocks. Still, I could not help but compare her resplendent wedding with my own grim rite, her shrewd banker father with improvident Jack Montgomery. Not until I read her autobiography, *Child Star*, in 1988 was I disabused of my high opinion of Shirley's father. At twenty-two she learned he had failed to make legally required deposits to her trust fund for a period of eight years, earning the gratitude of relatives and friends by magnanimously handing out nonrepayable personal loans. Shirley was told that only *three cents* on every dollar she earned over one nine-year period was saved. In 1950 thirty-seven cents on every dollar earned was actually lost. Perhaps it was her father's only way to escape being "Mr. Shirley Temple." Not knowing the whole story, I felt that while other child stars may have stumbled, I had failed. As a rabid Durbin fan once said to me, "It was positively wicked of Deanna Durbin to grow up!" Yes, it was wicked of—and for—all of us to grow up.

I invited Father, Neal Hart, and some of the other old movie cowboys to dinner at Kay's house often, priming them with carefully disguised interview questions in order to get down on paper some of the history of their tenure in Hollywood. I talked a little and listened a lot as they recalled forty years of bone-breaking stunts and falls and their lifelong running battle with C. B. DeMille. I had expected some bona fide historian would have long since rounded them up in a book as the rare sociological quarry they were. Since no one had, I decided to at least do an article on them myself. God knows, by their riding, stunts, driving of six-up teams, and their unfailing chivalry, they had earned an honored place in motion-picture history.

But despite my writing and my job, Hollywood evoked disturbing subliminal memories I was unable to face or come to terms with. Aunt Emma's sagacious warning came back to me. All the hard work and late hours would catch up with me when I was thirty, she had said. I was twenty-nine and beginning to come apart exactly as she predicted.

I wanted to run away, go somewhere else, face my future anywhere but here. But when I mentioned starting over in another town, my family and friends looked wise and murmured snidely, "Running away again?" Actually, I was trying to run toward something—some achievable goal as an adult.

What they didn't understand was that Baby Peggy had never believed she was loved for herself. Purely by means of constant performance and high wages was she worthy of her parents' affection, which she felt she did not otherwise possess or deserve. I had clung to the romantic fiction that only Gordon's love for me had been unconditional. With that illusion shattered I was inconsolable. Programmed since infancy to take the blame for whatever went wrong in my life, I was not really mourning Gordon's loss. I was blaming myself for not putting things to right. At precisely this moment, when I had reached my emotional nadir, a most unlikely liberator appeared.

40

If how elegantly a gift is wrapped bespeaks its worth, the one that fate now handed me gave no outward sign of its hidden value. What would turn out to be the gift of a whole new life for me came in a plain brown wrapper—the dark chocolate-brown habit of a Franciscan priest.

I had followed the canonization cause of Junípero Serra ever since my arrival in Carmel in 1943, when the body of the Spanish-born candidate for sainthood was officially exhumed and the cause entered an accelerated stage. It was now being directed by the energetic California-born Franciscan Father Eric O'Brien. I had just sold a piece to the *Saturday Evening Post* on the Gower Gulch cowboys, so in the spring of 1948 I set out to interview Father Eric for an in-depth article on his work and the cause for either the *Post* or *Esquire*.

At the time of my first interview with Father Eric at the Old Mission in Santa Barbara, where he was headquartered, tape recorders were very new and he was leery of them. If I would work from written notes, he would grant me as many sessions as I needed to get my facts right. Our follow-up interview took place at Kay's house, and on that occasion he brought along a confrere, Father Gracian Gabel.

From the outset Father Gracian sensed I was not just a reporter pursuing a story. As he told me later, he picked up on the way I seemed to avoid some subjects, and he believed I was going through an identity crisis and was in urgent need of professional help. When I completed my third interview with Father Eric in Santa Barbara, I asked to see Father Gracian in the mission parlor. Trusting him more than anyone I had ever met, I told him forthrightly I wanted out of Hollywood, was about to fall apart emotionally, and did not know which way to turn. He offered me immediate help and guidance and agreed to become my spiritual director.

Meeting Father Gracian changed the course of my future. Within six months I was living in Santa Barbara and working part-time in a used-book store. Once a week Father Gracian met with me for a ninety-minute session. Mostly he let me talk out my problems and then offered common-sense answers. In a very few simple words he enabled me to cut the bonds of guilt that kept me tied to my parents. "You can love them theologically," he said, "meaning you wish the best for them. But one doesn't always have common interests even with one's parents. You must love them, but you are not compelled to like them."

Like the caring father he was, he advised me to undergo my long-delayed tonsillectomy. At thirty it was not the simple surgery it would have been at seven, but I survived. Six months later, because of my experience with books and religious goods in my Los Angeles job, Father Gracian made me manager of the mission's Serra Gift Shop, which was then little more than a bare dark room with a few 1920s postcards and souvenirs. As he intended, under my direction it grew into two large well-lit rooms, attractively decorated and filled with a wide selection.

Meanwhile, Kay Hardy accepted a full-time position as secretary for the Serra cause, an enterprise that had grown beyond Father Eric's ability to handle alone. After selling her house in Hollywood, she moved to Santa Barbara, where we rented an apartment together. On the side I continued as a freelance writer and also wrote pieces about the cause, making the life and accomplishments of Serra better known through the secular press. I was also fortunate to have the historian Dr. Maynard Geiger, OFM, guide my study of Spanish, Mexican, and Californian history, much as Malcolm Wyer had done with Western Americana. I attended classes on colonial Mexican history at the University of California, Santa Barbara, although my sketchy educational background barred me from earning a credential.

For several years I worked as manager and buyer for the nonprofit Serra Shop, serving some three hundred thousand tourists each year and overseeing a staff of five full-time employees. I built it into a source of considerable revenue for the Franciscans, who had the financial burden of feeding, clothing, and providing medical care for eighty resident friars.

In 1950 Kay left to enter the Carmelite order's monastery in Carmel, and Father Eric went to Rome for the cause. I took on his program of speaking engagements before various California historical groups. I also became well-known to the local press for my goodwill role of promoting Santa Barbara through the Serra Shop. I became a staff correspondent, providing feature stories on Santa Barbara persons and events for the Los Angeles weekly archdiocesan newspaper.

But following my own protective instincts and Father Gracian's prudent advice, I never told my new friends about my movie past. Most saw me only as a "good Catholic girl" with a strong commitment to people and the Serra cause, but not of the timber to ever become a nun. As Father Gracian knew, I had no interest in religious life. I thoroughly enjoyed all my new and challenging activities which were forging a strong new identity, although its welds to Baby Peggy were still weak at the broken places. When Father Gracian was transferred to another city, I felt I was ready to make it on my own. I might have too if I had not been faced with the unlikeliest challenge of all. I fell in love.

While I had always preferred the company of men, my contact with them had been almost entirely on a professional level. I had never dated anyone but Gordon, and the only males I knew were chivalrous cowboys, on-the-make male extras, and a coterie of servicemen with whom I shared platonic USO friendships. What first attracted me to Phillip (not his real name) was his intellect. However ill or well other men had treated me, almost none had ever cracked a book, which made long-term communication with them slow going for a bookworm like me. To find such erudition in an otherwise ordinary man was an awe-inspiring experience.

My involvement with Phillip was ironic on several scores. He had studied for the priesthood, then dropped out in junior seminary. Father Gracian, a close friend and former classmate, introduced us. Phillip was a lawyer, held a key position in city politics, and was active and highly visible in its social affairs. A handsome, well-educated Irish Catholic of thirty-six, he was married to an irreproachable Catholic wife and was the father of two model children. My attraction to him was the serpent in my otherwise edenic Santa Barbara.

God knows, I had seen enough movies to know Phillip bristled with No Trespassing signs. No "other woman" could ever hope to break into the impregnable moral vault that was his marriage, and I, of all people, had no intention of trying. But Phillip had a rakish willfulness and was accustomed to running to ground any quarry on which he bent his charm, professionally or personally, which made him both dangerous and irresistibly attractive to a novice like me.

Once ignited, the flame of this perilous affair took on a life of its own, putting passion first, prudence last, and driving me to take ruinous risks. It burned at white heat for three torturous years, with no hope of resolution. Absorbed in his own demanding role, Phillip rarely asked how I was playing mine. He mouthed all the "good husband" lines: he was caught between his love for me, the true love he couldn't bear to lose, and the noble wife he couldn't bear to leave. I wanted to run, to Seattle one day, to Denver the next. At last I decided my best escape was to start a business of my own that could be run from any city I chose. Thus was the greeting-card firm of Serrana born.

Until the Second Vatican Council, the daily chores of running the Franciscan missions were assigned to brothers—laymen who took either simple or solemn vows but did not opt to be priests. They served as porters, sacristans, cooks, tailors, and, in California's Franciscan missions, tourist guides. With the strong postwar resurgence of religion among ex-servicemen, there was no shortage of applicants. One day a brother who guided tours at the mission showed me a watercolor painted by his friend Brother Solano, whom he had met when both were stationed at Mission San Luis Rey.

For months I had been trying to find an artist who could capture the Spanish baroque spirit of mission art. I intended to produce a series of greeting cards, each featuring a painting of one of the patron saints of the twenty-one California missions. Inside would be a thumbnail history and a sketch of each mission. Tourists were forever asking me the very questions these cards were designed to answer. The artistic style of the old brother at San Luis Rey had exactly the right eighteenth-century mixture of theatricality and naïveté I had been searching for.

I wrote Brother Solano immediately, asking him to send me sample drawings of the saints. Phillip was out of town for several weeks, working on a legal case, and the bracing effects of having our affair in remission made me more determined than ever to make the card business seaworthy enough to carry me safely out of Phillip's perilous world.

Not having anyone to staff the shop when I was out to lunch, I always closed at noon. One day as I returned I found a good-looking young man waiting in the mission corridor.

"Are you waiting for one of the fathers?" I asked, moving toward the shop.

"No," he replied. "I'm waiting for Miss Ayres to come back from lunch."

"*I'm* Miss Ayres."

He looked dumbfounded. "But you can't be. I'm looking for the—the elderly lady who runs the gift shop."

"Who are you?" I asked, mystified.

"I'm Brother Solano."

What he had envisioned as a prim, white-haired spinster turned out to be me, and what I had thought was a gnarled, white-bearded old friar turned out to be blond, six feet tall, and perhaps a year or two past thirty! More than that, he was now *former* brother Solano. Wanting to become a serious artist and finding he had no vocation for the religious life, he decided he would rather attend Chouinard Art Institute in Los Angeles on the GI Bill, and design cards for Serrana, than milk cows and paint murals on barns in praise of Lady Poverty.

Soon the former brother Solano, Bob Cary, and I were business partners and good friends. He was Cajun, had grown up in Los Angeles, and had a buoyant sense of humor. Nothing ever seemed to surprise him, including my battles with my family, my past identity, and even my fight to end my destructive entanglement with Phillip (a fiasco I had not confided to another soul). The cards sold well, but our distributor went out of business, leaving me with packing, shipping, and marketing, in addition to my full-time gift-shop job.

At last Bob left art school and moved from Los Angeles to Santa Barbara to help me pull the firm together. We worked very hard for Serrana, but we shared pleasures too. He was intelligent and widely read in history, art, philosophy, and literature, far more so than Phillip. An expert on baroque architecture and the restoration of antique paintings and statues, he was also an accomplished artist and designer. We went dancing together at least once a week, and he taught me how to laugh and have fun, carefree pleasures which had been in very short supply all my life.

Although I was trying desperately to distance myself from Phillip, he called me from a nearby town and begged me to come to him "one last time." To my sorrow, I did. After enduring the anguish of our final good-bye I returned home, more desolate than I had ever been. Suddenly I knew I simply could not face life without him. But conversely I knew the affair was destroying us both. It seemed crystal clear to me that *I* was the real problem, the obstacle that must be gotten rid of. By sundown every remaining light of hope had flickered out and black despair closed in.

I got into my car and drove to the beach. I couldn't swim a stroke, so I supposed if I just kept walking into the sunset, like Frederic March in *A Star Is Born,* I would go under painlessly. Phillip alone would know why and, in time, would thank me. Leaving my shoes on the beach, I waded out, numb, resolute, without any sense of melodrama and almost without fear. But just when I was waist deep, a late fisherman in a small skiff with a pitifully weak motor putt-putted slowly across in front of me. It was getting dark, so I had to wait to let him pass. But when I forged on again, the same presumptuous dinghy recrossed in front of me, putt-putting slowly the other way. After it happened five times, I figured it out. That fisherman was more persistent than a sheep dog driving a bummer lamb back to the flock. Suddenly chilled and afraid, I took the cue, waded back to the beach, and picked up my shoes.

Driving home, I remembered reading about a mountain man with a flint arrowhead buried in his chest, who clenched a twig between his teeth while his partner dug out the barb with a red-hot hunting knife. It would take that kind of pain to cut Phillip out of my life, but at least when it was over I'd be cured—and better still, alive!

Still badly shaken, I phoned Bob's apartment and confessed to him what an idiotic thing I had almost done. He arrived shortly with a bottle of dry sherry and a pack of Gypsy Witch fortune cards. Card by card he proceeded to foretell the riotously nonsensical future that lay ahead without my lawyer friend.

I chuckled. I laughed. Soon tears began streaming down my face. Suddenly I was backstage with the Russian gypsies, Earl Larson, Gus Fay, Larry Rich and Cheri. It was New Year's Eve 1926 in Houston all over again. My God, I thought triumphantly, I survived vaudeville. I can survive anything!

That was the unforgettable day when Baby Peggy—like some disembodied spirit from the other side—finally broke through all my denials and defenses to come to my aid. It took a while for me to appreciate what a powerful ally she was, and still could be, in getting me through the rest of my life. After all, I reminded myself, I had not survived vaudeville. She had! And in spite of the shabby way I had treated her, she was prepared to be generous with me, ready to hand over all her hard-won battle trophies and campaign ribbons without a word, as though they were mine.

That was also the moment I began falling in love with my irrepressibly cheerful partner, the art director of Serrana.

41

  I am in the process of writing . . . a book . . . "Whatever Became of . . . ?" After three years of research I can rattle off current data on all but two of 300 headline figures of yesterday. . . . One is the former child star Baby Peggy . . . the other the [notorious] slayer of two women, WINNIE RUTH JUDD [who] . . . walked out of the Arizona State Hospital [for the insane] in 1962. Anyone with knowledge of the latter's whereabouts should get in touch with . . . the FBI. Please do *not* call [radio station] WBAI. Unless, of course, you happen to be Baby Peggy.

This article in the *New York Times* came to me in June of 1966, in a letter from Richard Lamparski, soon after its publication. Through a former soldier friend, now in radio in New York, Lamparski had traced me to remote Cuernavaca, Mexico, where I had been living for almost a decade.

A movie buff and well-known interviewer on Pacifica Radio, Mr. Lamparski wanted an update on "life after Baby Peggy" and current photographs to include in his book. At the time I was writing an ambitious nonfiction book about Hollywood which, while not an autobiography, touched upon some of my childhood experiences. Instinctively fearful of publicity, and not sure of his motives in seeking me out, I was strongly tempted to refuse.

Was I ready to go public with all the same old problems, fielding the tired questions about childhood fame, my failure as an adult, and my parents' handling of my money? Most of all, was I prepared to reveal my whereabouts and forfeit the healing privacy my eight years in Mexico had accorded me?

Cuernavaca, a city located some fifty miles south of Mexico City, is best known as a resort town with a perpetual springtime climate. It was here that Helen Hayes and Merle Oberon maintained second homes and Tennessee Williams wrote *Night of the Iguana*. But because it harbored a few slick Mexican *politicos* and gringos on the dodge from someone or something in the States, it was also referred to as "a sunny place for shady people." Several stoic martyrs to free speech, who had been drummed out of Hollywood during Senator McCarthy's Red witch-hunt, were now also licking their wounds in nearby Mexico City.

While I was a freelancer, selling to American magazines, and had chosen Cuernavaca for its reliable post office, in one sense I was still on the run from my past. But as a writer and historian I had also come here to study Mexico's fascinating Spanish colonial past with an eye toward writing a trilogy of historical novels. Mexico served too as a wide moat between myself and my parents.

Not that they were hostile in their pursuit. When Bob and I were married in the spring of 1954, they happily attended our simple nuptial mass in Mission Santa Ines, near Santa Barbara. In a flared ivory gown and a white lace mantilla over a high Spanish comb, and carrying red roses, I was at last the radiantly happy bride I had never been. And this time my family showed no rancor. Father, with long sideburns grown for an upcoming Western, led me proudly down the aisle in his dark "cowboy funeral" suit and best steepheel boots. It was like a scene out of an old Tim McCoy Western in which he marries the California señorita and her hacendado father gives the bride away.

Over the months that followed, I visited my parents often in their home in the Valley. I couldn't help but note the slow erosion of the industry on which they had built their lives. Father had bought one of the earliest television sets on the market, and spent hours watching reruns of early Westerns, calling each actor, rider, and chase horse by name. He was seeing his own life on the open range and on film, along with the lives of his friends, being replayed on that greatly diminished screen. It held a unique fascination for him.

At first he did not see the new medium as the threat it really was, being completely addicted to it. At the same time he and Mother were working for higher wages than they had ever earned before. An extra's daily pay was no longer doled out at a cashier's window near the studio gate, after a tedious wait in line at the end of a grueling day: one five spot and two singles laid down silently, with the silver change sent clanging down the change slot. Checks were now mailed directly to the extra's home, tax and Social Security already deducted.

But soon Father began to talk about how long it would be before the bubble burst. "Hell, it costs a studio fifty dollars a day to put an empty horse on the set with a wrangler," he confided one day. "For straight riding or driving six-up, Hank Bell or I get thirty-three dollars and a lousy streetwalker gets twenty-five. I like the pay, but goddamn it I'm afraid the guild's gonna price us out of business. Pretty soon Republic and tight-assed directors like DeMille will refuse to pay such wages. Would you believe, for leading a camel, a 'gunsil' gets sixty-one dollars a day."

As Father had predicted, by the end of the fifties the industry was finding ways to circumvent the union's gains, and inadvertently pointed the way to countless other American industries in the decades that followed. "Runaway productions" went to countries like Italy, Spain, and Israel, which offered many hidden benefits along with spectacular locations. When Cecil B. DeMille filmed his monumental remake of *The Ten Commandments* in Israel, he hired locals who built pyramids, raced through the Red Sea, and worshiped the Golden Calf, all for fifty cents a day. Not only were the old cowboys getting long of tooth and brittle of bone, studios found their pay rate outrageous when crack Argentine, Spanish, or Mexican riders could be had on the spot, willing to jump their ponies over the moon for a couple of U.S. dollars.

Now too death began to claim Hollywood's fallen kings. In 1957 the pomp of Louis B. Mayer's funeral, as staged by David Selznick, scripted by two of L. B's best writers, acted by Spencer Tracy, and directed by Clarence Brown, rivaled a MacDonald-Eddy film's fountain-and-fire finale. Jeanette MacDonald reprised "Oh, Sweet Mystery of Life" from the choir loft, and high points of the fearsome monarch's long reign were recounted by silver-tongued "Rabbi to the Stars" Edgar Magnin.

Harry Cohn's obsequies were simpler, held on a soundstage of his own

Columbia. But even so, playwright Clifford Odets penned the eulogy that star Danny Kaye movingly delivered. There were other, less ostentatious funerals for the industry's founding fathers, but each bespoke the fall of empire, the passing of the industry's pioneers.

Movie attendance had dropped drastically since the war. By the mid-1950s it was a mere forty-five million, down from ninety million a decade earlier. The new generation of young parents were staying home with the kids, and their children were growing up without the neighborhood theater and Saturday-afternoon serial habit of that earlier generation. Convenient in-house TV was taking up the amusement slack as increased automobile traffic made going out to movies a chore. In newer suburbs drive-in theaters siphoned off some of the flood of moviegoers defecting to the tube. I was shocked when two American children visiting Cuernavaca went to the movies there, and upon their return said, "It's the first time we've ever been to a walk-in theater!"

Fearful for their own golden years in an industry that was dying, Father and Mother snapped up an offer of steady work from soon-to-be-opened Disneyland. Father was put in charge of a children's trail ride on gentle mules, while Mother got on as wardrobe mistress for six chorus girls dancing in the Golden Horseshoe Dance Hall. Invited to tour the new park, Bob and I found ourselves allergic to Disney's brand of capsulized "instant history." Unfortunately, after several months, Disney discovered that live animals were not nearly as tractable as electronic look-alikes. Father's mule train was discontinued as was his job.

In 1955 our greeting-card business was thriving, but when our Midwest and Eastern seaboard accounts complained about paying postage all the way across the continent, we dropped a few postal zones by moving from Santa Barbara to Santa Fe, New Mexico. Because of Bob's restoration skills, the Catholic bishop assigned him to the major project of restoring and gold-leafing a Spanish altar screen dating back to the 1720s. (It still stands in the side chapel of Our Lady of the Conquest in the cathedral.) At the same time, he was designing all of Serrana's cards, while I was busy running the business end and directing a nationwide sales force of two dozen regional representatives selling to the nation's leading gift, book, and department stores.

Our second summer in Santa Fe, we invited Mother to visit us. We were living in and running our business from a large two-hundred-year-old adobe house on unpaved Canyon Road, a quaint, quiet street lined with artists' studios and galleries. Mother took such a shine to the city, she said she'd love to live there. Bob and I discussed it and decided we should ask her to move in with us. This proved to be a disastrous mistake. Once installed, Mother became lonely and restless, missing the Hollywood studios and her old extra friends.

Later that summer, Father came to Santa Fe as part of the company of the Glenn Ford and Jack Lemmon Western *Cowboy*. Ironically, the film was almost a retelling of Father's early years of trailing longhorns and chuck wagons. Hired as a wrangler in charge of a small herd of *corriente* steers from Mexico, he was not put up by the studio at La Fonda with the cast, so we naturally invited him to stay with us.

Once Jack and Marian found themselves under the same roof, they turned the place into Fort Apache. Their fights revived my worst childhood memories of old courtroom quizzes escalating into screaming, door-slamming scenes. It grew so bad Bob and I had to leave and go driving in the hills to escape the turmoil in our own living room.

We were under added stress at this time because over the past year Hallmark Cards had bought up more than a hundred small studio card companies like our own. Because they bought paper, envelopes, and packaging in such volume, their costs were a fraction of ours. By autumn of 1957 we could plainly see Serrana's days were numbered and we would soon be forced to the wall. The only way to escape both that eventuality and our problem with my parents was to quit the card business, sell our inventory to the sales rep who wanted to buy it, and leave Santa Fe.

Ever since our marriage we had dreamed of moving to Mexico and devoting ourselves entirely to serious painting and writing. Now was the ideal time to undertake such an adventure, for in 1957 living costs there were so low, such a dream was actually feasible. Over the years various doctors had told me I would never be able to have children, so we knew we would have responsibility for no one but ourselves. When we told my parents we were going to Mexico, they deplored the fact we could be so "disloyal" as to live "outside America." But they had no hesitation about their own destination.

Returning to Hollywood, they sold their home in the Valley and rented a smaller house nearby. While Father soon moved to a small ranch in Sonora, California, Mother stayed put and hung on at Central Casting, even though runaway productions were now bringing back hard times for extras. She flatly refused to go ranching with Father again, having worked as hard as any of us in Wyoming, Montana, and Colorado, and for what?

Since Bob spoke fluent Spanish and knew the country's history well, we bought two one-way train tickets to Querétaro in the heartland of Mexico, taking only a box of paints, my portable typewriter, and two footlockers filled

with books and clothes. For the first three months we lived in the remote silver mining town of Guanajuato, then settled in Cuernavaca. I soon had
writing assignments from American magazines, and Cuernavaca's leading
gallery arranged for Bob to exhibit his paintings there year round, as well as
holding annual one-man shows of his work. Who could ask for more?

We were able to live simply but comfortably on our combined incomes
from articles and paintings. But after three years this delicate balance was upset
dramatically when my doctor stunned me with the news that I was pregnant.
We welcomed the birth of a son in 1961 as a miracle. Father was pleased, but
because of illness, he wrote, he had given up his ranch in Sonora and was back
in Hollywood. A letter from Louise disclosed that he was terminally ill. Difficult as the journey would be, I now felt compelled to make the train trip to
California with nine-month-old Mark, so Father could see him before he died.

Knowing we would be in Hollywood for Father's seventieth birthday, I
asked John and Dorothy Hampton of the Silent Movie Theater to arrange
a private screening that day. They had a rare print of *The Family Secret*, one
of three features I had made for Universal when I was about three and a half.
I sensed the biggest surprise and most satisfying birthday present I could give
him would be Baby Peggy.

A few lifelong cowboy and extra friends joined our entire family for the
afternoon screening. Father broke into occasional tears as the film progressed, at one point leaning over to tell me he regretted it wasn't in sound,
"because then I could have heard her sweet voice once more." His remark
confirmed what that long-ago reporter had stated so perceptively:

> [Baby Peggy] has not only been the darling of his heart—she has been
> his gold mine. Managing her has been his career, and in a way she has
> been the clay which he molded and through which he expressed him-
> self.

But this pleasant day had an unexpected denouement not even I could have
foreseen. We had just returned from the theater and gotten Father comfortably settled, with blond, blue-eyed Mark laughing and toddling around
his chair, when I noticed a sudden change in Father's attitude.

"Sharkey, come in here this minute!" he called to Mother, who hurried
into the living room from the kitchen.

"Yes, dear, what is it?"

"Just come here and look at this kid! Why, he's the spitting image of Peg
when she was his age. Just a little work and training and he would be a natural to star in movies and on television!"

I stiffened as Mother exclaimed, "You're absolutely right! Why didn't we notice it before?"

Instinctively, I moved closer to Mark, as if protecting him from an impending physical blow. "Oh, no," I found myself saying warningly. "Not my baby! I'll never permit such a thing to happen to him."

One of Mother's extra friends was standing nearby. "Why, Peg, you'd be crazy to refuse," Dorothy said enthusiastically. "With TV commercials and residuals, he could make a fortune—more than enough to put himself through college and travel around the world."

I couldn't believe my ears. Was I an eavesdropper standing outside the old Barn at Century while starstruck Margaret Campbell encouraged a young Marian Montgomery to put me in films with those very same words?

"Dorothy's right," Mother ventured almost petulantly. "Just because you don't like the industry for some reason, it's not fair to deny your only child his opportunity to make it big in movies!"

As I should have known, our visit was stressful. A day or two before Father entered the hospital and we had to depart, he confronted me with a legal document. I was stunned to learn I owed him something in the neighborhood of thirty-five hundred dollars! This sum, he said, I had borrowed from him ten years before. "I've got to leave your mother with some kind of security," he offered by way of explanation, "and it's high time I started getting back some of the money I've foolishly loaned out to other people over the years."

My clear memory of this transaction was that he had come to visit me in Santa Barbara during one of his separations from Mother and long before my marriage to Bob. He had just won fifteen hundred dollars playing poker on a six-week location job: on a John Ford location with John Wayne that was easy to do. Card winnings were what the cowboys called "calf money," because they were never reported to their wives or the IRS, and to justify these actions they promised themselves they would use it "to invest in a few weaner calves."

At the time I was preparing a line of greeting cards featuring famous mountain men for the dude ranch and national park market. Our guests had always asked me about these historical figures, and this was a succinct way to answer such vacationers' queries. When I mentioned my proposed line to Father, he volunteered to give me his calf money, saying that "Western cards" were something he could get behind. When I accepted, I took it to be his oblique way of making some small restitution for my lost childhood earnings. It made me happy for both of us. Now I was told I not only owed the original fifteen hundred dollars, but ten years' interest on it as well.

I accepted the obligation mutely, but it wounded me deeply and I alternately wept and raged over it after we returned to Mexico. Nevertheless, I contacted both Father Eric of the Serra cause and my old friend Jack Haley, asking them to please visit Father at the Motion Picture Home during his final days, since I could not be there.

To my own and everyone's astonishment, Father made a dramatic deathbed conversion to the Catholic faith two weeks before he died. "Peggy believes in this religion," he told Father Eric, who baptized him, "and I want to be sure I'm in the right pen."

Father Eric celebrated the solemn high requiem mass which all of Father's cowboy friends attended. Jack Haley, who together with Flo had been my model couple in vaudeville, visited Father several times. Haley later helped Mother with the details of transferring Father's grave to the cemetery at San Fernando Mission, the same mission we had used so long ago as a location for my Baby Peggy comedies.

Father's peaceful death was a great consolation. It released me from the last vestiges of his hold over me. I began to function as my own person at last, without the feeling I was under constant pressure to perform. With Bob's help, Hollywood and my career gradually came into perspective, and I began to see them through the eyes of a historian and not those of a child.

In a letter, Mother mentioned having seen Richard Lamparski interviewed on a television talk show for his first book, *Whatever Became of . . . ?* "And suddenly," she went on, "there you were, big as life on my TV, as Little Red Riding Hood!"

This had come about because Bob persuaded me to overcome my self-protective distrust of Lamparski (or any other stranger trying to draw me out). I had sent him the data and photos he requested. I had Richard to thank for this public resurrection of my long-buried self. Still, I was hardly prepared for what followed. He began forwarding a steady stream of fan letters sent in care of him but addressed simply to Baby Peggy!

PART 8
1954 – 1996

DESCENDING
FROM
MYSELF

42

Mother had always dreamed of taking a Caribbean cruise, but even when he could afford it, Father wouldn't be found dead on a cruise ship. To cheer her after the ordeal of his long illness and death, I invited her to spend three months with us in Cuernavaca. We took her to all the bright spots in Mexico City and to a hilltop restaurant in Taxco that had a stunning view, great martinis, and a marimba band. It wasn't a Caribbean cruise, but she had the time of her life.

But after her departure, the cost of our Mexican idyll began rising and our sources of revenue drying up. In the mid-1960s reasonable rentals like ours shot up overnight when American hippies began descending on Mexico en masse and thoroughly trashing the nicely furnished places they rented. Around the same time the U.S. passed a law limiting to five hundred dollars the value of merchandise its citizens could bring into the country from foreign lands without paying customs duties. Whereas a tourist may have purchased two or three of Bob's five-hundred-dollar canvases at a time, now Bob was lucky to sell even one. Also, many U.S. magazines, large and small, for which I wrote regularly, folded as their readers defected to TV, and the once-thriving Catholic press, another lucrative market for articles, was all but demolished by the changes of the Second Vatican Council.

For all these reasons it seemed a welcome bonanza when a blustering Texan, who vacationed part of the year in Cuernavaca, offered to take thirty of Bob's paintings to sell through an art gallery in Dallas. Bob worked day and night to turn out that many canvases. After agreeing to give him a 20 percent commission, he made a three-hundred-dollar deposit and set out for Texas in his station wagon, with fifteen thousand dollars' worth of paintings on consignment. (That was the last we saw or heard of him.)

After several weeks without any word and unable to reach the man at his Dallas address and phone, we became seriously alarmed. As his concern deepened, Bob developed a bleeding ulcer, and our American-trained doctor prescribed a new sedative medication to quiet his nerves. The ulcer healed, but Bob grew steadily weaker, until soon he was hardly able to get out of bed or walk to the front gate.

Worried, I contacted another doctor, who came to the house. After examining the patient, he turned to me and asked, "What kind of medication is he taking?"

"These," I said, showing him the bottle. "One pill three times a day."

After a pregnant pause he took the bottle, led me out of the bedroom, and shut the door behind us. "Señora, your doctor made a grave mistake. This is a massive depressant, to be taken before major surgery or to induce 'twilight sleep.' One pill is powerful enough to knock a patient out. Having taken three a day for three months, your husband is lucky to be still alive."

Setting the bottle down on a table, he continued. "This drug is also highly addictive, so we have to get him off it gradually, but soon. Since you tell me he's a veteran, I suggest you get him to the nearest U.S. veteran's hospital."

We were sorry to leave Mexico, for it had been one of the most enriching experiences of our lives. But we were both realists enough to know the circumstances that had made this Mexican interlude possible no longer prevailed. Mark's arrival had changed things too. Friends at the American embassy told us if children born abroad were taken back to the States, it should be done either when they were six or sixteen. Mark had just turned six.

Houston, with its large VA hospital, was our target city. Bob had family there, and it had the highest rate of employment in the nation. However, after we got ourselves on our feet, we intended to return to California. From the classified pages Bob's aunt sent, I picked a first-rate employment agency, sent them my résumé as journalist and bookseller, and told them to expect me in ten days. We returned by plane with the same paint box, portable typewriter, and two trunks with which we had left. The only additional baggage was one little boy.

The agency found me a good job as paperback book buyer at Post Oak Books. It was located within hailing distance of Neiman Marcus and shared their same haute clientele. After a few weeks as an outpatient, Bob was completely recovered and took a position with an art gallery and custom frame shop. My only dismaying surprise came when I discovered that *Paperback Books in Print,* which had counted barely two hundred titles ten years before, had skyrocketed to thirty-five thousand! Post Oak Books stocked the lion's share of these titles, and it was my responsibility to see they were kept in stock. There wasn't time to memorize a dozen publishers' catalogs, I was afraid of being fired for not knowing them already, and I couldn't risk losing this job. There were no shortcuts and of course computerized inventories for bookstores were only a scientist's dream.

Without consciously knowing I possessed such an inner mechanism, I fell back automatically on the same technique Baby Peggy had used at Century when she was a toddler: learning "in the round." I found myself visually and mentally locating and pulling information in from all sides, just as she had done, identifying and memorizing objects by their placement and distance from me. Having the signal advantage this time of also being able to read, I added an intense, one-stop system of memorizing title, author, and publisher as a single unit each time I shelved a book. Within three months I had virtually committed to memory the large store's entire inventory. Baby Peggy had not only come to my rescue, she had imparted to me her secret of how she had managed to function before a camera when she was only two.

Returning to what seemed more like a foreign country than the nation we remembered, we suffered from severe culture shock. Before we left the States, Americans were still being addressed as citizens: now they were universally referred to as "consumers." Even Post Oak patrons were said to be consumers instead of readers. I found that not only were Americans who had lived abroad for ten years considered "disloyal," they were suspected of having turned Communist as well. At the supermarket, not yet armed with a Texas driver's license and recognized credit cards, I used my passport for identification. The wary checker all but called the cops. It was clear to me anyone caught in Texas without at least six credit cards could be picked up for vagrancy.

Being parents of a suddenly uprooted child and holding down two de-

manding jobs in a strange city, after being a close-knit family working together at home in a pastoral environment, took their toll on all three of us.
I also discovered that not all my vaudeville ghosts had been laid to rest.
Piped-in music played all day long at Post Oak Books. Since we had not
owned a radio in Mexico, I had not heard most of these songs since childhood. Now, hearing my bow music, "Baby Face," and others after so many
years, I was drawn back to family crises I thought I had forgotten. All day
long the music kept nagging at me.

My emotional defenses already down, I was devastated by the news of
Judy Garland's death. We had been close friends at Lawlor's, where I learned
she knew a good deal about Baby Peggy long before we met. Her mother
had played piano for my films in the pit of the New Grand Theater back in
Grand Rapids, Minnesota. As she had to many other ambitious mothers,
Baby Peggy appealed early on to Ethel Gumm, bewitching her to brave child
stardom for her own Baby Gumm in far-off Hollywood.

But my fondest recollection of Judy was a night in 1939 at the Cliff
Dwellers, an informal café-club where Gordon and I were spending a rare
evening out. Judy, still in makeup and costume as Dorothy in *The Wizard
of Oz*, dropped by with her sister to visit the leader of the club's small band.
I went over to their table to congratulate Judy on her first big break. She
thanked me but confessed she was in the dumps about the studio handing
her "just one more dumb kid part." Glancing around the room, an idea
struck me. "Judy, this is your kind of crowd. Why don't you sing for them?
You know it always makes you feel better."

"You're right," she said, brightening, "I will!" Handing the pianist a
sheet of music, she stepped up onto the bandstand and announced, "Ladies
and gentlemen, I'd like to sing something for you this evening—it's a brand-
new song I just learned today at the studio."

She was not yet a recognized star, so the presence of Judy Garland meant
little to this uninterested crowd. But I was eager to see her shake it up the
way only she could do. Suddenly her marvelous voice filled the small room,
and with the opening bars of "Over the Rainbow," she had the blasé audience in her pocket.

When she finished, pandemonium broke out. Hearing her sing for the
very first time before a live audience what was to become her lifelong musical signature was an electrifying experience.

I had always felt protective of Judy because she seemed so vulnerable, and
I had followed her ups and downs from afar, understanding perhaps better
than most what she was going through. To me she symbolized all the captive

children of Hollywood, and for that reason her death seemed doubly sad. Suddenly I, who rarely wept, could not stop the tears. I was so distraught I could not go to work. I had not been so emotionally unstrung by anything since my divorce. After three days, I heeded Bob's advice to seek professional help.

A Houston psychotherapist I will call Dr. Forge had a fancy office and an even fancier bejeweled female receptionist. He charged fifty-five dollars an hour. This was my first time on the couch, and if I hadn't been so desperate to glue myself together fast, I would not have paid his ungodly fee.

Gingerly groping my way into his small office, I found it totally dark except for a psychedelic lampshade with a moving beacon inside that slowly scanned the room at programmed intervals. I sat down across the desk from the shadowy Dr. Forge, who uttered not a word. Seeing I was expected to make the first move, I took a deep breath and said, "Well, Doctor, I'll start at the beginning. I began working at the age of twenty months as a child star in Hollywood—"

"Oh, my Gawd!" the shadowy presence broke in disgustedly as the garish red, blue, and green light made its eerily timed sweep of the darkness. "Not *another* one of those!"

"How many have you had this week?" I shot back, suddenly enraged by the whole ludicrous setup. Without another word I got to my feet, turned my back on his pseudopsychological spook show, placed fifty-five dollars on the receptionist's desk, and stalked out. I felt better already. Sheer indignation must have cured me.

In watching American television, I was able to observe the vast changes the medium had wrought with the traditional movie child's image. In my day a child star was expected to be distinctive and perform heroic deeds, thereby serving as a role model for youngsters in the audience. At four, I bravely climbed the lighthouse stairs and lit the beacon to guide passing ships clear of the reef. In *How Green Was My Valley*, eleven-year-old Roddy McDowall risked his life to save his father, actor Donald Crisp, in a gripping dramatic scene.

The new TV youngsters dressed in look-alike T-shirts, shorts, and sneakers and bore a cookie-cutter likeness to each other. In soaps their role was to induce tears, but in sitcoms they were expected to get laughs by delivering wicked one-liners considerably too wise for their years. And when they grew too old, they were replaced by look-alike successors, much as the aging casts of Our Gang had, over the years, been replaced with reasonably accurate facsimiles of their predecessors. One thing was certain. Performing children were in greater demand than ever, and parents were still taking kids to Hollywood to see to it supply met the demand.

While we found Texas's climate purgatorial and deciphering the natives' spoken language a losing battle, Texans themselves were friendly and kind. However, on Christmas Day 1970, having endured enough Texas heat, humidity, torrential rains, blue northers, and hurricanes to last a lifetime, we headed back to California. An old friend and former classmate of Bob's at Chouinard Art Institute offered us her completely furnished vacation-cottage home, standing empty in a small beach town not far from La Jolla, until we found permanent jobs and decided where to settle. Here the loose ends of my own and all the other Hollywood childrens' lives were destined to come together at last.

43

After Houston, Encinitas offered a quiet breathing spell and a delightful climate. Mission San Luis Rey, where Bob had been Brother Solano in another life, was nearby and Los Angeles a convenient ninety miles away. I had considerable research to do in various Hollywood archives for a history I was planning to write, so having the film capital handy, but not oppressively close, was ideal. Mother had moved into the comfortable Motion Picture Home at Woodland Hills, where she was well cared for and surrounded by friends.

Bob found work at an art gallery in nearby La Jolla, but I spent the next six months collecting unemployment checks, being a full-time mother to Mark, and writing. One thing bookselling had taught me was how a smart author packages his material. In Mexico I had been trying to put together a massive volume from a mound of Hollywood material. In Texas I saw how a writer like Stephen Birmingham could get two and three best-sellers out of a single batch of his own distinctive literary dough. As a bookseller I had also met many ardent young students of film who had grown up watching classic black-and-white movies on television and were enthralled by Hollywood history. Now as soon as I began writing about the cowboys in Hollywood, I realized it was the germ of a book.

When it was finished and titled *The Hollywood Posse: The Story of a Gallant Band of Horsemen Who Made Movie History*, my agent sent it to twenty-three publishers. Twenty-two turned it down. All found it "unique," "fascinating," and "a singular look at Hollywood," but all rejected it on the grounds that a Hollywood book without gossip, scandal, sex, and a big-name star would not sell. I did not accept that argument as valid. From what film buffs had told me, they wanted little-known behind-the-scenes facts, presented by an honest and insightful author. My agent continued circulating the manuscript.

When I learned the campus bookstore at the University of California, San Diego, in La Jolla was looking for a trade-book buyer with experience outside the university system, I hastened to apply. While I approached this bastion of higher learning with some trepidation, knowing I had neither a college diploma nor a master's degree in journalism, I knew I had all the tools and expertise a good buyer needed. I brought a varied background and a wide field of reference to the job, having researched and written some four hundred non-fiction magazine articles on everything from eighteenth-century Mexico and the lives of the saints to early Hollywood and the great American West. After all, I mused, I'll bet not many learned faculty members on campus knew that Norma Shearer's only son, Irving Thalberg Jr. was a published professor of philosophy at a prestigious Eastern university! I was pleased to know that fact and proud to stock his book.

Confident, but determined to make sure, I included in my résumé a two-line reference to my film career. As good luck would have it, the head of campus personnel was a film buff and remembered me. Even the bookstore manager was almost as impressed by hiring a former movie star as he was by my bookselling credentials. I got the job, which came with enviable health benefits, a good retirement program, and opened up a whole new career in a university setting.

Richard Lamparski had moved to Hollywood and asked me to appear with him in a Canadian Broadcast Company documentary on early Hollywood. We were to meet at the Rainbow Dance Studio. Well, I certainly knew where *that* was, I told him. Hadn't I rehearsed my ill-fated musical there all one summer?

Bob and Mark came with me, and we parked in front of a well-remembered office building on Hollywood Boulevard. I ran up the stairs to the second floor but was stopped in my tracks by the darkness and giant padlocks and chains cordoning off all the upper floors. A warning sign, PROCEED AT YOUR OWN RISK!, was my first glimpse of the "new" Hollywood.

Baffled, I returned to the street, which was teeming with panhandlers, hustlers, and a few lionhearted tourists shopping for movie memorabilia or scanning the sidewalk for stars. A passerby directed me to the studio, which he said had relocated. A brass plaque by the door told me the Rainbow Studio had occupied this "new" site *for the past thirty years!* Inside I was greeted by Richard and the studio's owners, who turned out to be Will and Gladys Ahearn, a renowned dance team I had often worked with in vaudeville.

After the CBC filming, Bob, Mark, and I drove over to Sunset and Gower. The Napoli Cafe was gone, but the old Columbia drugstore still stood on the southeast corner. We lunched at the Copper Kettle, a restaurant that had replaced the bowling alley on the site of Century Studio. I told the waitress that I remembered when a studio stood on this lot. She looked at me with undisguised pity. "Ma'am, there never was no studio on this lot. The Copper Kettle's always been here!" I got the same sort of answer at Zinke's Shoe Repair on Selma Avenue when I mentioned to an employee that this was where the cowboys' earliest gathering place, the Waterhole, used to stand. Ah, sic transit gloria!

I had only been at UCSD a year when Bob suffered a serious heart attack. He made a good recovery but gave up making frames to teach an art history course at a San Diego community college. In 1974, Houghton Mifflin bought *The Hollywood Posse.* I was understandably pleased to be a published author at last, and the same publisher wanted a second book, an outline of which my editor had seen and liked immensely.

I immediately set to work researching and writing *Hollywood's Children: An Inside Account of the Child Star Era.* Although I put in forty hours a week at my highly demanding job, on weekends I worked another twenty on the book, editing what I had written on my lunch hours during the week.

Through Richard Lamparski I was able to recontact many of the performing children I had worked with or known at Lawlor's. Unfortunately, Frankie Darro was not only an alcoholic but too drunk to give a coherent interview. In the ultimate irony he was living out his last tragic years in the St. Francis Apartments on Hollywood Boulevard, in the very same apartment from which his own mother had stood at her window to watch him come and go from Lawlor's school.

I visited again with Edith Fellows and spoke to Anne Shirley by phone and to Jean Rouveral (the ingenue in *Growing Pains*), now a successful writer herself. Through Mother's connections at the Motion Picture Home I was able to locate and conduct an interview by telephone with Fred Fishbach's ailing widow, who seemed overjoyed to hear from me.

"Oh, how Fred loved you!" she exclaimed. "When he was shooting some special sequence, he would phone me over at Christie Studio to come across the street to Century and watch you work. He always said you did everything he ever asked and he was so proud of you!" I was deeply touched. She also gave me much otherwise unknown information about Fred Fishbach's early life and directorial career. Alf Goulding had recently died, but I had two enlightening interviews with his son, Alfie, a professional musician.

Gathering information on early influences in Jackie Coogan's life, I talked with Lillian Coogan, who was confined to a wheelchair. She was delighted when I asked her to tell me about her childhood working with her parents in vaudeville, billed as Baby Lillian, and later touring with Jack Senior. I learned that she lived in an apartment house in the Valley which Arthur Bernstein had left her as income property.

I attempted to reach Jackie, but a publicity woman who spoke for him kept me at bay. I learned he lived in Palm Springs (another of Arthur's real-estate acquisitions). Once the publicist said Jackie was visiting his property near San Diego. (His father's old ranch?) Another time she told me he was vacationing at his beach house in Malibu, which was odd, since others told me Jackie's income was steady but quite modest. It struck me that, however black Arthur's deeds may have been, he had not left the Coogans exactly homeless.

I finally gave up on Jackie, thinking he must be writing his own life story and was understandably wary of sharing his material with an outsider. (I'm sorry to say, I was wrong. To my great surprise he apparently left no written record of his life, which was both spectacular and sad.)

I was especially pleased when director Lewis Milestone, recently returned from years of living in Paris, granted me an interview. Unhappily, he was suffering from a painful back condition. When I asked if he remembered being my gagman at Century, he bristled visibly. "No! I only did that job for director William Seiter." I did not press the point. Although I owned a still showing Seiter directing me in a Century two-reeler called *The Poor Kid*, on balance we were both right. An Academy Award–winning director, and acclaimed throughout his long career, he had good reason to be proud of his accomplishments. Being a twenty-five-dollar-a-week gagman on lowly Poverty Row was certainly not one of them.

Finding Millie had no recollections of Century, I wrote Carl Laemmle Jr., asking if he had any memories of the lot that might otherwise be lost to history. In his brief reply he said he had none but closed with a suggestion that caused me to sink weakly into the nearest chair. "For information about Century," he wrote, "you should contact my uncle Julius Stern in Palm Springs."

Julius Stern was still alive! I was struck dumb. It was like hearing that Tutankhamen was still Egypt's reigning pharaoh. My own memories of him were as fresh as on the day I saw him last: starched collar, narrow tie, shirtsleeves with garters, and always sporting a straw boater or derby.

But on a subliminal level I was still afraid of Julius Stern. As president of Century he had been so all-powerful that even my own autocratic father submitted to his decrees. The realization that this despot was taking the winter sun less than eighty miles from where I sat filled me with a chilling sense of awe and foreboding. As *the* authority figure of my childhood, Julius still loomed large in my psyche.

Glancing at the telephone, I felt my hands turn to ice. Did I dare risk a call? How should I introduce myself, knowing what venomous words had passed between him and Father? But why was I so fearful? I asked myself. I was no longer the child whose fate this man held in his iron fist. Besides, being able to interview a movie pioneer like Julius Stern, one of Hollywood's original immigrant producers, was a film historian's dream.

Heart still pounding, I dialed the Racquet Club in Palm Springs and asked for the Sterns' cottage. In the time it took for two long rings, the perfect scenario popped into my head. When Edith Stern answered and told me Julius was resting, I explained I was an author writing a book about early Hollywood. If I sent him a list of questions in a letter, would he be willing to answer them by mail? I gave her my name, but as *The Hollywood Posse* was not yet published, I knew Diana Cary would ring no bells with either her or Julius.

Ten days later I received a reply with brief but descriptive answers to my questions. Overcoming my timidity, now that an adult connection had been established between us, I opened my letter of thanks with a revealing personal note.

"In my effort to be objective and ask questions without any personal bias, I did not mention that I myself grew up in the industry. But since I am now corresponding with the man whose productions helped me rise to fame, I thought you might be pleased to know me as the same Baby Peggy Fred Fishback discovered long ago in the old Century Barn."

A few days later I received a call from New York. The instant I heard his voice I knew it was Julius. Both the singsong speech and his heavily accented English remained unchanged. "Baby!" he addressed me excitedly. "Like I told my wife, 'Edith,' I said, 'the questions that woman is asking, I tell you, she's no stranger to Century. She knows too many inside things. She had to have worked on the lot!' "

He hesitated and then, as if seeking reassurance, asked half jokingly and half fearfully, "Do you remember, vee vass always . . . *good to you* at Century, vern't vee?" He paused expectantly. "Right, Baby?"

Sharp images of the lot, my stark dressing room, Joe Martin, Charley, and my many near-brushes with death all rose before me. Masking my sense of irony, and remembering too the romp it had been to make those wild "five-day wonders," I replied, "Yes, Julius, Century was very good to me."

Bob and I visited the Sterns in Palm Springs the following winter and again in New York City when I went back to consult with my publisher and appear on a talk show. Julius was well up in his eighties by then and he died not long after my visit, but his daughter and I still correspond.

In the course of researching *Hollywood's Children,* I was saddened to discover how much tragedy had befallen so many of them. With perhaps the exception of Jane Withers, Mickey Rooney, and Shirley Temple, all had faced a devastating sense of adult failure equal to, or worse than, my own. In San Diego I searched for and, after many months, finally found Charlotte Henry, who played the lead in *Growing Pains* and starred in the classic 1934 film version of *Alice in Wonderland.* In a sense I ressurected and gave her back to what she was amazed to find were her many loyal and devoted fans.

Badly wounded by her Hollywood experience, she had become almost a recluse, dropping out of sight for nearly forty years. Over lunch she told me that her debut film, far from launching her career, had in fact destroyed it. Even at sixteen I knew her as a recognized stage actress of great talent, experience, and promise. But she was so typecast as Alice, no studio could imagine her playing any other role.

Her license plate gave mute testimony to the strange alpha and omega of her acting career: across it was spelled out one word: ECILA, or ALICE spelled backwards. Richard Lamparski came to San Diego to interview her, and by including her in one of his *Whatever Became of . . . ?* series, brought her renewed recognition and many letters from her fans.

I was particularly dismayed at the struggles of Darla Hood, who enjoyed such a long and successful child-star career as the "sweetheart" of Our Gang and the later Little Rascals at MGM. When she was three, her mother, the frustrated and ambitious wife of a bank president in a small Oklahoma town, gazed into her beautiful little daughter's hazel eyes and said, "Darla, honey, you're my ticket out of Liddy!"

Dancing and singing lessons followed. On a trip to New York with her dancing teacher, Darla led the band and did a song and dance in the Edison Hotel dining room during dinner. A talent scout for Hal Roach saw her and arranged a test. She was with Our Gang for ten years, earning a steady six hundred dollars a week, but she said she never saw a penny of her earnings. Her paychecks gave her parents a life of ease and built them a handsome home. (Her father quit the bank and left benighted Liddy for Hollywood early on.) But that house was not Darla's to live in or sell.

Married and the mother of two children, the still attractive Darla was ignored by the industry. One day in Hollywood, still only in her forties, she was on her way to an interview, new professional portraits in hand, when she was stricken with agonizing stomach pains. Rushed to the hospital, she died a few hours later of a ruptured stomach ulcer. A mutual friend who attended her funeral told me he was standing near the casket when he noticed a woman lean over to view the deceased. He was close enough to hear her murmur through her tears. "Oh, Darla, Darla! You were such a good little girl, and you had such a hard life."

When the service ended, he went over to the woman, who was still seated in the chapel, and asked her softly, "I suppose you were one of Darla's studio teachers?"

The woman glanced up at him, surprised. "Oh, no," she replied. "I'm her mother!"

When *The Hollywood Posse* was published in the fall of 1975, the *Los Angeles Times* devoted the front page of their View section to a feature story telling how Baby Peggy had metamorphosed into the author Diana Serra Cary. I toured the West Coast with the book, giving television talk show interviews from San Diego to Seattle. It was widely and favorably reviewed, and as I had argued all along, readers did not miss the sex, gossip, scandals, and big-name stars.

As film critic Richard Schickel said, it was the very first book to portray "the working stiff's Hollywood." Other reviewers felt such incidents as the

Gower Gulch cowboys saving one another's lives in dangerous location chases and charges gave Westerns and moviemaking a whole new dimension. Their colorful language, customs, and chivalrous ways, carried with them from the open range, revealed a hidden, heroic side of Hollywood.

The cowboys' tradition of "passing the hat" on studio sets to pay a widow's fare home after her husband was killed on some riding job had never before been told. Few readers knew studios paid *no* hospital or funeral expenses for such victims: workers' compensation was unknown until the 1940s.

I watched many times as Father proudly passed his sixty-dollar, satin-lined chocolate-brown "dress" Stetson around the privileged circle where the highly paid director and stars sat, the silent ritual shaming them into donating as much as they should. Even in the worst of times, the cowboys agreed the collection had to at least add up to the cost of the dress Stetson being passed, which explains why mostly ten spots were dropped in by the cowboys themselves.

But some reviewers judged the book, which was based on Father's life as a cowboy and his years as stuntman and double, to be a daughter's unabashed tribute to the father she blindly adored. In truth, few people knew his foibles better than I, or had suffered from them more. But his life typified those of the men he rode with. They were a rare and picturesque band who deserved my praise, and it was meant for them all, Father included, not as model husbands and fathers perhaps, but as cowboys, on and off the screen.

Their philosophy was summed up in one of Father's cowboy songs, which he taught me when I was a very little girl.

> I dreamt that they held a great roundup
> Where all of the Range's top hands
> Were marked by the Riders of Judgment,
> Who are posted and know all the brands.
>
> Then Saint Peter stood up in the grandstand,
> A six-gun held up in each hand,
> And he sez, "Boys, we'll judge by the riding
> Who goes to that sweet Promised Land!"

The men of the Hollywood Posse asked only "to be judged by the riding." If in the end they were, then surely they had nothing to fear when it came time for them to "ford the Jordan"—as they put it, in their own distinctive lingo.

Indeed, almost all the old-timers among them had passed away by 1975, and were all sadly missed by me. But in a way I was glad they had not lived to see the terrible changes time had wrought in their former "second chance" frontier town.

44

The changes in both the motion-picture industry and the Hollywood I had grown up with proved to be much more radical and far-reaching than the mere physical rerouting of a few main thoroughfares to accommodate freeways. Disneyland had changed the entire landscape of Anaheim, formerly famous only for orange groves and a roadside shack where Knott's Berry Farm sold homemade jam. A wax museum of movie stars had opened near Disneyland and was vying for tourist dollars. Universal Studio's gargantuan version of Uncle Carl's twenty-five-cent "sugar-bowl money" tours had already reached mind-boggling proportions and charged a whopping entrance fee.

Noting the incredible prices such places were asking, I could not help contrasting the United States with Europe and Mexico. There pilgrims travel great distances to pray for grace at ancient shrines and cathedrals or to venerate the images of centuries-old Virgins and saints. Here most Americans—

especially those touring Hollywood—come not to pray but to see, spend, consume food, and above all else, have fun. It was difficult for me to follow their reasoning.

But trying to follow the changes in Hollywood during the seventies and eighties was even more puzzling. When I first read that the old pillared, ivy-covered Hal Roach Studio was being torn down, such mindless destruction of a treasured Hollywood landmark seemed unthinkable. But it soon became routine. My innate reverence for history was outraged by the new studio bosses' barbaric practice of reducing valuable movie artifacts to marketable kitsch. Once stripped of every salable object, all quickly disposed of at ghoulish public auctions, the gutted studio was razed for the lucrative bare ground beneath it.

Most tragic of all was the sorry fate of mighty MGM, once home of what was perhaps the most efficient studio system in the world. Under the auctioneer's hammer went the magnificent sets, period furniture, and incomparably beautiful, one-of-a-kind hand-stitched gowns and costumes. How could they sell such irreplaceable historical treasures for such a mess of pottage as one more garish hotel on the glitzy Vegas Strip?

Debbie Reynolds pleaded passionately with MGM's top brass to at least spare such unique outdoor gems as Judge Hardy's house and the *Raintree County* set. Knowing money was the motive behind the dismantlement, she urged them to convert all these back-lot landmarks into a Universal-like, moneymaking theme park. The studio brass heard her out but went their own way. After hawking everything *inside* the studio at a giant auction to the highest bidder, management callously bulldozed the sixty-five-acre back lot and sold the land for high-priced homes.

But perhaps MGM's ignoble end was no more reprehensible than the disastrous managerial and fiscal crises that had brought it on. Declaring such holdings an illegal monopoly, the government had stripped the Loew's corporation, MGM's parent company, of its fleet of American theaters some years earlier, a crippling blow for both the circuits and the studio. The overseas circuit went next.

For nearly fifty years the studio system had been the crown jewel of the Metro lot. But in these sad final days the lot was overrun by a gaggle of upstart independents. There were no tightly run production units anymore, and no control from the top. In this last bastion of contract security for major stars, management security itself was nonexistent.

For decades such reigning stars as Joan Crawford, Lana Turner, Clark Gable, Mickey Rooney, and Judy Garland had been shepherded around the

lot like children, led from picture to picture by wiser heads who knew precisely what was best for them. Of course a few stars had remonstrated against
this suffocating paternalism. But none ever had to hazard, on their own, the
slightest threat to their careers. Some member of the MGM family was always on hand to protect and advise and even fend off unwanted reporters.
Louis B. Mayer pampered and groomed his stars the way he did his thoroughbreds.

Suddenly driven out of their contractual Eden, MGM's biggest names
found themselves naked to the world. They no longer went from stage to
stage on their own home lot, greeted by the same trusted makeup people and
crew members they had worked with most of their lives. Both Joan Crawford and Judy Garland later admitted they were helpless outside those protective walls. Inexperienced at running their own careers, they turned to
equally unskilled but avaricious managers.

Now they were forced to make deals one picture at a time with hard-nosed
strangers heading companies that might fold their corporate tents after making only a single film. The new breed of movie producer took no interest in
grooming a stable of stars.

This lean new Hollywood was moribund and depressing, a place of carelessly discarded talent and razed studios. And yet talent continued to flourish here. Through a sort of random magic, some good films still managed
to be made and fine performances to be given by new generations of actors.

But the studios were not the only landmarks that fell victim to change.
On my visits to the city, I missed the old Hollywood Hotel that for so long
dominated the northwest corner of Hollywood Boulevard and Highland
Avenue. In memory's eye I could still see that sprawling three-story stucco
pile, its 1880s pseudo-California mission style ludicrously mismated with
Victorian Gothic turrets, cupolas, and a wide imitation Saratoga veranda.
From the high-backed, wicker rockers with arms that lined that veranda,
well-heeled, well-dressed Eastern visitors watched us make Baby Peggy
movies on the lawn while they basked in California's sunny winters, and in
the reflected glory of movie stars.

The hotel's liberal residents had been the first to take to their bosoms the
hardworking, hard-drinking camera gypsies. Treated as social pariahs in this
town, which was a bastion of temperance and moral rectitude, picture people were grateful for the hotel residents' nonjudgmental acceptance. Every
Thursday night the lobby rugs were all rolled back and the hotel orchestra
played while—a few of them secretly fortified with the contents of their own

silver flasks—these wickedly innocent revelers shimmied, waltzed, and tangoed the night away.

But the depression had wreaked havoc on the outmoded hotel's carriage trade. By 1940 it was a ghostly, black-windowed relic with no tourists as guests, occupied by a handful of tenacious old-timers, its awnings in shreds, lawns gone to crabgrass, and its huge vine-choked canary palms infested with rats. While I was in Mexico, it was condemned and ordered razed, despite the lamentations of its residents, many of whom had spent half a lifetime under its roof. While being forcibly evicted, one such movie-fan resident spoke for them all when she cried, "I don't want to go to heaven! I just want to stay on forever at the Hollywood Hotel!"

I visited Mother at the Motion Picture Home in Woodland Hills nearly every weekend from 1971 until her death in 1977. A haven to industry people, it was also, in a palpable sense, the Hollywood I had grown up with reduced to its distilled essence. Many survivors of my childhood were there, creating a society not unlike that of a movie set. Edward Earle, who had played my father in *The Family Secret,* was in residence. Familiar ghosts hovered over brass plaques bearing donors' names: Louis B. Mayer had given the theater and Rosabelle Laemmle (Uncle Carl's daughter) the library.

John Ford donated a white frame chapel not much bigger than a gardener's toolshed. Originally, he had it built to serve what he called his "family," a tightly knit band of skilled young men drawn from the industry, who had helped him film and edit his daring and dangerous wartime documentaries.

Ford envisioned setting up a kind of postwar Camelot where he could live surrounded by his own round-table knights. They would work with him on his films but, together with their wives and children, make their homes around his own. Deeply hurt when his "boys" chose to go their separate ways, he gave what was to have been the community's chapel to the home. There it stands aloof and forlorn, a prop department's miniature of a steepled New England church.

Lunching with me at Mother's table were "Curly," the last surviving member of the Three Stooges, director Mitch Leightner, and former RKO producer Gene Towne. Yes, the same Gene Towne who had told Walter Winchell he was giving Baby Peggy an important, nonexistent part in his film on its last day of shooting. Ironically, Gene was now Mother's closest friend, and neither of them even recalled the incident. Of course, I said nothing to remind them.

When the urbane Mitch Leightner spoke proudly of a particular film which had won him an Academy Award, Towne fixed him with a winner's eye and chortled, "Mitch, you may have won the Oscar, but I was the producer. I own the film."

Mother was proud of my success as a writer, reading and rereading those chapters of *The Hollywood Posse* that recounted her own pioneering days with Jack in Yosemite and the Grand Canyon. And yet she still seemed to think of me and treat me as a little girl.

When going through her things after her death, I came upon a folder containing a unique collection of photographs, all childhood portraits of me. Most I had never seen before, although I remember well posing for them. Only one was of Baby Peggy, dressed in period costume in Century's *Hansel and Gretel* comedy. Mother had loved the Dutch gown. All the others were pictures of a mother's very private little girl, without the usual makeup and wearing a rare party dress. All were posed at home in our Laurel Canyon house. They dated from early 1923, shortly before my fifth-birthday party, where Sol Lesser declared me public property by turning me into a golden egg. After that the child in these pictures was never seen again.

It seems to me Mother kept these portraits as reminders that this long-vanished child had once belonged to her. It caused me to ask myself a long-unanswered question: had she ever had regrets about putting me in films? Perhaps, but somehow I doubt it, for when I moved to Santa Barbara she did a most astonishing thing. Sensing I would never return to films, she reregistered at Central Casting under the name of "Peggy Montgomery," giving as her excuse that she was being confused with a certain "Marianne Montgomery" in the extra ranks. Her death certificate, dated February 7, 1977, gives mute testimony that I died before my time.

One of the even greater ironies about my mother's life was the amazing success of her first beau, later her brother-in-law, Ed Montgomery. After a long and happy but childless marriage, and twenty years spent eking out a living from a small-tool business in a Chicago suburb, the huge demands of large aircraft companies for small parts during the brief four years of World War II garnered him $2 million.

In 1957 he and his wife visited us in Santa Fe at the same time Jack and Marian were waging all-out war in our once-peaceful home on Canyon Road. Of course, in Uncle Ed's presence they became their always charming public selves. But Father did insist Ed drive him around the county in his custom-made Cadillac to look at promising ranch properties.

In 1972, soon after we returned to California and I took up my job at the

University Bookstore, Uncle Ed died of a heart attack while on a weekend fishing trip. When his lawyers wrote to say he had left six hundred thousand dollars to be divided among ten heirs—my mother, my sister, myself, and seven other nieces and nephews—I was stunned. My sixty-thousand-dollar share would put me beyond the reach of financial worry for the first time since the day I quit the act when I was ten! Like Uncle Ed's four-year wartime windfall, my neat six-hundred-thousand-dollar fortune had been racked up in only four years in vaudeville.

But that Baby Peggy movie version of riches-to-rags-to-riches was not to be a real-life scenario. The will remained in litigation for all of twelve years, and Mother died before it was settled. By the time Uncle Ed's estate was finally divided in 1984, the original ten shares of sixty thousand dollars each had been pared down to a paltry six thousand. Still, I was grateful. Except for a surprising five-hundred-dollar cash wedding gift from Father when Bob and I were married, the one-thousand-dollar bequest from my great-aunt Alice, and a stream of five-dollar checks Mother sent me in Mexico from her modest earnings as an extra, it was the only money I ever received from any member of my family.

45

Shortly after my second book, *Hollywood's Children*, was published in 1979, I received a surprising phone call at my bookstore office desk. "Is this Diana Cary?" a man asked in a clipped British accent. When I answered in the affirmative he added, "Are you sitting down?"

"Should I be?"

"Yes!" he said imperiously. "This is Roddy McDowall. I have just read your book. It's the sort of book I have always avoided, loathed, and sworn I would absolutely never read. Joan Rivers gave it to me for Christmas, but of course I set it aside. Then one day I got curious and began nibbling around the edges, because—well, I'd always wondered what ever happened to Baby Peggy."

Roddy paused to take a deep breath. "Anyway, I'm calling from Hunter's Bookstore in Beverly Hills, to let you know I've just bought ten copies, one for every friend of mine who was ever a child actor. I wanted to tell you personally I think it's a perfectly wonderful book, and you've done us all a great service!"

A few days later when I went up to Hollywood for talk shows and an autographing at Brentano's, a photographer with professional camera and gear was waiting for me in my hotel lobby. It was Roddy. We fell into each other's arms like twins separated at birth. In minutes we were fast friends.

I learned that Roddy's child-star days, like my own, had come to a swift and bitter end. One day when he was seventeen his studio boss called him in and told him flatly that child star Roddy McDowall was as good as dead.

He turned over to his mother his large home in Cheviot Hills and everything in it (which his earnings had paid for) and moved to New York to "make myself into an actor." Although anyone who saw *How Green Was My Valley,* made when he was eleven, would dispute that he ever had to learn to act, Roddy carved out a remarkable adult career for himself as a very fine and versatile actor. Over and above his long film career, his photographic portraits of celebrities, now in four published volumes, form an impressive second adult career. Many of these insightful portraits were the work of a camera-wise twelve-year-old anthropologist who began capturing the unique culture around him on film nearly half a century ago.

Hollywood's Children broke new ground in tracing the history of child stars in America, an era that began in 1853 with four-year-old Cordelia Howard playing the original Little Eva in the stage version of *Uncle Tom's Cabin.* In the California gold fields, Lotta Crabtree's long career and multimillion-dollar-fortune began in 1854 when she was seven: a miner tossed a fifty-dollar gold piece at her dancing feet, and her hawk-eyed mother picked it up. The era closed with Natalie Wood and Margaret O'Brien. Critics found this a "different" Hollywood book too—no gossip, no scandal, no sex. But they reviewed it even more widely and well than my first.

A New York sociologist-turned-producer approached me about doing an hour-long television documentary based on the book. Approving of his nonexploitive and compassionate approach to the subject, I worked as adviser on the script, and we both agreed Roddy should be the narrator. (It was well received and is still being aired by PBS stations.)

When it came time to shoot my segment, I went up to Hollywood, and had barely checked into my hotel room when I received a call from a man staying in the same hotel. He said his scenes were also being shot the following day and he was anxious to meet me. He proved to be someone I had always admired but never met: "Spanky" McFarland.

Moments later he appeared at my door, a stocky, heavy-jowled, middle-aged man with a twinkle in his eye and a tall drink in hand. As we talked I learned that George McFarland was no longer playing second fiddle to Spanky but that it had taken some doing to come to terms with that small stick of dynamite. By now I had grown accustomed to being an unofficial father confessor to former movie children, some of whom I knew from childhood, others strangers, but all of whom had read my book and completely trusted me.

Quietly, but with strong emotional undertones, George recounted the brief but pivotal event in his own stormy passage from Spanky to George. Returning from World War II, he had decided to head back to Hollywood and try a comeback in films. For six months he fried hamburgers, washed dishes, and almost starved to death, but there were no takers for a grown-up Spanky. Then, Darla Hood and two others of the Our Gang cast got together and hit upon a winning idea. They interested a novelty manufacturer in producing Our Gang lunch boxes and other commercial items whose original Hal Roach patents had expired. The idea was to sell them to the brand-new market of kid fans watching Little Rascal reruns on television. They signed what promised to be a lucrative contract, even when split four ways. Spanky called his sweetheart in Dallas and told her to join him, because he would soon have enough money to marry her.

"You understand, Diana," he confided, "all those years Hal Roach literally owned us, lock, stock, and barrel, and minted money on the side by selling the rights to our names and faces. Now it was our turn to make money on ourselves." He paused and took a sip of his screwdriver, looking very much like the downcast younger Spanky.

"Well, at this point Mr. Roach got wind of our deal and moved fast. He renewed his patents and signed with another firm, underbidding us on everything. My fiancée joined me, but by then the whole project was dead."

It was like a script from one of Spanky's own comedies. The Gang kids need to earn money, so they decide to pick a few lemons, make lemonade, and sell it to the neighbors. But the villainous and greedy banker co-opts their backyard enterprise and runs them out of business. It was clear to me that Roach was still a father figure in Spanky's eyes, and to have him deliberately scuttle their chances was tantamount to a father disowning his children.

Not long after our conversation, George McFarland was selected by a committee to present Hal Roach, then in his nineties, the industry's Lifetime Achievement Award. I knew this would be a critical and ironic moment for both Spanky and George. Watching the event on television, I could see how eager he was to receive a kind word from the man who for years had owned him, body and soul. Mr. Roach took his trophy from the former Spanky's hands with a wan, impersonal smile and said not a word to grown-up George.

It was dismaying to find my own and three younger generations of performing children struggling to survive a much worse child-star trip than mine. Drew Barrymore and Kristy McNichol were fighting drug and alcohol addiction in their early teens; Gary Coleman, estranged from his parents, was suing them for several million dollars of his earnings. Many were suicides or had died of drugs. Paul Peterson, a former TV child actor, put it aptly when he said, "Fame is a dangerous drug and should be kept out of the reach of children."

Three experienced family and child psychologists practicing in San Diego who read my book contacted me and formed the Project for Performing Children. One, who had enjoyed considerable success deprogramming young people brainwashed by religious cults, said he was game to take on Hollywood. He would get the word out that here was a group of professionals ready to offer special counseling to parents on how to cope with the peculiar difficulties a child's career places on themselves and their families.

Although he had high hopes, children's agents told him there *were* no family problems. The Screen Actors Guild refused to see him and every studio locked him out. The few parents he was able to contact by phone refused to listen or, God forbid, give him access to their little breadwinners. I should have known trying to reach such children would be every bit as difficult as trying to free a terrorist's hostage. Surrounded by exploitative parents, agents, producers, and managers, the child star has no one in his corner to advise or counsel him. Blocked at every turn, our project failed.

As a bookseller I was pleased to host many successful author autographings in the campus bookstore I had built up from 6,000 titles in 1971 to 100,000 twenty years later. Among my guests were Anne Edwards (Judy Garland's biographer), Bob Parrish (an old Lawlor's friend), former child star Dickie Moore, Roddy McDowall, and Richard Lamparski.

Having had a lot of experience selling other people's books, I was pleased when ninety-year-old Adela Rogers St. John, the doyenne of the Hollywood women's press corps, invited me to be the guest speaker at one of her monthly roundtable literary events in the Ambassador Hotel. Copies of *Hollywood's Children* would be on sale at the autographing.

I knew very well that in Ms. St. John I was dealing with "Mother Hollywood" incarnate. A veteran "sob sister" of the old movie-magazine school, she was accustomed to judging, scolding, and whenever possible, banishing intractable or unrepentant movie people from her sight. To forestall any ill will she might hold for me after reading my extremely outspoken book, I approached her where she was presiding like a queen seated in a thronelike chair on a platform elevated slightly above and directly behind the speaker's podium.

"Miss Saint John," I greeted her warmly, "it's a great pleasure to be your guest today. I believe we last met when you did a story on me for *Photoplay* in 1923. Remember?"

She nodded and smiled and we chatted briefly about our early days in Hollywood. With my volatile hostess thus safely disarmed, I went on to address the waiting audience. But I quickly learned I had underestimated the power of this tenacious Hollywood partisan, more used to dictating her own terms than listening to hard truths about her adored hometown that she felt could do no wrong.

Halfway through my talk she began rudely interrupting and heckling me. To my remarks about Judy Garland's tragic life, she injected a strident, "If she'd been any good, she'd still be around!" When I spoke of other child actors who had been "thrown away like used Dixie cups," she was outraged: "Hollywood never gets rid of good people," she shrilled. "Kids who didn't make it didn't have what it takes!"

I replied to each remark as graciously as possible, then went on with my talk. When I finished I got a standing ovation, but the indignant Adela would neither join me at the table where I was signing books nor bid me good-bye when I left. Her deeply embarrassed assistants did it for her.

Because of the interest in child stars generated by my book, I was asked by the National Film Society to host a panel of former child stars at their 1983 convention held for movie buffs in Studio City. One of those on my panel was Jackie Coogan. I had recently heard rumors he had suffered a heart attack or a stroke in Palm Springs. After that story leaked out, Jackie accused the hospital of damaging his career by giving out false reports about his health and threatened to sue them for $4 million, the exact sum for which he had sued Arthur Bernstein and his mother some forty-five years earlier!

I knew well that before the war he had unsuccessfully tried his hand at everything from selling kitchenware to heading a song-and-dance act, but nothing worked for him. As a glider pilot in Burma he was shot down behind the lines and decorated for heroism. Upon his return to Hollywood he set his sights on an adult film career, but with Louis B. Mayer's black curse still hanging over him, his comeback was confined to television. He played

Jack Webb's sidekick in *Dragnet* and starred as the ghoulish Uncle Fester in *The Addams Family*.

He married three times after he and Betty Grable parted, the fourth an enduring union. When his daughter, Leslie, was four years old, he told a columnist she was destined for stardom. "The world is ready to take another child star to its heart," he enthused. "I will form my own company and . . . I believe she should collect four hundred thousand dollars on her twenty-first birthday. Public adoration is the greatest thing in the world."

It was curious how differently Jackie and I looked back on our child-star careers. He seemed to have been so transfixed by early fame, he was ready to exploit his own daughter in order to recoup the adulation he prized. I was fiercely determined to protect my son Mark from every kind of damaging childhood pressure or exposure and give him a happy, well-structured upbringing.

But there had been many unexpected detours leading back to Baby Peggy along the otherwise happy road of our son's childhood. When Mark was three months old, my husband, who adored the baby, remarked to me in wonderment, "I know you love Mark as much as I do, but I've never seen you kiss him even once. How come?"

I was surprised by his observation but I knew why. I had never forgotten all those gushing grown-ups—strangers who had hugged and kissed me so inordinately as a child. "I want him to be a good friend when he grows up. It wouldn't be fair to impose upon him now when he can't defend himself."

During a visit Mother had once startled me by saying, "Enjoy the baby now, honey, while he's at this adorable age. Because later on, when they grow up, kids are nothing but grief." I had nodded understandingly but was amazed at the implications of her candor.

One afternoon when Mark was three, I remember glancing out the window to check on him in his sandbox. For a moment I watched him playing idly there and then was struck by an inexplicable mixture of deep contentment and sheer outrage. What was wrong? A longtime male friend of ours, an experienced social worker, was visiting us in Cuernavaca at the time. I turned to him and burst into tears. "Chris, I just had the most unsettling sensation. I'm so happy to see Mark playing out there, but at the same time I'm furious with him because—well—because he isn't working."

"He's doing you a great favor," Chris replied sagely. "He's just given you the carefree childhood you never had."

Jackie Coogan's daughter had not become a child star, but her son, Keith

Coogan, was a rising young television actor, and both were with Jackie at the convention. When I entered the hotel lobby where all three were sitting, Jackie was being interviewed by a reporter who had a copy of my book, heavily highlighted, open as a reference on a footstool beside her. I feared it was not a good omen, but I was wrong.

"Hi, sweetie!" was Jackie's unexpectedly cordial greeting as I approached. "It's good to see you!" He rose to his feet and embraced and kissed me. Later photographers took pictures of us, only the second time in our lives we were ever photographed together.

At my panel, Jackie spoke passionately about the so-called Coogan Law, passed in the wake of his lawsuit against his parents. That law required that in the future the parents of child actors who signed a studio contract must set aside 50 percent of his or her earnings in trust.

"But in today's world kids are not put under any contract for a TV commercial," Jackie told the audience. "The long-term contract was the only legal hook. Today a child can earn thirty-five thousand dollars in residuals for a two-minute cereal commercial and there's no hook at all. No law forces today's parents to put away a thin dime for the kid."

As he spoke I realized how weary he must be of fighting this same losing battle. I recalled how he once told an interviewer that his greatest achievement was never having been beaten at Scrabble, a game at which he excelled. Then, suddenly he corrected himself. "No, that's not what I'm proudest of." Glancing at a photo of himself with Charlie Chaplin in *The Kid*, he said fervently, "No matter what I do now, I was the first. Nobody can take that away from me."

Being "the first" was the single battle Jackie won; trying to recapture his childhood fame was the long war he waged for the rest of his life and lost. When he died in the spring of 1984, I sent a spray of carnations—all of them red—for courage.

During my own long climb back from obscurity, I had come across Jackie's picture in every major history of films. But almost without fail he appears with Charlie Chaplin in one of many scenes from *The Kid*. Although his solo movie career lasted a full dozen years thereafter, his fame was kept alive by being paired in the public's mind with Chaplin. Together they formed a single immortal icon that symbolized "child star." Our Gang stars and Shirley Temple became known to later generations of children by having their films rerun on television. Going it alone, with most of her films destroyed, Baby Peggy's filmic image had a rougher time surviving.

But curiously enough, my work as an author prompted a resurgence of interest in Baby Peggy's career among film buffs and historians. I was amazed to learn that collectors were now paying twenty-five hundred dollars and up for an original bisque-headed Baby Peggy doll, circa 1923. Letters come to me from all over Europe and America, written by film fans, young and old, who have read my books, seen my films at film festivals or on videotape or are seeking autographs. Many send me rare 1920s Baby Peggy postcards.

Fortunately I never became addicted to fame. Like someone innoculated against a deadly plague in early childhood, I grew up incapable of ever catching that disease. My first concerns as an adult have been devotion to my husband and son; after that to ply my trade as a writer and historian, and to do so in the most professional, even-handed manner possible. As in childhood, I still seek most of all to earn the respect of my coworkers, peers, and audience of readers.

Not long ago a silent film historian and Baby Peggy fan launched an all-out campaign to find my "lost" two-reel comedies. The New York Museum of Modern Art has so far turned up two early comedies, *Circus Clowns*, with Brownie, and *Miles of Smiles*.

The Library of Congress has prints of both *Captain January* and *Helen's Babies*. A thoughtful dealer in silent films sent me two recent Grapevine Videos, *The Family Secret* and *April Fool*, the latter made on Poverty Row in 1926. Like Roddy, I have also become an anthropologist of sorts, studying the artifacts, customs, and culture of the moviemaking tribe that not only built the unique industry and town which cradled me but erected the largest make-believe rainbow in the world.

Today, both with and without credit given, I find myself quoted in articles and books on performing children. I have spoken widely before teachers, students, child psychologists, and family counselors on the serious problems that child-star careers pose for both the children and their families.

While the joy of writing is its own reward, naturally I find this recognition gratifying. Now I consider my early years an archaeological dig, and my Baby Peggy self my most valued research assistant. Luckily for me she made a lot of field notes along the way. The skills she mastered early on have helped me immensely as an adult. Her preliterate trick of memorizing data "in the round," her self-discipline, perseverance, and willingness to delay gratification—these were all *her* hard-won accomplishments, handed on as outright gifts to me.

People often remark upon my tendency to sometimes speak of her as someone separate from me. Actually, she is and she isn't. I understand now that it was not Baby Peggy herself I was fighting throughout my adolescent and early adult years, but merely the long shadow her childhood fame cast over me. Her childhood and earthly life ended at ten years of age at that impromptu appearance on the New York Palace stage with the Duncan Sisters. That was her swan song. Enigmatically, she and I shared the same childhood, but I was the one who had to grow up and take the longer, harder road. Nevertheless, she earned the right to remain her own distinctive person. I also owe her a great debt, for in the end it was she who greatly helped me sort out and eventually forge my own identity.

A few years ago my sister, Louise, who for many years was so traumatized by what my career had done to her we were almost estranged, wrote a remarkably candid and conciliatory letter to the sibling whose early fame had overshadowed her.

> The other day I was struck by an important realization. When I think of the sacrifices you were forced to make and the responsibilities heaped on your tiny shoulders at an age when my own children had nothing more serious to contemplate than potty training, it makes me feel ashamed, not of the child I was, but that as an adult it never occurred to me.
>
> We were raised by parents who taught us by example that one's own immediate pain and anger are the most important things in life. Consequently something that has needed to be said never was, not by me or anyone else in our sick little family, and that is THANK YOU! Thank you for all the things you did without, things the average child and parent alike take as a child's birthright today. Mother always held "what you owe Peg" as a weapon over my head, making me feel both guilt and anger toward you. Father never seemed to think of it at all. Thanks again and be happy for us both.

Back in the 1930s one of those "Where are they now?" articles showing former child stars in "then" and "now" photos made a deep impression on me. A sharp baby picture of me was there, all right, but the "now" frame was a solid black square under which ran the eerie caption: "Vanished completely." That was not reassuring to a troubled adolescent trying to learn who she was and where she was going.

Another photo caption, dating from the same bleak period, I found equally disquieting at the time, but its curiously prophetic message has taken on greater significance over the years. My "comeback" photo showed a stylish thirteen-year-old girl in a white turtleneck sweater and tailored slacks. Under it ran this haunting observation: "Other actors and actresses have ancestors, but Baby Peggy is unique. She descended from herself."

While that caption may not have been entirely true back in 1932, it most certainly is now.

FILMOGRAPHY

I. CENTURY COMEDIES

Century Film Corporation. Released by Universal. Two reels.

Executive producers Julius and Abe Stern; production manager Sig Neufeld; executive secretary Zion Myers; animal trainers Charles Gay and Pete Morrison; chief electrician D. C. Stegal; assistant electricians Charles Gould, Walter Gould, and Harold Story; directors included J. G. Blystone, Tom Buckingham, James Davis, Harry Edwards, Fred C. Fishback, Arvid Gillstrom, Alf Goulding, Albert Herman, Fred Hibbard, Vin Moore, Zion Myers, Herman C. Raymaker, Chuck Reisner, David Smith, Noel Smith, Bert Sternbach, and William H. Watson.

The Century Film Corporation was founded in 1917 to produce comedies starring Alice Howell. By 1920 the studio was best known for its animal comedies featuring the Century lion, "wonder" dogs, mule, and trick horse. Century followed a strict "unit" system for the production of shorts. Each "unit" was built around a star comedian, such as Brownie the dog, and consisted of a self-contained production crew headed by a director who also acted as unit producer and scriptwriter. So crucial was the unit director to the creation of individual films at Century, and so small and overworked was the studio's directorial staff, that a director's disability during production could mean the cancellation or long-term shelving of a film. After a number of unbilled performances as the studio's "baby" and as a sidekick for the Century dog stars Brownie and Teddy,

Baby Peggy was made the star of her own "unit" in mid-1921. Directors Alf Goulding and Arvid Gillstrom were responsible for most of the official Baby Peggy productions. Personnel for the "Baby Peggy unit" included, at various times, assistant producer David Smith; chief cameraman Jerry Ash; assistant cameraman Roy Eslick; editor and title writer Joe W. Farnham; art director Tom O'Neil; property manager Chuck Harris; extra and production assistant Johnny Belasco; director of publicity Mrs. Maud Robinson Toombs; and actors Max Asher, Joe Bonner, Jack Earle, Inez McDonnell, Fred Spencer, and Blanche Payson.

A number of the Baby Peggy films were premiered in advance of their national release at important theaters in New York and Los Angeles, as means of enhancing their prestige and generating reviews which were later used to promote the films when they went into general release. Although this was a common practice among producers of short films at this time, Century president Julius Stern claimed it as a uniquely successful element in the studio's exploitation of its product.

With one exception, Baby Peggy's uncredited appearances as an extra are not included.

ETR = *Exhibitors Trade Review*
MPN = *Motion Picture News*
MPW = *Moving Picture World*

1921
Her Circus Man (9 March). Directed by James Davis.
On with the Show (20 April). Directed by James Davis.
The Kid's Pal (27 April). Directed by Tom Buckingham. With Brownie the dog, Florence Lee, Bud Jamison, Billy Engle. Review: *MPW*, 19 March 1921.
Playmates (18 May). Directed by Fred C. Fishback. With Brownie the dog.
On Account (8 June). Directed by William H. Watson.
Pals (15 June). Directed by Tom Buckingham. With Brownie the dog. Review: *MPW*, 14 May 1921.
Third Class Male (20 July). Directed by William H. Watson. With Charles Dorety.
The Clean Up (17 August). Directed by William H. Watson. With Charles Dorety.
Golfing (24 August). Written and directed by Fred C. Fishback. With Brownie the dog. Review: *MPW*, 3 September 1921.
Brownie's Little Venus (11 September, Rivoli Theater, New York; 14 September, nationwide). Directed by Fred Hibbard. With Brownie the dog. Reviews: *MPW*, 30 July 1921; *MPN*, 24 September 1921.
Sea Shore Shapes (18 September, Central Theater, New York; 19 October, nationide). Directed by Alf Goulding. With Teddy the dog, Louise Lorraine. Review: *ETR*, 29 Oct 1921.
A Week Off (28 September). Directed by Fred Hibbard. With Charles Dorety. Reviews: *ETR*, 8 October 1921; *MPW*, 15 October 1921.
A Muddy Bride (2 October, Central Theater, New York; 16 November, nationwide). Directed by Fred Hibbard. With Jackie Morgan. Review: *ETR*, 24 December 1921.
Brownie's Baby Doll (5 October). Directed by Alf Goulding. With Brownie the dog.
Teddy's Goat (30 November). Written and directed by Fred Hibbard. With Teddy the

dog, Charles Dorety, Bud Jamison, Viola Dolan. Reviews: *ETR/MPW*, 17 December 1921; *MPN*, 24 December 1921.

Get-Rich-Quick Peggy (23 October, Central Theater, New York; 7 December, nationwide). Directed by Alf Goulding. With Louise Lorraine, Aulbert Twins, Teddy the dog.

Chums (18 December, Rivoli Theater, New York; 28 December, nationwide). Directed by Fred Hibbard. With Brownie the dog. Reviews: *ETR/MPW*, 7 January 1922.

1922

The Straphanger (11 January). Directed by Fred Hibbard. With Lee Moran, Bartine Burkett. Review: *ETR*, 21 January 1922.

Circus Clowns (25 January). Directed by Fred Hibbard. With Brownie the dog, William Irving. Review: *MPN*, 11 February 1922. Preserved by Museum of Modern Art, New York.

Little Miss Mischief (15 February). Directed by Arvid Gillstrom. Reviews: *ETR*, 25 February 1922; *MPN*, 18 March 1922.

Peggy, Behave! (27 February, Central Theater, New York; 15 March, nationwide). Written and directed by Arvid Gillstrom. Review: *ETR*, 25 March 1922.

The Little Rascal (23 April, Rivoli Theater, New York; 24 May, nationwide). Written and directed by Arvid Gillstrom. With Blanche Payson. Production title: *The Little Angel*.

Tips (11 June 1922, Rivoli Theater, New York; 25 July 1923, nationwide). Directed by Arvid Gillstrom. With Fred Spencer, Jack Henderson, Inez McDonnell, Pal the dog. Locations: the Ambassador Hotel, Los Angeles.

1923

Peg o' the Movies (28 January, Rivoli Theater, New York; 28 March, nationwide). Directed by Alf Goulding. With Alf Goulding Jr., Max Asher, Joe Bonner. Reviews: *ETR*, 10 February and 24 March 1923: *MPW*, 10 February 1923. Production title: *The Baby Star*.

Sweetie (11 February, Criterion Theater, New York; 25 April, nationwide). Directed by Alf Goulding. With Louise Lorraine, Max Asher, Jennie the organ grinder monkey. Reviews: *ETR/MPN/MPW*, 24 February 1923. Production title: *Peggy Immigrates*. Preserved by Museum of Modern Art, New York.

The Kid Reporter (30 May). Directed by Alf Goulding. With Blanche Payson, Albert Willis, Jim Kelly, Buddy Williams. Reviews: *ETR/MPN/MPW*, 9 June 1923. Production titles: *Peggy's Scoop; The Cub Reporter*. Preserved by National Film Archive, London.

Taking Orders (27 June). Directed by Alf Goulding. With Dick Smith Fred Spencer, Juanita Vaughn, Max Asher. Reviews: *MPN*, 23 June 1923; *MPW*, 7 July 1923. Production titles: *Peggy's Busy Day; Peggy's Restaurant*.

Carmen, Jr. (28 June on the Loew's circuit; 29 August, nationwide). Directed by Alf Goulding. Titles by Joe W. Farnham. With Lillian Hackett, Inez McDonnell, Thomas Wonder. Location: the mission at San Fernando Rey. Production titles: *The Señorita; Sunny Smiles*.

Nobody's Darling (15 July, Rivoli Theater, New York; 29 September, nationwide). Directed by Alf Goulding and Harry Edwards. Written by William Friedle. With Lillian Worth, Charlotte Rich, John Ralston. Reviews: *ETR/MPN/MPW*, 4 August 1923. Production title: *The Orphan.*

Little Miss Hollywood (31 October). Written and directed by Albert Herman. Titles by Joe W. Farnham. With Fred Spencer, Dick Smith, Joe Bonner, Florence Lee, Mary Pickford, Douglas Fairbanks, Charles Ray. [Note: After the production of Baby Peggy's "last" short comedy, Century put together this "tour" of various Hollywood studios using stock footage.]

Miles of Smiles (28 November). Directed by Alf Goulding. Reviews: *ETR*, 27 October and 1 December 1923; *MPN*, 1 December 1923. Preserved by Museum of Modern Art, New York, and Nederlands Filmmuseum, Amsterdam.

Hansel and Gretel (26 December). Written and directed by Alf Goulding. With Jack Earle, Buddy Williams, Blanche Payson, Jim Kelly. Review: *ETR*, 29 December 1923.

1924

Such Is Life (30 January). Directed by Alf Goulding. With Joe Bonner, Thomas Wonder, Jack Henderson, Arnold MacDonald, Paul Stanhope. Reviews: *ETR/MPW*, 2 February 1924. Production titles: *The Little Match Girl; Little Miss Spunk.*

Peg o' the Mounted (27 February). Directed by Alf Goulding. Story "Sweetheart of the Mounted" by Bert Sterling. With Bert Sterling, Jack Earle, Tiny Tim the pony. Reviews: *ETR*, 3 November 1923; *MPN/MPW*, 1 March 1924. Locations: Camp Curry, Yosemite National Park; the Mission San Fernando Rey. Production title: *Peggy of the Mounted.*

Our Pet (11 May). Directed by Herman Raymaker. With Newton Hall, Winston Radom, Verne Winter, Donald Condon. Production titles: *Too Many Lovers; Five After One.*

The Flower Girl (25 May). Directed by Herman Raymaker. With Billy Franey, Jack Earle, Joe Moore.

Stepping Some (8 June). Directed by Arvid Gillstrom.

Poor Kid (22 June). Directed by Arvid Gillstrom. With Max Asher.

Jack and the Beanstalk (7 July). Written and directed by Alf Goulding. With Jack Earle, Blanche Payson, Buddy Williams.

1925

Little Red Riding Hood (21 November). Written and directed by Alf Goulding. With Peter the Great (the dog), Louise Lorraine, Arthur Trimble, Johnny Fox, Alf Goulding Jr. Review: *ETR*, 5 December 1925. [Note: This film was heavily promoted as the first in a prestigious series of Baby Peggy "fairy tales" for distribution in the fall of 1922; however, production problems, including a fire at the studio which damaged the original negative, delayed its release until after Baby Peggy had left the studio.]

II. UNREALIZED CENTURY COMEDIES

Grandma's Girl (in production 1922). Written and directed by Alf Goulding. With Florence Lee, Jimmy Kelly. [Note: This production, a satire of Harold Lloyd's hit

Grandma's Boy, was first shut down when illness struck Baby Peggy and Alf Goulding, and was then canceled after a fire at the studio.]

The Messenger Boy (in production 1922). Written and directed by Arvid Gillstrom. With Ena Gregory, Inez McDonnell, Max Mogi, Tom Dempsey, Harry Asher, Blanche Payson. Location: The Bernheimer Estate, Hollywood. Production title: *Western Union*. [Note: There is no record of a Baby Peggy release with this title; however, evidence suggests that this may be *Stepping Some*, released in 1924.]

III. NEWSREEL APPEARANCES

Screen Snapshots, second series, number 14. December 1921. Produced by Screen Snapshots Inc. Distributed states rights by Federated Exchanges of America, Inc. Baby Peggy appears at home. Other celebrities featured include Wallace Reid, Harry Carey, Mary MacLaren, Richard Barthelmess, Mary Pickford and Douglas Fairbanks [Sr.], Constance Talmadge, Bessie Love, Pal the dog. Review under the title "There's No Place Like Home": *MPN*, 17 December 1921. Preserved by Library of Congress, Washington, D.C.

Screen Snapshots, third series, number 3. July 1922. Produced by Screen Snapshots Inc. Distributed states rights by Pathé Exchanges, Inc. Other celebrities featured include Buster Keaton, Snub Pollard, Marie Mosquini, Nell Shipman, Colleen Moore, Bryant Washburn, Pauline Stark, Ruth Clifford, Bessie Love, Carmel Myers. Review: *MPW*, 1 July 1922.

Screen Snapshots, third series, number 21. March 1923. Produced by Screen Snapshots Inc. distributed states rights by Pathé Exchanges, Inc. Baby Peggy is mobbed by "fans" Harold Lloyd, William Desmond, Gaston Glass. Other celebrities featured include Edna Flugrath, Shirley Mason, Viola Dana, Marion Davies, Louise Lovely, Milton Sills, Betty Compson, Jesse Lasky, Adolf Zukor, Marcus Loew. Reviews: *ETR/MPW*, 10 March 1923.

International News, number 23. 13 March 1923. Produced by International News Reel Corp. Distributed by Universal. Baby Peggy appears with Irene Castle and at home with her sister, Louise. Press releases: *ETR*, 24 March 1923; *MPN*, 31 March 1923.

Screen Snapshots, fourth series, number 3. November 1923. Produced by Screen Snapshots Inc. Distributed states rights by C.B.C. Film Sales Inc. Other celebrities featured include Douglas Fairbanks Jr., Charles Ray, Wallace Beery, Teddy the dog. Review: *MPN*, 17 November 1923.

Screen Snapshots, fourth series, number 8. January 1924. Produced by Screen Snapshots Inc. Distributed states rights by C.B.C. Film Sales Inc. Baby Peggy visits New York City. Other celebrities featured include Rudolph Valentino, Bobby Vernon, Dorothy Dalton, Agnes Ayres, Earle Kenton, Creighton Hale, Wandy Hawley, Richard Dix, Lottie Pickford, Dagmar Godowsky, Irving Cummings, Herbert Rawlinson, Hope Hampton, Bessie Love. Press release: *MPN*, 5 January 1924.

Screen Snapshots, fourth series, number 16. April 1924. Produced by Screen Snapshots Inc. Distributed states rights by C.B.C. Film Sales Inc. Other celebrities featured include Jackie Coogan, Mae Murray, Marguerite De La Motte, David Warfield, Douglas Fairbanks [Sr.]. Press release: *MPN*, 26 April 1924.

[*Life in Hollywood*] (ca 1923–1924) Goodwill Pictures Inc. Produced by L. M. BeDell. With Lon Chaney, Ed Brady, Pat O'Malley, Bob Hill, Max Davidson, Neely Edwards, Bert Roach, Hobart Henley, King Baggott, Irving Cummings, Harry Pollard, Pete Morrison, Emmett Corrigan, Edward Sedgwick, Hoot Gibson, Mary Philbin, Margaret Morris, Reginald Denny, Joe Martin. [Note: Baby Peggy is featured together with director Jesse Robbins on the set of *The Law Forbids*. Original production credits for this tour of Universal studios are lacking on the reissued sound version in circulation on video.]

IV. SILENT FEATURES

Penrod. 1922. Marshall Neilan Productions/Associated First National Pictures. Directed by Marshall Neilan. Screenplay by Lucita Squier, based on Booth Tarkington's "Penrod" and "Penrod, a Comedy in Four Acts." Photographed by David Kesson and Ray June. With Wesley Barry, Tully Marshall, Claire McDowell, John Harron, Sunshine Morrison.

Fool's First. 1922. Marshall Neilan Productions/Associated First National Pictures. Directed by Marshall Neilan. Screenplay by Marion Fairfax. Based on the short story "Fool's First" by Hugh MacNair Kahler. Titles by Hugh Wiley. Photographed by David Kesson and Karl Struss. With Richard Dix, Claire Windsor, Claude Gillingwater, Raymond Griffith.

Hollywood. 1923. Famous Players Lasky/Paramount Pictures. Directed by James Cruze. Story by Frank Condon. Adaptation by Tom Geraghty. Photographed by Karl Brown. With Hope Drown, Luke Cosgrave, George K. Arthur, and over seventy guest stars and celebrities including Baby Peggy as herself.

The Darling of New York. 1923. Universal Pictures. Directed by King Baggot. Story by King Baggot. Screenplay by Raymond L. Schrock. Photographed by John Stumar. With Sheldon Lewis, Gladys Brockwell, Pat Hartigan, Frank Currier, Junior Coughlan. Production titles: *Wanted, a Home; Whose Baby Are You?*

The Law Forbids. 1924. Universal Pictures. Directed by Jesse Robbins. Story by Bernard McConville. Screenplay by Lois Zellner and Ford I. Beebe. Photographed by Charles Kaufman and Jack Stevens. With Robert Ellis, Elinor Fair, Winifred Bryson, James Corrigan. Production titles: *Settled Out of Court; The Right to Love*.

Captain January. 1924. Principal Pictures. Directed by Edward F. Cline. Screenplay by Eve Unsell and John Grey. Photographed by Glen MacWilliams. With Hobart Bosworth, Irene Rich, Lincoln Stedman, Harry T. Morey. Location: Laguna Beach, California. Preserved at Archives du Film du CNC, Bois d'Arcy, France; Library of Congress, Washington, D.C.

The Family Secret. 1924. Universal Pictures. Directed by William A. Seiter. Based on Frances Hodgson Burnett's "Editha's Burglar." Screenplay by Lois Zellner. Photographed by John Stumar. With Gladys Hulette, Edward Earle, Frank Currier, Cesare Gravina. Production title: *The Burglar's Kid*.

Helen's Babies. 1924. Principal Pictures. Directed by William A. Seiter. Adaptation by Hope Loring and Louis D. Lighton. Photographed by William Daniels and Glen MacWilliams. With Clara Bow, Jean Carpenter, Edward Everett Horton, Claire Adams. Preserved by Library of Congress, Washington, D.C.; National Film Archive, London.

April Fool. 1926. Chadwick Pictures. Directed by Nat Ross. Screenplay by Zion Myer.

Photographed by L. William O'Connell. With Alexander Carr, Duane Thompson, Mary Alden, Raymond Keane.

V. SOUND FILMS

Off His Base. 1932. Educational Pictures Inc. Produced by Norman L. Sper and James Gleason. Story by Charles W. Paddock. Directed by James Gleason. With James Gleason, Lucille Gleason, Russell Gleason, Eugene Palette. Two reels.

Hollywood on Parade. 1932. Paramount Pictures. With Frankie Darro and the Our Gang kids. One reel.

Eight Girls in a Boat. 1934. Charles R. Rogers Productions, Inc./Paramount Productions, Inc. Directed by Richard Wallace. Story by Helmut Brandis. Adaptation by Lewis Foster. Screenplay by Casey Robinson. Photographed by Gilbert Warrenton. With Dorothy Wilson, Douglas Montgomery, Kay Johnson. (Baby Peggy appears as a Swiss boarding-school girl.)

Ah! Wilderness. 1935. Metro-Goldwyn-Mayer. Directed by Clarence Brown. Based on the play by Eugene O'Neill. Screenplay by Frances Goodrich and Albert Hackett. Photographed by Clyde de Vinna. With Wallace Beery, Lionel Barrymore, Aline MacMahon, Mickey Rooney. (Baby Peggy appears as a schoolgirl in the graduation sequence.)

Girls' Dormitory. 1936. Twentieth Century-Fox. Directed by Irving Cummings. Screenplay by Gene Markey. Photographed by Merritt Gerstad. With Herbert Marshall, Tyrone Power, Ruth Chatterton, Simone Simone. (Baby Peggy appears as a schoolgirl.)

VI. TELEVISION APPEARANCES

1974: *What Ever Became of Hollywood?* Canada. CBC. Documentary on child stars.

1975: *Babes in Hollywood*. Great Britain. BBC. Directed by Cris Cook.

1976: *To Tell the Truth*. USA. Game show, syndicated.

1979: *The Joyce Davidson Show*. Canada. National TV. Two-part interview, 16–17 March.

1982: *Hollywood's Children*. USA. Wombat Productions/PBS broadcast.

1985: *60 Minutes*. Australia. Interview.

1989: *When We Were Young*. USA. PBS fund-raiser on child stars.

Allen, Fred. *Much Ado about Me*. New York: Atlantic, Little, Brown, 1956.

Black, Shirley Temple. *Child Star*. New York: McGraw-Hill, 1988.

Brownlow, Kevin. *Hollywood: The Pioneers*. London: Collins, 1979.

Cary, Diana Serra. *Hollywood's Children: An Inside Account of the Child Star Era*. Boston: Houghton Mifflin, 1979.

————. *The Hollywood Posse: The Story of a Gallant Band of Horsemen Who Made Movie History*. Boston: Houghton Mifflin, 1975.

Bell, Monta, and William Wyler. "Griffithiana." *Journal of Film History* 17 (October 1994): 18–19.

Coghlan, Frank "Junior." *They Still Call Me Junior*. Jefferson, N.C.: McFarland, 1993.

Drimmer, Frederick. *Very Special People*. New York: Amjon, 1973.

Drinkwater, John. *The Life of Carl Laemmle*. New York: G. P. Putnam's Sons, 1931.

Fountain, Leatrice Gilbert. *Dark Star: The Untold Story of the Meteoric Rise and Fall of the Legendary John Gilbert*. New York: St. Martin's Press, 1985.

Gabler, Neal. *An Empire of Their Own: How the Jews Invented Hollywood*. New York: Crown, 1988.

Goldbeck, Willis. "Seen but Not Heard: An Interview with Baby Peggy." *Motion Picture Classic*, October 1922.

Green, Abel, and Joe Laurie Jr. *Show Biz: From Vaude to Video*. New York: Henry Holt, 1951.

Harmetz, Aljean. *The Making of "The Wizard of Oz."* New York: Alfred A. Knopf, 1977.

Howe, Herbert. "What's Going to Happen to Jackie Coogan?" *Photoplay*, December 1923.

Janis, Elsie. *So Far, So Good*. New York: E. P. Dutton, 1932.

Jennings, Dean. "The Private Life of a Giant" [article on the later life of Jake Earle]. *Saturday Evening Post*, 4 November 1950.

Lee, Raymond. *Not So Dumb*. New York: Castle Books, 1970.

Magley, Guy. *Down Memory Lane* [listing of vaudeville bills for various venues during New Year's week, 1926]. Hollywood, Calif.: Magley Realty Company, 1964.

Marx, Samuel. *Mayer and Thalberg: The Make-Believe Saints*. New York: Random House, 1975.

Meyer, Nicholas E. *Magic in the Dark*. New York: Facts on File, 1985.

Milestone, Lewis "Millie." Interview by author. Beverly Hills, Calif., summer 1976.

Moore, Dick "Dickie." *Twinkle, Twinkle, Little Star*. New York: Harper and Row, 1984.

Naylor, David. *American Picture Palaces: The Architecture of Fantasy*. New York: Van Nostrand Reinhold, 1981.

Palmer, Ethel Fishbach. Letter to author, 1975.

————. Telephone conversation with author, 1975.

Rooney, Mickey. *I.E.: An Autobiography*. New York: G. P. Putnam's Sons, 1965.

Rubin, Jay. "Jay Rubin Interviews Jackie Coogan." *Classic Film Collector* 52 (October 1976): 4, 7–9.

Schatz, Thomas. *The Genius of the System*. New York: Pantheon, 1988.

Sennett, Mack. *The King of Comedy*. New York: Doubleday, 1954.

Stern, Julius. Interview by author. Palm Springs, Calif., 1975.

Thomas, Bob. *King Cohn*. New York: G. P. Putnam's Sons, 1967.

Wagner, Walter. *You Must Remember This: Oral Reminiscences of the Real Hollywood*. New York: G. P. Putnam's Sons, 1975.

Wanamaker, Marc. "The Encyclopedia of American Motion Picture Studios: Century Film Company (1917–1926), Stern Film Corporation (1927–1932), Alexander Brothers (1932–1943)." Manuscript.

Zierold, Norman J. *The Child Stars*. New York: Coward-McCann, 1965.

————. *The Moguls*. New York: Coward-McCann, 1969.

INDEX

Because Baby Peggy's father, mother, and sister (Jack, Marian, and Louise Montgomery) appear on virtually every page of the first three-fourths of the text, their names have not been included here.